THE MORMONS,

OR

LATTER-DAY SAINTS:

A CONTEMPORARY HISTORY.

THE EXPULSION OF THE MORMONS FROM NAUVOO.

AMS PRESS

NEW YORK

" One of the gang raised him up and placed him against a well, and while in this position, four others among the mob advanced to the front rank with loaded muskets, and fired at the " Prophet. "—*Page* 162.

THE MORMONS:

OR

LATTER-DAY SAINTS.

WITH MEMOIRS OF

THE LIFE AND DEATH OF JOSEPH SMITH,

THE " AMERICAN MAHOMET."

BY
HENRY MAYHEW

ILLUSTRATED WITH FORTY ENGRAVINGS.

LONDON:

OFFICE OF THE NATIONAL ILLUSTRATED LIBRARY,

198, STRAND.

Reprinted from the edition of 1852, London

First AMS edition published 1971

Manufactured in the United States of America

International Standard Book Number: 0-404-08440-0

Library of Congress Catalog Card Number: 71-134398

AMS PRESS INC.
NEW YORK, N, Y, 10003

PREFACE.

IN the summer of the year 1850, during the course of an inquiry in which he was engaged on the subject of " LABOUR AND THE POOR," the author of this volume had occasion to direct his particular attention to the amount of Emigration from the port of Liverpool. While pursuing his researches, he learned that, independently of the general emigration of English and Irish, amounting, during the fine season, to nearly 20,000 persons per month, there was a peculiar, but smaller stream of emigration, carried on in behalf of the religious sect known by the name of the " Mormons," or " Latter-Day Saints." He was informed that many years ago these people had established an Emigrational Agency in Liverpool, having ramifications in all parts of England, Wales, and Scotland, and that the number of Mormon emigrants sailing from that port to New Orleans, on their way to the Great Salt Lake Valley, in California, during the year 1849, had been no less than 2,500, chiefly consisting of farmers and mechanics of a superior class, from Wales, Lancashire, Yorkshire, Staffordshire, and the southern counties of Scotland ; and that since 1840 the total emigration of the sect from great Britain had amounted to between 13,000 and 14,000 persons. He was led, in consequence, to devote his attention to the history of the origin and progress of this singular sect, of which comparatively little was known. The results of his investigations were published in the *Morning Chronicle* a short time afterwards, in three letters of the well-known series undertaken by that Journal. The subject, however, was too interesting, important, and extensive to be thoroughly handled in the limited space at the disposal of a newspaper, and the writer was. in consequence, induced—having received, in the meantime, a large accession of new, valuable, and authentic materials—to extend these slight sketches into the volume now offered to the public. It presents the history of Joseph Smith, a great impostor, or a great visionary,—perhaps both—but in either case one of the most remarkable persons who has appeared on the stage of the world in modern times. The author has endeavoured to disencumber the conflicting accounts of his disciples on the one hand, and of his enemies on the other, of all exaggeration for him, or against him, and to state with fairness what appeared to him to be the truth. As far as he is aware, it is the first time that anything which can be called a history of this new religion and its founder has been offered to the public, either in this country, or in the cradle of the Mormons—the United States of America.

With respect to the Illustrations of this Volume, it may be stated, that embracing, as they do, views of remote places not hitherto pourtrayed, and representations of events in a wild and very partially settled country, they have, nevertheless, been derived from authentic sources, having been drawn from the rude sketches, or minute descriptions, of persons to whom the spots were familiar, and who were, in many cases, eye-witnesses of the incidents depicted. Such Portraits of the leading Mormons as it has been possible to procure, are from the pencil of a Mormon artist, and other subjects have been copied from prints published under the sanction of the sect.

LONDON, *June* 1851.

CONTENTS.

CHAPTER V.

CHAPTER VI.

CHAPTER VII.

CHAPTER VIII.

CHAPTER IX.

CHAPTER X.

LIST OF ILLUSTRATIONS.

LIST OF ILLUSTRATIONS.

THE MORMONS.

CHAPTER I.

BIRTH AND PARENTAGE OF JOSEPH SMITH, THE MORMON PROPHET—HIS "REMARKABLE
VISIONS"—HIS CONSECRATION TO THE PRIESTHOOD—ALLEGED APPEARANCE OF JOHN
THE BAPTIST TO JOSEPH AND HIS CONFEDERATES—THE GOLDEN PLATES OF THE HILL
OF CUMORAH—THE BOOK OF MORMON—THE MORMON WITNESSES OF ITS AUTHENTICITY
—THE WITNESSES WHO ASSERT IT TO BE A FRAUD—STATEMENTS OF PROFESSOR ANTHON
—THE SPAULDING FAMILY—MRS. DAVISON AND SIDNEY RIGDON.

IN the year 1825 there lived, in a small village in the United States
of America, an obscure young man—of little or no education—of no
fortune, and of but indifferent character. That obscure young man
had meditated for five years before this time the establishment of a
new religion. In 1830, being then in the twenty-fifth year of his age,
he began to carry his design into effect. In the following year he
became the head of a sect numbering five persons; amongst whom
were included his father and three brothers. In the course of a few

weeks, the number of his adherents increased to thirty. At the present time, the sect so established numbers 300,000 people; has its own Bible, and zealous missionaries to preach it in every part of the Christian world, and besides this, inhabits and possesses a fertile and beautiful territory almost as large as England, and aspires to obtain admission, on equal terms, as a free State, into the great confederation of American Republics. The name of this young man was Joseph Smith —of his new Bible, the " Book of Mormon"—of his sect, the " Church of Jesus Christ of Latter-Day Saints,"—or in the parlance of those not members of it—The Mormons, or Mormonites; and of the state or territory of which they have taken possession, Utah or Deseret, in New California. The Mormons have thriven amid oppression of the most cruel and pertinacious kind ; they have conquered the most astonishing difficulties ; they have triumphed over the most vindictive enemies, and over the most unrelenting persecution ; and from the blood of their martyrs have sprung the courage, the zeal, and the success of their survivors. They can boast not only an admirable and complete organization, but the possession of worldly wealth, influence, and power. Their progress within the last seven years has been rapid to a degree unparalleled in the history of any other sect of religionists. The remarkable career of Joseph Smith, the Prophet of the Mormons, and the story of the rise of the sect which he founded, is one of the most curious episodes in the modern history of the world. To trace that history with all its fanaticism, all its zeal, all its genuine and sincere faith, all its folly and all its virtue, and to carry it through all the touching scenes in the varied and surprising fortunes of the people who believe in Joseph Smith as the prophet of God, from the day in which the doctrine was first broached amid the hatred and the derision of a few, to the present day, when the sect is too powerful and too sincere to be derided, is the object of the following pages.

To avoid the appearance of unfriendliness towards men who— whatever the character or views of their former leaders may have been, or whatever may be thought of their own fanaticism—are carrying on a great and remarkable work, but little understood, or even heard of, in this country, beyond the limits of their own body, we shall whenever it is possible to do so, present their history in the words of their own writers, appending such statements on the other side as may be necessary for the exposition of the truth. The following particulars of the origin of the Book of Mormon, of the early life of Joseph Smith, and of his first appearance in the character of a man divinely inspired—to be the new Moses, or Mahomet of his generation —are extracted from the " Remarkable Visions," of Mr. Orson Pratt. his gentleman was formerly their emigrational agent at Liverpool,

and styles himself, in the title-page, " One of the twelve Apostles of
the Church of Jesus Christ of Latter-day Saints :"—

" Mr. Joseph Smith, jun.," says this friendly narrator, " was born
in the town of Sharon, Windsor County, Vermont, on the 23d December,
1805. When ten years old, his parents, with their family, moved to
Palmyra, New York, in the vicinity of which he resided for about
eleven years, the latter part in the town of Manchester. He was a
farmer by occupation. His advantages for acquiring scientific knowledge were exceedingly small, being limited to a slight acquaintance
with two or three of the common branches of learning. He could
read without much difficulty, and write a very imperfect hand, and
had a very limited understanding of the elementary rules of arith-
metic. These were his highest and only attainments, while the rest
of those branches so universally taught in the common schools
throughout the United States were entirely unknown to him. When
somewhere about fourteen or fifteen years old, he began seriously to
reflect upon the necessity of being prepared for a future state of
existence ; but how, or in what way to prepare himself, was a question as yet undetermined in his own mind. He perceived that it was
a question of infinite importance, and that the salvation of his soul
depended upon a correct understanding of the same. He retired to a
secret place in a grove, but a short distance from his father's house,
and knelt down and began to call upon the Lord. At first he was
severely tempted by the powers of darkness, which endeavoured to
overcome him, but he continued to seek for deliverance until darkness
gave way from his mind, and he was enabled to pray in fervency of
the spirit, and in faith ; and while thus pouring out his soul, anxiously
desiring an answer from God, he at length saw a very bright and
glorious light in the heavens above, which at first seemed to be at a
considerable distance. He continued praying, while the light appeared to be gradually descending towards him ; and as it drew
nearer it increased in brightness and magnitude, so that by the time
it reached the tops of the trees the whole wilderness around was
illuminated in a most glorious and brilliant manner. He expected to
see the leaves and boughs of the trees consumed as soon as the light
came in contact with them ; but perceiving that it did not produce
that effect, he was encouraged with the hopes of being able to endure
its presence. It continued descending slowly, until it rested upon the
earth, and he was enveloped in the midst of it. When it first came
upon him, it produced a peculiar sensation throughout his whole
system ; and immediately his mind was caught away from the natural
objects with which he was surrounded, and he was enwrapped in a
heavenly vision, and saw two glorious personages, who exactly re-

B

sembled each other in their features or likeness. He was informed that his sins were forgiven. He was also informed upon the subjects which had for some time previously agitated his mind—namely, that all the religious denominations were believing in incorrect doctrines, and consequently that none of them was acknowledged of God as his church and kingdom. And he was expressly commanded to go not after them ; and he received a promise that the true doctrine, the fulness of the Gospel, should at some future time be made known to him. After which the vision withdrew, leaving his mind in a state of calmness and peace indescribable. Some time after having received this glorious manifestation, being young, he was again entangled in the vanities of the world, of which he afterwards sincerely and truly repented.

✗   "And it pleased God, on the evening of the 21st September, A.D. 1823, to again hear his prayer. It seemed as though the house was, filled with consuming fire. This sudden appearance of a light so bright, as must naturally be expected, occasioned a shock of sensation visible to the extremities of the body. It was, however, followed by calmness and serenity of mind, and an overwhelming rapture of joy, that surpassed understanding, and, in a moment, a Personage stood before him.

"Notwithstanding the brightness of the light which previously illuminated the room, yet there seemed to be an additional glory surrounding or accompanying this Personage, which shone with an increased degree of brilliancy, of which he was in the midst, and though his countenance was as lightning, yet it was of a pleasing, innocent, and glorious appearance, so much so, that every fear was banished from his heart, and nothing but calmness pervaded his soul.

"The stature of this Personage was a little above the common size of men in his age ; his garment was perfectly white, and had the appearance of being without seam.

"This glorious being declared himself to be an angel of God, sent forth by commandment to communicate to him that his sins were forgiven, and that his prayers were heard ; and also to bring the joyful tidings that the covenant which God made with ancient Israel concerning their posterity was at hand to be fulfilled : that the great preparatory work for the second coming of the Messiah was speedily to commence ; that the time was at hand for the gospel, in its fulness, to be preached in power unto all nations, that a people might be prepared with faith and righteousness for the Millennial reign of universal peace and joy.

"He was informed that he was called and chosen to be an instrument in the hands of God, to bring about some of his marvellous purposes in this glorious dispensation. It was also made manifest to him that the 'American Indians' were a remnant of Israel; that when they first emigrated to America they were an enlightened people, possessing a knowledge of the true God, enjoying his favour and peculiar blessings from his hand; that the prophets and inspired writers among them were required to keep a sacred history of the most important events transpiring among them, which history was handed down for many generations, till at length they fell into great wickedness. The greatest part of them were destroyed, and the records were safely deposited, to preserve them from the hands of the wicked, who sought to destroy them. He was informed that these records contained many sacred revelations pertaining to the Gospel of the kingdom, as well as prophecies relating to the great events of the last days; and that to fulfil his promises to the ancients, who wrote the records, and to accomplish his purposes in the restitution of their children, they were to come forth to the knowledge of the people. If faithful, he was to be the instrument who should be thus highly favoured in bringing these sacred writings before the world. After giving him many instructions concerning things past and to come, he disappeared, and the light and glory of God withdrew, leaving his mind in perfect peace, while a calmness and serenity indescribable pervaded his soul. But before morning the vision was twice renewed, instructing him further and still further concerning the great work of God about to be performed on the earth. In the morning he went out to his labour as usual, but soon the vision was renewed—the angel again appeared, and having been informed, by the previous visions of the night, concerning the place where those records were deposited, he was instructed to go immediately and view them.

" Accordingly he repaired to the place, a brief description of which shall be given in the words of a gentleman named Oliver Cowdery, who has visited the spot:—

" ' As you pass on the mail-road from Palmyra, Mayne county, to Canandigua, Ontario county, New York, before arriving at the little village of Manchester, say from three to four, or about four miles from Palmyra, you pass a large hill on the east side of the road.

" ' It was at the second-mentioned place where the record was found to be deposited, on the west side of the hill, not far from the top, down its side; and when myself visited the spot in the year 1830 there were several trees standing—enough to cause a shade in summer, but not so much as to prevent the surface being covered with grass—which was also the case when the record was first found.

" ' How far below the surface these records were placed I am unable to say, but from the fact that they had been some fourteen hundred years buried, and that, too, on the side of a hill so steep, one is ready to conclude that they were some feet below, as the earth would naturally wear, more or less, in that length of time. But being placed towards the top of the hill, the ground would not remove as much as two-thirds, perhaps. Another circumstance would prevent another wearing of the earth—in all probability, as soon as timber had time to grow, the hill was covered, and the roots of the same would hold the surface.

"'However, on this point I shall leave every man to draw his own conclusion, and form his own speculation : but, suffice to say, a hole of sufficient depth was dug. At the bottom of this laid a stone of suitable size, the upper surface being smooth. At each edge was placed a large quantity of cement, and into this cement, at the four edges of this stone were placed erect four others, their bottom edges resting in the cement at the outer edges of the first stone. The four last named when placed erect, formed a box ; the corners, or where the edges of the four came in contact, were also cemented so firmly that the moisture from without was prevented from entering. It is to be observed also that the inner surfaces of the four erect or side stones were smooth. This box was sufficiently large to admit a breastplate such as was used by the ancients to defend the chest from the arrows and weapons of their enemy. From the bottom of the box, or from the breastplate, arose three small pillars, composed of the same description of cement used on the edges ; and upon these three pillars were placed the records. ' This box containing the records was covered with another stone, the bottom surface being flat, and the upper crowning.'

" When it was first visited by Mr. Smith, on the morning of the 22nd of September, 1823, 'a part of the crowning stone was visible above the surface, while the edges were concealed by the soil and grass.' From which circumstance it may be seen 'that, however deep this box might have been placed at first, the time had been sufficient to wear the earth, so that it was easily discovered, when once directed, and yet not enough to make a perceivable difference to the passer-by.' ' After arriving at the repository, a little exertion in removing the soil from the edges of the top of the box, and a light lever, brought to his natural vision its contents.' While viewing and contemplating this sacred treasure, with wonder and astonishment—behold ! the angel of the Lord, who had previously visited him, again stood in his presence, and his soul was again enlightened as it was the evening before, and he was filled with the Holy Spirit, and the heavens were opened, and the glory of the Lord shone round about and rested upon him. While he thus stood gazing and admiring the angel said, 'Look!' And, as he thus spake, he beheld the Prince of Darkness, surrounded by his innumerable train of associates. All this passed before him, and the heavenly messenger said, 'All this is shown, the good and the evil, the holy and impure, the glory of God and the power of darkness, that you may know hereafter the two powers, and never be influenced or overcome by the wicked one. You cannot at this time obtain this record, for the commandment of God is strict, and if ever these sacred things are obtained, they must be by prayer and faithfulness in obeying the Lord. They are not deposited here for the sake of accumulating gain and wealth for the glory of this world; they were sealed by the prayer of faith, and because of the knowledge which they contain; they are of no worth among the children of men only for their knowledge. In them is contained the fulness of the Gospel of Jesus Christ, as it was given to his people on this land; and when it shall be brought forth by the power of God, it shall be carried to the Gentiles, of whom many will receive it, and after will the seed of Israel be brought into the field of their Redeemer by obeying it also.

" During the period of the four following years, he frequently received instruction from the mouth of the heavenly messenger. And on the morning of the 22nd of September, A.D., 1827, the angel of the Lord delivered the records into his hands.

" These records were engraved on plates, which had the appearance of gold. Each plate was not far from seven by eight inches in width and length, being not quite as thick as common tin. They were filled on both sides with engravings in Egyptian characters, and bound together in a volume as the leaves of a book, and fastened at one edge with three rings running through the whole. This volume was something near six inches in thickness, a part of which was sealed. The characters or letters upon the unsealed part were small and beautifully engraved. The whole book exhibited many marks of antiquity in its construction, as well as much skill in the art of engraving. With the records was found 'a curious instrument, called by the ancients the Urim and Thummim, which consisted of two transparent stones, clear as crystal, set in the two rims of a bow. This was in use in ancient times, by persons called seers. It was an instrument by the use of which they received revelation of things distant, or of things past or future.'

" Having provided himself with a home, he commenced translating the record, by the gift and power of God, through the means of the Urim and Thummim ; and being a poor writer, he was under the necessity of employing a scribe to write the translation as it came from his mouth.

" In the meantime, a few of the original characters were accurately described and translated by Mr. Smith, which, with the translation, were taken by a gentleman, by the name of Martin Harris, to the city of New York, where they were presented to a learned gentleman of the name of Anthon, who professed to be extensively acquainted with many languages, both ancient and modern. He examined them, but was unable to decipher them correctly; but he presumed that if the original records could be brought, he could assist in translating them.

" But to return—Mr. Smith continued the work of translation, as his pecuniary circumstances would permit, until he finished the unsealed part of the records. The part translated is entitled the ' Book of Mormon,' which contains nearly as much reading as the Old Testament.

" After the book was translated, the Lord raised up witnesses to the nations of its truth, who, at the close of the volume, send forth their testimony, which reads as follows :—

" ' TESTIMONY OF THREE WITNESSES.

" ' Be it known unto all nations, kindreds tongues, and people, unto whom this work shall come, that we, through the Grace of God the Father, and our Lord Jesus Christ, have seen the plates which contain this record, which is a record of the people of Nephi and also of the Lamanites, their brethren, and also of the people of Jared, who came from the tower of which hath been spoken ; and we also know that they have been translated by the gift and power of God, for his voice hath declared it unto us; wherefore we know of a surety that the work is true, and we also testify that we have seen the engravings which are upon the plates ; and they have been shown unto us by the power of God, and not of man. And we declare, with words of soberness, that an angel of God came down from heaven, and he brought and laid before our eyes, that we beheld and saw the plates, and the engravings thereon ; and we know that it is by the grace of God the Father, and our Lord Jesus Christ, that we beheld and bear record that these things are true, and it is marvellous in our eyes; nevertheless, the voice of the Lord commanded us that we should bear record of it; wherefore, to be obedient unto the commandments of God, we bear testimony of these things. And we know that if we are faithful in Christ we shall rid our garments of the blood of all men, and be found spotless before the judgment seat of Christ, and shall dwell with him eternally in the heavens. And the honour be to the Father, and to the Son, and to the Holy Ghost, which is one God. Amen.

" ' OLIVER COWDERY.
DAVID WHITMER.
MARTIN HARRIS.

" ' TESTIMONY OF EIGHT WITNESSES.

" ' Be it known unto all nations, kindreds, tongues and people, unto whom this work shall come, that Joseph Smith, jun., the translator of this work has shown unto us the plates of which hath been spoken, which have the appearance of gold : as many of the leaves as the said Smith has translated we did handle with our hands ; and we also saw the engravings thereon, all of which have the appearance of ancient work, and of curious workmanship.   And this we bear record with words of soberness, that the said Smith has shown unto us, for we have seen and lighted, and know of a surety that the said Smith has got the plates of which we have spoken · and we give our names unto the world of that which we have seen ; and we lie not, God bearing witness of it.

> " 'John Whitmer.
> Christian Whitmer.
> Jacob Whitmer.
> Peter Whitmer, jun.
> Hiram Page.
> Joseph Smith, sen.
> Hyrum Smith.
> Samuel H. Smith.' "

Such is the story of a friend, derived from statements made at various times by the " Prophet" himself.   It will be seen that the witnesses of its truth were principally of the two families of Whitmer and Smith.   The Smiths were the father and brothers of Joseph. Who the Whitmers were is not clear—and all clue to their character and proceedings since this date, though probably known to the Mormons themselves, is undiscoverable by the " profane vulgar."   As, in the history of an imposture so remarkable as this, the narrative of the principal actor becomes both curious and important, the following account of the matter is extracted from the autobiography of Joseph Smith, which was published in the *Millennial Star* :—

" So great was the confusion and strife among the different religious denominations, that it was impossible for a person, young as I was, and so unacquainted with men and things, to come to any certain conclusion who was right and who was wrong.   My mind at different times was greatly excited, the cry and tumult was so great and incessant.   The Presbyterians were most decided against the Baptists and Methodists, and used all their powers of either reason or sophistry to prove their errors, or at least to make the people think they were in error.   On the other hand, the Baptists and Methodists in their turn were equally zealous to establish their own tenets and disprove all others.

" In the midst of this war and tumult of opinions, I often said to myself, what is to be done ?   Who of all these parties are right ? or are they all wrong together ?   If any one of them be right, which is it, and how shall I know it ?

" While I was labouring under the extreme difficulties, caused by the contests of these parties of religionists, I was one day reading the epistle of James, first chapter and fifth verse, which reads, 'If any of you lack wisdom, let him ask of God, that giveth unto all men liberally and upbraideth not, and it shall be given him.' Never did any passage of Scripture come with more power to the heart of man than this did at this time to mine. It seemed to enter with great force into every feeling of my heart. I reflected on it again and again, knowing that if any person needed wisdom from God, I did; for how to act I did not know, and unless I could get more wisdom than I then had, would never know; for the teachers of religion of the different sects understood the same passage so differently as to destroy all confidence in settling the question by an appeal to the Bible. At length I came to the conclusion that I must either remain in darkness and confusion, or else I must do as James directs, that is, ask of God. I at length came to the determination to 'ask of God,' concluding that if he gave wisdom to them that lacked wisdom, and would give liberally and not upbraid, I might venture. So, in accordance with this my determination to ask of God, I retired to the woods to make the attempt. It was on the morning of a beautiful clear day, early in the spring of eighteen hundred and twenty. It was the first time in my life that I had made such an attempt, for amidst all my anxieties I had never yet made the attempt to pray vocally.

"After I had retired into the place where I had previously designed to go, having looked around me and finding myself alone, I kneeled down and began to offer up the desires of my heart to God. I had scarcely done so, when immediately I was seized upon by some power which entirely overcame me, and had such astonishing influence over me, as to bind my tongue, so that I could not speak. Thick darkness gathered around me, and it seemed to me for a time as if I were doomed to sudden destruction. But exerting all my powers to call upon God to deliver me out of the power of this enemy which had seized upon me, and at the very moment when I was ready to sink into despair and abandon myself to destruction, not to an imaginary ruin, but to the power of some actual being from the unseen world, who had such a marvellous power as I had never before felt in any being. Just at this moment of great alarm, I saw a pillar of light exactly over my head, above the brightness of the sun, which descended gradually until it fell upon me. It no sooner appeared than I found myself delivered from the enemy which held me bound. When the light rested upon me, I saw two personages, whose brightness and glory defy all description, standing above me in the air. One of them spake unto me, calling me by name, and said (pointing to the other)—'this is my beloved son, hear him.'

"My object in going to inquire of the Lord, was to know which of all the sects was right, that I might know which to join. No sooner, therefore, did I get possession of myself, so as to be able to speak, than I asked the personages who stood above me in the light, which of all the sects was right (for at this time it had never entered into my heart that all were wrong), and which I should join. I was answered that I must join none of them, for they were all wrong, and the personage who addressed me said, ' that all their creeds were an abomination in his sight ; that those professors were all corrupt, they draw near to me with their lips, but their hearts are far from me; they teach for doctrine the commandments of men, having a form of godliness, but they deny the power thereof.' He again forbade me to join with any of them : and many other things did he say unto me which I cannot write at this time. When I came to myself again, I found myself laying on my back, looking up into heaven. Some few days after I had this vision, I happened to be in company with one of the Methodist preachers who was very active in the before-mentioned religious excitement, and conversing with him on the subject of religion, I took occasion to give him an account of the vision which I had had. I was greatly surprised at his behaviour; he treated my communication not only lightly, but with great contempt, saying it was all of the devil, that there were no such things as visions or revelations in these days; that all such things had ceased with the apostles, and that there never would be any more of them. I soon found, however, that my telling the story had excited a great deal of prejudice against me among professors of religion, and was the cause of great persecution, which continued to increase ; and though I was an obscure boy, only between fourteen and fifteen years of age, and my circumstances in life such as to make a boy of no consequence in the world, yet men of high standing would take notice sufficient to excite the public mind against me, and create a hot persecution, and this was common among all the sects : all united to persecute me. It has often caused me serious reflection, both then and since, how very strange it was that an obscure boy of a little over fourteen years of age, and one, too, who was doomed to the necessity of obtaining a scanty maintenance by his daily labour, should be thought a character of sufficient importance to attract the attention of the great ones of the most popular sects of the day, so as to create in them a spirit of the hottest persecution and reviling. But strange or not, so it was, and was often cause of great sorrow to myself. However, it was nevertheless a fact that I had had a vision. I have thought since that I felt much like Paul when he made his defence before king Agrippa, and related the account of the vision he had when he 'saw a light and heard a voice,' but still there were but few who believed him; some said he was dishonest, others said he was mad, and he was ridiculed and reviled; but all this did not destroy the reality of his vision. He had seen a vision, he knew he had, and all the persecution under heaven could not make it otherwise; and though they should persecute him unto death, yet he knew, and would know unto his latest breath, that he had both seen a light and heard a voice speaking to him, and all the world could not make him believe otherwise —So it was with me: I had actually seen a light, and in the midst of that light I saw two personages, and they did in reality speak unto me, or one of them did; and though I was hated and persecuted for saying that I had seen a vision, yet it was true; and while they were persecuting me, reviling me, and speaking all manner of evil against me falsely for so saying, I was led to say in my heart, why persecute for telling the truth? I have actually seen a vision, and 'who am I that I can withstand God?' or why does the world think to make me deny what I have actually seen? for I had seen a vision; I knew it, and I knew that God knew it, and I could not deny it, neither dare I do it; at least, I knew that by so doing I would offend God and come under condemnation. I had now got my mind satisfied, so far as the sectarian world was concerned, that it was not my duty to join with any of them, but continue as I was until further directed." *

Without stopping to inquire whether Joseph were a knave or a lunatic—a cool, calculating impostor—or a weak minded enthusiast, who, in the visions of a distempered brain, fancied and believed that he saw things which he has thus reported, we proceed to the next incident. Having seen God the Father and God the Son, he was in a short time afterwards, as he tells the world, favoured with a visit and a communication from John the Baptist! The circumstance is thus recorded by himself in the *Millennial Star*, vol. iii. page 148:—

" While we (Joseph Smith and Oliver Cowdery) were thus employed (in the work of translation), praying and calling upon the Lord, a messenger from heaven descended in a cloud of light, and having laid his hands upon us, he ordained us, saying unto us, ' Upon you, my fellow-servants, in the name of the Messiah, I confer the priesthood of Aaron, which holds the keys of the ministering of angels, and of the gospel of repentance, and of baptism by immersion for the remission of sins; and this shall never be taken again from the earth until the sons of Levi do offer again an offering unto the Lord in righteousness.' He said this Aaronic priesthood had not the power of laying on of hands for the gift of

---

* History of Joseph Smith, *Millennial Star*, vol. iii., No. 2, p. 21.

the Holy Ghost, but that this should be conferred on us hereafter; and he commanded us to go and be baptized, and gave us directions that I should baptize Oliver Cowdery, and afterwards that he should baptize me. Accordingly, we went and were baptized. I baptized him first, and afterwards he baptized me. After which I laid my hands upon his head, and ordained him to the Aaronic priesthood; afterwards he laid his hands on me, and ordained me to the same priesthood, for so we were commanded. The messenger who visited us on this occasion, and conferred this priesthood upon us, said that his name was John, the same that is called John the Baptist in the New Testament, and that he acted under the direction of Peter, James, and John, who held the keys of the priesthood of Melchizedek, which priesthood, he said, should in due time be conferred on us, and that I should be called the first elder, and he the second. It was on the 15th day of May, 1829, that we were baptized and ordained under the hand of the messenger."

The scheme was now ripe for a fuller development; but as we have hitherto had the story as in the words of Joseph himself, and of his ardent disciples, Mr. Orson Pratt and the "witnesses," it is necessary to go back a little, and narrate a few circumstances relative to one of the most important of these witnesses, and to the manner in which he was originally induced to become a believer in the "prophet" and his book. It will also be necessary to inquire whether the statements of Mr. Pratt, with reference to Professor Anthon, were admitted by that gentleman.

Joseph Smith having made known his doctrine to various persons, the wonderful plates began to be talked about. Among the persons who were originally most disposed to join the new sect was the Mr. Martin Harris whose name appears along with those of other witnesses in the above testimony. This Martin Harris was a farmer, who appears to have been possessed of more money than wit, and of more credulity than judgment. His religious opinions were unsettled, as he was at one time a member of the Society of friends, afterwards a Wesleyan, then a Baptist, and, at the time when Joseph Smith made his acquaintance, a Presbyterian. He was at once captivated by the doctrines and pretensions of Joseph, and lent the 'prophet' the sum of fifty dollars to enable him to publish his new Bible. Joseph, though asked by Martin Harris to show the plates, refused, on the pretence that he was not pure of heart enough to be allowed a sight of such treasures; but he generously made a transcript of a portion of them upon paper, which he told him to submit to any learned scholar in the world, if he wished to be satisfied. Martin Harris was an earnest man, and he set out from Palmyra to New

York, to visit Professor Anthon, a gentleman of the highest reputation, both in America and Europe, and well known for his valuable and correct editions of the classics. He found the Professor, and submitted the plates to him. The Mormons at this time were too insignificant to excite attention, and the result of Martin Harris's interview with the learned man was not known until three or four years afterwards, when a report having been spread abroad by the Mormons that the Professor had seen the plates, and pronounced the inscriptions to be in the Egyptian character, that gentleman was requested by a letter, directed to him by Mr. E. D. Howe, of Painesville, Ohio, to declare whether such was the fact? Professor Anthon returned the following answer, detailing his interview with the simple-minded Mr. Harris:—

"*New York, Feb.* 17, 1834.

"Dear Sir.—I received your letter of the 9th, and lose no time in making a reply. The whole story about my pronouncing the Mormonite inscription to be 'Reformed Egyptian Hieroglyphics,' is perfectly false. Some years ago a plain, apparently simple-hearted, farmer called on me with a note from Dr. Mitchell, of our city, now dead, requesting me to decypher, if possible, a paper which the farmer would hand me. Upon examining the paper in question, I soon came to the conclusion that it was all a trick, perhaps a hoax. When I asked the person who brought it how he obtained the writing, he gave me the following account:—A 'gold book,' consisting of a number of plates fastened together by wires of the same material, had been dug up in the northern part of the State of New York, and along with it an enormous pair of 'spectacles!' These spectacles were so large, that if any person attempted to look through them, his two eyes would look through one glass only; the spectacles in question being altogether too large for the human face. 'Whoever,' he said, 'examined the plates through the glasses was enabled not only to read them, but fully to understand their meaning. All this knowledge, however, was confined to a young man, who had the trunk containing the book and spectacles in his sole possession. This young man was placed behind a curtain, in a garret, in a farm-house, and being thus concealed from view, he put on the spectacles occasionally, or rather, looked through one of the glasses, deciphered the characters in the book, and having committed some of them to paper, handed copies from behind the curtain to those who stood outside. Not a word was said about their having been decyphered by the 'gift of God.' Everything in this way was effected by the large pair of spectacles. The farmer added, that he had been requested to contribute a sum of money towards the publication of the 'golden book,' the contents of which would, as he was told, produce an entire change in the world, and save it from ruin. So urgent had been these solicitations, that he intended selling his farm, and giving the amount to those who wished to publish the plates. As a last precautionary step, he had resolved to come to New York, and obtain the opinion of the learned about the meaning of the paper which he had brought with him, and which had been given him as part of the contents of the book, although no translation had at that time been made by the young man with the spectacles. On hearing this odd story, I changed my opinion about the paper, and instead of viewing it any longer as a hoax, I began to regard it as part of a scheme to cheat the farmer of his money, and I communicated my suspicions to him, warning him to beware of rogues. He requested an opinion from me in writing, which of course I declined to give, and he then took his leave, taking his paper with him.

"This paper, in question, was in fact a singular scroll. It consisted of all kinds of crooked characters, disposed in columns, and had evidently been prepared by some person who had before him at the time a book containing various alphabets, Greek and Hebrew letters, crosses, and flourishes; Roman letters inverted or placed sideways, were arranged and placed in perpendicular columns; and the whole ended in a rude delineation of a circle, divided into various compartments, decked with various strange marks, and evidently copied after the Mexican Calendar, given by Humboldt, but copied in such a way as not to betray the source whence it was derived. I am thus particular as to the contents of the paper, inasmuch as I have frequently conversed with my friends on the subject since the Mormon excitement began, and well remember that the paper contained anything else but 'Egyptian Hieroglyphics.'

"Some time after the same farmer paid me a second visit. He brought with him the 'gold book' in print, and offered it to me for sale. I declined purchasing. He then asked permission to leave the book with me for examination. I declined receiving it, although his manner was strangely urgent. I adverted once more to the roguery which, in my opinion, had been practised upon him, and asked him what had become of the gold plates. He informed me that they were in a trunk with the spectacles. I advised him to go to a magistrate and have the trunk examined. He said, 'The curse of God' would come upon him if he did. On my pressing him, however, to go to a magistrate, he told me he would open the trunk if I would take the 'curse of God' upon myself. I replied I would do so with the greatest willingness, and would incur every risk of that nature, provided I could only extricate him from the grasp of rogues; he then left me. I have given you a full statement of all that I know respecting the origin of Mormonism, and must beg you, as a personal favour, to publish this letter immediately, should you find my name mentioned again by these wretched fanatics.

"Yours respectfully,

"CHARLES ANTHON.'

This letter speaks for itself, and needs no comment. The following summary of the contents of the Book of Mormon, thus strangely issued into the world, is from a publication called the *Voice of Warning*, by Parley P. Pratt, another apostle:—

"The Book of Mormon contains the history of the ancient inhabitants of America, who were a branch of the house of Israel, of the tribe of Joseph; of whom the Indians are still a remnant; but the principal nation of them having fallen in battle, in the fourth or fifth century, one of their prophets, whose name was Mormon, saw fit to make an abridgment of their history, their prophecies, and their doctrine, which he engraved on plates, and afterwards, being slain, the record fell into the hands of his son Moroni, who, being hunted by his enemies, was directed to deposit the record safely in the earth, with a promise from God that it should be preserved, and should be brought to light in the latter days by means of a Gentile nation, who should possess the land. The deposit was made about the year 420 on a hill then called Cumora, now in Ontario county, where it was preserved in safety until it was brought to light by no less than the ministry of angels, and translated by inspiration. And the great Jehovah bore record of the same to chosen witnesses, who declare it to the world."

The question will be asked, could Joseph Smith, a notoriously illiterate, though clever man, really write the Book of Mormon? Without pretending to state positively that Joseph Smith was not the sole author of the volume, or that he was not aided by other persons in its composition, we present the following short history, which the American opponents of Mormonism consider to be a true statement of its origin.

It is stated by them that, in the year 1809, a man of the name of Solomon Spaulding, who had formerly been a clergyman, failed in business at a place called Cherry Vale, in the State of New York. Being a person of literary tastes, and his attention having been directed to the notion which at that time excited some interest and discussion, namely, that the North American Indians were the descendants of the lost ten tribes of Israel, it struck him that the idea afforded a good groundwork for a religious tale, history, or novel. For three years he laboured upon this work, which he entitled *The Manuscript Found.* "Mormon" and his son "Moroni," who act so large a part in Joseph Smith's *Book of Mormon,* were two of the principal characters in it. In 1812 the MS. was presented to a printer or bookseller, named Patterson, residing at Pittsburgh Pennsylvania, with a view to its publication. Before any satisfactory arrangement could be made, the author died, and the manuscript remained in the possession of Mr. Patterson, apparently unnoticed and uncared for. The printer also died in 1826, having previously lent the manuscript to one Sidney Rigdon, a compositor in his employ, who was at the time a preacher in connection with some Christian sect, of which the proper designation is not very clearly stated. This Rigdon afterwards became, next to Joseph Smith himself, the principal leader of the Mormons. How Joseph Smith and this person became connected is not known, and which of the two originated the idea of making a new Bible out of Solomon Spaulding's novel is equally uncertain. The wife, the partner, several friends, and the brother of Solomon Spaulding, affirmed, however, the identity of the principal portions of the *Book of Mormon* with the novel of *The Manuscript Found*, which the author had from time to time, and in separate portions, read over to them. John Spaulding, brother to Solomon, declared upon oath that his brother's book was an historical romance of the first settlers in America, endeavouring to show that the American Indians are the descendants of Jews, or the lost ten tribes. He stated that it gave a detailed account of their journey from Jerusalem by land and by sea, till they arrived in America under the command of Nephi and Lehi; and that it also mentioned the Lamanites. He added that " he had recently read the *Book of Mormon*, and, to his great surprise, he found nearly the same historical matter and names as in his brother's writings. To the best of his recollection and belief, it was the same that his brother Solomon wrote, with the exception of the religious matter."

The widow of Solomon Spaulding afterwards married a Mr. Davison ; and a statement, purporting to have been made by her in the following words, was published in a Boston newspaper in May, 1839 :—

" As the *Book of Mormon*, or *Golden Bible* (as it was originally called) has excited much attention, and is deemed by a certain new sect of equal authority with the Sacred Scriptures, I think it a duty which I owe to the public to state what I know touching its origin.

" That its claims to a divine origin are wholly unfounded needs no proof to a mind unperverted by the grossest delusions. That any sane person should rank it higher than any other merely human composition is a matter of the greatest astonishment; yet it is received as divine by some who dwell in enlightened New England, and even by those who have sustained the character of devoted Christians. Learning recently that Mormonism had found its way into a church in Massachusetts, and has impregnated some with its gross delusions, so that excommunication has been necessary, I am determined to delay no longer in doing what I can to strip the mask from this mother of sin, and to lay open this pit of abominations.

" Solomon Spaulding, to whom I was united in marriage in early life, was a graduate of Dartmouth College, and was distinguished for a lively imagination, and a great fondness for history. At the time of our marriage, he resided in Cherry Valley, New York. From this place, we removed to New Salem, Ashtabula County, Ohio, sometimes called Conneaut, as it is situated on Conneaut Creek. Shortly after our removal to this place, his health sunk, and he was laid aside from active labours. In the town of New Salem there are numerous mounds and forts supposed by many to be the dilapidated dwellings and fortifications of a race now extinct. These ancient relics arrest the attention of the new settlers, and become objects of research for the curious. Numerous implements were found, and other articles evincing great skill in the arts. Mr. Spaulding being an educated man, and passionately fond of history, took a lively interest in these developments of antiquity ; and in order to beguile the hours of retirement, and furnish employment for his lively imagination, he conceived the idea of giving an historical sketch of this long lost race. Their extreme antiquity led him to write in the most ancient style, and as the Old Testament is the most ancient book in the world, he imitated its style as nearly as possible. His sole object in writing this imaginary history was to amuse himself and his neighbours. This was about the year 1812. Hull's surrender at Detroit occurred near the same time, and I recollect the date well from that circumstance. As he progressed in his narrative, the neighbours would come in from time to time to hear portions read, and a great interest in the work was excited among them. It claimed to have been written by one of the lost nation, and to have been recovered from the earth, and assumed the title of ' Manuscript found.' The neighbours would often inquire how Mr. Spaulding progressed in deciphering the manuscript ; and when he had a sufficient portion prepared, he would inform them, and they would assemble to hear it read. He was enabled, from his acquaintance with the classics and ancient history, to introduce many singular names, which were particularly noticed by the people, and could be easily recognised by them. Mr. Solomon Spaulding had a brother, Mr. John Spaulding, residing in the place at the time, who was perfectly familiar with the work, and repeatedly heard the whole of it read. From New Salem we removed to Pittsburgh, in Pennsylvania. Here Mr. Spaulding found a friend and acquaintance, in the person of Mr. Patterson, an editor of a newspaper. He exhibited his manuscript to Mr. Patterson, who was very much pleased with it, and borrowed it for perusal. He retained it for a long time, and informed Mr. Spaulding that if he would make out a title page and preface, he would publish it, and it might be a source of profit. This Mr. Spaulding refused to do. Sidney Rigdon, who has figured so largely in the history of the Mormons, was at that time connected with the printing office of Mr. Patterson, as is well known in that region, and as Rigdon himself has frequently stated, became acquainted with Mr. Spaulding's manuscript, and copied it. It was a matter of notoriety and interest to all connected with the printing establishment. At length the manuscript was returned to its author, and soon after we removed to Amity, Washington county, &c., where Mr. Spaulding deceased in 1816. The manuscript then fell into my hands, and was carefully preserved. It has frequently been examined by my daughter Mrs. M'Kenstry, of Monson, Massachusetts, with whom I now reside, and by other friends.

"After the book of Mormon came out, a copy of it was taken to New Salem, the place of Mr. Spaulding's former residence, and the very place where the manuscript found was written. A woman preacher appointed a meeting there ; and in the meeting read and repeated copious extracts from the book of Mormon. The historical part was immediately recognised by all the older inhabitants, as the identical work of Mr. Spaulding, in which they had all been so deeply interested years before. Mr. John Spaulding was present and recognised perfectly the work of his brother. He was amazed and afflicted that it should have been perverted to so wicked a purpose. His grief found vent in a flood of tears, and he arose on the spot, and expressed to the meeting his sorrow and regret that the writings of his deceased brother should be used for a purpose so vile and shocking. The excitement in New Salem became so great, that the inhabitants had a meeting, and deputed Dr. Philastus Hurlbut, one of their number, to repair to this place, and to obtain from me the original manuscript of Mr. Spaulding, for the purpose of comparing it with the Mormon Bible, to satisfy their own minds, and to prevent their friends from embracing an error so delusive. This was in the year 1834. Dr. Hurlbut brought with him an introduction and request for the manuscript, which was signed by Messrs. Henry Lake, Aaron Wright, and others, with all of whom I was acquainted, as they were my neighbours when I resided at New Salem. I am sure that nothing would grieve my husband more, were he living, than the use which has been made of his work. The air of antiquity which was thrown about the composition doubtless suggested the idea of converting it to the purposes of delusion. Thus, an historical romance, with the addition of a few pious expressions, and extracts from the sacred Scriptures, has been construed into a new Bible, and palmed off upon a company of poor deluded fanatics as Divine. I have given the previous brief narration, that this work of deep deception and wickedness may be searched to the foundation, and the authors exposed to the contempt and execration they so justly deserve.

"MATILDA DAVISON."

The Dr. Hurlbut mentioned in Mrs. Davison's statement was once a believer in Joseph Smith, and a member of the church. According to his own account, he seceded, because his eyes were opened to the imposture and delusion of which he had been the victim. According to the Mormon account, he was expelled for adultery and other immorality. With this preface, the following coarse denial of Mrs. Davison's statement, and fierce denunciation of Dr. Hurlbut, will be intelligible. The denial was made by Sidney Rigdon, who was himself accused of being the principal agent of the fraud, and was addressed, on the 27th of May, 1839, to the editors of the *Boston Journal*. It will be seen from the tone and spirit, no less than from the grammatical construction of the letter, that Sidney Rigdon, although a compositor, was by no means so well educated as the bulk of his fellow-workmen in that intellectual branch of mechanical industry, and that his literary abilities were of the meanest order:—

"*Commerce, May* 27, 1839.

"Messrs. BARTLETT and SULLIVAN,—In your paper of the 18th instant, I see a letter signed by somebody calling herself Matilda Davison, pretending to give the origin of Mormonism, as she is pleased to call it, by relating a moonshine story about a certain Solomon Spaulding, a creature with the knowledge of whose earthly existence I am entirely indebted to this production; for surely, until Doctor Philastus Hurlbut informed me that such a being lived, at some former period, I had not the most distant knowledge of his existence; and all I now know about his character is, the opinion I form from what is attributed to his wife, in obtruding my name upon the public in the manner in which she is said to have done it, by trying to make the public believe that I had knowledge of the ignorant, and, according to her own testimony, the lying scribblings of her deceased husband; for if her testimony is to be credited, her pious husband, in his lifetime, wrote a bundle of lies, for the righteous purpose of getting money. How many lies he had told for the same purpose while he was preaching, she has not so kindly informed us; but we are at liberty to draw our own conclusions, for he that would write lies to get money, would also preach lies for the same object. This being the only information which I have, or ever had, of the said Rev. Solomon Spaulding, I, of necessity, have but a very light opinion of him as a gentleman, a scholar, or a man of piety; for had he have been either, he certainly would have taught his pious wife not to lie, nor unite herself with adulterers, liars, and the basest of mankind.

"It is only necessary to say, in relation to the whole story about Spaulding's writings being in the hands of Mr. Patterson, who was in Pittsburgh, and who is said to have kept a printing office, and my saying that I was concerned in the said office, &c., &c., is the most base of lies, without even the shadow of truth. There was no man by the name of Patterson, during my residence at Pittsburgh, who had a printing office; what might have been before I lived there I know not. Mr. Robert Patterson, I was told, had owned a printing office before I lived in that city, but had been unfortunate in business, and failed before my residence there. This Mr. Patterson, who was a Presbyterian preacher, I had a very slight acquaintance with during my residence in Pittsburgh. He was then acting under an agency, in the book and stationery business, and was the owner of no property of any kind, printing office or anything else, during the time I resided in the city.

"If I were to say that I ever heard of the Rev. Solomon Spaulding and his hopeful wife, until Dr. P. Hurlbut wrote his lie about me, I should be a liar like unto themselves. Why was not the testimony of Mr. Patterson obtained to give force to this shameful tale of lies? The only reason is, that he was not a fit tool for them to work with; he would not lie for them, for if he were called on he would testify to what I have here said.

"Let me here, Gentlemen, give a history of this Dr. P. Hurlbut and his associates, who aided in getting up and propagating this batch of lies.

"I have seen and heard, at one time and another, by the persecutors and haters of the truth, a great deal about the eminent physician, Dr. Hurlbut. I never thought the matter worthy of notice, nor probably ever should, had it not made its appearance in your paper, or some one of equal respectability. And I believe, Gentlemen, had you known the whole history of this budget of lies, it would never have found a place in your paper. But to my history.

"This said Doctor was never a physician at any time, nor anything else but a base ruffian.   He was the seventh son, and his parents called him Doctor : it was his name, and not the title of his profession.

" He once belonged to the Methodist church, and was excluded for immoralities.   He afterwards imposed himself on the church of Latter-Day Saints, and was excluded for using obscene language to a young lady, a member of the said church, who resented his insult with indignation, which became both her character and profession.

" After his exclusion he swore—for he was vilely profane—that he would have revenge, and commenced his work.   He soon found assistance ; a pious old deacon of the Campbellite church, by the name of Onis Clapp, and his two sons, Thomas J. Clapp and Matthew S. Clapp, both Campbellite preachers, abetted and assisted by another Campellite preacher by the name of Adamson Bentley.   Hurlbut went to work, catering lies for the company.   Before Hurlbut got through, his conduct became so scandalous that the company utterly refused to let his name go out with the lies he had collected, and which he and his associates had made, they therefore substituted the name of E. D. Howe.   The change, however, was not much better.   There were scandalous immoralities about the Howe family of so black a character, that they had nothing to lose, and became good tools for this holy company to work with.   A man of character would never have put his name to a work which Hurlbut was concerned in.   But while Hurlbut was busily employed in the service of the company, old Deacon Clapp was employed in taking care of his wife.   How many others of the company aided in this business must be left to futurity to disclose.   At a certain time, Hurlbut being out till a late hour in the night, returned to his house, and in going to his bed-room where his wife was, behold, and lo! there was the pious old deacon, either in bed with his wife or at the side of it.   He had a five-dollar bank note in his hand, and his dress was rather light to suit the Doctor's taste, for he was not quite as well off as was Aaron when he offered sacrifice, not even having on a pair of 'linen breeches.'   Hurlbut laid hold of him and called for help, which soon came to his assistance.   The pious old deacon was arraigned before a justice of the peace, and was on the eve of being bound over for his appearance to the county court, when, to put an end to the evils which might result from his pious care of Mrs. Hurlbut, he kindly offered a yoke of oxen and a hundred dollars.   This was accepted.   Hurlbut took his wife, and left the country forthwith ; and the pious old deacon and his sons, and the good Mr. Bentley, are left to wear out the shame of their great effort to destroy the character of innocent men whom they never dare meet in argument.   The tale in your paper is one hatched up by this gang before the time of their explosion.

" It has always been a source of no ordinary satisfaction to me to know that my enemies have no better weapon to use against me, or the cause in which I am engaged, than lies ; for if they had any better they would certainly use them.   I must confess, however, that there is some consistency in our persecutors, for as truth can never destroy truth, it would be in vain for our persecutors to use truth against us, for this would only build us up ; this they seem to know, and lay hold of the only available means they have, which are lies; and this indeed is the only weapon which can be, or ever has been, used against the truth. As our persecutors are endeavouring to stop the progress of truth, I must confess that they act with a degree of consistency in the choice of means, namely, lies; but if truth would do it, they would surely not have recourse to lies.

" In order to give character to their lies, they dress them up with a great deal of piety : for a pious lie, you know, has a great deal more influence with an ignorant people, than a profane one. Hence their lies came signed by the pious wife of a pious deceased priest. However, his last act of piety seems to have been to write a bundle of lies, themselves being witnesses; but then his great piety sanctifies them, and lies become holy things in the hands of such excessive piety, particularly when they are graced with a few Reverends; but the days have gone by when people are to be deceived by these false glossings of Reverend's sanctions; the intelligent part of the communities of all parts of the country, know that Reverends are not more notorious for truth than their neighbours.

"The only reason why I am assailed by lies is, that my opposers dare not adventure on argument, knowing that if they do they fall. They try, therefore, to keep the public from investigating, by publishing and circulating falsehoods. This I consider a high encomium on both myself and the cause I defend. Respectfully,

" S. RIGDON."

We believe that upon this evidence, the question of the authorship of the original romance on which the *Book of Mormon* was founded, will be decided by the reader in favour of Solomon Spaulding. As regards the *Book of Mormon* itself, Joseph Smith and the vulgar and abusive Sidney Rigdon seem to have acted in concert in its concoction from materials thus provided for them. The religious matter derived from the Old and New Testaments is engrafted upon the original romance in a manner that shows the ignorant and the illiterate workman. Such phrases as the following are of frequent occurrence :—" Ye are are like unto they"—" Do as ye hath hitherto done"— " I—the Lord delighteth in the chastity of women"—" I saith unto them"—" I who ye call your King"—" These things had not ought to be"—" Ye saith unto him"—" For a more history part are written upon my other plates." Anachronisms are also frequent; but all errors of grammar, all anachronisms, all contradictions, are admitted by the Mormons. They allege that the Old and New Testaments contain ungrammatical passages, and yet are holy, and the undoubted word of God; and that anachronisms and contradictions do not militate against the plenary inspiration either of the Bible or of the *Book of Mormon*. They acknowledge all possible faults and objections which mere critics may start; but treat them as of no account. Joseph Smith, they say, was the chosen vessel of grace, and it was not necessary, in the inscrutable purposes of the Lord, that he should write or speak correct English; or that he should not make a few human mistakes in his rendering of the divine word. All such objections they laugh to scorn.

Joseph Smith, who, on all occasions of doubt, silenced the uninformed, and amazed the educated, by the boldness of his own self-sufficiency, and the boundless resources of his impudence, was often asked, both by friends and foes, the meaning of the word " Mormon." The following reply, as published in a letter to the editor of the *Times and Seasons* is highly characteristic:—

" SIR,—Through the medium of your paper, I wish to correct an error among men that profess to be learned, liberal, and wise; and I do it the more cheerfully, because I hope sober-thinking and sound reasoning people will sooner listen to the voice of truth, than be led astray by the vain pretensions of the self-wise. The error I speak of is the definition of the word ' Mormon.' It has been stated that this word was derived from the Greek word *mormo*. This is not the case. There was no Greek or Latin upon the plates from which I, through the grace of God, translated the Book of Mormon. Let the language of that book speak for itself. On the 523rd page of the fourth edition, it reads :—' And now behold we have written the record according to our knowledge in the characters, which are called among us the Reformed Egyptian, being handed down and altered by us according to our manner of speech; and if our plates were sufficiently large, we should have written in Hebrew. Behold ye would have had no imperfections in our record, but the Lord knoweth the things which we have written, and also, that none other people knoweth our language ; therefore he hath prepared means for the interpretation thereof.

" Here, then, the subject is put to silence, for ' none other people knoweth our language;' therefore the Lord, and not man, hath to interpret, after the people were all dead. And, as Paul said, ' the world by wisdom know not God,' and the world by speculation are destitute of revelation; and as God, in his superior wisdom, has always given his saints, wherever he had any on the earth, the same spirit, and that spirit (as John says) is the true spirit of prophecy, which is the testimony of Jesus, I may safely say that the word Mormon stands independent of the learning and wisdom of this generation. Before I give a definition, however, to the word, let me say that the Bible, in its widest sense, means good; for the Saviour says, according to the Gospel of St. John, ' I am the good shepherd;' and it will not be beyond the common use of terms to say, that good is amongst the most important in use, and though known by various names in different languages, still its meaning is the same, and is ever in opposition to bad. We say from the Saxon, *good ;* the Dane, *god ;* the Goth, *goda ;* the German, *gut ;* the Dutch, *goed ;* the Latin, *bonus ;* the Greek, *kalos ;* the Hebrew, *tob ;* and the Egyptian, *mon.* Hence, with the addition of more, or the contraction *mor*, we have the word Mormon, which means, literally, *more good.* Yours JOSEPH SMITH."

JOSEPH SMITH.   HYRUM SMITH.

(From the busts by Gahagan.)

CHAPTER II.

THE BOOK OF DOCTRINES AND COVENANTS; OR, THE "REVELATIONS" OF JOSEPH SMITH—
MORMON HYMNS AND POEMS—MATERIALISM—THE AARONIC AND MELCHIZIDEK PRIEST-
HOOD—CONFESSION OF FAITH—MORMON CLAIMS TO WORK MIRACLES AND TO CAST OUT
DEVILS—SCENES IN LEAMINGTON AND WALES.

IN addition to the *Book of Mormon*, Joseph Smith originated and
partly composed a book of *Doctrines* and *Covenants*, purporting to
be direct revelations from heaven upon the temporal government
of their church, the support of the poor, the tithing or taxation of
the members, the establishment of cities and temples, the allotment
of lands, the emigration of the "saints," the education of the people,
the gathering of moneys, and other matters. This book abounds in
grammatical inaccuracies, even to a greater extent than the *Book of
Mormon:*—"God, that knowest thy thoughts"—"a literal descendant
of Aaron"—"an hair of his head shall not fall"—"your Father who
art in heaven knoweth"—"and the spirit and the body is the soul of
man"—"the stars also giveth their light as they roll upon their wings
in glory"—"her who sitteth upon many waters"—"thou shalt not
covet thine own property, but impart it freely to the printing of the
Book of Mormon"—form but a sample of hundreds of similar phrases
that might be culled, were it worth while. A few specimens of

the kind of "Revelations," and of the style in which Joseph Smith represented the Almighty as speaking to him in his early revelations, will show what men will assert and believe under the influence of fanaticism. The following is part of a revelation purporting to have been given by Jesus Christ, in February, 1831. In these revelations God the Father and God the Son are invariably represented as giving Joseph his proper designation of Smith, *junior*, that he might not be mistaken for his father, Joseph Smith, *senior* :—

" Hearken, oh ye elders of my church, who have assembled yourselves together in my name, even Jesus Christ, the Son of the living God, the Saviour of the world. Behold, verily I say unto you, I give unto you this first commandment, that you shall go forth in my name, every one of you, except my servants, Joseph Smith, jun., and Sidney Rigdon. . . . If there shall be properties in the hands of the church, or any individuals of it, more than is necessary for their support, it shall be kept to administer to those who have not."

The following is part of a revelation given to Joseph Smith in March, 1829, when Martin Harris desired to see the golden plates, and before he was deluded with the paper transcript, which he showed to Professor Anthon. It will be seen that Joseph was not at a loss to parry the inconvenient curiosity of his then doubting, but afterwards faithful, disciple :—

" Behold, I say unto you, that as my servant Martin Harris has desired a witness at my hand, that you my servant, Joseph Smith, jun., have got the plates of which you have testified and borne record that you have received of me ; and now, behold, this shall you say unto him—' He who spake unto you said unto you, I the Lord am God, and have given those things unto you, my servant, Joseph Smith, jun., and have commanded you that you should stand as a witness of these things ; *and I have caused you that you should enter into a covenant with me that you should not show them except to those persons that I commanded you ; and you have no power over them except I grant it you.*' . . And now, again I speak unto you my servant Joseph, concerning the man that denies the witness. Behold, I say unto him, he exalts himself, and does not sufficiently humble himself before me. But if he will bow down before me, and humble himself in mighty prayer and faith, in the sincerity of his heart, then will I grant unto him a view of the things which he desires to see."

Poor Martin Harris never got the promised glimpse of the plates. He did not behave himself properly ; and Joseph found an opportunity to reprimand and quarrel with him. But, in fact, Joseph and his principal assistant, Sidney Rigdon, appear to have quarrelled with all the "witnesses." The first witness to the truth of this *Book of Mormon* was declared by Smith himself, in a revelation given in November, 1831, to be unfit to be trusted with " moneys :"—

" Hearken unto me, saith the Lord your God, for my servant Oliver Cowdery's sake. It is not wisdom in me that he should be entrusted with the
commandments, *and the moneys* which he shall carry into the land of Zion,
except one go with him who shall be true and faithful."

In a paper drawn up by Sidney Rigdon in June, 1838, when the
great schism took place in the church, which led to the secession of
Dr. Hurlbut, and the exposure made by Mrs. Davison, it is stated
that Oliver Cowdery, David Whitmer, and another, were united with
a gang of "counterfeiters, thieves, liars, and blacklegs of the deepest
dye, to deceive, cheat, and defraud the saints." Martin Harris, the
last of the three, is spoken of, at the time of the schism, by Joseph
himself, in the following terms, in a paper called the *Elder's
Journal:*—" There are negroes who wear white skins, as well as black
ones. Grames Parish and others who acted as lackies, such as Martin
Harris, &c., but they are so far beneath contempt that a notice of them
would be too great a sacrifice for a gentleman to make."

While, by means of "revelations," those who were not longer to
be trusted were pointed out to the notice and condemnation of true
believers, Joseph Smith took care to have special "revelations" upon
matters relating to his own comfort. "It is meet," says a "revelation" of the Lord in February, 1831, "that my servant Joseph
Smith, jun., should have a house built, in which to live and translate." A second "revelation" of the same month says: "If ye desire
the mysteries of my kingdom, provide for him (Joseph Smith, jun.)
food and raiment, and whatsoever thing he needeth." Nor was
Joseph, according to the "Revelations," to labour for his living. "In
temporal labours," says another "revelation" of July, 1830, "thou
shalt not have strength; for that is not thy calling. Attend to thy
calling, and thou shalt have wherewith to magnify thine office, and
to expound all scriptures."

In a revelation given to Joseph Smith and Sidney Rigdon, in December, 1830, when the scheme was yet in its first infancy, the Lord
is represented as saying:—

" Behold, verily, verily, I say unto my servant Sidney, I have looked
upon thee and thy works. I have heard thy prayers, and prepared thee for
a great work. Thou art blessed, for thou shalt do great things. Behold
thou wast sent forth, even as John, to prepare the way before me, and before
Elijah, which should come, and thou knew it not. Thou didst baptize by
water unto repentance, but thou receivedst not the Holy Ghost; but now I
give unto thee a commandment, that thou shalt baptize by water, and they
shall receive the Holy Ghost by the laying on of the hands, even as the
apostles of old.

"And it shall come to pass, that there shall be a great work in the land, even among the Gentiles : for their folly and their abominations shall be made manifest in the eyes of all people ; for I am God, and mine arm is not shortened, and I will show miracles, signs, and wonders, unto all those who believe in my name. And whoso shall ask in my name, in faith, they shall cast out devils, they shall heal the sick, they shall cause the blind to receive their sight, and the deaf to hear, and the dumb to speak, and the lame to walk ; and the time speedily cometh, that great things are to be shown forth unto the children of men ; but without faith shall not anything be shown forth, except desolations upon Babylon—the same which has made all nations drink of the wine of the wrath of her fornication. And there are none that doeth good, except those who are ready to receive the fulness of my Gospel, which I have sent forth to this generation.

"Wherefore, I have called upon the weak things of the world—those who are unlearned and despised, to thresh the nations by the power of my Spirit : and their arm shall be my arm, and I will be their shield and their buckler, and I will gird up their loins, and they shall fight manfully for me, and their enemies shall be under their feet ; and I will let fall the sword in their behalf, and by the fire of mine indignation will I preserve them. And the poor and the meek shall have the Gospel preached unto them, and they shall be looking forth for the time of my coming, for it is nigh at hand : and they shall learn the parable of the fig-tree : for even now already summer is nigh, and I have sent forth the fulness of the Gospel by the hand of my servant Joseph : and in weakness have I blessed him, and I have given unto him the keys of the mystery of those things which have been sealed, even things which were from the foundation of the world, and the things which shall come from this time until the time of my coming, if he abide in me ; and if not, another will I plant in his stead.

"Wherefore, watch over him, that his faith fail not ; and it shall be given by the Comforter the Holy Ghost, that knoweth all things : and a commandment I give unto thee, that thou shalt write for him : and the Scriptures shall be given, even as they are in mine own bosom, to the salvation of mine own elect ; for they will hear my voice, and shall see me, and shall not be asleep, and shall abide the day of my coming, for they shall be purified, even as I am pure. And now I say unto thee, tarry with him, and he shall journey with you ;—forsake him not, and surely these things shall be fulfilled. And inasmuch as ye do not write, behold it shall be given unto him to prophesy : and thou shalt preach my Gospel, and call upon the holy prophets to prove his words, as they shall be given him. Keep all the commandments and covenants by which ye are bound, and I will cause the heavens to shake for your good : and Satan shall tremble, and Zion shall rejoice upon the hills and flourish ; and Israel shall be saved in mine own due time. And by the keys which I have given, shall they be led, and no more be confounded at all. Lift up your heads and be glad : your redemption draweth nigh. Fear not, little flock—the kingdom is yours until I come. Behold, I come quickly : even so. Amen."

In another revelation, also given in December, 1830, the voice of the Lord to Edward Partridge was :—

"Thus saith the Lord God, the mighty one of Israel, Behold, I say unto you, my servant Edward, that you are blessed, and your sins are forgiven you, and you are called to preach my Gospel as with the voice of a trumpet; and I will lay my hand upon you by the hand of my servant Sidney Rigdon, and you shall receive my Spirit, the Holy Ghost, even the Comforter, which shall teach you the peaceable things of the kingdom : and you shall declare it with a loud voice, saying, Hosannah, blessed be the name of the most high God.

"And now this calling and commandment give I unto you concerning all men, that as many as shall come before my servants Sidney Rigdon and Joseph Smith, jun., embracing this calling and commandment, shall be ordained and sent forth to preach the everlasting Gospel among the nations, crying, Repentance : saying, Save yourselves from this untoward generation, and come forth out of the fire, hating even the garments spotted with the flesh.

"And this commandment shall be given unto the elders of my church, that every man which will embrace it with singleness of heart, may be ordained and sent forth, even as I have spoken. I am Jesus Christ, the Son of God: wherefore gird up your loins, and I will suddenly come to my temple : even so. Amen."

An extract from one more "revelation" will suffice for the present. It purports to have been given, in July, 1830, to Emma Smith, the wife of Joseph, through Joseph himself:—

"The office of thy calling shall be for a comfort unto my servant Joseph Smith, jun., thy husband. And thou shall go with him at the time of his going, and be unto him for a scribe, while there is no one to be a scribe for him, that I may send my servant Oliver Cowdery whithersoever I will. And it shall be given to thee also to make a selection of sacred hymns, as it shall be given thee, which is pleasing unto me to be had in my church."

The hymn-book of Emma Smith does not appear to have been published; but a little hymn-book, containing hymns selected by Brigham Young, the present head of the church, and successor of Joseph Smith, has gone through eight editions. The eighth was published in Liverpool, in 1849. A few extracts will not be out of place. The following hymn, which is sometimes sung on shipboard in Liverpool prior to the departure of Mormon emigrants, is, in point of literary merit, among the best in the volume :—

> "Yes, my native land, I love thee ;
>   All thy scenes, I love them well ;
> Friends, connections, happy country,
>   Can I bid you all farewell ?
>   Can I leave thee,
>   Far in distant lands to dwell ?

" Home ! thy joys are passing lovely,
　　Joys no stranger heart can tell ;
Happy home ! 'tis sure I love thee,
　　　Can I—can I—say ' Farewell ?'
　　　　　Can I leave thee,
　　　Far in distant lands to dwell ?

" Holy scenes of joy and gladness
　　Every fond emotion swell ;
Can I banish heartfelt sadness,
　　　While I bid my home farewell ?
　　　　　Can I leave thee,
　　　Far in distant lands to dwell ?

" Yes ! I hasten from you gladly,
　　From the scenes I love so well ;
Far away, ye billows, bear me,
　　　Lovely native land, farewell !
　　　　　Pleased I leave thee,
　　　Far in distant lands to dwell.

" In the deserts let me labour,
　　On the mountains let me tell
How he died—the blessed Saviour,
　　　To redeem a world from hell !
　　　　　Let me hasten,
　　　Far in distant lands to dwell !

" Bear me on, thou restless ocean,
　　Let the winds my canvas swell ;
Heaves my heart with warm emotion,
　　　While I go far hence to dwell !
　　　　　Glad I bid thee,
　　Native land, farewell ! farewell !"

The next is a hymn for the Twelve Apostles, who have been sent
to different parts of Europe, to " gather" the Saints to the Salt Lake
Valley in Deseret :—

" Ye chosen twelve, to ye are given
　　The keys of this last ministry—
To every nation under heaven,
　　From land to land, from sea to sea.

" First to the Gentiles sound the news,
　　Throughout Columbia's happy land ;
And then before it reach the Jews,
　　Prepare on Europe's shores to stand.

> " Let Europe's towns and cities hear
>   The Gospel tidings angels bring ;
> The Gentile nations far and near,
>   Prepare their hearts His praise to sing.
>
> " India and Afric's sultry plains
>   Must hear the tidings as they roll—
> Where darkness, death, and sorrow reign,
>   And tyranny has held control.
>
> " Listen ! ye islands of the sea,
>   For every isle shall hear the sound ;
> Nations and tongues before unknown,
>   Though long since lost, shall soon be found.
>
> " And then again shall Asia hear,
>   Where angels first the news proclaimed ;
> Eternity shall record bear,
>   And earth repeat the loud Amen.
>
> " The nations catch the pleasing sound,
>   And Jew and Gentile swell the strain,
> Hosannah o'er the earth resound,
>   Messiah then will come to reign."

Many of their fugitive hymns and songs, not included in their hymn-book, are adapted to popular tunes, such as " The sea, the sea, the open sea ;" " Away, away to the mountain's brow," &c.   One to the first-mentioned tune is inserted in the *Times and Seasons*, page 895, and commences :—

> " The sky, the sky, the clear blue sky,
>   Oh, how I love to gaze upon it !
> The upper realms of deep on high,
>   I wonder when the Lord begun it !"

The following additional specimens of Mormon devotional poetry appear in their authorized organ, the *Times and Seasons*.   The first is sung to the tune of a pirate song by Mr. Henry Russell, called, " I'm afloat, I'm afloat," and written by Miss Eliza Cook :—

> " I'm a Saint, I'm a Saint, on the rough world wide,
> The earth is my home, and my God is my guide !
> Up, up with the truth, let its power bend the knee :
> I am sent, I am sent, and salvation is free.
> I fear not old priestcraft, its dogmas can't awe :
> I've a chart for to steer by, that tells me the law,—
> And ne'er as a coward to falsehood I'll kneel,
> While Mormon tells truth, or God's prophets reveal !

Up, up with the truth, let its power touch the mind,
And I'll warrant we'll soon leave the selfish behind.
Up, up with the truth, let its power bend the knee,
I am sent! I am sent! dying Bab'lon to thee,
I am sent! I am sent! take this warning and flee.

" The arm of the tyrant, fell terror may spread,
Yet, tho' they oppose us, their strongholds we'll tread;
What to us is the scorn of the selfish and vain ?
We have borne it before, and we'll bear it again.
The fire-gleaming bolts of oppression may fall,
And kill off the body, death can't us appal !
With Heaven above us, and all Hell below,
Thro' the wide field of error, right onward we'll go !
Come on! my brave comrades, now's the time you should speak,
The storm-fiend is roused from his long dreamy sleep.
Our watch-word, for safety in Zion, shall be,
I am sent! I am sent! dying Bab'lon to thee,—
I am sent! I am sent! take this warning and flee."

But the following, to the tune of " The rose that all are praising,"
is, perhaps, the most characteristic; and with it we may conclude the
specimens of Mormon devotional poetry :—

" The God that others worship is not the God for me;
He has no parts nor body, and cannot hear nor see;
  But I've a God that lives above—
  A God of Power and of Love—
A God of Revelation—oh, that's the God for me;
Oh, that's the God for me; oh, that's the God for me!

" A church without apostles is not the church for me;
It's like a ship dismasted, afloat upon the sea;
  But I've a church that's always led
  By the twelve stars round its head;
A church with good foundations—oh, that's the church for me;
Oh, that's the church for me; oh, that's the church for me !

" A church without a prophet is not the church for me ;
It has no head to lead it, in it I would not be;
  But I've a church not built by man,
  Cut from the mountain without hands;
A church with gifts and blessings—oh, that's the church for me ;
Oh, that's the church for me; oh, that's the church for me.

" The hope that Gentiles cherish is not the hope for me;
It has no hope for knowledge, far from it I would be;

But I've an hope that will not fail,
That reaches safe within the veil ;
Which hope is like an anchor—oh, that's the hope for me ;
Oh, that's the hope for me ; oh, that's the hope for me !

" The heaven of sectarians is not the heaven for me ;
So doubtful its location, neither on land nor sea ;
But I've an heaven on the earth,
The land and home that gave me birth ;
A heaven of light and knowledge—oh, that's the heaven for me ;
Oh, that's the heaven for me ; oh, that's the heaven for me !

" A church without a gathering is not the church for me ;
The Saviours would not order it, whatever it might be ;
But I've a church that's called out,
From false traditions, fear, and doubt,
A gathering dispensation—oh, that's the church for me ;
Oh, that's the church for me ; oh, that's the church for me !"

The following summary of the Mormon creed is given in their own periodicals, as the recognised " FAITH OF THE LATTER-DAY SAINTS :"—

" We believe in God the eternal Father, and his Son Jesus Christ, and in the Holy Ghost.

" We believe that men will be punished for their own sins, and not for Adam's transgressions.

" We believe that through the atonement of Christ all mankind may be saved, by obedience to the laws and ordinances of the Gospel.

" We believe that these ordinances are :—1st, Faith in the Lord Jesus Christ. 2nd, Repentance. 3rd, Baptism by immersion for the remission of sins. 4th, Laying on of hands for the gift of the Holy Spirit. 5th, The Lord's Supper.

" We believe that men must be called of God by inspiration, and by laying on of hands by those who are duly commissioned to preach the Gospel, and administer in the ordinances thereof.

" We believe in the same organization that existed in the primitive church viz., apostles, prophets, pastors, teachers, evangelists, &c.

" We believe in the powers and gifts of the everlasting Gospel, viz., the gift of faith, discerning of spirits, prophecy, revelation, visions, healing, tongues and the interpretation of tongues, wisdom, charity, brotherly love, &c.

" We believe in the Word of God recorded in the Bible ; we also believe the Word of God recorded in the Book of Mormon, and in all other good books.

" We believe all that God has revealed ; all that he does now reveal ; and we believe that he will yet reveal many more great and important things pertaining to the Kingdom of God, and Messiah's second coming.

" We believe in the literal gathering of Israel, and in the restoration of the ten tribes; that Zion will be established upon the western continent; that Christ will reign personally upon the earth a thousand years; and that the earth will be renewed, and receive its paradisaical glory.

" We believe in the literal resurrection of the body, and that the dead in Christ will rise first, and that the rest of the dead live not again until the thousand years are expired.

" We claim the privilege of worshipping Almighty God according to the dictates of our conscience unmolested, and allow all men the same privilege, let them worship how or where they may.

" We believe in being subject to kings, queens, presidents, rulers, and magistrates, in obeying, honouring, and sustaining the law.

" We believe in being honest, true, chaste, temperate, benevolent, virtuous, and upright, and in doing good to all men; indeed, we may say that we follow the admonition of Paul, we 'believe all things,' we 'hope all things,' we have endured very many things, and hope to be able to 'endure all things.' Everything virtuous, lovely, praiseworthy, and of good report, we seek after, looking forward to the 'recompense of reward.' "

The Mormons recognise two orders of priesthood, the " Aaronic" and the " Melchizidek." They are governed by a prophet or president, twelve apostles, the " seventies," and a number of bishops, highpriests, deacons, elders, and teachers; they assert, as will be seen from the last hymn, and their Confession of Faith, that the gifts of prophecy and the power of working miracles have not ceased; that Joseph Smith and many other Mormons wrought miracles and cast out devils; that the end of the world is close at end; and that they are the " saints" spoken of in the Apocalypse, who will reign with Christ in a temporal kingdom in this world. They assert also, in more precise terms than they employ in their printed " Confession of Faith," that the seat of this kingdom is to be either Missouri—the place originally intended—or their present location of the Great Salt Lake Valley of Deseret. They allege that their *Book of Mormon* and the " Doctrine" and " Covenants" form the fulness of the Gospel; that they take nothing from the Old or the New Testament, both of which they complete. They seem, however, not to have formed the same ideas of God which are promulgated in the Gospel, but to acknowledge a material deity. This idea appears in the song or hymn to the tune of " The rose that all are praising," already quoted; but is stated more broadly in the *Times and Seasons*, and other works. The following extract from the authorized documents, signed by Orson Spencer, one of the apostles of the church, gives the views of the sect upon this and other subjects:—" In some, and indeed in many respects, do we differ from some sectarian denominations. We believe that God is a being who hath both body and parts, and also passions. Also of the existence of the gifts, in the true church, spoken of in Paul's letter to the Corinthians. I do not believe that the career of Sacred Scripture was closed with the Revelation of John, but that wherever God has a true church, there he makes frequent revelations of his will; and as God takes cognizance of all things, both temporal and spiritual, his revelations will pertain to all things whereby his glory may be promoted."

Joseph Smith is more explicit. The following passage occurs in the *Millennial Star*, vol. vi., under the "prophet's" authority, and signed with his name :—

"What is God? He is a material organized intelligence, possessing both body and parts. He is in the form of a man, and is, in fact, of the same species, and is a model or standard of perfection, to which man is destined to attain, he being the Great Father and Head of the whole family. This being cannot occupy two distinct places at once, therefore he cannot be everywhere present.

"What are Angels? They are intelligences of the human species. Many of them are the offspring of Adam and Eve—of men, it is said, ' being Gods, or sons of God, endowed with the same powers, attributes, aud capacities, that their Heavenly Father and Jesus Christ possess.'

"The weakest child of God, which now exists upon the earth, will possess more dominion, more property, more subjects, and more power and glory, than is possessed by Jesus Christ or by his Father; while, at the same time, Jesus Christ and his Father will have their dominion, kingdom, and subjects, increased in proportion." *

Joseph Smith and his more immediate followers and disciples always laid claim to the power of working miracles. Many ludicrous stories are told of the attempts made by Joseph and others, to get out of difficulties with their own people, after having promised too much in this respect. These stories are, of course, considered false and scandalous by the Mormons. It is neither necessary nor desirable to reproduce them; but we may select, in preference, a specimen of their

---

* The following extracts from *The Latter-Day Saints' Catechism, or Child's Ladder*, by Elder David Moffat, explain still more fully the ideas of the Mormons on this subject :—

"28. *What is God?*
He is a material intelligent personage, possessing both body and parts.

29. *Could he be a being without body and parts?*
No. Verily, no.

30. *What form is he of?*
He is in the form of man, or rather man is in the form of God.

31. *Where do you find these proofs?*
In the Scriptures of the Old and New Testament.

32. *Can you prove, then, that man is in the form of God?*
Yes. Genesis, v, 1. In the day that God created man, in the likeness of God made he nim.

33. *Can you mention the parts of his body from the Scriptures?*
Yes. Exodus, xxxiii. 22, 23. And I will cover thee with my hand; and I will take away my hand, and thou shalt see my back parts, but my face shall not be seen.

"miracles," as recorded by themselves in their own publication, the *Millennial Star*. It will answer the purpose far better than any statement made by their opponents. In a letter addressed to Mr. Orson Spencer, and published in the *Millennial Star*, for August 1, 1847, the writer, a Mormon, who dates from Leamington Spa, Warwickshire, England, after detailing the attempts made to ordain one Currell to the Mormon priesthood,—attempts which were defeated by the devil, says—

"When we laid our hands upon him, the devil entered him, and tried to prevent us from ordaining him; but the power of Jesus Christ in the holy priesthood was stronger than the devil, and after all the endeavours of the powers of darkness to prevent us;—in the name of Jesus Christ, we ordained brother Richard Currell to the office of a priest in the Church of Jesus Christ of Latter-Day Saints. In consequence of what had taken place, many came to our meeting in the

34. *Can you mention any more parts of his body?*
Yes. Exodus, xxiv. 10. And they saw the God of Israel, and there was under his feet as it were a paved work of a sapphire stone.

35. *Did ever any man speak face to face with God?*
Yes.

36. *To whom did he speak?*
To Moses.

37. *Can you repeat it?*
Yes. Exodus, xxxiii. 11. And the Lord spake unto Moses face to face, as a man speaketh to his friend.

38. *As the God of Heaven possesses body and parts, doth he also possess passions?*
Yes. He eats, he drinks, he loves, he hates.

39. *Where have you an account of his eating?*
When he appeared to his servant Abraham on the plains of Mamre. Genesis, xviii.

39. *Did Abraham know that the Lord desired to eat when he appeared unto him?*
Yes. Genesis, xviii. 5. And I will fetch a morsel of bread, and comfort ye your hearts, for therefore are ye come to your servant.

40. *Can you point out the object of his love?*
Yes. Malachi, i. 2. Was not Esau Jacob's brother, saith the Lord, yet I love Jacob.

41. *What were the things of his hatred?*
The palaces of Jacob.

42. *Can you prove it?*
Yes. Amos, vi. 8. The Lord hath sworn by himself, saith the Lord of Hosts. I abhor the excellency of Jacob, and hate his palaces.

43. *Can this Being (God) occupy two distinct places at once?*
No.

44. *Can he move from planet to planet with facility and ease?*
Yes. Genesis, xi. 5. And the Lord came down to see the city and the tower which the children of men builded.

45. *With whom did the Lord converse?*
With his servant Abraham.

46. *Upon what things did they converse?*
About the destruction of Sodom and Gomorrah.

47. *Doth the Lord also reason with men?*
Yes. Isaiah, i. 18. Come let us reason together, saith the Lord."

D

evening, and paid great attention. The scenes of the 20th of June will long be remembered by us as a day of rejoicing in the glorious manifestation of the power of God, confirming the faith of the saints, and spreading the sound of the Gospel further than we could have done it in a long time.

"I should inform you that when the devil found he was defeated in brother C., he entered a sister. The devils kept coming in for several hours. As fast as one lot were expelled, another lot entered; at one time we counted twenty-seven come out of her. When we rebuked them, they would come out, but as soon returned again. How was it they could acknowledge the power, and yet would damn our power, damn our Gospel, and tear and bite? The sight was awful, but it has done us all good. I may as well say that the devils told us they were sent some by Cain, some by Kite, Judas, Kilo, Kelo, Kalmonia, and Lucifer. Some of these, they informed us, were presidents over seventies in hell. The last that came, previous to our going to prison, told us he was Kilo, one of the presidents, and had six councillors. We cast them out thirty times, and had three hundred and nineteen devils, from three to thirty-seven coming out at a time. I shall feel obliged for any instruction you can give me on this subject."

Another scene of the casting out of devils, related by one Daniel or Dan Jones, a Welsh Saint, dating from Merthyr Tydvil, January 6th, 1849, is still more outrageous. Its recital in the words of the principal actor will amuse the reader who feels inclined to laugh at the extent of human folly, while it may sadden those who are more disposed to grieve at and deplore the fanaticism, which defies the common sense and common decency of mankind. The story occurs in the eleventh volume of the *Millennial Star*, pages 39 and 40:—

"In the afternoon of the 21st of December, 1848, the power of God and also the Power of Darkness showed a wide and marvellous contrast. Whilst I was describing the beauties of Zion, together with the importance of building up there a temple to the Most High God, and the resulting consequences thereof to the Saints' glory and the overthrow of Babylon, the Prince of Darkness thought that I was getting to be too traitorous in the midst of his dominions. He could not bear such good and powerful truths, so he sent a legion of evil spirits into the hall at that time, as though he was determined with one grand rally to storm our little fortress, and demolish our citadel with impunity. In five minutes after their arrival, which was seen by some, three females were possessed, and many more nearly as bad. However, I perceived the enemy's design, and having command of the post, I lost no time in returning him a heavy broadside with the artilleries of heaven, by commanding every evil spirit in

the place to depart in the name of Jesus Christ, which was responded
to by all the audience with such powerful Amens! that the neighbours thought it thundered, and all the devils, except three, run away
in a fright; and the echoes opened the windows of heaven, so that the
power of God was felt and seen by all others in the place, and some of
our worst persecutors, having come there with evil intent, confessed
that God was with us, and shouted Amen as loud as any. There were
hundreds of young Saints who had never witnessed the like, and who
were rather timid, which caused me to maintain the platform for more
than an hour, to teach them the wiles of the devil, and to encourage
them to be brave in the power of God. In the meantime I had sent
some elders to those possessed, to rebuke the spirits, who were all
this time making the loudest noise with me and each other, calling
out—'Old Captain, have you come to trouble us? D——d old Captain, we will hold you a battle.' Many other expressions used would
be indecent to utter, and others useless, I suppose; but some spoke
English through one that knew no English of herself, and revealed
many mysteries; others spoke in tongues, praying for a reinforcement
of their kindred spirits, and chiding some dreadfully by name, such
as Borona, Menta, Philo, &c., for not obeying their mandates with
greater alacrity and courage. The spirits left one of the three females
at the first rebuke, but the others cursed all the elders, calling many
by names with which the females were totally unacquainted. They
said they were at Carthage in the slaughter of the prophets; we compelled them to acknowledge the authority of the priesthood, loudly, to
the astonishment of all. They swore that they would not depart without
'Old Brigham Young, from America, would come;—that they would
have to obey him; but that they held an office higher than any others.' I
questioned one of them on that, 'whether he had ever possessed any other
person in Wales?' 'Yes! very many!' was the reply. I asked, 'Did
you ever leave one unless compelled?' He replied, 'No; nor will I go from
here either.' Then I rebuked him for telling a falsehood, inasmuch as
that Brigham Young had never visited Wales, and that he had better
business than to come and wait on such beings as him; at which he
sneered and laughed, that echoed through the hall and alarmed many;
at the same time, the streets were crowded with strangers and police-
men, drawn there by the noise, and shortly the whole town was in an
uproar, like Ephesus of old. They derided us shamefully for our dis-
appointment in our expectation of the 'Old Apostle to the Conference.'
But enough of this comedy, I must hasten to more important subjects
lest I weary your patience, for I have much more to say; I will only
add the sequel, which was as follows:—Having understood that these
two females had been frequently possessed elsewhere, had the spirits

D 2

rebuked out of them as frequently by the power of the priesthood, and again giving way to them, and living in transgression, I found out the reason why the spirits assured us so often 'that they had a right to them, and that they (the females) had broken their covenant.' The instructions of our beloved brother Hyde to me, 'to cut off such after the third offence,' came forcibly to my mind, the which, before I uttered it, the evil spirits told loud enough to all, which, together with many other instances which they gave vent to, prove, to a demonstration, that these spirits have a way of knowing one's mind. The spirits said we could not cast them out, because some doubted in their minds; and one of them told me to my face, in a harsh voice, 'You doubt yourself;' which was too true, because that I saw the Lord had no alternative under the circumstances, but either to turn a deaf ear to our prayers, or disregard the counsel of Brother Hyde; and I was pretty confident that he would do the former, though to our great annoyance and mortification for the time. I had not understood all about these females at that time, or I would have chosen another and surer method. The next thing I did was to close the meeting, and call the elders together with the females (who were all this time biting, kicking, and swearing, most awfully, and being held by men), and explain to them the principle above alluded to; and when I proposed to cut the females off from the Church, all agreed to it; and after laughing, deriding, and saying that that was what they wanted, the spirits left them both in less than five minutes; so that the females recovered themselves, and went home without any inconvenience. On their way home they were informed that they had been excommunicated, which they had not previously understood, though done over their heads, and they both wept bitterly.

"In that night's meeting our hall was more crowded than before. if possible, and I took the liberty to show the cunning craft of the devil; to caution the Saints not to give a place for evil spirits by transgression, and made an example of the foregoing, to prove to the world that the very devils incarnate testified to the divinity of this Church and Gospel, and that the evil spirits had given the 'old Captain' such a strong testimony and good recommendation as their inveterate foe. I had the satisfaction to know that even the devils, by this affair, had done much good to the Saints and sinners, proving that 'all things work together for good to those that love the Lord;' and this affair, too! During all this time the spirit had led one of the females back, though late, but the place was too crowded for her to get inside, and he kept her running about the streets in front of our hall, shrieking, cursing, barking, and howling the most hideous noises imaginable, which at times penetrated the assembly, but failed to get inside, so that we had a glorious meeting in despite of him and all his legions; and after speaking with my whole strength for seven hours and a half, with but little cessation, I closed the meeting, and disbanded our noble battalion, fully determined to be more valiant than ever."

The familiarity with which fanatics of all kinds speak of the Supreme Being, was never more grossly displayed than in this recital. The profanity of Mr. Dan Jones would be ludicrous, if it were not shocking, when he asserts that he remonstrated for seven hours and a half with the devils, and that he knew the Lord had no alternative but to act under such and such circumstances in such and such a manner. But such a spectacle is, after all, more calculated to excite pity than indignation.

From a mass of instances cited by the Mormons, in proof of their possession of the gift of miraculous healing, a very few will suffice. A preacher of the name of Westwood, writing in the first number of the eleventh volume of the *Millennial Star*, says :—" A woman in the Wesleyan Connexion, by the name of Richardson, who has had a running disease of the legs for some years, heard me preach once; she told her friends she was sure I was a servant of the Lord, and such was her faith, that if she could but touch me, she should be healed. She obtained her desire, and is healed of her disease. Still she has not obeyed the Gospel, but has turned round, persecuting those who would obey; and those who witness the miracle of healing, imbibe the same spirit as in the days of Christ, when they said, 'He casteth out devils by Beelzebub, the prince of devils.'"

Another Mormon preacher of the name of Nibley, dating from Huddersfield, December 12th, 1848, says in the same publication:—" On Sunday the 3rd of December, at three o'clock in the afternoon, I was seized with cholera of a most virulent kind: bowel complaint, vomiting, and cramp, in which I laboured in a most painful condition for some time, until the elder was relieved from preaching at seven at night, who, being called on then, came to my assistance, joined in prayer, and then anointed me with oil, and when the brethren laid on hands, I was immediately restored. On Sunday the 10th of December, Sister Morrison was seized with the same complaint, whereupon I was called to attend her. I administered the ordinance morning and night, and she was also healed. Such is the way the Lord hath dealt with us."

But whether the patients upon whom the Mormons operate, recover or die, it is equally a miracle in the estimation of the true believers, as the following case, which occurred in Glasgow, exemplifies in an amusing manner. A paragraph having appeared in a Glasgow newspaper under the date of February 2nd, 1849, stating that two young girls, attacked with cholera, had died under the treatment of a Latter-Day Saint and several assistant elders, the following explanation was offered on behalf of the Mormons. It is to be found, like the cases already cited, in the eleventh volume of the *Millennial Star :*—

"The two sisters (Mary and Elizabeth Murray) worked in a mill in Govan. About four o'clock P.M., on the 15th of last month, Elizabeth was seized with the cholera while at work in the mill. She and her sister Mary immediately started for home. The afternoon was wet, and the poor girl was soon almost perished with cold. They called at several houses on the way, and asked for the privilege of a fire ; but instead of granting their request, the inmates drove them into the street, and shut their doors upon them. By the time they got to Brother Stewart's (which was directly on their way home), Elizabeth was so overcome, she could go no farther. Here they were kindly taken in. The sisters in the neighbourhood immediately gathered. The poor girl was soon relieved of her wet clothes, and put into a warm bed. The elders were sent for, and they came and anointed her with oil in the name of the Lord Jesus, laid their hands upon her, and prayed the Lord to make manifest his power in her behalf, and rescue her from the grasp of the destroyer. During the night, Mary was also seized with the same disease, but was not laid in the same bed. They bore their sufferings patiently for a short time, but soon they became weary of suffering, and besought the elders present to lay their hands upon them, and pray the Lord to take them to himself, for they had suffered enough. The brethren did so. They were eased from pain, and went off so calmly and quietly, that those around could hardly tell when the last breath left the body.

"This case soon created quite a stir. The doctors were sharp set after the affair, determined, in their holy zeal, to bring the whole matter before the authorities, and inflict the condign punishment upon Elder Stewart, that all persons might hereafter take warning, and suffer no one to leave the world without their assistance, that their exodus from the stage of action might be scientifically attended to, and heavy fees thereby secured to themselves. It is truly a horrible affair for a person in this enlightened age to call on the Lord instead of a doctor —to put their trust in the arm of Jehovah, rather than the arm of flesh.

"Brother Stewart was accordingly arrested, and brought before the magistrates to answer to the charge of culpable homicide. He bore himself nobly, faced his accusers boldly, preached the Gospel to them in his defence, until they were ashamed of themselves, and were glad to dismiss the matter."

But our readers will probably exclaim that they have had enough of the Mormon miracles, and of Mormon doctrine, at least for the present. We proceed to detail the personal history of the "prophet," and the progress of the sect, from 1830 to the present time.

THE MOB TARRING JOSEPH SMITH.

CHAPTER III.

FIRST PERSECUTIONS OF THE SECT—EXPLORATORY JOURNEY TO THE FAR WEST—ESTA-
BLISHMENT IN MISSOURI—THE PROPHET "LYNCHED" BY THE POPULACE—QUARRELS
WITH THE "GENTILES"—THE NEW ZION—PERSECUTIONS IN MISSOURI.

THE truth that no absurdity of fanaticism is too outrageous to attract
believers, finds continual corroboration. The learned and the unlearned,
the rich and the poor, the gentle and the simple, alike break through
the trammels of reason, and become the dupes of religious impostors,
or of persons who are still more dangerous—the religious maniacs, who
strengthen their cause by their own conscientious belief in it. To
whichever of these two classes Joseph Smith is most properly con-
signable, it is certain that his doctrine was no sooner preached than
he began to make converts of the people around him. The idea of the
"Latter Days," or days immediately prior to the second coming of
Christ to establish the Millenium, is one that has a great hold upon
the imagination of large classes of persons. Joseph Smith worked upon
this idea, and every earthquake recorded in the newspapers, every

new comet discovered, every falling meteor that was observed, every
war and rumour of a war in Europe or America, every monstrous birth
among inferior animals, every great public calamity, tempest, fire,
or explosion, was skilfully and pertinaciously adduced as a proof
and a warning of the "Latter Days." He had two great elements of success in his favour, sufficient novelty and unconquerable
perseverance. His doctrine was both old and new. It had sufficient of the old to attract those who would have been repelled by
a creed entirely new, and it had sufficient of the new to rivet the
attention and inflame the imagination of those on whose minds an old
creed, however ably preached, would have fallen and taken no root.
Basing his doctrine upon isolated passages of the Bible; claiming
direct inspiration from the Almighty; promising possession of the
earth, all temporal power and glory, and the blessing of Heaven upon
true believers; and being gifted with a courage and audacity that
despised difficulty and danger; Joseph Smith soon found himself the
recognised head of a small but increasing body of ardent disciples. On
the 1st of June, 1830, the first conference of the sect, as an organized
church, was held at Fayette, which place was for some time the
"prophet's" residence, and the head-quarters of the sect. The numbers of the believers, including the whole family of the Smiths, was
thirty. Even at this early period in the history of the sect, they met
considerable opposition from the people. Joseph ordered the construction of a dam across a stream of water, for the purpose of bap-
tizing his disciples. A mob collected, and broke it down, and used
language towards Joseph that was anything but flattering to him or
his followers, threatening him with violence and assassination, and
accusing him of robbery and swindling. He was nothing daunted,
however. With a rare tact, as well as courage, he broke the keen
edge of detraction, by confessing boldly that he had once led an improper and immoral life; but, unworthy as he was, "the Lord had
chosen him—had forgiven him all his sins, and intended, in his own
inscrutable purposes, to make him—weak and erring as he might have
been—the instrument of his glory." Unlettered and comparatively
ignorant he acknowledged himself to be; but then—was not St. Peter
illiterate? Were not St. John, and the other apostles of Christ, men of
low birth and mean position, before they were called to the ministry?
And what had been done before, might it not be done again, if God
willed it? By arguments like these, he strengthened the faith of those
inclined to believe in the divinity of his mission, and foiled the logic
of his opponents. But the more difficult that it became for the
preachers of rival sects to meet him on Scriptural grounds, and to disprove his pretensions, either by his unworthiness as a man—which he

owned, or his incompetency as a scholar—which he as freely admitted, the more virulent became their animosity; until, at last, the family of the Smiths, father and brothers, who all joined in the scheme of Joseph for founding a new religion, removed from Palmyra and Fayetteville to Kirtland, in Ohio. The attention of the little band was directed, from the very commencement of their organization, to the policy and expediency of fixing their head-quarters in the Far West, in the thinly-settled and but partially explored territories belonging to the United States, where they might squat upon, or purchase good lands at a cheap rate, and clear the primeval wilderness. They required " elbow room," and rightly judged that a rural population would be more favourable than an urban one to the reception of their doctrine. Oliver Cowdery having been sent on an exploratory expedition, reported so favourably of the beauty, fertility, and cheapness of the land in Jackson County, Missouri, that Joseph Smith, after remaining but a few weeks in Kirtland, determined to visit this land of promise himself. Leaving his family and principal connections in Kirtland, he proceeded with Sidney Rigdon and some others upon a long and arduous journey to the wilderness, to fix upon a site for the " New Jerusalem;" the future city of Christ, where the Lord was to reign over the Saints as a temporal king in " power and great glory."

CINCINNATI.

They started about the middle of June, travelling by waggons or canal boats, and sometimes on foot, as far as Cincinnati. From this place they proceeded by steamer to Louisville and St. Louis. At the last-mentioned village all further means of transport failed them, and they walked a distance of three hundred miles to Independence, in Jackson County, Missouri, the seat of the promised inheritance of the Saints. They arrived at their destination foot-sore and weary, in the middle of July. Joseph was in raptures with the beauty of the country, and his delight broke out into the following description, which occurs in his Autobiography, published in the *Times and Seasons :—*

" Unlike the timbered states in the east, except upon the rivers and water-courses, which were verdantly dotted with trees from one to three miles wide, as far as the eye can glance, the beautiful rolling prairies lay spread around like a sea of meadows. The timber is a mixture of oak, hickory, black walnut, elm, cherry, honey locus, mulberry, coffee bean, hackberry, box, elder, and bass wood, together with the addition of cotton wood, button wood, pecon—soft and hard maples upon the bottoms. The shrubbery was beautiful, and consisted in part of plums, grapes, crab apples, and parsimmons. The prairies were decorated with a growth of flowers that seemed as gorgeous and grand as the brilliancy of the stars in the heavens, and exceed description. The soil is rich and fertile, from three to ten feet deep, and generally composed of a rich, black mould, intermingled with clay and sand. It produces, in abundance, wheat, corn, and many other commodities, together with sweet potatoes and cotton. Horses, cattle, and hogs, though of an inferior breed, are tolerably plenty, and seem nearly to raise themselves by grazing in the vast prairie range in summer, and feeding upon the bottoms in winter. The wild game is less plenty where man has commenced the cultivation of the soil, than it is a little distance further in the wild prairies. Buffalo, elk, deer, bears, wolves, beaver, and many lesser animals, roam at pleasure. Turkies, geese, swans, duck—yea, a variety of the feathered race, are among the rich abundance that graces the delightful regions of this goodly land of the heritage of the children of God. Nothing is more fruitful, or a richer stockholder in the blooming prairies, than the honey bee ; honey is but about twenty-five cents per gallon.

" The season is mild and delightful nearly three quarters of the year, and as the land of Zion is situated at about equal distances from the Atlantic and Pacific Oceans as well as from the Alleghany and Rocky Mountains, in the thirty-ninth degree of north latitude, and between the tenth and twentieth degrees of west longitude, it bids fair to become one óf the most blessed places on the globe."

The longer he staid in Missouri, the more delighted he was with the "location" fixed upon for the Saints ; and that there might be no difference of opinion upon the subject in the church, he had a direct

" revelation" from the Almighty upon the subject; establishing it as the future Zion, and setting forth his views relative to the organization of the church, the building of a temple, the allotment of lands, and the means of living of the people. So early in his career did this remarkable man begin to exercise authority over his followers, so bold and daring were his designs, and so confident was he in himself. This extraordinary document ran as follows :—

" Hearken, O ye elders of my church, saith the Lord your God, who have assembled yourselves together, according to my commandments, in this land which I have appointed and consecrated for the gathering of the Saints; wherefore this is the land of promise, and the place for the city of Zion. And thus saith the Lord your God, if you will receive wisdom, here is wisdom. Behold, the place which is now called Independence, is the centre place, and a spot for the temple is lying westward, upon a lot which is not far from the court-house: wherefore it is wisdom that the land should be purchased by the Saints ; and also every tract lying westward, even unto the line running directly between Jew and Gentile. And also every tract bordering by the prairies, inasmuch as my disciples are enabled to buy lands. Behold, this is wisdom, that they may obtain it for an everlasting inheritance.

" And let my servant, Sidney Gilbert, stand in the office which I have appointed him, to receive moneys, to be an agent unto the church, to buy land in all the regions round about, inasmuch as can be in righteousness, and as wisdom shall direct.

" And let my servant, Edward Partridge, stand in the office which I have appointed him, to divide the Saints their inheritance, even as I have commanded ; and also those whom he has appointed to assist him.

" And, again, verily I say unto you, let my servant, Sidney Gilbert, plant himself in this place, and establish a store, that he may sell goods without fraud; that he may obtain money to buy lands for the good of the Saints ; and that he may obtain whatsoever things the disciples may need to plant them in inheritance. And also let my servant, Sidney Gilbert, obtain a licence that he may send goods also unto the people, even by whom he will, as clerks employed in his service, and thus provide for my Saints, that my Gospel may be preached unto those who sit in darkness, and in the region and shadow of death.

" And, again, verily I say unto you, let my servant, William W. Phelps, be planted in this place, and be established as a printer unto the church ; and lo, if the world receiveth his writings, let him obtain whatsoever he can obtain in righteousness, for the good of the Saints. And let my servant, Oliver Cowdery, assist him, even as I have commanded, in whatsoever place I shall appoint unto him, to copy, and to correct, and select, that all things may be right before me, as it shall be proved by the Spirit through him. And thus let those of whom I have spoken to be planted in the land of Zion, and speedily as can be, with their families, to do those things even as I have spoken.

"And now, concerning the gathering. Let the bishop and the agent make preparations for those families which have been commanded to come to this land, as soon as possible, and plant them in their inheritance. And unto the residue of both elders and members, further directions shall be given hereafter. Even so. Amen."

JOSEPH SMITH PREACHING IN THE WILDERNESS.

On the first Sunday after their arrival Joseph preached in the wilderness to a crowd of Indians, squatters, and, as he himself records, "to quite a respectable company of negroes." He made a few converts, and had another revelation from the Lord, to the effect that an angel should be appointed to receive money, and that Martin Harris should "be an example to the church in laying his moneys before the bishops

of the church. I ask that lands should be purchased for the place of
the storehouse, and also for the house of the printing." On the 3rd of
August, after a sojourn of less than three weeks, the spot for the
temple was solemnly laid out, and dedicated to the Lord; and Joseph
in a day or two afterwards, having completed all his arrangements,
established a bishop, and acquired, as he thought, a firm footing for
his sect in this remote but lovely and fertile spot, prepared to return
into Ohio, to look after his business in Kirtland. He was accompanied by ten elders of the church. " We started down the river," says
Joseph in his Autobiography, " in sixteen canoes, and went the first
day as far as Fort Osage, where we had a wild Turkey for supper.
Nothing very important occurred until the third day, when many of
the dangers so common upon the western waters manifested themselves; and, after we had encamped upon the bank of the river,
Brother Phelps, in open vision by daylight, saw the destroyer (the
Devil) ride upon the waters. Others," he adds, "heard the noise,
but saw not the vision." They arrived safely at Kirtland, after a
journey of twenty-four days. Some dispute, of which the nature is
not clearly known, appears 'to have arisen between Joseph and his
friend Sidney Rigdon before their return. It is probable, from the
course of subsequent events, that Sidney, even at this time, aspired to
greater power in the church than suited the purposes of the " prophet;" but, whatever the disagreement was, Joseph thought fit to
rebuke his chief disciple by a revelation from heaven, in which he
accused him of " being exalted in his heart, and despising the counsel
of the Lord." They afterwards became reconciled, and in partnership
or conjunction of some kind, and by the aid of other members and
elders of the church, they established a mill and a store in Kirtland,
and set up a bank. Joseph appointed himself its president, and entrusted Sidney Rigdon with the office of cashier. To Kirtland, they
gave the name of a "stake," or support of Zion, intending to remain
there for at least five years, "and make money," until the wilderness
was cleared and the temple built in Zion.

From this time until January, 1832, Joseph continued preaching
in various parts of the United States, making converts with great
rapidity. He found it necessary, however, to check the presumption
of some new and indiscreet converts who also had revelations from the
Lord, which they endeavoured to palm off upon the public, asserting
that they were quite as good as those of the prophet. Among others,
one Mr. E. Maclellan was rebuked. " This Maclellan," says Joseph,
" as a wise man in his own estimation, and having more learning than
sense, endeavoured to write a commandment like unto one of the least
of the Lord's, but failed. It was an awful responsibility to write in

the name of the Lord. The elders and all present, who witnessed the
vain attempt of this man to imitate the language of the Lord Jesus
Christ, renewed their faith in the revelation which the Lord had given
through my instrumentality." Joseph, at the same time, was obliged
to combat some charges which were brought against his character by
one Ezra Booth, formerly in his council, and whom he denounced as
an apostate, and as a man who, by the exposure of his own wickedness and folly, had left himself " a monument of shame for the whole
world to wonder at." His strange doctrines, and these charges against
his character, brought forward by men who had once been in his
confidence, united to the hatred with which other fanatics more
violent than himself regarded his preaching, created much ill-feeling
against him. On the 25th of January, being then resident at a
village called " Hiram," he was dragged out of his bed at midnight,
from the side of his wife, " by a mob of Methodists, Baptists, Camp-
bellites," and miscellaneous ruffians, who stripped him naked and
tarred and feathered him. Sidney Rigdon was similarly treated by
the same lawless and cowardly assemblage.

The following account of this outrage, the first of a long series, was
given by Joseph some years afterwards:—

" According to previous calculations, we now began to make preparations to visit the brethren, who had removed to the land of Missouri. Before going to Hiram to live with Father Johnson, my wife had
taken two children (twins) of John Murdock to bring up. She received
them when only nine days old, and they were now nearly eleven
months. I would remark that nothing important had occurred since
I came to reside in Father Johnson's house in Hiram. I had held meetings on the Sabbaths and evenings, and baptized a number. Father
Johnson's son, Olmsted Johnson, came home on a visit, during which
I told him that if he did not obey the Gospel, the spirit he was of
would lead him to destruction ; and then he went away. He would
never return to see his father again. He went to the Southern States
and Mexico ; on his return, took sick, and died in Virginia. In addition to the apostate Booth, Simmonds Rider, Eli Johnson, Edward
Johnson, and John Johnson, junior, had apostatized.

" On the 25th of March, the twins before mentioned, which had
been sick of the measles for some time, caused us to be broke of our
rest in taking care of them, especially my wife. In the evening, I told
her she had better retire to rest with one of the children, and I would
watch with the sickest child. In the night, she told me I had better
lay down on the trundle-bed, and I did so, and was soon after awoke
by her screaming *murder !* when I found myself going out of the door
in the hands of about a dozen men ; some of whose hands were in my

hair, and some had hold of my shirt, drawers, and limbs. The foot of the trundle bed was towards the door, leaving only room enough for the door to swing. My wife heard a gentle tapping on the windows, which she then took no particular notice of (but which was unquestionably designed to ascertain whether we were all asleep), and soon after the mob burst open the door, and surrounded the bed in an instant, and, as I said, the first I knew, I was going out of the door in the hands of an infuriated mob. I made a desperate struggle, as I was forced out, to extricate myself, but only cleared one leg, with which I made a pass at one man, and he fell on the door-steps. I was immediately confined again; and they swore by God they would kill me if I did not be still, which quieted me. As they passed around the house with me, the fellow that I kicked came to me, and thrust his hand into my face all covered with blood (for I hit him on the nose), and with an exulting horse laugh muttered: ' *Ge, Gee, God d——n ye, I'll fix ye.*'

" They then seized my throat, and held on till I lost my breath. After I came to, as they passed along with me, about thirty rods from the house, I saw Elder Rigdon stretched out on the ground, whither they had dragged him by the heels. I supposed he was dead.

" I began to plead with them, saying : ' You will have mercy, and spare my life, I hope!' To which they replied, ' *God d—n ye*, call on your God for help, we'll show you no mercy;' and the people began to show themselves in every direction : one coming from the orchard had a plank, and I expected they would kill me, and carry me off on the plank. They then turned to the right, and went on about thirty rods further, about sixty rods from the house, and thirty from where I saw Elder Rigdon, into the meadow, where they stopped ; and one said, ' Simmonds, Simmonds' (meaning, I suppose, Simmonds Rider), ' pull up his drawers, pull up his drawers, he will take cold.' Another replied, '*A'nt ye going to kill him ? a'nt ye going to kill him ?*' when a group of mobbers collected a little way off, and said, ' Simmonds, Simmonds, come here;' and Simmonds charged those who had hold of me to keep me from touching the ground (as they had done all the time), lest I should get a spring upon them. They went and held a council, and as I could occasionally overhear a word, I supposed it was to know whether it was best to kill me. They returned after a while, when I learned that they had concluded not to kill me, but pound and scratch me well, tear off my shirt and drawers, and leave me naked. One cried, ' Simmonds, Simmonds; *where's the tar bucket?*' ' I don't know,' answered one, ' *where 't is, Eli's left it.*' They ran back, and fetched the bucket of tar, when one exclaimed,

' *God d——n it, let us tar up his mouth ;*' and they tried to force the tar-paddle into my mouth; I twisted my head around, so that they could not; and they cried out : ' *God d——n ye, hold up your head, and let us give ye some tar.*' They then tried to force a phial into my mouth, and broke it in my teeth. All my clothes were torn off me except my shirt collar; and one man fell on me and scratched my body with his nails like a mad cat, and then muttered out : ' *God d——n ye, that's the way the Holy Ghost falls on folks.*'

"They then left me and I attempted to rise, but fell again; I pulled the tar away from my lips, &c., so that I could breathe more freely, and after a while I began to recover, and raised myself up, when I saw two lights. I made my way towards one of them, and found it was Father Johnson's. When I had come to the door I was naked, and the tar made me look as though I had been covered with blood; and when my wife saw me, she thought I was all smashed to pieces, and fainted. During the affray abroad, the sisters of the neighbourhood had collected at my room. I called for a blanket; they threw me one, and shut the door; I wrapped it around me and went in.

" In the meantime, Brother John Poorman heard an outcry across the cornfield, and running that way met Father Johnson, who had been fastened in his house at the commencement of the assault, by having his door barred by the mob; but, on calling to his wife to bring his gun, saying he would blow a hole through the door, the mob fled, and Father Johnson seizing a club ran after the party that had Elder Rigdon, and knocked one man down, and raised his club to level another, exclaiming, ' *What are you doing here ?*' They then left Elder Rigdon and turned upon Father Johnson, who, turning to run towards his own house, met Brother Poorman coming out of the cornfield; each supposing the other to be a mobber, an encounter ensued, and Poorman gave Johnson a severe blow on the left shoulder with a stick or stone, which brought him to the ground. Poorman ran immediately towards Father Johnson's, and arriving while I was waiting for the blanket, exclaimed, 'I'm afraid I've killed him.' 'Killed who?' asked one; when Poorman hastily related the circumstances of the rencounter near the cornfield, and went into the shed and hid himself. Father Johnson soon recovered so as to come to the house, when the whole mystery was quickly solved concerning the difficulty between him and Poorman, who, on learning the facts, joyfully came from his hiding-place.

" My friends spent the night in scraping and removing the tar, and washing and cleansing my body; so that by morning I was ready to be clothed again. This being Sabbath morning, the people assembled for meeting at the usual hour of worship, and among those came also the mobbers; viz., Simmonds Rider, a Campbellite preacher, and leader of the mob; one McClentic, son of a Campbellite minister; and Pelatiah Allen, Esq., who gave the mob a barrel of whiskey to raise their spirits; and many others. With my flesh all scarified and defaced, I preached to the congregation as usual, and in the afternoon of the same day baptized three individuals.

"The next morning I went to see Elder Rigdon, and found him crazy, and his head highly inflamed, for they had dragged him by his heels, and those, too, so high from the earth he could not raise his head from the rough frozen surface, which lacerated it exceedingly; and when he saw me he called to his wife to bring him his razor. She asked him what he wanted of it? and he replied to kill *me*. Sister Rigdon left the room, and he asked *me* to bring his razor; I asked him what he wanted of it? and he replied he wanted to kill his wife; and he continued delirious some days. The feathers which were used with the tar on this occasion, the mob took out of Elder Rigdon's house. After they had seized him, and dragged him out, one of the banditti returned to get some pillows; when the women shut him in, and kept him some time."

Joseph, after this cruel treatment, thought it high time to absent himself for a little, and on the 2nd of April he started, in company with some of his adherents, for Missouri, "to fulfil the revelation." Although he left secretly, his inhuman persecutors received notice of his design, and tracked him for several hundred miles, until he arrived at Louisville, where he was sheltered and protected from his assailants by the captain

LOUISVILLE.

F.

of a steam-boat. He arrived at " Zion," or Independence, on the 26th, where he was enthusiastically received by a large congregation of thriving " Saints," and solemnly acknowledged as prophet and seer, and president of the high priesthood of the church. He found that in his absence, but in obedience to a revelation which he had given, a printing-press had been procured, and a monthly newspaper or magazine established by W. W. Phelps, the " printer to the church," under the title of the *Evening and Morning Star*. A weekly paper was also planned and established, called the *Upper Missouri Advertiser*. Both of these journals were exclusively devoted to the interests of Mormonism, which by this time numbered between 2,000 and 3,000 disciples, principally in Missouri. The number of the Saints in Kirtland, including women and children, was but one hundred and fifty. Joseph, however, had his mill, his store, and his farm to look after at Kirtland; and although, while in that town, he lived among enemies, it was necessary that he should return to it. He therefore left Zion, with the full confidence that all was going on prosperously. In January, 1833, while attending to his worldly business, a schism broke out in " Zion " itself, which threatened, and, in combination with other circumstances, ultimately produced, the greatest calamities, and led to the violent expulsion of the Mormons from the whole State of Missouri. The manner in which the Mormons behaved in their " Zion " was not calculated to make friends. The superiority they assumed gave offence, and the rumours that were spread by their opponents, as well as by some false friends, who had been turned out of the church for misconduct, excited against them an intense feeling of alarm and hatred. They were accused of Communism, and not simply of a community of goods and chattels, but of wives. Both these charges were utterly unfounded; but they were renewed from day to day, and found constant believers, in spite of denials and refutations on the part of the Mormons. Joined to the odium unjustly cast upon them for these reasons, they talked so imprudently of their determination to possess the whole State of Missouri, and to suffer no one to live in it who would not conform to their faith, that a party was secretly formed against them, of which the object was nothing less than their total and immediate expulsion from their promised " Zion." In a letter to Mr. Phelps, the editor of the Mormon paper— the *Morning and Evening Star*, dated from Kirtland Mill, Joseph threatened the vengeance of God upon all the schismatics of " Zion." " I say to you (and what I say to you I say to all), hear the warning voice of God, lest Zion fall, and the Lord swear in his wrath the inhabitants of Zion shall not enter into my rest. The brethren in Kirtland pray for you unceasingly; for, knowing the terrors of the Lord, they greatly fear for you." Some of the Missouri Saints, it appeared, had accused Joseph Smith of aiming at " monarchical power and authority ;" and two of the high priests, in a letter written at the time in support of the rebuke of the prophet to these " rebels," speak of " low, dark, and blind insinuations against Joseph's character and intentions."

Whatever Joseph's views in this respect may have been, he found it necessary to take the sting out of this accusation, by associating with him in the supreme government of the church his old colleague, Sidney Rigdon, and another Saint named Williams. As usual, when any great movement was to be made, he had a " revelation." Under the date of the 8th of March, 1833, the Lord is represented as declaring that the sins of Sidney Rigdon and Frederick G. Williams were forgiven, and " that they were henceforth to be accounted as equal with Joseph Smith, jun., in holding the keys of His last kingdom." As it appears that Sidney Rigdon was too ambitious of power to be safely trusted among the Saints of Missouri, he was commanded by this revelation to remain in Kirtland. The bishop was also ordered by the same authority to " search diligently for an agent," who was to be a " man who *had got riches in store—a man of God, and of strong faith*, that thereby he might be enabled to discharge every debt, that the storehouse of the Lord might not be brought into disrepute before the people." Joseph also condescended to forgive the rebellious of Zion. " Behold, I say unto you," said the revelation, " your brethren in Zion begin to repent, and the angels rejoice over them. Nevertheless, I am not well pleased with many things, and I am not well pleased with my servant William E. Maclellan, neither with my servant Sidney Gilbert, and the bishop also; and others have many things to repent of. But verily I say unto you, that I the Lord will contend with Zion, and plead with her strong ones, and chasten her, until she overcomes and is clean before me, for she shall not be removed out of her place. I the Lord have spoken it. Amen." On the same day Joseph " laid his hands on Brothers Sidney and Frederick, and ordained them to take part with him in holding the keys of the last kingdom, and to assist in the presidency of the high priesthood as his councillors. After which he exhorted the brethren to faithfulness and diligence in keeping the commandments of God; and gave much instruction for the benefit of the Saints, with a promise that the pure in heart should see a heavenly vision, and after remaining a short time in secret prayer, the promise was verified. He then blessed the bread and wine, and distributed a portion to each, after which many of the brethren saw a heavenly vision of the Saviour and concourses of angels, and many other things."

But although the dissensions in the church were apparently healed by the judicious step thus taken, the old settlers of Missouri caused Joseph much alarm by the daily increasing hostility they expressed against the whole sect.

"In the month of April," says Joseph in his Autobiography, "the first regular mob rushed together, in Independence (Zion), to consult upon a plan for the removal, or immediate destruction, of the church in Jackson county. The number of the mob was about three hundred. A few of the first elders met in secret, and prayed to Him who said to the wind 'Be still,' to frustrate them in their wicked design. They therefore, after spending the day in a fruitless endeavour, to unite upon a general scheme for 'moving the Mormons out of their diggings,' as they asserted, and becoming a little the worse for liquor, broke up in a regular Missouri 'row,' showing a determined resolution that every man would 'carry his own head.'"

The Mormon paper of June, 1833, published an article entitled "Free people of colour," which roused against the sect the hostility of the whole pro-slavery party—then, as now, peculiarly sensitive upon the question of Abolition. The anti-Mormon press contained at the same time an article entitled "Beware of false prophets," written by a person whom Joseph called "a black rod in the hand of Satan." This article was distributed from house to house in Independence and its neighbourhood, and contained many false charges against Smith and his associates, reiterating the calumny about the community of goods and wives. The Mormons were insulted and sometimes beaten in the streets and highways, and quarrels and fights were of frequent occurrence. In the beginning of April, a meeting of three hundred people, enemies of the Mormons, was held in Independence, or "Zion," itself, at which the resolution referred to by Joseph, "that the Mormons should be removed out of their diggings," was unanimously passed. After the publication of these two articles, other meetings were held in various parts of Jackson county, at which still more violent resolutions were agreed to. A general meeting of the citizens of Jackson county, expressly convened, as the requisition stated, "for the purpose of adopting measures to rid themselves of the sect of fanatics called Mormons," was held on the 20th of July. Between four and five hundred people attended from every part of the county, and an address to the public was agreed upon. The address stated that little more than two years previously, "some two or three of these people made their appearance in Missouri; that they now numbered upwards of 1,200; that each successive autumn and spring poured forth a new swarm of them into the country, as if the places from which they came were flooding Missouri with the very dregs of their composition; that they were but little above the condition of the blacks in regard to property and education; and that, in addition to other causes of scandal and offence, they exercised a corrupting influence over the slaves." The sanguine boast and sincere belief of the Mormons, that the whole country of Missouri was their destined inheritance, and that all the "Gentiles," or unbelievers in Joseph Smith, were to be cut off in the Lord's good time, was not forgotten. The address concluded—

"Of their pretended revelations from heaven—their personal intercourse with God and his angels—the maladies they pretend to heal by the laying on of hands—and the contemptible gibberish with which they habitually profane the Sabbath, and which they dignify with the appellation of unknown tongues, we have nothing to say: vengeance belongs to God alone. But as to the other matters set forth in this paper, we feel called on, by every consideration of self-preservation, good society, public morals, and the fair prospects that, if they are not blasted in the germ, await this young and beautiful country, at once to declare, and we do hereby most solemnly declare—

"That no Mormon shall in future move and settle in this country.

"That those now here, who shall give a definite pledge of their intention within a reasonable time to remove out of the country, shall be allowed to remain unmolested until they have sufficient time to sell their property and close their business without any material sacrifice.

"That the editor of the *Star* be required forthwith to close his office, and discontinue the business of printing in this country; and, as to all other stores and shops belonging to the sect, their owners must in every case comply with the terms of the second article of this declaration, and upon failure prompt and efficient measures will be taken to close the same.

"That the Mormon leaders here, are required to use their influence in preventing any further emigration of their distant brethren to this country, and to council and advise their brethren here to comply with the above requisitions.

"That those who fail to comply with these requisitions be referred to those of their brethren who have the gifts of divination and of unknown tongues, to inform them of the lot that awaits them."

This sarcastic, but very earnest and emphatic, address, was unanimously adopted. The meeting adjourned for two hours, and a deputation waited upon Mr. Phelps, the Mormon editor, upon Mr. Partridge, the bishop, and upon the keeper of the Mormon store, and urged upon them the expediency of complying with these terms. The deputation reported to the meeting that they could not procure any direct answer, and that the Mormons wished an unreasonable time for consultation upon the matter, not only among themselves in Independence, but with Joseph Smith, their prophet, in Kirtland. It was therefore resolved, *nem. con.*, that the *Star* printing-office should be immediately razed to the ground, and the types and presses secured.

" This resolution," said the anti-Mormons, in an account of the occurrence published under their authority, " was, with the utmost order,
and the least noise and disturbance possible, forthwith carried into
execution, *as also some other steps of a similar tendency,* but no blood
was spilled, nor any blows inflicted." The meeting then adjourned
for three days, to give the Mormons an opportunity of considering
what their fate was likely to be in case they should ultimately refuse
to leave the country.

The " other steps of a similar tendency," alluded to in this extract, appear to have been the tarring and feathering of two Mormons.
Phelps, the editor, managed to escape from the mob, but Partridge,
the Mormon bishop, and another Saint named Allen, were not so fortunate. These two were seized, according to the established back-wood
or Lynch fashion, stripped naked, tarred and feathered, and set loose.
The Lieutenant-Governor of the State of Missouri, Lilburn W. Boggs
—a man who from thenceforward appears to have pursued the Mormons with unrelenting hostility—was in the immediate neighbourhood
of the riot, but declined to take any part in preserving the peace.
Joseph Smith afterwards stated that he actually looked on, and aided
the movement, saying to the Mormons, " You know what we Jackson
boys can do. You must all leave the country." A Presbyterian
preacher is also reported to have declared from the pulpit that " the
Mormons were the common enemies of mankind, and ought to be destroyed." On the morning of the 23rd of July, the meeting again
assembled. It was composed of several hundred persons, well armed,
and bearing the red flag in sign of vengeance. They declared their
intention of driving the whole sect forcibly out of Missouri, if they
would not depart peaceably. The Mormons saw that it was useless to
resist, and their leaders agreed, if time were given, that the people
should remove westward into the wilderness. It was arranged, and an
agreement was duly signed to that effect, that one half of the Mormons,
with their wives and families, should depart by the 1st of January, and
the other half by the 1st of April next ensuing; that the paper should
be discontinued; and that no more Mormons should be allowed to come
into the country in the interval. The opposite party pledged themselves that no violence should be done to any Mormon, provided these
conditions were complied with.

In these distressing and perilous circumstances, Oliver Cowdery
was despatched to Kirtland with a message to the " Prophet." On
his arrival, it was resolved, in solemn conclave, Joseph himself presiding, that the *Morning and Evening Star* should be published in
Kirtland, and that a new paper, to be called the *Latter-Day Saints'
Messenger and Advocate,* should be forthwith started. It was also re-

solved to appeal for protection to Mr. Dunklin, the governor of the State of Missouri, and to demand justice for the outrages inflicted upon the sect. Joseph himself did not venture into " Zion," in the dangerous circumstances of his people, but undertook a journey to Canada with Sidney Rigdon and another, where they made some converts. In the meantime, Governor Dunklin wrote a sensible and conciliatory letter in reply to the Mormon petition, in which he stated that the attack upon them was illegal and unjustifiable, and recommended them to remain where they were, and to apply for redress to the ordinary tribunals of the country. This letter was widely circulated, and the Mormons, upon the strength of it, resolved to remain in Missouri, and " proceed with the building up of Zion." They commenced actions against the ringleaders of the mob, and engaged, for a fee of 1,000 dollars, the best legal assistance they could procure to support their case. But on the 30th of October, the mob was once again in arms to expel them. Ten houses of the " Saints" were unroofed and partially demolished at a place called Big Blue; and on the following days several houses were sacked at Independence. The Mormons, in some instances, defended their property, and a regular battle ultimately ensued between thirty of the Saints, armed with rifles, and a large company of their opponents, also well armed. In this encounter two of the anti-Mormons were killed. Things at last assumed so alarming an aspect, that the militia, under the command of Lieutenant-Governor Boggs, was called out. The militia, however, was anti-Mormon to a man, and the unhappy Saints saw that they had no alternative but in flight. The blood that had been shed had caused such an exasperation against them, that it was unsafe for a solitary Mormon to show himself in the towns or villages. The women first took the alarm, and fled, with their children, across the Missouri river.

" On Thursday, Nov. 7th," says the account in the *Times and Seasons*, "the shore began to be lined on both sides of the ferry with men, women, and children, goods, waggons, boxes, chests, provisions; while the ferrymen were busily engaged in crossing them over; and when night again closed upon the Saints, the wilderness had much the appearance of a camp meeting. Hundreds of people were seen in every direction, some in tents, and some in the open air, around their fires, while the rain descended in torrents. Husbands were inquiring for their wives, and women for their husbands; parents for children, and children for parents. Some had the good fortune to escape with their family, household goods, and some provisions; while others knew not the fate of their friends, and had lost all their goods. The scene was indescribable, and would have melted the hearts of any people upon

earth except the blind oppressor, and prejudiced and ignorant bigot.
Next day the company increased, and they were chiefly engaged in
felling small cotton trees, and erecting them into temporary cabins, so
that when night came on, they had the appearance of a village of
wigwams, and the night being clear, the occupants began to enjoy
some degree of comfort. The Saints who fled took refuge in the
neighbouring counties, mostly in Clay county, which received them
with some degree of kindness. Those who fled to the county of Van
Buren were again driven and compelled to flee, and those who fled to
Lafayette county were soon expelled, or the most of them, and had to
move wherever they could find protection."

ENCAMPMENT OF MORMONS ON THE MISSOURI RIVER

THE DISCOVERY OF THE "LAMANITE" SKELETON

CHAPTER IV.

JOURNEY OF THE PROPHET INTO MISSOURI—THE LAMANITE SKELETON—THE SHOWER OF
METEORS—FINAL REMOVAL OF JOSEPH FROM KIRTLAND, OHIO—PERSECUTIONS IN MIS-
SOURI—MASSACRE AT HAUN'S MILL—THE DANITE BAND—EXPULSION FROM MISSOURI.

THE public authorities of the State of Missouri, and, indeed, all the
principal people, except those of Jackson county, were scandalized at
these lawless proceedings, and sympathized with the efforts made by
the Mormon leaders to obtain redress. The Attorney-General of the
State wrote to say that if the Mormons desired to be re-established in
their possessions, an adequate public force would be sent for their
protection. He also advised that the Mormons should remain in
the State, and organize themselves into a regular company of militia,
in which case they should be supplied with public arms. The
"Prophet," having by this time returned to Kirtland, wrote to his
people in their distress, though he did not take the bold step
of personally appearing among them. He reiterated that "Inde-

pendence," or "Zion," was the place divinely appointed by God for the inheritance of the Saints; that, therefore, they should not sell any land to which they had a legal title within its boundaries, but hold on "until the Lord in his wisdom should open a way for their return." He also advised that they should, if possible, purchase a tract of land in Clay county, for present emergencies. He also had a revelation in which the Lord was represented as saying that these calamities were a punishment on the Saints for their "jarrings, contentions, and envying, and strifes, and lustful and covetous desires." Zion, however, was the appointed place, and thither, in due time, the Saints should return "with songs of everlasting joy." The revelation, which was of unusual length, and contained a long parable, commanded the Saints to "importune at the feet of the Judge; and if he did not heed, to importune at the feet of the Governor; and if the Governor did not heed, to importune at the feet of the President of the United States; and if the President did not heed, then the Lord God Himself would arise and come forth out of His hiding-place, and in His fury vex the nation."

The Saints, however, did not succeed in their object. They never returned to their "Zion," but remained for upwards of four years in Clay county. It was mostly uncleared land where they settled or squatted, but being a most industrious and persevering people, they laid out farms, erected mills and stores, and carried on their business successfully. They also laid the foundation of the towns of Far West and Adam-On-Diahman; but their fanaticism here, as well as in their former location, soon proved the cause of their expulsion from the whole State of Missouri. The slavery question, the calumny about their open adulteries and community of wives, their loud vaunts of their supreme holiness, their continually repeated declarations that Missouri was to be theirs by Divine command, and the quarrels that were the constant result, led to the same ill-feeling in Clay county, as had been exhibited elsewhere. But before the final consummation, when, as one of their hymns says—

> " Missouri,
> Like a whirlwind in its fury,
> And without a judge or jury,
> Drove the Saints and spilled their blood"—

various interesting events in their history took place. On the 5th May, 1834, Joseph resolved to proceed to Clay county, and put the affairs of the scattered and dispirited church into order. Having organized a company of one hundred persons, mostly young men, and nearly all elders, priests, deacons, and teachers, he started at their head for Missouri.

They travelled on foot; several waggons with their baggage and provisions, and relief to the destitute Saints in Clay county, following
behind. They were well provided with "fire-arms and all sorts of
munition of war of the most portable kind for self-defence." They
were joined in two days by fifty more " Saints," similarly armed.
Their baggage waggons now amounted to twenty. Joseph divided
his band into companies of twelve, consisting of two cooks, two fire-
men, two tent makers, two watermen, one runner or scout, one com-
missary, and two waggoners. Every night, " at the sound of the
trumpet, they bowed down before the Lord in their several tents; and
at the sound of the morning trumpet, every man was again on his
knees before the Lord." They passed through extensive wilds, and
forded many streams and rivers; and though, as Joseph says, " their
enemies were continually breathing threats of violence, the Saints did
not fear, neither did they hesitate to prosecute their journey, for God
was with them, and his angels were before them, and the faith of the
little band was unwavering. We knew," he added, " that angels were
our companions, for we saw them."

On their arrival in June at the Illinois river, the people were very
anxious to know who and what they were. Many questions were
asked, but the Mormons evaded them all, and gave no information as
to their names, profession, business, or destination. Joseph himself
travelled *incognito*, and though the settlers in Illinois vehemently sus-
pected the band to be Mormons, they did not think it prudent to
molest them. Having been safely ferried over the river, with all their
baggage, they encamped two days afterwards amid some mounds, or
ancient burial-places of the Indians. Here Joseph played the " prophet," and gave his followers an additional proof of the authenticity
of the Book of Mormon, and of the history of the Lamanites, the
descendants of the Jews, therein recorded. This was a master-stroke
of policy. " The contemplation of the scenery," says Joseph, " produced peculiar sensations in our bosoms. The brethren procured
a shovel and a hoe, and removing the earth of one of the mounds, to
the depth of about a foot, discovered the skeleton of a man almost
entire, and between his ribs was a Lamanitish arrow. The visions of
the past being opened to my understanding, by the spirit of the Almighty, I discovered that the person whose skeleton was before us was
a white Lamanite, a large thick-set man, and a man of God. He was
a warrior and chieftain under the great prophet Omandagus, who was
known from the hill Cumorah, or Easter Sea, to the Rocky Mountains.
His name was Zelph. He was killed in battle by the arrow found
among his ribs, during the last great struggle of the Lamanites and
Nephites." On the next day, refreshed by this incident, and marvel-

lously confirmed in the faith by the wisdom and knowledge of their Prophet, they moved onwards, and crossed the Mississippi river, into the limits of the State of Missouri.

The following extracts from the journal or diary of one of the elders who accompanied the Prophet, will show the influence he exercised, and the manner in which his singular journey was conducted :—

" This day, June 3rd, while we were refreshing ourselves and teams, about the middle of the day, Brother Joseph got up in a waggon and said that he would deliver a prophecy. After giving the brethren much good advice, exhorting them to faithfulness and humility, he said ' the Lord had told him that there would be a scourge come upon the camp, in consequence of the fractious and unruly spirits that appeared among them, and they should die like sheep with the rot ; still, if they would repent and humble themselves before the Lord, the scourge, in a great measure, might be turned away : but, as the Lord lived, the camp would suffer for giving way to their unruly temper,' which afterwards actually did take place, to the sorrow of the brethren.

" The same day, when we had got within one mile of the Snye, we came to a very beautiful little town called Atlas. Here we found honey for the first time on our journey, that we could buy ; we purchased about two-thirds of a barrel. We went down to the Snye and crossed over that night in a ferry-boat. We encamped for the night on the bank of the Snye. There was a great excitement in the country through which we had passed, and also a-head of us ; the mob threatened to stop us. Guns were fired in almost all directions through the night. Brother Joseph did not sleep much, if any, but was through the camp pretty much during the night.

" We pursued our journey on the 4th, and encamped on the bank of the Mississippi river. Here we were somewhat afflicted, and the enemy threatened much that we should not cross over the river out of Illinois into Missouri. It took us two days to cross the river, as we had but one ferry-boat, and the river was one mile and a half wide. While some were crossing, many others spent their time in hunting and fishing, &c. When we had all got over, we encamped about one mile back from the little town of Louisiana, in a beautiful oak grove, which is immediately on the bank of the river. At this place there was some feelings of hostility manifested by Sylvester Smith, in consequence of a dog growling at him while he was marching his company up to the camp, he being the last that came over the river. The next morning Brother Joseph said that he would descend to the spirit that was manifested by some of the brethren, to let them see the folly of their wickedness. He rose up, and commenced speaking by saying, ' If any man insults me, or abuses me, I will stand in my own defence at the expense of my life; and if a dog growl at me, I will let him know that I am his master.' At this moment Sylvester Smith, who had just returned from where he had turned out his horses to feed, came up, and hearing Brother Joseph make these remarks, said, 'If that dog bites me, I'll kill him.' Brother Joseph turned to Sylvester and said, 'If you kill that dog, I'll whip you,' and then went on to show the brethren how wicked and unchristian-like such conduct appeared before the eyes of truth and justice.

"On Friday, the 6th, we resumed our journey. On Saturday, the 7th, at night we camped among our brethren at Salt River, in the Allred settlement, in a piece of woods by a beautiful spring of water, and prepared for the Sabbath. On the Sabbath we had preaching. Here we remained several days, washing our clothes, and preparing to pursue our journey. Here we were joined by Hyrum Smith and Lyman Wight, with another company. The camp now numbered two hundred and five men, all armed and equipped as the law directs. It was delightful to see the company, for they were all young men, with one or two exceptions, and in good spirits."

Another entry in the same diary will be interesting to those who wish to trace the slight incidents upon which strong fanaticism supports itself. The meteors of the 13th of November, which are annually looked for by the observers of the heavens, were to the Mormons then, as they are now, convincing proofs of the truth of Mormonism, and signs of the Latter Days:—

"*November* 13th.—About 4 o'clock A.M. I was awakened by Brother Davis knocking at my door, and calling on me to arise and behold the signs in the heavens. I arose, and, to my great joy, beheld the stars fall from heaven like a shower of hail-stones; a literal fulfilment of the word of God, as recorded in the Holy Scriptures, as a sure sign that the coming of Christ is close at hand. In the midst of this shower of fire, I was led to exclaim: How marvellous are thy works, O Lord! I thank thee for thy mercy unto thy servant; save me in thy kingdom, for Christ's sake. Amen.

" The appearance of these signs varied in different sections of the country: in Zion, all heaven seemed enwrapped in splendid fireworks, as if every star in the broad expanse had been suddenly hurled from its course, and sent lawless through the wilds of ether; some at times appeared like bright shooting meteors with long trains of light following in their course, and in numbers resembled large drops of rain in sunshine. Some of the long trains of light following the meteoric stars were visible for some seconds; these streaks would curl and twist up like serpents writhing. The appearance was beautiful, grand, and sublime beyond description; as though all the artillery and

fire-works of eternity were set in motion to enchant and entertain the
Saints, and terrify and awe the sinners on the earth.   Beautiful and
terrific as was the scenery, which might be compared to the falling
figs or fruit when the tree is shaken by a mighty wind; yet, it will
not fully compare with the time when the sun shall become black like
sack-cloth of hair, the moon like blood (Rev. vi. 13); and the stars
fall to the earth, as these appeared to vanish when they fell behind
the trees, or came near the ground."

J oseph was now on a dangerous territory, and chose twenty men for
his body-guard, appointing his brother Hyrum Smith as their captain,
and another brother, George Smith, as his armour-bearer.   He also appointed a "general," who daily inspected the little army, examined their
fire-locks, and drilled them on the prairies.   The people of Jackson county,
by this time, were informed of Joseph Smith's arrival with his army.
A deputation of them, who were in Clay county, to submit a proposal for
the purchase of all the Mormon lands in Independence, no sooner heard
that the Prophet was in the field in person, than they returned towards their own county to raise a force with which to meet and
chastise him.   One of their leaders, named Campbell, swore, as he ad-
justed his pistols in his holsters, "that the eagles and turkey buzzards
should eat his flesh if he did not, before two days, fix Joe Smith and
his army, so that their skins should not hold shucks."   Joseph, who
relates this story, adds, that Campbell and his men " went to the ferry
and undertook to cross the Missouri river after dusk; but the angel of
God saw fit to sink the boat about the middle of the river, and seven
out of the twelve that attempted to cross were drowned.   Thus suddenly and justly," he adds, with great complacency, "they went to
their own place by water.   Campbell was among the missing.   He
floated down the river some four or five miles, and lodged upon a pile
of drift wood, where the eagles, buzzards, ravens, crows, and wild animals, ate his flesh from his bones, to fulfil his own words, and left him
a horrible-looking skeleton of God's vengeance, which was discovered
about three weeks afterwards by one Mr. Purtle."

Joseph, much delighted at the death of Campbell and his men, and
at the discovery of the fleshless bones of his enemy by " Mr. Purtle," continued his march, and had a new " revelation " from the Lord, to comfort
and excite his people.   The cholera, however, broke out in his camp on
the 24th of June, and Joseph attempted to cure it by " laying on of his
hands and prayer."   He failed, however, to do any good, and accounted
for his failure by stating that " he quickly learned by painful experience that when the Great Jehovah decrees destruction, man must not
attempt to stay his hand."   Though he could not cure the cholera, he
endeavoured to maintain his influence over the minds of his followers,

and impress them more forcibly with the miraculous nature of his mission, by stating that the enemies of the Mormons would suffer more severely from the visitation than the Mormons themselves. He laid particular stress upon the case of a woman who refused a Saint some water to drink. "Before a week," said the prophet, "the cholera entered that house, and that woman and three others of the family were dead." Joseph lost thirteen of his band by the ravages of the disease. On the 1st of July he crossed into Jackson county, with a few friends, " to set his feet once more on that goodly land;" and, after remaining one day, proceeded with the remainder of his company to Clay county. He did not remain long with the Saints, for we find that he arrived on the 2nd, and started back for Kirtland on the 9th. It was not prudent, it appears, that he should make himself too familiar with his believers. The great man was not to be seen too closely with impunity, for some of his travelling companions began to accuse him of " prophesying lies in the name of the Lord," and also of appropriating "moneys" to which he had no right. But Joseph Smith was not a man to be daunted by domestic treason or enemies in his own camp; and short as was the time he stayed, he did not depart without organizing and encouraging the main body of the fugitives from Jackson county, and establishing the community in Clay county on a better footing than when he arrived. On his return to Kirtland, his first step was to bring to trial before his church the brother who accused him of " prophesying lies," and of appropriating moneys. The brother confessed his error, retracted his charge, and was forgiven.

The history of the sect for the next three years is one of strife and contention with their unrelenting and vindictive enemies in Missouri. The numbers of the Mormons increased with the numbers of their opponents; and the warfare raged so bitterly that the whole people of Missouri were ranged either on one side or the other. In the autumn of 1837, Joseph's bank at Kirtland stopped payment; the district was flooded with its worthless paper, and Joseph had a " revelation " commanding him to depart finally for Missouri, and live among the Saints in the land of their inheritance. Joseph obeyed the " revelation " by departing secretly in the night. His enemies assert that he went " between two days," as it is called in America, and that he left his creditors to their remedy. He found the affairs of his church in considerable confusion on his arrival. The Saints formed a numerous and powerful body, but they did not agree among themselves; and occasional seceders and deserters from their camp — many of them consisting of men who were ashamed of their previous delusions, and of others who were actuated by vindictive motives or disappointed ambition — spread abroad all sorts of rumours and stories to the disadvantage of the sect. The great schism, already alluded to, broke out in 1838, when Joseph Smith found it necessary to denounce some of his oldest confederates, among others "Oliver Cowdery," one of the three witnesses to the authenticity of the Book of Mormon, and the existence of the gold plates; Martin Harris, another witness; Sidney Rigdon, his co-equal in the government of the church, and various disciples and apostles. Sidney Rigdon was afterwards forgiven, being too important a personage to be converted into an enemy. In the midst of these squabbles, the people of Jackson county, joined by the people of Clay county, Caldwell county, and other districts, made a series of pertinacious efforts to expel them finally from Missouri.

A very clear narrative of these events was given in evidence upon oath by Hyrum, the brother of Joseph Smith, at one of the numerous criminal trials, which were instituted against the members of the sect. It appears from this statement that at a popular election in 1838, at Gallatin, in Davis county, the old ill-feeling having arisen with more than its usual virulence, the mob would not allow any Mormons to exercise their privilege of voting; and that a desperate fight, in which two men were killed, and many persons seriously hurt, was the result. Both parties armed to defend themselves, and carried on a guerilla warfare for several weeks. The cry was raised by the anti-Mormons, that there would be no peace in the country as long as a single Mormon was allowed to remain within it. Early in the September of that year, the mob assembled at a place called Millport, near Adam-On-Diahman—"and," to use the words of Hyrum Smith, "commenced making aggressions upon the Mormons, taking away their hogs and cattle, and threatening them with extermination, or utter extinction; saying that they had a cannon, and there should be no compromise only at its mouth: frequently taking men, women, and children prisoners, whipping them and lacerating their bodies with hickory withes, and tying them to trees and depriving them of food until they were compelled to gnaw the bark from the trees to which they were bound, in order to sustain life; treating them in the most cruel manner they could invent or think of, and doing everything they could to excite the indignation of the Mormon people to rescue them, in order that they might make that a pretext of an accusation for the breach of the law, and that they might the better excite the prejudice of the populace, and thereby get aid and assistance to carry out their hellish purposes of extermination." We continue the narrative as given in Hyrum Smith's evidence:—"Immediately on the authentication of these facts, messengers were despatched from Far West to Austin A. King, Judge of the district, and to Major-General Atchison, Commander-in-Chief of that division, and Brigadier-General Doniphan, demanding immediate assistance. General Atchison returned with the messengers, and went immediately to Diahman, and from thence to Millport, and he found the facts were true as reported to him;—that the citizens of that county were assembled together in a hostile attitude to the amount of two or three hundred men, threatening the utter extermination of the Mormons, he immediately returned to Clay county, and ordered out a sufficient military force to quell the mob. Immediately after they were dispersed, and the army returned, the mob commenced collecting again soon after. We again applied for military aid, when General Doniphan came out with a force of sixty armed men to Far West; but they were in such a state of insubordination that he said he could not control them.

"After witnessing the distressed situation of the people in Diahman, my brother Joseph Smith, Senior, and myself, returned back to the city of Far West, and immediately despatched a messenger, with written documents, to General Atchison, stating the facts as they did then exist, praying for assistance if possible, and requesting the editor of *The Far West* to insert the same in his newspaper ; but he utterly refused to do so. We still believed that we should get assistance from the Governor, and again petitioned him, praying for assistance, setting forth our distressed situation ; and in the meantime the presiding Judge of the County Court issued orders—upon affidavits made to him by the citizens—to the Sheriff of the county, to order out the militia of the county to stand in constant readiness, night and day, to prevent the citizens from being massacred, which fearful situation they were exposed to every moment.

" It was on the evening of the 30th of October, according to the best of my recollection, that the army arrived at Far West, the sun about half an hour high. In a few moments afterwards, Cornelius Gillum arrived with his army, and formed a junction. This Gillum had been stationed at Hunter's Mills for about two months previous to that time—committing depredations upon the inhabitants —capturing men, women, and children, and carrying them off as prisoners, lacerating their bodies with hickory withes. The army of 'Gillum' were painted like Indians, some of them were more conspicuous than others, and were designated the red spots ; he, also, was painted in a similar manner, with red spots marked on his face, and styled himself the 'Delaware Chief.' They would whoop, and hollow, and yell as near like Indians as they could, and continued to do so all that night. In the morning early, the Colonel of Militia sent a messenger into the camp with a white flag, to have another interview with General Doniphan. On his return he informed us that the Governor's

orders had arrived. General Doniphan said that 'the order of the
Governor was, to exterminate the Mormons by God, but he would be
damned if *he* obeyed *that order*, but General Lucas might do what he
pleased.' We immediately learned from General Doniphan that 'the
Governor's order that had arrived was only a copy of the original, and
that the original order was in the hands of Major-General Clark,
who was on his way to Far West, with an additional army of six
thousand men.' Immediately after this, there came into the city a
messenger from Haun's Mill, bringing the intelligence of an awful
massacre of the people who were residing in that place, and that a

MASSACRE OF MORMONS AT HAUN'S MILL.

force of two or three hundred, detached from the main body of the
army, under the superior command of Colonel Ashley, but under the
immediate command of Captain Nehemiah Compstock, who, the day
previous, had promised them peace and protection, but on receiving a
copy of the Governor's order 'to *exterminate or to expel*' from the
hands of Colonel Ashley, he returned upon them the following day,
and surprised and massacred the whole population, and then came
on to the town of Far West, and entered into conjunction with
the main body of the army. The messenger informed us that he

himself with a few others fled into the thickets, which preserved them from the massacre, and on the following morning they returned and collected the dead bodies of the people, and cast them into a well. There were upwards of twenty who were dead or mortally wounded. One, of the name of Yocum, has lately had his leg amputated, in consequence of wounds he then received. He had a ball shot through his head, which entered near his eye, and came out at the back part of his head, and another ball passed through one of his arms.

" The army, during all the while they had been encamped in Far West, continued to lay waste fields of corn, making hogs, sheep, and cattle common plunder, and shooting them down for sport. One man shot a cow, and took a strip of her skin, the width of his hand, from her head to her tail, and tied it around a tree, to slip his halter into, to tie his horse to. The city was surrounded with a strong guard, and no man, woman, or child was permitted to go out or come in, under the penalty of death. Many of the citizens were shot in attempting to go out to obtain sustenance for themselves and families."

It was not to be expected that the Mormons, exposed to a series of persecutions and outrages like these, and in a country so utterly lawless, should not take measures to defend themselves. As it was unsafe for a Mormon to stir abroad, a body of them, instituted expressly for the defence of the sect, and possibly on the recommendation of the Governor of Missouri given to them some years before, was organized under the name of the " Danite Band," or, as they were sometimes called, the " Destroying Angels." An affidavit made before a justice of the peace in Ray county, Missouri, on the 24th of October, 1838, and sworn by a man named Marsh, who had held office in the Mormon church, and another affidavit, signed by Orson Hyde, an ex-apostle of the church, alleged the following facts with reference to the " Danites," and their proceedings :—

" They have among them a company, consisting of all that are considered true Mormons, called the Danites, who have taken an oath to support the heads of the church in all things that they say or do, whether right or wrong. Many, however, of this band are much dissatisfied with this oath, as being against moral and religious principles. On Saturday last, I am informed by the Mormons that they had a meeting at Far West, at which they appointed a company of twelve, by the name of the Destruction Company, for the purpose of burning and destroying ; and that if the people of Buncombe came to do mischief upon the people of Caldwell, and committed depredations upon the Mormons, they were to burn Buncombe ; and if the people of Clay and Ray made any movement against them, this destroying company were to burn Liberty and Richmond. The plan of said Smith, the prophet, is to take this State ; and he professes to his people to intend taking the United States, and

ultimately the whole world. This is the belief of the church, and my own
opinion of the prophet's plans and intentions. The prophet inculcates the
notion, and it is believed by every true Mormon, that Smith's prophecies are
superior to the law of the land. I have heard the prophet say that he would
yet tread down his enemies, and walk over their dead bodies : that if he was
not let alone, he would be a second Mahomet to this generation, and that he
would make it one gore of blood from the Rocky Mountains to the Atlantic
Ocean; that, like Mahomet, whose motto, in treating for peace, was 'the Al-
coran or the sword,' so should it be eventually with us, 'Joseph Smith or the
sword.' These last statements were made during the last summer. The
number of armed men at Adam-On-Diahman was between three and four
hundred.

"THOMAS B. MARCH.

" Sworn to and subscribed before me, the day herein written.
" HENRY JACOBS, J.P., Ray county, Missouri.

" *Richmond, Missouri, October* 24, 1838."

"AFFIDAVIT OF ORSON HYDE.*

" The most of the statements in the foregoing disclosure of T. B. March
I know to be true ; the remainder I believe to be true.
" ORSON HYDE, *Richmond, Oct.* 24, 1838.

" Sworn to and subscribed before me on the day above written.
" HENRY JACOBS, J.P."

"CERTIFICATE OF THOMAS C. BURCH AND OTHERS.

" The undersigned committee, on the part of the citizens of Ray county,
have no doubt but Thomas B. March and Orson Hyde, whose names are signed
to the foregoing certificates, have been members of the Mormon church in
full fellowship until very recently, when they voluntarily abandoned the
Mormon church and faith, and that said March was, at the time of his dis-
senting, the president of the Twelve Apostles, and president of the church at
Far West; and that said Hyde was at that time one of the Twelve Apostles,
and that they left church, and abandoned the faith of the Mormons, from a
conviction of their immorality and impiety.

" THOMAS C. BURCH.
WILLIAM HUDGINS.
HENRY JACOBS.
GEORGE WOODWARD.
J. R. HENDLEY.
C. R. MOREHEAD.

" *Richmond, October* 24, 1838." O. H. SEARCY."

These and other statements of a similar kind, many of which were
doubtless highly exaggerated, were daily inculcated, and produced

---

* This Orson Hyde appears to have rejoined the Mormons, and to have been present
at the trial of Sidney Rigdon, after the death of Joseph Smith.

the effect of still further exasperating the people against Joseph and his disciples. The Mormons, seeing the law broken by their opponents, refused obedience to the law themselves. They fortified their farms and towns, and treated with contempt the legal processes which it was attempted to serve upon them. The militia of the State was again called out, under the command of General Doniphan. His measures were so vigorous, and the fury of the people against Joseph was so great, that the Mormons, dreading the general massacre of their sect, so long threatened, laid down their arms, and finally resolved to leave the State of Missouri and take refuge in Illinois, then very partially cleared and settled.

The following address, which is of itself sufficient evidence of the cruelty and injustice with which the sect was treated, was delivered at Far West, by Major-General Clark, to the Mormons, after they had surrendered their arms, and declared themselves prisoners of war:—

"Gentlemen,—You whose names are not attached to this list of names will now have the privilege of going to your fields to obtain corn for your families, wood, &c. Those that are now taken will go from thence to prison, be tried, and receive the due demerit of their crimes; but you are now at liberty, all but such as charges may be hereafter preferred against. It now devolves upon you to fulfil the treaty that you have entered into, the leading items of which I now lay before you. The first of these you have already complied with, which is, that you deliver up your leading men to be tried according to law. Second, that you deliver up your arms—this has been attended to. The third is, that you sign over your properties to defray the expenses of the war—this you have also done. Another thing yet remains for you to comply with—that is, that you leave the State forthwith; and whatever your feelings concerning this affair, whatever your innocence, it is nothing to me. General Lucas, who is equal in authority with me, has made this treaty with you. I am determined to see it executed. The orders of the Governor to me were, that you should be exterminated, and not allowed to continue in the State; and had your leader not been given up, and the treaty complied with, before this, you and your families would have been destroyed, and your houses in ashes.

"There is a discretionary power vested in my hands, which I shall try to exercise for a season. I did not say that you shall go now; but you must not think of staying here another season, or of putting in crops; for the moment you do, the citizens will be upon you. I am determined to see the Governor's Message fulfilled, but shall not come upon you immediately—do not think that I shall act as I have done any more—but if I have to come again, because the

treaty which you have made here shall be broken, you need not
expect any mercy, but extermination ; for I am determined the
Governor's order shall be executed.   As for your leaders, do not once
think—do not imagine for a moment—do not let it enter your mind—
that they will be delivered, or that you will see their faces again ; for
their fate is fixed, their die is cast, their doom is sealed.

   " I am sorry, gentlemen, to see so great a number of apparently
intelligent men found in the situation that you are ;—and, oh ! that I
could invoke the spirit of the unknown God to rest upon you, and deliver you from that awful chain of superstition, and liberate you from
those fetters of fanaticism with which you are bound.   I would advise you to scatter abroad, and never again organize with bishops, presidents, &c., lest you excite the jealousies of the people, and subject
yourselves to the same calamities that have now come upon you.   You
have always been the aggressors, you have brought upon yourselves
these difficulties by being disaffected, and not being subject to rule—
and my advice is, that you become as other citizens, lest by a recur-
rence of these events, you bring upon yourselves irretrievable ruin."

   While the great body of the Mormons were thus barbarously dealt
with, and while General Clark so coolly spoke of their "extermination"
as a result which they might expect, the Prophet himself, was betrayed into the hands of his enemies, and taken into custody, to answer
the various charges of treason, murder, and felony, which were brought
against him.   His brother Hyrum, and three other leaders of the sect,
were apprehended at the same time.   The "treason" was for making
war against the State of Missouri, the "murder" was the death of
the two men in the affray at Gallatin, and the "felony" was the
destruction and robbery of property committed by the Danite band.
Though Joseph at first anticipated an acquittal upon the whole of these
charges, the mob breathed such vengeance against him that he made
an attempt to escape after he had been a few weeks in prison.   His
attempt, however, was discovered and foiled, partly by the breaking
of an auger with which he was at work, and partly by the indiscretion
of his friends outside.

   Hyrum Smith, in a " Communication to the Saints scattered
abroad," published in the first volume of the *Times and Seasons*, a
year after the events described, gave a painfully interesting account
of the sufferings and persecutions which he and other members of the
sect underwent at this time, in which he recapitulated the main portion
of the evidence from which we have quoted, and added many other facts,
which are necessary to the proper understanding of the narrative.

   " It would be unnecessary for me," he said, " to enter into the particulars prior to my settlement in Missouri, or give an account of my journey

to that State; suffice it to say, that after having endured almost all manner of abuse, which was poured out upon the Church of Latter-Day Saints, from its commencement, by wicked and ungodly men, I left Kirtland, Ohio, the beginning of March, 1838, with a family consisting of ten individuals, and with means only sufficient to take us one half the way. The weather was very unpropitious, and the roads were worse than I had ever seen them before. However, after enduring many privations and much fatigue, through the kind providence of God, I arrived with my family in Far West, the latter part of May, where I found many of my friends who had borne the heat and burthen of the day, and whose privations and sufferings for Christ's sake had been great, with whom I fondly hoped and anticipated the pleasure of spending a season in peace, and having a cessation from the troubles and persecutions to which we had been subject for a number of years. The prospect was truly flattering; we were the owners of almost the entire county; many of the brethren had already opened very extensive farms; nature was propitious, and the comforts of life would have soon been realized by every industrious person. But notwithstanding these favourable auspices, a storm arose, before whose withering blast our fair and reasonable prospects were blasted and ruined : anarchy and dismay were spread through that county, as well as the adjoining ones, in which our brethren had found a resting-place.

"The inhabitants of the upper counties, jealous of the increasing number of the Saints, thinking, like some in ancient times, that if they were to let us alone, we should take away their place and nation, soon began to circulate reports prejudicial to us, and after threatening us with mobs for some time, at last put their threats into execution, and proceeded to drive off our cattle, and burn down our houses, while helpless females, with their tender offspring, had to flee into the wilderness, and wander to a considerable distance for shelter. This state of things continued until, from false representations, and a wicked desire to overthrow the Saints, the Governor called out the militia, and gave orders for our extermination.

" Soon after the arrival of the militia at Far West, my brother Joseph, with several others, who were considered leading characters in the church, were betrayed into their hands, and the day after Colonel George Hinckle, who had always been a professed friend, but who had now turned traitor, came with a company of the enemy to my house, and told them I was the person whom they sought. They told me I must go with them to the camp. I inquired when I could return, my family being in a situation that I knew not how to leave them; but could get no answer. Remonstrance was in vain, so I was obliged to go with them. I was aware of the hostile feelings of our enemies, and their hatred to all those who professed the faith of the Church of Latter-Day Saints; and I can assure my brethren that I would as soon have gone into a den of lions, as into that host, who had orders from the executive of the State to put us to death, and who had every disposition to do so. However, I was enabled to put my trust in the Lord, knowing that he who delivered Daniel out of the den of lions, could deliver me from cruel and wicked men. When I arrived at the camp, I was put under the same guard with my brother Joseph and my other friends, who had been taken the day previous.

"That evening a court-martial was held, to consult what steps should be taken with the prisoners, when it was decided that we were to be shot the next morning, as an ensample to the rest of the church. Knowing that I had done nothing worthy of 'death or of bonds,' and feeling an assurance that all things would work together for our good, I remained quite calm, and felt altogether unmoved. When I heard of their unjust and cruel sentence, 'my heart was fixed, trusting in the Lord.'

"The next morning came on, when (according to the sentence of the court) we were to be shot. It was an important time; thousands were anticipating the event with fiendish joy, and seemed to long for the hour of execution, while our friends and brethren were beseeching a throne of grace on our behalf, and praying for our deliverance. The time at length arrived when their sentence was to be carried into effect: but in consequence of General Doniphan protesting against the unlawfulness of the proceedings, and, at the same time, threatening to withdraw his troops, if they should offer to carry into effect their murderous sentence, the court rescinded their resolution; and thus their purposes were frustrated, and our bitterest enemies were disappointed. The prayers of our friends were answered, and our lives spared. Notwithstanding the discomfiture of their plans, yet our destruction was determined upon by a vast majority, who, thinking they could better carry into effect their purposes, ordered us to be conveyed to Jackson county, where they were well aware our most cruel persecutors resided. Before starting, I got permission to visit my family, but had only time to get a change of clothes, and then was hurried away from them, while they clung to my garments, they supposing it would be the last time they would see me in this world. While getting into the waggon which was to convey us to our destination, four men rushed upon us, and levelled their rifles at us, seemingly with a determination to shoot us. But this was not permitted them to do. No! their arms were unnerved, and they dropped their pieces and slunk away. While thus exposed, I felt no tremour or alarm; I knew I was in the hands of God, whose power was unlimited.

"While on our way to Jackson county we excited great curiosity

At our stopping places, people would flock to see us from all quarters, a great number of whom would rail upon us, and give us abusive language, while a few would pity us, knowing that we were an injured people. When we arrived at Independence, the county seat of Jackson county, the citizens flocked from all parts of the county to see us. They were generally very abusive : some of the most ignorant gnashed their teeth upon us; but all their threats and abuse did not move me, for I felt the spirit of the Lord to rest down upon me, and I felt great liberty in speaking to those who would listen to the truth. Notwithstanding the determination of our enemies, they were not suffered to carry out their designs in that county; for, after enduring considerable hardships, we were removed back as far as Richmond, in Ray county, where, for the first time in my life, I was put into prison. My feet were hurt with the fetters; and I remained in this situation for fourteen days. I endeavoured to bear up under my sufferings and wrongs, but at the same time could not help but feel indignant at those who treated us with such cruelty, and who pretended to do it under the sanction of the laws. After many attempts to destroy us by the military, in all of which they were unsuccessful, we were at length delivered up to the civil law, soon after which, a court of inquiry was held. A great deal of false testimony was given prejudicial to my brethren ; but all the testimony they could produce against me was, that I was one of the presidency of the church, and a firm friend to my brother Joseph. This the court deemed sufficient to authorize my committal to prison. I was then, with my brethren, removed to Liberty, in Clay county, where I was confined for more than four months, and suffered much for want of proper food, and from the nauseous cell in which I was confined, but still more so on account of my anxiety for my family, whom I had left without any protector, and who were unable to help themselves. My wife was confined while I was away from home, and had to suffer more than tongue can tell. She was not able to sit up for several weeks, and to heighten my affliction, and the sufferings of my helpless family, my goods were unlawfully seized upon and carried off, until my family had to suffer in consequence thereof. Nor were the Missourians my only oppressors; but those with whom I had been acquainted from my youth, and who had ever pretended the greatest friendship towards me, came to my house while I was in prison, and ransacked and carried off many of my valuables; this they did under the cloak of friendship. Amongst those who treated me thus, I cannot help making particular mention of Lyman Cowdery, who, in connection with his brother Oliver, took from me a great many things; and, to cap the climax of his iniquity, compelled my aged father, by threatening to bring a mob upon him, to deed over to him, or his brother Oliver, about 160 acres of land, to pay a note, which he said I had given to Oliver, for 165 dollars. Such a note I confess I was, and still am, entirely ignorant of; and after mature consideration, I have to say, that I believe it must be a forgery.

" These circumstances, with the afflicting situation of my family, served greatly to heighten my grief; indeed, it was almost more than I could bear up under. I traversed my prison-house for hours, thinking of their cruelty to my family, and the afflictions they brought upon the Saints of the Most High. They forcibly reminded me of the children of Edom, when the Jews were destroyed by their enemies; and the language of the prophet Obadiah to Edom is, I think, so very much in point, that I cannot refrain from inserting it : —

" ' For thy violence against thy brother Jacob, shame shall cover thee, and thou shalt be cut off for ever.

" ' In the day thou stoodest on the other side, in the day that the strangers carried away captive his forces, and foreigners entered into his gates, and cast lots upon Jerusalem, even thou wast as one of them.

" ' But thou shouldest not have looked on the day of thy brother, in the day that he became a stranger; neither shouldst thou have rejoiced over the children of Judah in the day of their destruction; neither shouldst thou have spoken proudly in the day of distress.

" ' Thou shouldst not have entered into the gate of my people in the day of their calamity ; yea, thou shouldst not have looked on their affliction in the day of their calamity, nor have laid hands on their substance in the day of their calamity. Neither shouldst thou have stood in the crossway, to cut off those of his that did escape; neither shouldst thou have delivered up those of his that did remain in the city of distress.'

" After being in the hands of our enemies for about six months, the time of our deliverance at length arrived. You may judge what my feelings were when I escaped from those whose feet were fast to shed blood, and when I was again privileged to see my beloved family, who had suffered so many privations and afflictions, not only while in Far West, but likewise in moving away in that inclement season of the year.

" Thus, I have endeavoured to give you a short account of my sufferings while in the state of Missouri ; but how inadequate is language to express the feelings of my mind while under them, knowing that I was innocent of crime, and that I had been dragged from my family at a time when my assistance was most needed ; that I had been abused and thrust into a dungeon, and confined for months on account of my faith, and the ' testimony of Jesus Christ.' However, I thank God that I felt a determination to die rather than deny the things which my eyes had seen, which my hands had handled, and which I had borne testimony to, wherever my lot had been cast ; and I can assure my beloved brethren, that I was enabled to bear as strong a testimony when nothing but death presented itself as ever I did in my life. My confidence in God was likewise unshaken. I knew that He who suffered me, along with my brethren, to be thus tried, could, and would, deliver us out of the hands of our enemies ; and in His own due time He did so, for which I desire to bless and praise His holy name.

" From my close and long confinement, as well as from the sufferings of my mind, I feel my body greatly broken down and debilitated, my frame has received a shock from which it will take a long time to recover. Yet, I am happy to say that my zeal for the cause of God, and my courage in defence of the truth, are as great as ever. ' My heart is fixed ;' and I yet feel a determination to do the will of God, in spite of persecutions, imprisonments, or death. I can say with Paul, ' None of these things move me, so that I may finish my course with joy.'

" Your brother in the Kingdom and patience of Jesus Christ,

" HYRUM SMITH."

" *Dec.* 1839."

A document of still more interest was issued by the two brothers while in prison, and signed by them and three other members of the church. The unflinching courage of Joseph while surrounded with difficulties and perils of no ordinary kind, and his firm reliance upon the ultimate triumph of his doctrine, compel admiration, and would almost justify the supposition, that he had taught his imposture so long, and lived so thoroughly in it, by it, and with it, as to have ended by believing it. The document ran as follows :—

" *Liberty Jail, Clay Co., Missouri.*

" To Bishop Partridge, and to the Church of Jesus Christ of Latter-Day Saints, in Quincy, Illinois, and to those scattered abroad, throughout all the regions round about.

" Your humble servant Joseph Smith, jr., prisoner for Christ's sake, and the Saints, taken and held by the power of mobocracy under the exterminating reign of his excellency Governor Lilburn W. Boggs, in company with his fellow-prisoners and beloved brethren, Caleb Baldwin, Lyman Wight, Hyrum Smith, and Alexander McRae, send unto you greeting : May the grace of God the Father, and the Lord and Saviour Jesus Christ, rest upon you all, and abide with you for ever ; and may faith, virtue, knowledge, temperance, patience, godliness, brotherly-kindness, and charity, dwell in you and abound, so that you may not be barren and unfruitful.

" We know, that the greater part of you are acquainted with the wrongs, high-toned injustice, and cruelty which are practised upon us; we have been taken prisoners, charged falsely with all kind of crimes, and thrown into a prison enclosed with strong walls, and are surrounded with a strong guard who are as indefatigable in watching us, as their master is in laying snares for the people of God. Therefore, under these circumstances, dearly beloved brethren, we are the more ready to claim your fellowship and love. Our situation is calculated to awaken our minds to a sacred remembrance of your affection and kindness; and we think that your situation will have the same effect; therefore, we believe, that nothing can separate us from the love of God, and our fellowship one with another; and that every species of wickedness and cruelty practised upon us, will only tend to bind our hearts and seal them together in love.

" It is probably as unnessary for us to say, that we are thus treated and held in bonds without cause, as it would be for you to say, that you were smitten and driven from your homes without any provocation; we mutually understand and verily know, that if the citizens of the State of Missouri had not abused the Saints, and had been as desirous of peace as we were, there would have been nothing but peace and quietude to this day, and we should not have been in this wretched place, and burthened with the society of demons in human form, and compelled to hear nothing but oaths and curses, and witness scenes of drunkenness and debaucheries of every description; neither would the cries of orphans and widows have ascended to God, or the blood of the Saints have stained the soil, and cried for vengeance against them. But ' we dwell with those who hate peace; and who delight in war; and surely their unrelenting hearts—their inhuman and murderous disposition—and their cruel practices, shock humanity, and defy description! It is truly a tale of *sorrow, lamentation,* and *woe,* too much for humanity to contemplate. Such a transaction cannot be found where kings and tyrants reign, or among the savages of the wilderness, or even among the ferocious beasts of the forest. To think that man should be mangled for sport, after being cruelly put to death, and that women should have their last morsel stolen from them, while their helpless children were clinging around them and crying for food—and then, to gratify the hellish desires of their more than inhuman oppressors, be violated, is horrid in the extreme.

" They practice these things upon the Saints, who have done them no wrong, have committed no crime, and who are an innocent and virtuous people; and who have proved themselves lovers of God by forsaking and enduring all things for His sake. ' It must needs be that offences come, but wo to those by whom they come.'

"O God! where art thou? and where is the pavilion that covereth thy hiding-place? how long shall thy hand be stayed, and thy pure eyes behold from the heavens the wrongs and sufferings of thy people, and of thy servants; and thine ears be penetrated with their cries? How long, O Lord! shall they thus suffer, before thine heart shall be softened towards them, and thy bowels be moved with compassion towards them? O Lord God Almighty, maker of heaven, earth, and seas, and of all things that in them is, and who controlleth and subjecteth the devil and the dark and benighted dominions of Satan, stretch forth thy hand, let thine eye pierce, let thy pavilion be taken up, let thy hiding-place no longer be uncovered, let thine ear be inclined, let thine heart be softened, and thy bowels moved with compassion towards thy people; and let thine anger be kindled against our enemies, and in thy fury let fall the sword of thine indignation, and avenge us of our wrongs. Remember thy suffering Saints, O our God! and thy servants will rejoice in thy name forever.

"Dearly beloved brethren, we realize that perilous times have come, as have been testified of in ancient days, and we may look with certainty and the most perfect assurance for the rolling in of all those things which have been spoken of by all the holy prophets: lift up your eyes to the bright luminary of day, and you can say, Soon thou shalt veil thy blushing face, for at the behest of HIM who said, 'Let there be light, and there was light,' thou shalt withdraw thy shining. Thou moon, thou dimmer light, and luminary of night, shalt turn to blood. We see that the prophecies concerning the last days are fulfilling, and the time shall soon come when the 'Son of man shall descend in the clouds of heaven, in power and great glory.'

"We do not shrink, nor are our hearts and spirits broken at the grievous yoke which is put upon us. We know that God will have our oppressors in derision, that he will laugh at their calamity, and mock when their fear cometh. We think we should have got out of our prison house, at the time Elder Rigdon got a writ of habeas corpus, had not our own lawyers interpreted the law contrary to what it reads, and against us, which prevented us from introducing our witnesses before the mock court; they have done us much harm from the beginning; they have lately acknowledged that the law was misconstrued, and then tantalized our feelings with it, and have now entirely forsaken us, have forfeited both their oaths and their bonds, and are co-workers with the mob. From the information we received, the public mind has been for some time turning in our favour, and the majority is now friendly, and the lawyers can no longer browbeat us by saying, that this or that is a matter of public opinion, for public opinion is not willing to brook all their proceedings, but is beginning to look with feelings of indignation upon our oppressors. We think that truth, honour, virtue, and innocence, will eventually come out triumphant.

"We should have taken out a writ of habeas corpus, and escaped the mob in a summary way, but unfortunately for us, the timber of the wall being very hard, our auger handles gave out, which hindered us longer than we expected. We applied to a friend for assistance, and a very slight uncautious act gave rise to suspicion, and before we could fully succeed, our plan was discovered. We should have made our escape, and succeeded admirably well, had it not been for a little imprudence, or over anxiety on the part of our friend.

"The sheriff and jailor did not blame us for our attempt; it was a fine breach, and cost the county a round sum; public opinion says we ought to have been permitted to have made our escape, but then the disgrace would have been on us, but now it must come on the State. We know that there cannot be any charge sustained against us, and that the conduct of the mob—the murders at Haun's Mill, the exterminating order of Governor Boggs, and the one-sided, rascally proceedings of the Legislature, have damned the State of Missouri to all eternity. General Atchison has proved himself to be as contemptible as any of our enemies. We have tried a long time to get our lawyers to draw us some petitions to the supreme judges of this State, but they have utterly refused; we have examined the laws, and drawn the petitions ourselves, and have obtained abundance of proof to counteract all the testimony that is against us, so that if the judges do not grant us our liberty they have got to act contrary to honour, evidence, law, or justice, merely to please the mob; but we hope better things, and trust that before many days, God will so order our case, that we shall be set at liberty, and again enjoy the society of the Saints. We received some letters from our friends, last evening, one from Emma, one from D. C. Smith, and one from Bishop Partridge, all breathing a kind and consoling spirit; we had been a long time without information from our friends, and when we read those letters they were refreshing to our souls, as the gentle air and refreshing breeze; but our feelings of joy were mingled with feelings of pain and sorrow on account of the sufferings of the poor and much injured Saints, and we need not say unto you that the flood-gates of our hearts were open, and our eyes were a fountain of tears. Those who have not been inclosed in the walls of a prison, without cause or provocation, can have but little idea how sweet the voice of a friend or one token of friendship is, from any source whatever, and awakens and calls into action every sympathetic feeling of the human heart; it brings to review everything that has passed, it seizes the present with the velocity of lightning, and grasps after the future with fond anticipation; it fills the mind with tenderness and love, until all enmity, malice, hatred, past differences, misunderstandings, and mismanagements, are entirely forgotten, or are slain victims at the feet of love. When the heart is sufficiently contrite, then the voice of inspiration steals along and whispers, My son, peace be unto thy soul;—thine adversity and thy afflictions shall be but for a moment; and then, if thou art faithful and endure, God shall exalt thee on high, thou shalt triumph over all thy foes, thy friends shall stand by thee, and shall hail thee again with warm hearts: thou art not yet as Job, thy friends do not contend against thee, neither do they charge thee with transgression; and those who do charge thee with transgression, their hope shall be blasted, and their prospects melt away, as the hoar frost melteth before the rays of the rising sun. It likewise informs us that God has set his hand to change the times and the seasons, and to blind the minds of the wicked, that they may not understand his marvellous workings, that he may take them in their own craftiness, because their hearts are corrupt, and the distress and sorrow which they seek to bring upon the saints, shall return upon them double; and, not many years hence, they and their posterity shall be destroyed from under heaven. Cursed are all those that shall lift up the heel against mine anointed, saith the Lord, for they have not sinned before me, saith the Lord, but have done that which was meet in mine eyes, and which I commanded them, saith the Lord. Those who cry transgression do it because they are the servants of sin, and are the children of disobedience themselves, and swear falsely against my servants, that they may bring them into bondage and death. Wo unto them, because they have offended my little ones; they shall be severed from the ordinances of mine house, their basket shall not be full, their houses and their lands shall be empty, and they themselves shall be despised by those who have flattered them. They shall not have right to the priesthood, nor their posterity after them, from generation to generation; and it would have been better for them that a mill-stone had been hung about their necks, and they drowned in the depths of the sea. Wo unto all those who drive, and murder, and testify against my people, saith the Lord of hosts, for they shall not escape the damnation of hell: behold mine eye seeth, and I know all their works, and I have in reserve a swift judgment in the season thereof, and they shall be rewarded according to their works.

"God has said he would have a tried people, and that he would purify them as gold is purified; now, we think he has chosen his own crucible to try us, and if we should be so happy as to endure and keep the faith, it will be a sign to this generation, sufficient to leave them without excuse; and that it will be a trial of our faith equal to that of Abraham or any of the ancients, and that they will not have much cause to boast over us, in the persecutions and trials they endured. After passing through so much suffering and sorrow, we trust that before long a ram may be caught in the thicket, so that the sons and daughters of Abraham may be relieved from their fears and anxiety, and that their faces may once more be lighted up with joy and salvation, and be enabled to hold out unto everlasting life.

"Now, concerning the places for the location of the Saints, we would say that we cannot council you in this thing as well as if we were with you; and as to the things written to you before, we did not consider them binding; we would advise, that while we remain in prison and in bondage, that the affairs of the church be conducted by a general conference of the most faithful and respectable of the authorities of the church, and that the proceedings of the same be forwarded to your humble servants; and if there be any corrections by the word of the Lord, they shall be freely transmitted, and we will cheerfully approve of all things which are acceptable to God. If anything should have been suggested by us, or any names mentioned except by commandment, or ' thus saith the Lord,' we do not consider it binding; therefore we shall not feel grieved if you should deem it wisdom to make different arrangements. We would respectfully advise the brethren to be aware of an aspiring spirit, which has frequently urged men forward to make foul speeches, and beget an undue influence in the minds of the Saints, and bring much sorrow and distress in the church. We would likewise say, be aware of pride; for truly hath the wise man said, ' Pride goeth before destruction, and an haughty spirit before a fall.' Outward appearance is not always a criterion for us to judge our fellow-man by; but the lips frequently betray the haughty and overbearing mind. Flattery also is a deadly poison; a frank and open rebuke provoketh a good man to emulation, and in the hour of trouble he will be your best friend; but rebuke a wicked man, and you will soon see manifest all the corruption of a wicked heart—the poison of asps is under their tongue, and they cast the Saints in prison, that their deeds be not reproved. A fanciful, flowery, and heated imagination be aware of; for the things of God are of vast importance, and require time and experience, as well as deep and solemn thought, to find them out; and if we would bring souls to salvation, it requires that our minds should rise to the highest heavens, search into and contemplate the lowest abyss, expand wide as eternity, and hold communion with Deity. How much more dignified and noble are the thoughts of God than the vain imaginations of the human heart! How vain and trifling have been our spirits in our conferences and council meetings, as well as in our public and private conversations! Too low and condescending for the dignified characters of the called and chosen of God, who have been set apart in the mind of God before the foundation of the world, to hold the keys of the mysteries of those things which have been kept hid for ages and generations, which have been revealed to babes, yea, to the weak, obscure, and despisable ones of the earth. We would beseech you to bear with the infirmities of the weak, and at the same time exhort one another to a reformation, both teachers and taught, male and female; so that honesty, sobriety, candour, solemnity plainness, meekness, and virtue, may characterize us from henceforth and that we be like little children, without malice, guile, or hypocrisy. And now, brethren, after your tribulation, if you do these things, and exercise fervent prayer in the sight of God always, he shall give unto you knowledge, by his Holy Spirit; yea, he shall pour out the Holy Ghost in such copious effusion as has not been since the creation until now; yea, the fulness of that promise which our fathers have waited for with such anxious expectation, which was to be revealed in the last days, and held in reserve until a time when nothing shall be withheld; when all the glories of earth and heaven, time and eternity, shall be manifest to all those who have endured valiantly for the Gospel of Jesus Christ. If there be bounds set to the heavens, the seas, the dry land, they shall be manifest, as well as the various revolutions of the sun, moon, and planets; and a full development of all the glorious laws by which they are governed shall be revealed in the 'dispensation of the fulness of times,' according to that which was ordained in the midst of the council of heaven in the presence of the eternal God, before this world was.

"Ignorance, bigotry, and superstition are frequently in the way of the prosperity of this church, and are like the torrent of rain rushing down from the mountains, which floods the clear stream with mire and dirt; but when the storm is over, and the rain has ceased, the mire and dirt are washed away, and the stream again is pure and clear as the fountain, so shall the church appear when ignorance, superstition, and bigotry are washed away. What power can stay the heavens? As well might man stretch forth his puny arm to stop the mighty Missouri river in its course, as to hinder the Almighty from pouring down knowledge from heaven upon the hearts of the Latter-Day Saints! What are the governor and his murderous party, but willows on the shore to stop the waters in their progress? As well might we argue that water is not water, because the mountain torrent sends down mire, and riles the crystal stream; or that fire is not fire, because it is quenchable; as to say that our cause is down

G

because renegadoes, liars, priests, and murderers, who are alike tenacious
of their crafts and creeds, have poured down upon us a flood of dirt
and mire from their strongholds. No, they may rage, with all the
powers of hell, and pour forth their wrath, indignation, and cruelty,
like the burning lava of Mount Vesuvius, yet shall Mormonism stand.
Truth is Mormonism, and God is its author; by HIM we received our
birth, by HIM we were called to a dispensation of his gospel, in the
beginning of the fulness of times; it was by him we received the Book
of Mormon, by him we remain unto this day, and shall continue to
remain, if it be to his glory; we are determined to endure tribulation, as
good soldiers, unto the end: when you read this, you will learn that
prison walls, iron doors, screeching hinges, guards and jailors, have
not destroyed our confidence, but we say, and that from experience,
that they are calculated in their very nature to make the soul of an
honest man feel stronger than the powers of hell. But we must bring
our epistle to a close, and send our respects to fathers, mothers, wives,
and children, brothers, and sisters, and be assured we hold them in
sacred remembrance.

" We should be glad to hear from Elder Rigdon, George W. Robinson and Elder Cahoon. We remember them, and would like to jog
their memory a little on the fable of the bear and the two friends, who
mutually agreed to stand by each other. We could also mention Uncle
John Smith and others. A word of consolation and a blessing would
not come amiss from anybody, while we are so closely whispered by
the bear. Our respects and love to all the virtuous saints. We are,
dear brethren, your fellow-sufferers, and prisoners of Jesus Christ for
the Gospel's sake, and for the hope of glory which is in us. Amen.

" JOSEPH SMITH, JR.
HYRUM SMITH.
LYMAN WIGHT.
CALEB BALDWIN.
ALEXANDER MCRAE."

While Joseph and Hyrum remained in prison, and thus endeavoured to arouse the zeal of such men as Sidney Rigdon, men who
knew too much to be thoroughly trusted, and who required the goad
to keep them faithful; the Mormons, unable to cope with their enemies, were hunted out of Missouri, no opportunity being allowed them
to sell their farms, or enter into arrangements for the disposal of their
property. In the midst of an inclement winter, in December, 1838,
and January, 1839, men, women, and children—the sick and the aged
as well as the young and strong—were turned out into the prairies or
forests, without food or sufficient protection from the weather. In

this miserable plight they arrived in Illinois in small detachments, and were most kindly received by the settlers, as well as by the Indians. Subscriptions were entered into for their relief, and many of them procured situations in farms, mills, and stores. After a time they began to hold up their heads again. Their numbers became formidable in their new settlements. Persecution did its ordinary work in making proselytes, and the congregations of the Saints were increased daily by new converts from among the people of Illinois. Early in the spring of 1839, the Prophet, more successful than in his first attempt, when his auger broke, escaped from prison, and made his appearance among his followers at a place called Quincy. His rude but touching eloquence, his confident appeals to Heaven, his magnificent promises, his tact and skill, and the joy of the true believers that he was once more among them, all combined to restore confidence. The great bulk of the Mormons speedily gathered about a village called "Commerce," just above the Desmoines Rapids, on the Mississippi river. Here they soon made arrangements for settling down. The Saints joined them from various parts of the United States, many of them bringing considerable sums of money. Their surprising fortunes in their new home will be more fully detailed in the next chapter. In order, however, to complete the history of the sufferings and persecution they endured in Missouri, we reproduce the petition presented by Sidney Rigdon to the State of Pennsylvania, craving redress. The petition is well worded; and although its language is strong, the facts it narrates are fully corroborated by other parties, not connected with the Mormons.

" TO THE HONOURABLE THE SENATE AND HOUSE OF REPRESENTATIVES OF PENNSYLVANIA, IN LEGISLATIVE CAPACITY ASSEMBLED.

" YOUR memorialist, a member of the Church of Jesus Christ of Latter-Day Saints, and now an exile in the State of Illinois, begs leave most respectfully to represent to your honourable body, that he was born in the State of Pennsylvania, on the 19th of February, A.D 1793, in Alleghany county, and township of Saint Clair; that he continued his permanent residence in said State until the year 1826, when he moved into the State of Ohio. In 1831 he went into the State of Missouri, and, in connection with other members of said Church of Jesus Christ of Latter-Day Saints, became the owner of real estate in the county of Jackson in said state; but by reason of the violence of a formidable mob, and the unwillingness of the authorities of Missouri to protect your memorialist, and those connected with him in the possession of their rights, they were forbidden the privilege of enjoying their property, or receiving any benefit therefrom; that in the month of April 1838, your memorialist moved with his family into the State of Missouri, into Caldwell county, and became the owner of real estate in the said county of Caldwell, without, however, being

privileged to enjoy the benefit of his lands in Jackson county. All the lands
owned by your memorialist and his brethren in Jackson county were purchased
from the United States, for which payment had been made in full; the benefits
of which payment the United States now enjoy, and has ever since the purchase.
There had a large number of the Church of Jesus Christ of Latter-Day Saints
settled in Caldwell county at the time your memorialist went into that county,
as also many in Davies county in said State. We commenced building houses
and improving our lands; building mills and other machinery for our mutual
benefit; quietly and peaceably enjoying our new homes, and using much industry and economy to render the desolate waste, whither we had been driven,
a pleasant habitation for man. The toils of the day were followed by the sound
of the hammer, the noise of the plane, and the hum of the wheel at night.
Day and night all was bustle, all was stir; every hour of the day and many of
the night brought forth the fruits of industry for the benefit of the settlers, and
additional improvement, beauty, and comfort to our new homes.   Our
social circles, however, were not unfrequently disturbed by the tears and sobbings
of some disconsolate widow, or the weeping of some bereaved orphan, bewailing
the loss of a husband or a father, who had fallen a victim to the violence of
the Jackson and Clay county mobs. Jackson county was the place of our
choice, and nothing but violence could have caused our people to leave it.
Their hearts were set upon it, and all their feelings associated with that place,
as the future home of themselves and their posterity. The location in Caldwell and Davies counties was only made by our people by reason of violence
and lawless outrages committed upon them It was always received by us as
a place of exile, and not of choice, and in despite of all our efforts at cheerfulness, at times the mind would be almost overwhelmed with melancholy, and
we would say in our hearts, and often with our lips, ' What availeth us that our
ancestors bled, and our fathers fought for liberty, while we are as captives in a
strange land ?' and like Israel along the streams of Babylon, we would be almost
ready to hang our harps on the willows, and refuse to sing the song of Zion.
Oh, where is the patrimony our fathers bequeathed to us ? Where is the liberty
they purchased with their blood ?   Fled ! alas, fled ! but we hope not for ever.

   " But the wants of our families would dissipate our feelings; we would engage
in the labours of the day and the toils of the night with untiring perseverance,
and struggle with all the powers of both mind and body, to render our families
comfortable, and make our homes pleasant. But, alas ! this privilege was not
allowed us. Our quiet industry and untiring perseverance soon awakened the
jealousy of our enemies, and the cry went forth, that if the Mormons (as they
called us) were let alone, Caldwell county would in five years be the most
wealthy and populous county in the State. This our enemies could not endure;
and a regular system of mobocracy, of violence, and plunder, was formed to
check us in our course to wealth and greatness, as our enemies supposed ; and
indeed, they had some reason to think so ; for an extent of improvement had
been made in this remote and wild region, in the space of a few months, which
had no parallel in the history of our western settlements, and I strongly doubt
whether anywhere else.

" This banditti of marauders increased in numbers and violence, until by device and stratagem, duplicity and falsehood, they got the authorities of the State to interfere and aid them in their diabolical purposes ; and the then Governor of the State, Lilburn W. Boggs, actually sent a large military force into the county, with orders to exterminate us and confiscate our property ; or such was the authority the commanders of the military array claimed, by virtue of the order received from the Governor. Suffice it to say, that our settlements were broken up, our towns plundered, our farms laid waste, our crops ruined, our flocks and herds either killed or driven away, our houses rifled, our goods, money, clothing, provisions, and all we had carried away ; men were shot down like wild beasts, or had their brains dashed out ; women were insulted and ravished, until they died in the hands of their destroyers ; children were killed while pleading for their lives. All entreaties were vain and fruitless ; men, women, and children, alike fell victims to the violence and cruelty of these ruffians. Men moving into the county with their families were shot down ; their waggons, teams, and loading, taken by the plunderers as booty, and their wives with their little ones ordered out of the State forthwith, or suffer death, as had their husbands, leaving them no means of conveyance but their feet, and no means of subsistence but begging. Soldiers of the revolution were slain in the most brutal manner while pleading for their lives in the name of American citizens. Many were thrown into prison to endure the insults of a mock trial, that would have disgraced an Inquisition. This last part of the scene was doubtless designed to make the distant public believe that there was some excuse for all this outrage and violence. Among the number of those cast into prison was your memorialist, who had to endure four months' imprisonment, part of the time in chains.

" To give your honourable body a correct idea of the origin of these scenes of cruelty and woe, we will here transcribe the preamble to a set of resolutions passed by these plunderers at their first meeting, held in Jackson county, for the purpose of taking measures for the expulsion of our people from that county. It is as follows :

" ' We the undersigned, citizens of Jackson county, believing that an important crisis is at hand as regards our civil society, in consequence of a pretended religious society of people that have settled and are still settling in our county, styling themselves Mormons ; and intending, as we do, to rid our society, peaceably if we can, forcibly if we must, and believing, as we do, that the arm of the civil law does not afford us a guarantee, or at least a sufficient one, against the evils which are now inflicted on us, and seem to be increasing, by the said religious sect, deem it expedient and of the highest importance to form ourselves into a company for the better and easier accomplishment of our purpose, which, we deem it almost superfluous to say, is justified as well by the law of nature as by the law of self-defence.'

" Your honourable body will see by the above that the reason assigned for the formation of the company (and this was the first that was formed), was the want of power in the civil law to enable them to effect their own object. Hear their own words : ' And believing, as we do, that the arm of the civil law does

not afford us a guarantee, or at least a sufficient one, against the evils which
are now inflicted on us.' What were the evils complained of? Strange must
be the answer, themselves being judges; the existence of a religious society
among them—a society, too, against which even envy and malice themselves
could not find an accusation, or ferret out a lawless impropriety, or one act
which the laws recognised as crime. For, say the complainants, we form
ourselves into a company, because the laws do not provide for the evils which
afflict us; or this is in effect what they say. If any individual or individuals
of said society, or the society as a body, had transgressed the laws, had not the
State power to lawfully inflict the punishment due to said offence? The
sequel shows they had. What are the facts, then, of the case, our enemies being
the judges themselves? They are, that our people had so deported themselves
as to be justified by the laws, claiming no rights but such as the laws guaran-
teed, exercising no power beyond the limits set for them by the laws of the
country; and this was the reason why our enemies formed themselves into a
company for our expulsion, or at least they so say. If our people had been
transgressors of the laws, no need then for the people of Jackson county to
form themselves into a company to drive us from our homes; they could have
done this lawfully: no need of a company being formed; all could have been
done without that humanity could have demanded.

" By virtue, then, of the unholy determination, as stated above, our people
were attacked indiscriminately, men, women, and children, their houses were
rifled; the inmates driven out into open fields or wild prairies; their farms
desolated; their crops all destroyed; their goods and chattels carried off or otherwise destroyed; men were caught, tied up, and whipped, until some died in
their hands; others had to tie handkerchiefs round their bodies to keep their
bowels from falling out; others were shot down, their wives and little ones
driven from their habitation. And this often in the night, having nothing but
their night-clothes on; their houses would be set on fire and all consumed,
leaving hundreds of women and little children thus destitute and naked, wandering bare-footed and nearly naked in the darkness of night and dead of
winter, in the fields and open prairies without any covering but the heavens,
or any bed but the earth; and their condition so terrible, that they might be
followed by their blood, which flowed from their lacerated and bleeding feet.
Females in this heart-rending condition gave birth to children in the open air,
and exposed to the inclemencies of the winter. The consequences were, that
many sickened and many died. And if we ask, Why all this abuse? the answer
must be, Because the people had not transgressed the laws; if they had, their
persecutors would have punished them by the laws; but they had not done it,
and for this cause they must suffer all the cruelties which the most inhuman
barbarity could invent. The lands which your memorialist and his brethren
had purchased from the general government, and on which large improvements
were made, were thus taken possession of by our persecutors, and the same
are held by them till this day, and we are forbid the privilege of enjoying them,
or any benefit arising from them—I mean, the lands in Jackson county.

" After wandering about for a length of time, those that were thus unlawfully deprived of their earthly all, and cruelly driven from their homes, got into Clay county in said State of Missouri, and again began to get homes; but in a short time the same scenes began to be acted in Clay, as had been in Jackson county, and the people were again driven and got into Caldwell, or what was afterwards Caldwell county, and into Davies county, or a large majority of them, and here again purchased lands from the general government.

" To give your honourable body a correct idea of how those who had been thus driven and stripped of their all were enabled again to purchase, it is only necessary to say, that there was a constant emigration into the country of the members of the Church of Jesus Christ of Latter-Day Saints ; many of those had money, and they loaned part of what they had to those who had none, and enabled them to purchase homes. The lands soon began to rise in value, and the first purchasers were enabled to sell part of what they had purchased-for enough to pay for the whole and save themselves a home, some more and some less. There were few, if any, who did not in this way get homes, but were privileged only a very short time to enjoy them. We were followed into Caldwell and Davies counties by the same relentless spirit, and by the same persecutors who had desolated our people in Jackson county, under the command of Major-General Lucas, of Independence, Jackson county, seat of the first mob, and the place where the first company was formed for our destruction. He was joined on his way hither by many of other counties, and invaded our towns and settlements, laid all waste, and drove us into exile.

" Lilburn W. Boggs, who was Lieutenant-Governor of the State when the persecution first commenced, and one of the principal actors in the persecution, was now (1838) Governor of the State, and used his executive and influence to have us all massacred or driven into exile ; again taking all we had, and holds it till this day ; and all this because we were not lawless and disobedient. For if the laws had given them a sufficient guarantee against the evils complained of by the existence of our religious society among them, then would they have had recourse to the laws. If we had been transgressors of law, our houses would not have been rifled, our women ravished, our farms desolated, and our goods and chattels destroyed, our men killed, our wives and children driven into the prairies, and made to suffer all the indignities that the most brutal barbarity could inflict ; but would only have had to suffer that which the laws would inflict, which were founded in justice, framed in righteousness, and administered in humanity. But, scourged by this banditti without the forms of law, and, according to their own declaration, in violation of all law or the principles of humanity, we were doomed to suffer all kinds of cruelty which barbarity or inhumanity could invent. And they have gravely told the world that they deem it almost superfluous to say that their cause was justified, as well by the law of nature as by the law of self-defence. Now, in the name of all humanity, what law of nature justified, or law of self-defence required, the infliction of such shameless cruelties ? In so saying, they show most assuredly but very little respect to the intelligence or humanity of American citizens ; and in the eyes of the civilised world have cast a shade, and a dark one too, on the character of the sons of a noble ancestry ; for they

have virtually said that Americans look upon such cruelties as the acts of
virtue and the fatherly chastisements of humanity.

"During the whole progress of those scenes of cruelty, from the beginning
we petitioned the authorities of the State of Missouri for protection and redress.
In the name of American citizens we appealed to their patriotism, to their justice,
to their humanity, and to their sacred honours; but they were deaf to our
'entreaties, and lent a listless ear to our petitions. All attempts at redress or
protection were vain; and they heeded us not, until we were exiles in a strange
land, though one (and to its honour be it spoken) where we found both friends
and a home. But since our residence in Illinois, Missouri has followed us
with the same relentless spirit of persecution. Warrants have been sent by
the Governor of Missouri to the Governor of Illinois, demanding the body of
your memorialist and a number of others; for that of Joseph Smith three
several warrants have been sent, all of which have been set aside by the legal
authorities of Illinois; and yet they cease not their persecution. Our people
are kidnapped and carried into Missouri, and there insulted and whipped (as
many have been), and cast into prison, and left to get out as they could. All
this without the forms of trial. Missouri is by these brutal means endeavouring to make the public think that they have cause for this barbarity. But,
let me ask your honourable body, what excuse can be pled for such inhuman
barbarity and brutal recklessness? Let me further ask the attention of your
honourable body to the fact, that all the before-described outrages were committed by a body of men calling themselves militia, called out by order of
the Governor for the professed object of seeing that the laws were kept, and
their supremacy maintained. Such was their pretended object, and under this
cover they put at defiance the laws of both God and man, of nature, humanity,
and decency; and in these unhallowed abuses of all the laws of civilized society
in the world, they were upheld by the authorities of the state, and actually
paid by the State for committing theft, robbery, rapine, violence, rape, and
murder, with innumerable cruelties painful to mention. And when we made
application to the authorities for redress, we were insulted instead of receiving
common civilities. The constitution of the United States provides, that the
United States shall give to each state a republican form of government. Is
it a republican form of government where such outrages can be committed in
the face of the authorities, and yet no redress can be had? where all law is
suspended to give place to cruelty, barbarity, and inhumanity? Let your
honourable body answer.

"Her statesmen in the national councils may attempt to plead excuses for
these diabolical outrages; but all they can do is to stamp infamy on their own
characters, and engrave disgrace on the urn that contains their ashes after
they sleep. What, I ask your honourable body, can be pled in extenuation of
crimes so barbarous, cruelties so infamous, and outrages so violent? What
crime can any man commit, it matters not how flagrant, which can, according
to the laws of the civilized world, subject his wife to insult, his daughters to
rape, his property to public plunder, his children to starvation, and himself
and family to exile. The very character of the outrage is all the testimony

I think your honourable body can ask—that it was without provocation on the part of the sufferers ; for if there had been provocation, then would the transgressors have had to suffer the penalty of broken laws ; but their punishment, if such it can be called, was not the penalty inflicted for the breach of any law, for no law in existence knows such a penalty or penalties. Why, then, all this cruelty ? Answer, because the people had violated no law ; and they could not be restrained by law, nor prevented from exercising the rights which they (according to the laws) enjoyed, and had a right to be protected in, in any State in the Union.

" Being refused redress by the authorities of Missouri, to whom shall your memorialist look ?   He answers, to the people of his native State, and through them to the general government ; and where can he look with more confidence than to the patriots of Pennsylvania, the State of his nativity, and the place of the sepulchres of his fathers ? Yes, your memorialist says in his heart, ' I will tell my wrongs and grievance, and that of my brethren, in Pennsylvania ; I will publish them in the streets, highways, and high places of the " Key-Stone State," that her statesmen may plead the cause of suffering innocence in the halls of the National Legislature ; her matrons may arise in the strength of patriotism ; her fair ones in virtuous indignation, and their united voices cease not until the cause of the innocent shall be heard, and their most sacred rights restored.' To your honourable body, then, the representatives of the people of his native State, your memorialist utters his complaining voice ; to you he tells the tale of his wrongs and his woes, and that of his brethren, and appeals to your honourable body as one of Pennsylvania's native sons, and asks you in the name of all that is patriotic, republican, and honourable, to instruct the whole delegation of Pennsylvania in Congress, to use all lawful and constitutional means to obtain for us redress for our wrongs and losses ; believing, as your memorialist does, that the general government has not only power to act in the premises, but are bound by every sacred obligation by which American citizens are bound to one another in our national compact, to see that no injury is inflicted without redress being made.

" Weak indeed must be our republican institutions, and as contemptible our national capacity, if it is a fact that American citizens, after having purchased lands from the government, and received the government guarantee to be protected in the enjoyment of them, they can be lawlessly and causelessly driven off by violence and cruelty, and yet the government have no power to protect them or redress their wrongs. Tell not this in Pennsylvania, publish it not in the streets of Harrisburgh, for surely the sons of the ' Key-Stone State' will feel themselves insulted.

" Well may the nations of the old world ridicule the weakness and impotency of our free institutions,—a government not able to protect its own citizens ! A government,—it must be famous indeed in the annals of history, and a pattern to the world, which is so governed as to admit of the most flagrant abuses known to the civilized world, and acknowledged by all to be such, and yet no power to redress them ! Hear it, O ye barbarians ! Listen to it, O ye savages ! and hasten, yea, hasten all of you to America ; there you can glut your avarice by plunder, and riot in the blood of innocence till you are satisfied, and the government has no power to restrain, nor strength to punish, nor yet ability to redress, the sufferers at your hands.

" From the acquaintance which your memorialist has with the history of his native State, he has been induced to make his appeal to your honoured body:—a State whose people are noted for their civic virtues and zealous attachment to the principles of civil and religious liberty,—a people venerable from the beginning of our national existence, whose virtuous efforts to the sacred principles of freedom, religious, civil, and political, have obtained for themselves imperishable laurels in the history of our country's glory,—a people whose colonial organization was based upon the holy principles of equal rights and equal privileges,—a people whose national escutcheon has never been stained with the martyr's blood,—a people whose statesmen, divines, and heroes, laboured in the cabinet, the desk, and the field, to secure and hand down to their posterity, in all succeeding ages, the boon of heaven, the sacred rights of freemen.

" It was in the honoured metropolis of Pennsylvania, the seat of the first colonial Congress, when the principles of liberty were matured, from whence emanated the voice of independence, whose echoes rolled and reverberated till it reached the circumference of the colonial settlements, and inspired the sons of freedom, until there was but one voice heard, ' Freedom or death !' It was there, when the leaders and heroes of the revolution pledged their lives, their fortunes, and their sacred honours to each other, to be scourged by a tyrant's sceptre no longer, until all they had, and all they were, were offered on the altar of freedom.

" Not only were the principles of equal rights inscribed in legible characters on the flags which floated on her towers in the incipient stages of our national existence, but they were engraven on the hearts of the people with an impression which could not be obliterated. All who collected in her towers or fought under her banners could contend and fight for freedom only. Her teachers of religion, whose influence in the pulpit and eloquence in public assemblies, wielded an overwhelming influence in forwarding the cause of liberty,—did they use this influence in securing to themselves governmental patronage or religious preferences ? All acquainted with the history of the times answer *No.* They were citizens of Pennsylvania, and the immortal *Penn* had inscribed on every pot and bell in the colony, ' Civil and Religious Liberty.' The patriotism of Pennsylvania's religious teachers was pure. They threw in their whole weight of character and influence to promote a cause which made others equal with themselves,—for the glorious privilege of seeing a people free. Her heroes bore the horrors of war, not to sway the tyrant's sceptre or enjoy a lordling's wealth ; but to found an asylum for the oppressed, and prepare a land of freedom for the tyrant's slave. Her statesmen, while in the councils of the nation, devoted all their wisdom and talents to establish a government where every man should be free ; the slave liberated from bondage, and the coloured African enjoy the rights of citizenship ; all enjoying equal rights to speak, to act, to worship—peculiar privileges to none

Such were Pennsylvania's sons at the beginning, and surely *their* sons and successors must have degenerated, lamentably degenerated from the purity and patriotism of their fathers and predecessors, if crimes and cruelties, such as your memorialist complains of, go unheeded and unregarded. Honourable regard for the people of my native State forbids the thought.

" In confidence of the purity and patriotism of the representatives of the people of his native State, your memorialist comes to your honourable body through this his winged messenger, to tell you that the altar which was erected by the blood of your ancestors to civil and religious liberty, from whence ascended up the holy incense of pure patriotism and universal good will to man into the presence of Jehovah, a savour of life, is thrown down, and the worshippers thereat have been driven away, or else they are laying slain at the place of the altar. He comes to tell your honourable body that the temple your fathers erected to freedom, whither their sons assembled to hear her precepts and cherish her doctrines in their hearts, has been desecrated, its portals closed, so that those that go up hither are forbidden to enter.

" He comes to tell your honourable body that the blood of the heroes and patriots of the revolution, who have been slain by wicked hands for enjoying their religious rights,—the boon of heaven to man,—has cried, and is crying, in the ears of the Lord of Sabaoth, saying : ' Redress, redress our wrongs, O Lord God of the whole earth !'

" He comes to tell your honourable body that the dying groans of infant innocence, and the shrieks of insulted and abused females, and many of them widows of revolutionary patriots, have ascended up into the ears of Omnipotence, and are registered in the archives of eternity, to be had in the day of retribution as a testimony against the whole nation, unless their cries and groans are heard by the representatives of the people, and ample redress made, as far as the nation can make it, or else the wrath of the Almighty will come down in fury against the whole nation.

" Under all these circumstances, your memorialist prays to be heard by your honourable body touching all the matters of his memorial, and as a memorial will be presented to Congress this session for redress of our grievances, he prays your honourable body will instruct the whole delegation of Pennsylvania, in both houses, to use all their influence in the national councils, to have redress granted.

" And, as in duty bound, your memorialist will ever pray.

SIDNEY RIGDON, P. M."

THE TEMPLE AT NAUVOO.

CHAPTER V.

Establishment of the Sect in Illinois—Building of the City and Temple of Nauvoo
—Joseph a Lieutenant-General—The Prophet's Right-hand Man—The Mormons in England—Prosperity of Nauvoo.

In the course of a few months after their expulsion from Missouri,
the number of Mormons that found refuge in Illinois amounted to
fifteen thousand souls, including men, women, and children. Many
of these had never resided in Missouri, but flocked to the new location
of the sect from all parts of the Union, and even from England, to
make a last stand against oppression, and to support their prophet
against his enemies. The organization of the sect began to be more
fully and admirably developed; and the Mormons were even at this
early period of their career, a pre-eminently industrious, frugal, and
pains-taking people. They felt the advantages of co-operation.

Though robbed and plundered, they did not lose their time in vain repinings, but set themselves to repair the calamities they had suffered. The needy were aided by the more affluent in the purchase of land, and in the plenishing of their farms ; and the inducements which they held out to skilled mechanics and others to join them, were not merely of a religious and spiritual, but of a social and worldly character. The Mormons as a body understood the dignity and the holiness of hard work, and they practised to the fullest extent the duty of self-reliance. They soon found themselves so numerous in the vicinity of the village of "Commerce," that their leaders conceived the project of converting it first into a town, and afterwards into a city. They gave it the name of "Nauvoo," or the "Beautiful," a word that occurs in the Book of Mormon. In the course of a year and a half they erected about 2,000 houses, besides schools and other public buildings, and called the place the "Holy City." Joseph Smith was appointed its Mayor, and for a brief period in his troubled career enjoyed the supremacy, which was the great object of his existence, and the darling dream of his ambition. His word was law. ' He was both the temporal and spiritual head of his people, and enjoyed, beside the titles of "Prophet," "President," and "Mayor," the military title of "General" Smith, in right of his command over a body of militia, which he organized under the name of the Nauvoo Legion.

It was shortly previous to this time that the sect first began to be heard of in England. In a short sketch of the rise, progress, and faith of the Mormons, inserted in the fifth volume of the *Times and Seasons,* it is stated that in 1837 the first mission to England was undertaken, under the direction of Elders O. Hyde, the same whose signature appears to the disparaging affidavit relative to the Danite Band already quoted, and H. C. Kimball. These two baptized two thousand people into the Mormon faith, chiefly in Manchester, Birmingham, Leeds, Liverpool, Glasgow, and South Wales. In 1843, the number of the sect in England had increased to upwards of 10,000. In 1844, Elder Lorenzo Snow, being then in England, forwarded, by desire of the "Prophet," a copy of the Book of Mormon to Queen Victoria, and another to his Royal Highness Prince Albert, a circumstance at which the Saints in Nauvoo seemed greatly to rejoice. A Mormon poet exclaimed, in reference to it—

> " Oh! would she now her influence lend—
> The influence of royalty—
> Messiah's kingdom to extend,
> And Zion's nursing mother be.

"Then with the glory of her name
    Inscribed on Zion's lofty spire,
She'd win a wreath of endless fame,
    To last when other wreaths expire."

LORENZO SNOW.

Joseph became rather chary of giving forth "revelations" after
he finally left Kirtland, but it was necessary to have a revelation
with reference to the Holy City. It was published accordingly in
the month of January, 1841, and directed the building of a magnificent temple, to which all the Saints were to contribute a tithe
of their possessions, or of their time and labour. "Let all my Saints
come from afar," said this revelation, the last that the prophet appears to have issued, "and send ye swift messengers, yea, chosen messengers, and say unto them, 'Come ye with all your gold, and your
silver, and your precious stones, and with all your antiquities, and
with all who have knowledge of antiquities, that will come, may
come; and bring the box tree, and the fir tree, and the pine tree, to-

gether with all the precious trees of the earth, and with iron, and with copper, and with brass, and with zinc, and with all your precious things of the earth, and build a house to my name for the Most High to dwell therein.'" The Saints were also commanded to build "a boarding-house" for the boarding of strangers. "Let it be built in my name, and let my name be named upon it, and let my servant Joseph Smith and his house have place therein from generation to generation, for ever and ever, saith the Lord; and let the name of the house be called the Nauvoo House, and let it be a delightful habitation for man, and a resting-place for the weary traveller, that he may contemplate the glory of Zion, and the glory of this, the corner-stone thereof." This "revelation" was the most elaborate of all the compositions issued under this name. It was divided into forty-six heads or paragraphs, and entered minutely into directions for raising the funds for these undertakings, and also for governing the church in all its various departments.

The building of the temple was immediately commenced. The site chosen was exceedingly fine, being on a hill commanding a magnificent view on every side. It was built of a polished white lime-stone, almost as hard as marble, and is described as having been 138 feet in length by 88 in breadth. It was surmounted by a pyramidal tower, ascending by steps 170 feet from the ground, and the internal decorations were very costly. The Mormons having grown rich and powerful under persecution, expended nearly a million of dollars upon this edifice.

The foundation-stone was laid with much pomp on the 6th of April, 1841, within less than two years and a half after the expulsion of the sect from Missouri. A writer in the Mormon paper, the *Times and Seasons*, described the ceremony as one of the most magnificent that had ever been witnessed in America. At an early hour on the appointed day, the prophet, who then enjoyed the title of Lieut.-General Smith "was informed that the legion was ready for review, and accompanied by his staff, consisting of four aides-de-camp and twelve guards, nearly all in splendid uniforms, took his march to the parade ground. On their approach they were met by the band, beautifully equipped, who received them with a flourish of trumpets, and a regular salute, and then struck up a lively air, marching in front to the stand of the Lieut.-General. On his approach to the parade ground the artillery were again fired, and the legion gave an appropriate salute. This," said the Mormon reporter, "was indeed a glorious sight, such as we never saw, nor did we ever expect to see such a one in the west. The several companies presented a beautiful and interesting spectacle, several of them being uniformed and equipped, while

the rich and costly dresses of the officers would have become a
Buonaparte or a Washington.

"After the arrival of Lieut.-General Smith, the ladies, who had
made a beautiful silk flag, drove up in a carriage to present it to the
legion. Major-General Bennett very politely attended on them, and
conducted them in front of Lieut.-General Smith, who immediately
alighted from his charger, and walked up to the ladies, who presented
the flag, making an appropriate address. Lieut.-General Smith
acknowledged the honour conferred upon the legion, and stated that
as long as he had the command it should never be disgraced, and then
politely bowing to the ladies, gave it into the hands of Major-General
Bennett, who placed it in possession of Cornet Robinson, and it was
soon seen gracefully waving in front of the legion. During the time
of presentation the band struck up a lively air, and another salute
was fired from the artillery.

"After the presentation of the flag, Lieut.-General Smith, accompanied by his suit, reviewed the legion, which presented a very imposing appearance, the different officers saluting as he passed. Lieut.-
General Smith then took his former stand, and the whole legion passed
before him in review."

A procession was then formed with Joseph at its head, followed by
Aides-de-Camp—Brigadiers—a military band—a body of infantry—
and of cavalry—and a troop of young ladies eight a-breast. On its
arrival at the temple block, the generals with their staffs, and the
strangers present, took their position inside the foundation ; the
ladies formed on the outside, immediately next the walls, the gentlemen and infantry behind, and the cavalry in the rear.

The assembly being stationed, the choristers sung an appropriate
hymn. Sidney Rigdon then ascended a platform, which had been
prepared for the purpose, and delivered an oration, which lasted for
an hour ; in which he passed in review " the scenes of tribulation and
anguish through which the Saints had passed, the barbarous cruelties
inflicted upon them for their faith and attachment to the cause of their
God, and for the testimony of Jesus, which they endured with patience,
knowing that they had in heaven a more enduring substance—a crown
of eternal glory. In obedience to the commandments of their Heavenly
Father, and because that Jesus had again spoken from the heavens,
were they engaged in laying the foundation of the Temple, that
the Most High might have an habitation, and where the Saints might
assemble to pay their devotions to his holy name. He rejoiced at the
glorious prospect which presented itself of soon completing the edifice,
as there were no mobs to hinder their labours, consequently their circumstances were very different than before."

After the address the choir sung a hymn. Sidney Rigdon then invoked the blessings of Almighty God upon the assembly, and upon those who should labour upon the building. This done the Prophet went through the principal ceremony of the day, and said that the first corner stone of the Temple of Almighty God was laid. He prayed with much solemnity that the building might soon be completed, that the Saints might have an habitation to worship the God of their fathers.

"It was a gladsome sight," said the *Times and Seasons,* "and extremely affecting, to see the old revolutionary patriots, who had been driven from their homes in Missouri, strike hands and rejoice together, in a land where they knew they would be protected from mobs, and where they could again enjoy the liberty for which they had fought many a hard battle.

"The day was indeed propitious—heaven and earth combined to make the scene as glorious as possible."

Shortly before the foundation-stone of the temple was laid, Joseph attracted the attention of a personage, whom he appointed to a military command in Nauvoo, and who figures as Major-General Bennett in the Mormon report of that ceremonial which has just been quoted. This Bennett, being ambitious, unscrupulous, and unprincipled, seems to have had an idea that by means of Mormonism he might become of importance in America ; and, without mincing the matter by fine words, he wrote to the Prophet to propose himself as his "right-hand man." "You know," said he to Joseph, "that Mahomet had his right-hand man ;" and why, he suggested, should not the new Mahomet or Moses have his right-hand man also? This curious letter ran as follows:—

"*Arlington House, Oct.* 24*th,* 1843.

"DEAR GENERAL,—I am happy to know that you have taken possession of your new establishment, and presume you will be eminently successful and happy in it, together with your good lady and family. You are no doubt already aware that I have had a most interesting visit from your most excellent and worthy friend, President B. Young, with whom I have had a glorious frolic in the clear, blue ocean; for most assuredly a frolic it was, without a moment's reflection or consideration. Nothing of this kind would in the least attach me to your person or cause. I am capable of being a most *undeviating friend,* without being governed by the smallest religious influence.

"As you have proved yourself to be a *philosophical divine,* you will excuse me when I say that we must leave their influence to the mass. The boldness of your plans and measures, together with their unparalleled success so far, are calculated to throw a charm over your whole being, and to point you out as the most extraordinary man of the present age. But my mind is of so mathematical and philosophical a cast, that the divinity of Moses makes no impres-

II

sion on me ; and you will not be offended when I say that I rate you higher as a legislator than I do Moses, because we have you present with us for examination, whereas Moses derives his chief authority from prescription and the lapse of time. I cannot, however, say but you are both right, it being out of the power of man to prove you wrong. It is no mathematical problem, and can therefore get no mathematical solution. I say, therefore, go-a-head—you have my good wishes. You know Mahomet had his '*right-hand man*.'

"The celebrated Thomas Brown, of New York, is now engaged in cutting your head on a beautiful cornelian stone, as your private seal, which will be set in gold to your order, and sent to you. It will be a gem, and just what you want. His sister is a member of your church. The expense of the seal set in gold will be about forty dollars, and Mr. Brown assures me that if he were not so poor a man, he would present it to you free. You can, however, accept it or not, as he can apply it to another use. I am myself short for cash ; for although I had some time since 2,000 dollars paid me by the Harpers, publishers, as the first instalment on the purchase of my copyright, yet I had got so much behind during the hard times, that it all went to clear up old scores. I expect 38,000 dollars more, however, in semi-annual payments, from those gentlemen, within the limits of ten years, a large portion of which I intend to use in the State of Illinois, in the purchase and conduct of a large tract of land ; and, therefore, should I be compelled to announce in this quarter that I have no connection with the Nauvoo Legion, you will, of course remain silent, as I shall do it in such a way as will make all things right.

"I may yet run for a high office in your State, when you would be sure of my best services in your behalf; therefore, a known connection with you would be against our mutual interest. It can be shown that a commission in the legion was a Herald hoax, coined for the fun of it, by me, as it is not believed even now by the public. In short, I expect to be yet, through your influence, Governor of the State of Illinois.

"My respects to Brothers Young, Richards, Mrs. Emma, and all friends.
                       "Yours, most respectfully,
                              "JAS. ARLINGTON BENNETT."
"Lieut. General Smith."

"P.S. As the office of Inspector-General confers no command on me, being a mere honorary title, if, therefore, there is any gentlemen in Nauvoo who would like to fill it in a practical way, I shall with great pleasure and good will resign it to him, by receiving advice from you to that effect. It is an office that should be filled by some scientific officer.
                                      "J. A. B."

Joseph's reply to this singular and too candid epistle was quite as singular and infinitely more amusing. Joseph was too cunning a man to accept, in plain terms, the rude but serviceable offer ; and he rebuked the vanity and presumption of Mr. Bennett, while dexterously retaining him for future use. He was not at all angry, though he endeavoured to appear so.

" DEAR SIR,—Your letter of the 24th ult. has been regularly received; its contents duly appreciated, and its whole tenor candidly considered; and, according to my manner of judging all things in righteousness, I proceed to answer you; and shall leave you to meditate whether mathematical problems, founded upon the truth of revelation, or religion as promulgated by me, or Moses, can be solved by rules and principles existing in the systems of common knowledge.

" How far you are capable of being ' a most undeviating friend, without being governed by the smallest religious influence,' will best be decided by your survivors, as all past experience most assuredly proves.   Without controversy, that friendship, which intelligent beings would accept as sincere must arise from love, and that love grow out of virtue, which is as much a part of religion as light is a part of Jehovah.   Hence the saying of Jesus :— ' Greater love hath no man than this, that a man lay down his life for a friend.'

" You observed, ' as I have proven myself to be a *philosophical divine*, I must excuse you when you say that we must leave these *influences* to the mass.'   The meaning of ' philosophical divine' may be taken in various ways.   If, as the learned world apply the term, you infer that I have achieved a victory, and been strengthened by a scientific religion, as practised by the popular sects of the age, through the aid of colleges, seminaries, Bible societies, missionary boards, financial organizations, and gospel money schemes, then you are wrong; such a combination of men and means shows the form of godliness without the power; for is it not written, ' I will destroy the wisdom of the wise; beware lest any man spoil you through philosophy and vain deceit, after the rudiments of the world and not after the doctrines of Christ.' But if the inference is, that by more love, more light, more virtue, and more truth from the Lord, I have succeeded as a man of God, then you reason truly, though the weight of the sentiment is lost, when the ' *influence is left to the mass.*'   Do men gather grapes of thorns, or figs of thistles ?

" Of course, you follow out the figure, and say, ' the boldness of my plans and measures, together with their unparalleled success so far, are calculated to throw a charm over my whole being, and to point me out as the most extraordinary man of the present age.'   *The boldness of my plans and measures* can readily be tested by the touch-stone of all schemes, systems, projects, and adventures—*truth*, for truth is a matter of fact; and the fact is, that by the power of God I translated the Book of Mormon from hieroglyphics, the knowledge of which was lost to the world : in which wonderful event, I stood alone, an unlearned youth, to combat the worldly wisdom and multiplied ignorance of eighteen centuries with a new revelation, which (if they would receive the everlasting Gospel) would open the eyes of more than eight hundred millions of people, and make ' plain the old paths,' wherein if a man walk in all the ordinances of God blameless, he shall inherit eternal life; and Jesus Christ, who was, and is, and is to come, has borne me safely over every snare and plan, laid in secret or openly, through priestly hypocrisy, sectarian prejudice, popular philosophy, executive power, or law-defying mobocracy, to destroy me.

"If, then, the hand of God, in all these things that I have accomplished, towards the salvation of a priest-ridden generation, in the short space of twelve years, through the boldness of the plan of preaching the Gospel, and the boldness of the means of declaring repentance and baptism for the remission of sins, and a reception of the Holy Ghost, by laying on of the hands, agreeably to the authority of the priesthood, and the still more bold measures of receiving direct revelation from God, through the Comforter, as promised, and by which means all holy men, from ancient times till now, have spoken and revealed the will of God to men, with the consequent 'success' of the gathering of the Saints, throws any 'charm' around my being, and 'points me out as the most extraordinary man of the age,' it demonstrates the fact, that truth is mighty, and must prevail; and that one man empowered from Jehovah has more influence with the children of the kingdom than eight hundred millions led by the precepts of men. God exalts the humble, and debases the haughty. But let me assure you in the name of Jesus, who spake as never man spake, that the 'boldness of the plans and measures,' as you term them, but which should be denominated the righteousness of the cause, the truth of the system, and power of God, which, 'so far,' has borne me and the church (in which I glory in having the privilege of being a member) successfully through the storm of reproach, folly, ignorance, malice, persecution, falsehood, sacerdotal wrath, newspaper satire, pamphlet libels, and the combined influence of the powers of earth and hell, I say these powers of righteousness and truth are not the decrees or rules of an ambitious and aspiring Nimrod, Pharaoh, Nebuchadnezzar, Alexander, Mahomet, Buonaparte, or other great sounding heroes, that dazzled forth with a trail of pomp and circumstances for a little season, like a comet, and then disappeared, leaving a wide waste where such an existence once was, with only a name; nor were the glorious results of what you term 'boldness of plans and measures,' with the attendant 'success,' matured by the self-aggrandizing wisdom of the Priests of Baal, the Scribes and Pharisees of the Jews, Popes and Bishops of Christendom, or Pagans of Juggernaut; were they extended by the divisions and sub-divisions of a Luther, a Calvin, a Wesley, or even a Campbell, supported by a galaxy of clergymen and churchmen, of whatever name or nature, bound apart by cast-iron creeds, and fastened to set stakes by chain-cable opinions, without revelation; nor are they the lions of the land, nor the leviathans of the sea, moving among the elements, as distant chimeras to fatten the fancy of the infidel; but they are as the stone cut out of the mountain without hands, and will become a great mountain, and fill the whole earth. Were I an Egyptian, I would exclaim, *Jah-oh-eh, Enish-go-on-dosh, Flo-ees, Flos-is-is.* [O the earth! the power of attraction, and the moon passing between her and the sun.] A Hebrew, *Haueloheem yerau ;* a Greek, *O theos phos esi ;* a Roman, *Dominus regit me ;* a German, *Gott gebe uns das licht ;* a Portugee, *Senhor Jesu Christo e libordade ;* a Frenchman, *Dieu defend le droit ;* but as I am, I give God the glory, and say, in the beautiful figure of the poet—

>" ' Could we with ink the ocean fill,
> Was the whole earth of parchment made,
> And every single stick a quill,
> And every man a scribe by trade,
> To write the love of God above
> Would drain the ocean dry,
> Nor could the whole upon a scroll
> Be spread from sky to sky.'

" It seems that your mind is of such ' a mathematical and philosophical cast, that the divinity of Moses makes no impression upon you, and that I will not be offended when you say, that you rate me higher as a legislator than you do Moses, because you have me present with you for examination;' that 'Moses derives his chief authority from prescription and the lapse of time; you cannot, however, say but we are both right, it being out of the power of man to prove us wrong. It is no mathematical problem, and can therefore get no mathematical solution.'

" Now, Sir, to cut the matter short, and not dally with your learned ideas for fashion's sake you have here given your opinion, without reserve, that revelation, the knowledge of God, prophetic vision, the truth of eternity, cannot be solved as a mathematical problem. The first question, then, is, what is a mathematical problem? And the natural answer is, a statement, proposition, or question, that can be solved, ascertained, unfolded, or demonstrated, by knowledge facts of figures; for 'mathematical' is an adjective derived from *Mathesis* (Gr.), meaning in English, learning or knowledge. ' Problem ' is derived from *probleme* (French), or probleme (Latin, Italian, or Spanish), and in each language means a question or proposition, whether true or false. ' Solve ' is derived from the Latin verb *solvo*, to explain or answer. One thing more, in order to prove the work as we proceed; it is necessary to have witnesses, two or three of whose testimonies, according to the laws or rules of God and man are sufficient to establish any one point.

" Now for the question. How much are one and one? Two. How much is one from two? One. Very well, one question or problem is solved by figures. Now let me ask one for facts: Was there ever such a place on the earth as Egypt? Geography says Yes; ancient history says Yes; and the Bible says Yes. So three witnesses have solved that question. Again, Lived there ever such a man as Moses in Egypt? The same witnesses reply *Certainly*. And was he a prophet? The same witnesses, or a part, have left on record that Moses predicted in Leviticus that if Israel broke the covenant they had made, the Lord would scatter them among the nations, till the land enjoyed her Sabbaths; and subsequently these witnesses have testified of the captivity in Babylon, and other places, in fulfilment. But, to make assurance doubly sure, Moses prays that the ground might open, and swallow up Korah and his company for transgression, and it was so : and he endorses the prophecy of Balaam, which said, Out of Jacob shall come he that shall have dominion, and shall destroy him that remaineth of the city ; and Jesus Christ, as him that ' had dominion,' about fifteen hundred years after, in accordance with this and the prediction of Moses, David, Isaiah, and many others, came, saying : Moses wrote of me, declaring the dispersion of the Jews, and the utter destruction of the ' city ; ' and the apostles were his witnesses, unimpeached, especially Jude, who not only endorses the facts of Moses' ' divinity,' but also the events of Balaam, and Korah, with many others, *as true.* Besides these tangible facts, so easily proven and demonstrated by simple rules and testi- mony unimpeached, the art (now lost) of embalming human bodies, and pre- serving them in the catacombs of Egypt, whereby men, women, and children, as *mummies,* after a lapse of near three thousand five hundred years, come forth among the living, and although dead, the papyrus which has lived in their bosoms unharmed, speaks for them, in language like the sound of an earth- quake : *Ecce veritas ! Ecce cadaveros !* Behold the truth ! Behold the mum- mies ! Oh, my dear Sir, the sunken Tyre and Sidon, the melancholy dust where ' the city ' of Jerusalem once was, and the mourning of the Jews among the nations, together with such a ' cloud of witnesses,' if you had been as well acquainted with your God and Bible as with your purse and pence table, the ' divinity ' of Moses would have dispelled the fog of five thousand years, and filled you with light ; for facts, like diamonds, not only cut glass, but they are the most precious jewels on earth. The spirit of prophecy is the testimony of Jesus.

" The world at large is ever ready to credit the writings of Homer, Hesid, Plutarch, Socrates, Pythagoras, Virgil, Josephus, Mahomet, and a hundred others ; but where, tell me where, have they left a line, a simple method of solving the truth of the plan of eternal life ? Says the Saviour, ' If any man will do his (the Father's) will, he shall know the doctrine, whether it be of God, or whether I speak of myself.' Here then is a method of solving the ' divinity ' of men by the divinity within yourself, that as far exceeds the calculation of numbers, as the sun exceeds a candle. Would to God that all men understood it, and were willing to be governed by it, that when one had filled the measure of his days, he could exclaim like Jesus, ' *Veni mori, et revi- viscere !'*

" Your good wishes to ' go a-head,' coupled with Mahomet and a ' right- hand man,' are rather more vain than virtuous. Why, Sir, Cæsar had his right-hand Brutus, who was his ' left-hand' assassin ; not, however, applying the allusion to you.

" As to the private seal you mention, if sent to me, I shall receive it with the gratitude of a servant of God, and pray that the donor may receive a reward in the resurrection of the just.

" The summit of your future fame seems to be hid in the political policy of a ' mathematical problem' for the chief magistracy of this State, which, I sup- pose, might be solved by ' double position,' where the *errors* of the *supposition* are used to produce a true answer.

" But, Sir, when I leave the dignity and honour I received from hea- ven to hoist a man into power, through the aid of my friends, where the evil and designing, after the object has been accomplished, can lock up the clemency intended as a reciprocation for such favours, and where the wicked and unprincipled, as a matter of course, would seize the opportunity to flintify the hearts of the nation against me for dabbling at a sly game in politics; verily, I say, when I leave the dignity and honour of heaven to gratify the ambition and vanity of man or men, may my power cease, like the strength of Samson, when he was shorn of his locks, while asleep in the lap of Delilah! Truly said the Saviour, Cast not your pearls before swine, lest they trample them under their feet, and turn again and rend you.

"Shall I, who have witnessed the visions of eternity, and beheld the glories of the mansions of bliss, and the regions and the misery of the damned, shall I turn to be a Judas? Shall I, who have heard the voice of God, and communed with angels, and spake, as moved by the Holy Ghost, for the renewal of the everlasting covenant, and for the gathering of Israel in the last days, shall I worm myself into a political hypocrite? Shall I, who hold the keys of the last kingdom, in which is the dispensation of the fulness of all things spoken by the mouths of all the holy prophets, since the world began, under the sealing power of the Melchizidek priesthood—shall I stoop from the sublime authority of Almighty God to be handled as a monkey's catspaw, and pettify myself into a clown to act the farce of political demagoguery? No, verily no! The whole earth shall bear me witness that I, like the towering rock in the midst of the ocean, which has withstood the mighty surges of the warring waves for centuries, *am impregnable*, and am a faithful friend to virtue, and a fearless foe to vice; no odds, whether the former was sold as a pearl in Asia, or hid as a gem in America, and the latter dazzles in palaces, or glimmers among the tombs.

"I combat the errors of ages; I meet the violence of mobs; I cope with illegal proceedings from executive authority; I cut the Gordian knot of powers; and I solve mathematical problems of Universities: WITH TRUTH, *diamond truth, and God is my 'right-hand man.'*

"And to close, let me say in the name of Jesus Christ to you, and to Presidents, Emperors, Kings, Queens, Governors, Rulers, Nobles, and Men in Authority everywhere, do the works of righteousness, execute justice and judgment in the earth, that God may bless you, and her inhabitants; and

> "'The laurel that grows on the top of the mountain,
> Shall green for your fame while the sun sheds a ray;
> And the lily, that blows by the side of the fountain,
> Will bloom for your virtue till earth melts away.'

"With due consideration and respect,

"I have the honour to be your most obt. servant,

"JOSEPH SMITH."

"Gen. J. A. Bennett, Arlington House, N. Y."

"P.S. The Court Martial will attend to your case in the Nauvoo Legion.

"J. S."

A letter signed VERITAS, published in the *New York Herald* described not only the general appearance, but gave some particulars of

the physical as well as moral weight of the leading Mormons at this
time :—

"It may not be uninteresting to you to have a few lines from your
correspondent in Zion—the city of the Saints—the 'nucleus of a western empire.' In this communication I purpose giving you a description
of the first presidency of the Mormon hierarchy, which consists of
four dignitaries, to wit, a principal prophet, a patriarch, and two councillors.

"Joseph Smith, the president of the church, prophet, seer, and
revelator, is thirty-six years of age, six feet high in his pumps, weighing
two hundred and twelve pounds. He is a man of the highest talent
and great independence of character, firm in his integrity, and devoted to his religion ; in one word he is a *per se*, as President Tyler
would say ; as a public speaker, he is bold, powerful, and convincing,
possessing both the *suaviter in modo* and the *fortiter in re ;* as a leader,
wise and prudent, yet fearless ; as a military commander, brave and
determined ; as a citizen, worthy, affable, and kind ; bland in his manners, and of noble bearing. His amiable lady, too, the *Electa Cyria*,
is a woman of superior intellect and exemplary piety ; in every respect suited to her situation in society, as the wife of one of the most
accomplished and powerful chiefs of the age.

"Hyrum Smith, the patriarch of the church and brother of Joseph,
is forty-two years of age, five feet eleven and a half inches high,
weighing one hundred and ninety-three pounds. He, too, is a prophet, seer, and revelator, and is one of the most pious and devout
Christians in the world. He is a man of great wisdom and superior
excellence, possessing great energy of character, and originality of
thought.

"Sidney Rigdon, one of the councillors, prophet, seer, and revelator,
is forty-two years of age, five feet nine and a half inches high, weighing one hundred and sixty-five pounds ; his former weight, until reduced by sickness, produced by the Missouri persecution, was two
hundred and twelve pounds. He is a mighty man in Israel, of varied
learning, and extensive and laborious research. There is no divine in
the west more deeply learned in biblical literature, and the history of
the world, than he ; an eloquent orator, chaste in his language, and
conclusive in his reasoning ; any city would be proud of such a man.
By his proclamation, thousands on thousands have heard the glad
tidings and obeyed the word of God ; but he is now in the 'sear and
yellow leaf,' and his silvery locks fast ripening for the grave.

"William Law, the other councillor, is thirty-two years of age, five
feet eight and a half inches high, weighing one hundred and seventy
five pounds. He is a great logician and profound reasoner ; of correct

business habits, and great devotion to the service of God. No man could be better fitted to his station—wise, discreet, just, prudent—a man of great suavity of manners and amiability of character.

" All these men are Boanerges of the church, thundering in the western forests, and hurling arguments and reasons against the sectaries of the age, like the thunderbolts of Jupiter. Their wives and children present, likewise, a pleasing spectacle of intellect, goodness, hospitality, and kindness seldom witnessed."

It is necessary to append to this rather flattering statement, that with the exception of Hyrum Smith, every other " Boanerges" of the Church here mentioned was afterwards expelled or withdrew from it, and that the adventurer, General Bennett, did not long remain among the Saints. The "right-hand man" was made useful for a time ; but not being trusted to the extent he desired, he probably lost interest in the fortunes of Joseph Smith, and transferred his patronage elsewhere.

A letter from an officer of the United States' Artillery, who was travelling westward in September, 1842, described a grand review of the Mormon legion at Nauvoo, of which he was an eye-witness, and ventured on a prediction which subsequent events very singularly verified :—

" Yesterday," he says, " was a great day among the Mormons. Their legion, to the number of two thousand men, was paraded by Generals Smith, Bennett, and others, and certainly made a very noble and imposing appearance. The evolutions of the troops directed by Major-General Bennett, would do honour to any body of armed militia in any of the States, and approximates very closely to our regular forces. What does all this mean ? Why this exact discipline of the Mormon corps ? Do they intend to conquer Missouri, Illinois, Mexico ? It is true they are part of the militia of the State of Illinois, by the charter of their legion ; but then there are no troops in the States like them in point of enthusiasm and warlike aspect, yea, warlike character. Before many years this legion will be twenty, and perhaps fifty, thousand strong, and still augmenting. A fearful host, filled with religious enthusiasm and led on by ambitious and talented officers, what may not be effected by them ? Perhaps the subversion of the constitution of the United States ; and if this should be considered too great a task, foreign conquests will most certainly follow. Mexico will fall into their hands, even if Texas should first take it.

" These Mormons are accumulating like a snowball rolling down an inclined plane, which, in the end, becomes an avalanche. They are enrolling among their officers some of the first talent in the country, by titles or bribes, it don't matter which. They have appointed your namesake, Captain Bennett, late of the army of the United States, Inspector-General of their legion, and he is commissioned as such by Governor Carlin. This gentleman is known to be well skilled in fortification, gunnery, ordinance, castrametation, and military engineering generally, and I am assured that he is now under pay, derived from the tithings of this warlike people. I have seen his plans for fortifying Nauvoo, which are equal to any of Vauban's.

" Only a part of their officers, regents, and professors, however, are Mormons, but they are all united by a common interest, and will act together, on main points, to a man. Those who are not Mormons when they come here, very soon become so, either from interest or conviction.

" The Smiths are not without talent, and are said to be as brave as lions. Joseph, the chief, is a noble-looking fellow, a Mahomet every inch of him. The postmaster, Sidney Rigdon, is a lawyer, philosopher, and saint. Their other generals are also men of talent, and some of them men of learning. I have no doubt that they are all brave, as they are most unquestionably ambitious, and the tendency of their religious creed is to annihilate all other sects; you may, therefore, see that the time will come when this gathering host of religious fanatics will make this country shake to its centre. A western empire is certain. Ecclesiastical history presents no parallel to this people, inasmuch as they are establishing their religion on a learned footing. All the sciences are taught, and to be taught in their colleges, with Latin, Greek, Hebrew, French, Italian, Spanish, &c. The mathematical sciences, pure and mixed, are now in successful operation, under an extremely able professor of the name of Pratt, and a graduate of Trinity College, Dublin, is president of their University.

" Now, Sir, what do you think of Joseph, the modern Mahomet?

" I arrived here *incog.*, on the 1st instant, and from the great preparation for the military parade, was induced to stay to see the turnout, which I confess has astonished and filled me with fears for future consequences. The Mormons, it is true, are now peaceable, but the lion is asleep. Take care and don't rouse him.

" The city of Nauvoo contains about ten thousand souls, and is rapidly increasing. It is well laid out, and the municipal affairs appear to be well conducted. The adjoining country is a beautiful prairie. Who will say that the Mormon Prophet is not among the great spirits of the age?

" The Mormons number in Europe and America about one hundred and fifty thousand, and are constantly pouring into Nauvoo and the neighbouring country. There are probably in and about this city and adjacent territories, not far from thirty thousand of these warlike fanatics, this place having been settled by them only three years ago."

A public lecturer, of the name of Newhall, published, in the *Salem* (Massachusetts) *Advertiser*, an account of a visit made to Nauvoo, in 1843. He described the Temple as a very "magnificent structure, different from anything in ancient or modern history," and "General" Smith's legion as a very fine body of men. He was present at a grand review of the corps by Joseph himself, accompanied by "six ladies on horseback—who were dressed in black velvet, and wore waving plumes of white feathers, and rode up and down in front of the regiment."

GENERAL JOSEPH SMITH REVIEWING THE NAUVOO LEGION.

He described Joseph as "very sociable, easy, cheerful, obliging and kind, and very hospitable—in a word a jolly fellow—and one of the last persons whom he would have supposed God would have raised up as a prophet or a priest." Another account of Joseph was published about the same time by a Methodist preacher of the name of Prior.

"I will not attempt," said this writer, "to describe the various feelings of my bosom as I took my seat in a conspicuous place in the congregation, who were waiting in breathless silence for his appearance. While he tarried, I had plenty of time to revolve in my mind the character and common report of that truly singular personage. I fancied that I should behold a countenance sad and sorrowful, yet containing the fiery marks of rage and exasperation. I supposed that I should be enabled to discover in him some of those thoughtful and reserved features, those mystic and sarcastic glances, which I had fancied the ancient sages to possess. I expected to see that fearful, faltering look of conscious shame which, from what I had heard of him, he might be expected to evince. He appeared at last; but how was I disappointed when instead of the heads and horns of the beast and false prophet, I beheld only the appearance of a common man, of tolerably large proportions. I was sadly disappointed, and thought that, although his appearance could not be wrested to indicate anything against him, yet he would manifest all I had heard of him when he began to preach. I sat uneasily, and watched him closely. He commenced preaching, not from the Book of Mormon, however, but from the Bible; the first chapter of the first of Peter was his text. He commenced calmly, and continued dispassionately to pursue his subject, while I sat in breathless silence, waiting to hear that foul aspersion of the other sects, that diabolical disposition of revenge, and to hear that rancorous denunciation of every individual but a Mormon. I waited in vain; I listened with surprise; I sat uneasy in my seat, and could hardly persuade myself but that he had been apprised of my presence, and so ordered his discourse on my account, that I might not be able to find fault with it; for instead of a jumbled jargon of half-connected sentences, and a volley of imprecations, and diabolical and malignant denunciations, heaped upon the heads of all who differed from him, and the dreadful twisting and wresting of the Scriptures to suit his own peculiar views, and attempt to weave a web of dark and mystic sophistry around the Gospel truths, which I had anticipated, he glided along through a very interesting and elaborate discourse with all the care and happy facility of one who was well aware of his important station, and his duty to God and man."

The same writer thus describes Nauvoo:—

"At length the city burst upon my sight. Instead of seeing a few miserable log cabins and mud hovels, which I had expected to find, I was surprised to see one of the most romantic places that I had visited in the west. The buildings, though many of them were small, and of wood, yet bore the marks of neatness which I have not seen equalled in this country. The far-spread plain at the bottom of the hill was

JOSEPH SMITH PREACHING.

dotted over with the habitations of men, with such majestic profusion, that I was almost willing to believe myself mistaken, and instead of being in Nauvoo of Illinois, among Mormons, that I was in Italy at the city of Leghorn, which the location of Nauvoo resembles very much. I gazed for some time with fond admiration upon the plain below. Here and there arose a tall majestic brick house, speaking loudly of the genius and untiring labour of the inhabitants, who have snatched the place from the clutches of obscurity, and wrested it from

the bonds of disease; and in two or three short years, rescued it from
a dreary waste to transform it into one of the first cities in the west.
The hill upon which I stood was covered over with the dwellings of
men, and amid them was seen to rise the hewn stone and already
accomplished work of the Temple, which was now raised fifteen or
twenty feet above the ground. The few trees that were permitted to
stand are now in full foliage, and are scattered with a sort of fantastic
irregularity over the slope of the hill.

"But there was one object which was far more noble to behold,
and far more majestic than any other yet presented to my sight, and
that was the wide-spread and unrivalled father of waters, the Mississippi river, whose mirror-bedded waters lay in majestic extension before the city, and in one general curve, seemed to sweep gallantly by
the beautiful place. On the farther side was seen the dark green
woodland, bending under its deep foliage, with here and there an in-
terstice bearing the marks of cultivation. A few houses could be seen
through the trees on the other side of the river, directly opposite to
which is spread a fairy isle, covered with beautiful timber. The isle
and the romantic swell of the river soon brought my mind back to
days of yore, and to the bright emerald isles of the far-famed fairy
land. The bold and prominent rise of the hill, fitting to the plain
with exact regularity, and the plain pushing itself into the river,
forcing it to bend around its obstacle with becoming grandeur, and
fondly to cling around it to add to the heightened and refined lustre
of this sequestered land.

"I passed on into the more active parts of the city, looking into
every street and lane to observe all that was passing. I found all the
people engaged in some useful and healthy employment. The place
was alive with business—much more so than any place I have visited
since the hard times commenced. I sought in vain for anything that
bore the marks of immorality, but was both astonished and highly
pleased at my ill success. I could see no loungers about the streets
nor any drunkards about the taverns. I did not meet with those dis-
torted features of ruffians, or with the ill-bred and impudent. I heard
not an oath in the place, I saw not a gloomy countenance; all were
cheerful, polite, and industrious."

The following letter, purporting to be written by an "Englishman,"
was published about the same time by most of the American newspapers, and gave some further particulars of this extraordinary people,
and the beautiful city which they founded. It is doubtful, however,
whether the writer were quite such a stranger among the Mormons
as he was willing to make the world believe.

"Having, whilst in my native land, heard a great deal said re-

specting the people called Mormons, I thought it would be well, in
the course of my rambles (or tour) to visit their city, hold converse
with them, investigate their principles, and judge for myself. I
had heard, previous to my leaving England, some of their missionaries, among whom were Elders Woodruff, Richards, and Young.
I thought they were setters forth of strange doctrine, yet it had
an influence on my mind, so that I felt determined, as soon as
opportunity served, to hear both sides of the question, as well from
the Missourians as from any other source, with an unprejudiced mind.
I had, previous to this time, been a member of the Methodist church;
but having observed that there existed in the breasts of those people
a very strong prejudice with respect to the Mormons, I could not
give full credence to their statements, neither could I rest satisfied
with the statement of the Mormons; I thought it was possible that
they might dissemble in England, but, as a people, they could not do
so at home, their actions would appear ungarnished; they would there
act out their principles, and their moral and religious influence would
there be seen as clear as the sun at noon-day; but, above all, I wanted
to know something concerning the Missourian persecution; so, after having overcome all opposition (some of my friends being greatly alarmed
lest I should become a follower of Joe, as they termed it), I took ship and
arrived in safety at New Orleans. I then sailed up the Mississippi, and
landed at St. Louis. As soon as I had taken lodgings, I commenced my
inquiries respecting the Mormons. What think you of the Mormons? I
asked. I had scarcely spoken before my ears were saluted from all
quarters, from high and low, rich and poor. The Mormons! The
mean Mormons! The G——d d——d Mormons! The deluded Mormons, &c. I heard them calumniated and vilified—nay, abused beyond
belief. They informed me that their crimes were of the deepest dye,
that polygamy was not only tolerated, but practised amongst them;
that they would rob and plunder, and that blood and murder was to
be found in their skirts; that after they had stripped the poor stranger of his all, they confined him in a kind of dungeon, underneath
the Temple, where he was fed upon bread and water, until death put
a period to his sufferings—left to die alone without a kind friend by
him to perform the last sad offices, or to see him consigned to the
silent tomb; but like a dog he was left to die, and like a dog he was
buried. Well, one would have thought that after having heard all
this my courage must have failed, and that I would at once have
given up the search; but I called to mind the old adage—'Nothing
venture nothing have.' History also informed me of the wonderful
exploits performed in days of yore by the chivalrous and noble
knights of England, and so I felt determined to see and behold the

wonderful place, with the history of which I had become acquainted. I had, however, determined within myself to sell my liberty and life as dearly as I could, in case the reports I had heard should prove true; but the fact was, I did not place much confidence in their Jack-the-Giant-Killer's tales, looking upon them as being too marvellous to be true.

" I landed at Nauvoo on a beautiful morning in the summer season. I felt a degree of superstitious dread creep over me as I set my foot upon the shore. Presently I discovered some armed men advancing towards where I was, but immediately perceived that they were peaceable citizens of the place, engaged in a pleasure party. As I walked onward, I felt myself comparatively at home, as I now and again met with an Englishman that I once had gazed upon in my native land. I directed my course towards the Temple, and after having gazed upon and thoroughly examined every part of it, I was soon led to the conclusion that there was not much danger to be apprehended from being confined in its subterranean vaults or dungeons; I took up my abode as convenient to the edifice as I could, in order that I might be the better enabled to take cognizance of every circumstance which might come under my observation; I had resolved to keep upon a strict look-out, and to keep my head and understanding from being confused, in order that I might be enabled to judge correctly, and have a true and correct report to send to my native land, should I be permitted to reach its shores in safety.

" The city is of great dimensions, laid out in beautiful order; the streets are wide, and cross each other at right angles, which will add greatly to its order and magnificence when finished. The city rises on a gentle incline from the rolling Mississippi, and as you stand near the temple, you may gaze on the picturesque scenery around; at your side is the temple, the wonder of the world; round about, and beneath, you may behold handsome stores, large mansions, and fine cottages, interspersed with varied scenery; at the foot of the town rolls the noble Mississippi, bearing upon its bosom the numerous steam-ships which are conveying the Mormons from all parts of the world to their home. I have seen them landed, and I have beheld them welcomed to their homes with the tear of joy and the gladdening smile, to share the embrace of all around. I have heard them exclaim, How happy to live here! how happy to die here! and then how happy to rise here in the resurrection! It is their happiness; then why disturb the Mormons so long as they are happy and peaceable, and are willing to live so with all men? I would say, ' Let them live.'

" The inhabitants seem to be a wonderfully enterprising people. The walls of the temple have been raised considerably this summer; it is calculated, when finished, to be the glory of Illinois. They are endeavouring to establish manufactories in the city. They have enclosed large farms on the prairie ground, on which they have raised corn, wheat, hemp, &c.; and all this they have accomplished within the short space of four years. I do not believe that there is another people in existence who could have made such improvements in the same length of time, under the same circumstances. And here allow me to remark, that there are some here who have lately emigrated to this place, who have built themselves large and convenient houses in the town; others on their farms on the prairie, who, if they had remained at home, might have continued to live in rented houses all their days, and never once have entertained the idea of building one for themselves at their own expense.

" Joseph Smith, the Mormon prophet, is a singular character; he lives at the ' Nauvoo Mansion House,' which is, I understand, intended to become a home for the stranger and traveller; and I think, from my own personal observation, that it will be deserving of the name. The Prophet is a kind, cheerful, sociable companion. I believe that he has the good-will of the community at large, and that he is ever ready to stand by and defend them in any extremity; and as I saw the Prophet and his brother Hyrum conversing together one day, I thought I beheld two of the greatest men of the nineteenth century. I have witnessed the Mormons in their assemblies on a Sunday, and I know not where a similar scene could be effected or produced. With respect to the teachings of the Prophet, I must say that there are some things hard to be understood; but he invariably supports himself from our good old Bible. Peace and harmony reigns in the city. The drunkard is scarcely ever seen, as in other cities, neither does the awful imprecation or profane oath strike upon your ear; but, while all is storm, and tempest, and confusion abroad respecting the Mormons, all is peace and harmony at home."

HYRUM SMITH.　　JOSEPH SMITH.

CHAPTER VI.

FOR a time after the establishment of the Mormons at Nauvoo, the "Prophet" and his followers were warned by sad experience, and were less haughty, less overbearing, and less presumptuous, in their intercourse with the "Gentiles." But the prosperity which attended them in Illinois, and the rapid growth of Nauvoo, soon filled them again with insolence and spiritual pride. The dissensions, which had subsided in adversity, were renewed in prosperity. The power and influence of Joseph were too great not to excite envy, and Sidney Rigdon did great mischief by introducing a novelty called the "spiritual wife" doctrine. This caused great scandal, both among the Mormons and among their enemies. Joseph himself appears, unless he has been grievously maligned, and unless the affidavits published by his opponents were forgeries, to have had as great a *penchant* for a plurality of wives as Mahomet himself. Sidney Rigdon, according to the same authority, outdid him in this respect, and had "revelations" of his own, which he made subservient to the gratification of his passions. There was possibly some exaggeration in these stories, but they do not appear to have been wholly unfounded, as far as Rigdon, and some others, were concerned.

Joseph was now at the climax of his earthly glory, and might have been comparatively happy even amid the persecutions of his neighbours the "Gentiles," had it not been for secessions from his church, and the annoyances springing out of the "spiritual wife" doctrine of his indiscreet friend Rigdon. The population of Nauvoo was almost wholly composed of Mormons. The corporation over which he presided as mayor, assumed a jurisdiction independent of, and sometimes hostile to, that of the State of Illinois. They denied validity to the legal documents of the State, unless countersigned by Joseph, as mayor of Nauvoo, and they passed a law to punish any stranger in the city who should use disrespectful language in speaking of the Prophet. As time wore on, hostility against the sect increased. They waged a constant warfare with the nine counties that adjoin Handcock county, in which Nauvoo is situated, and their old feud with Missouri was kept up by legal proceedings, which, in a somewhat vexatious manner, were instituted against Smith. Lieutenant-Governor Boggs, of Missouri, was fired at through a window and narrowly escaped assassination. He swore that, to the best of his belief, Joseph Smith was a party to this attempt to murder him. The legal proceedings consequent upon this charge, tended to excite and maintain the bitterest animosity between the "Saints" and the "Gentiles." But the "spiritual wife" doctrine of Sidney Rigdon was the cause of the greatest scandal, and ultimately produced an unlooked-for catastrophe.

Nevertheless, the wealth and power of the sect continued to increase, their numbers being augmented from time to time by the English immigration from Liverpool. The *Times and Seasons* of the 15th of May in that year, announced to the Saints "that Nauvoo was becoming a large city, that a number of splendid houses were erected,

I 2

and that three ships' companies had arrived in the spring from England, and the Prophet was in good health and spirits." In 1844, they carried their heads so high that they put Joseph forward as a candidate for the Presidentship of the United States, and his still faithful Sidney Rigdon as a candidate for the Vice-Presidentship.

The *Times and Seasons* declared for Joseph Smith as President in the following address :—

"The question arises, whom shall the Mormons support?—General Joseph Smith. A man of sterling worth and integrity, and of enlarged views; a man who has raised himself from the humblest walks in life to stand at the head of a large, intelligent, respectable, and increasing society, that has spread, not only in this land, but in distant nations; a man whose talents and genius are of an exalted nature, and whose experience has rendered him every way adequate to the onerous duty. Honourable, fearless, and energetic, he would administer justice with an impartial hand, and magnify and dignify the office of chief magistrate of this land; and we feel assured that there is not a man in the United States more competent for the task.

"One great reason that we have for pursuing our present course is, that at every election we have been made a political target for the filthy demagogues in the country to shoot their loathsome arrows at. And every story has been put into requisition to blast our fame, from the old fabrication of 'walk on the water,' down to 'the murder of ex-Governor Boggs.' The journals have teemed with this filthy trash, and even men who ought to have more respect for themselves, men contending for the gubernatorial chair, have made use of terms so degrading, so mean, so humiliating, that a Billingsgate fisherwoman would have considered herself disgraced with. We refuse any longer to be thus bedaubed for either party; we tell all such, to let their filth flow in its own legitimate channel, for we are sick of the loathsome smell.

"Gentlemen, we are not going either to 'murder ex-Governor Boggs,' nor a Mormon in this State 'for not giving us his money;' nor are we going to 'walk on the water,' nor 'drown a woman;' nor 'defraud the poor of their property;' nor send 'destroying angels after General Bennett to kill him;' nor 'marry spiritual wives;' nor commit any other outrageous act this election, to help any party with : you must get some other persons to perform these kind offices for you for the future. We withdraw.

"Under existing circumstances we have no other alternative, and if we can accomplish our object, well; if not, we shall have the satisfaction of knowing that we have acted conscientiously, and have used our best judgment; and if we have to throw away our votes, we had better do so upon a worthy rather than upon an unworthy individual, who might make use of the weapon we put in his hand to destroy us with.

"Whatever may be the opinions of men in general in regard to Mr. Smith, we know that he need only to be known to be admired; and that is the principles of honour, integrity, patriotism, and philanthropy, that has elevated him in the minds of his friends, and the same principles, if seen and known, would beget the esteem and confidence of all the patriotic and virtuous throughout the Union.

" Whatever, therefore, be the opinions of other men, our cause is marked out, and our motto from henceforth will be GENERAL JOSEPH SMITH."

Joseph allowed his name to be put forward without any hope of his success, but was evidently proud of occupying so prominent a position; especially as, to use his own expression, it " riled " his enemies in general, and his old Missourian persecutors in particular. He thought it incumbent upon him, under the circumstances, to imitate the example of other great political characters, and he accordingly issued an address to the American people, in which he declared his views on various weighty matters. This singular document ran as follows:—

" GENERAL SMITH'S VIEWS OF THE GOVERNMENT AND POLICY OF THE UNITED STATES.

" Born in a land of liberty, and breathing an air uncorrupted with the sirocco of barbarous climes, I ever feel a double anxiety for the happiness of all men, both in time and in eternity. My cogitations, like Daniel's, have for a long time troubled me, when I viewed the condition of men throughout the world, and more especially in this boasted realm, where the Declaration of Independence ' holds these truths to be self-evident, that all men are created equal : that they are endowed by their Creator with certain inalienable rights; that among these are life, liberty, and the pursuit of happiness ;' but, at the same time, some two or three millions of people are held as slaves for life, because the spirit in them is covered with a darker skin than ours : and hundreds of our own kindred, for an infraction, or supposed infraction, of some over-wise statute, have to be incarcerated in dungeon glooms, or suffer the more moral penitentiary gravitation of mercy in a nut-shell ; while the duellist, the debauchee, and the defaulter for millions, and other criminals, take the uppermost rooms at feasts, or, like the bird of passage, find a more congenial clime by flight.

" The wisdom which ought to characterize the freest, wisest, and most noble nation of the nineteenth century, should, like the sun in his meridian splendour, warm every object beneath its rays; and the main efforts of her officers, who are nothing more or less than the servants of the people, ought to be directed to ameliorate the condition of all, black or white, bond or free ; for the best of books says, ' God hath made of one blood all nations of men, for to dwell on all the face of the earth.'

" Our common country presents to all men the same advantages, the same facilities, the same rewards ; and without hypocrisy, the Constitution, when it says, ' We, the people of the United States, in order to form a more perfect union, establish justice, ensure tranquillity, provide for the common defence, promote the general welfare, and secure the blessings of liberty to ourselves and our posterity, do ordain and establish this Constitution for the United States of America,' meant just what it said, without reference to colour or condition: *ad infinitum.* The aspirations and expectations of a virtuous people, environed with so wise, so liberal, so deep, so broad, and so high a character of *equal rights,* as appears in said Constitution, ought to be treated by those to whom the administration of the laws are entrusted with as much sanctity as the prayers of the saints are treated in heaven, that love, confidence, and union, like the sun, moon, and stars, should bear witness,

" '(For ever singing as theyshine,)
The hand that made us is divine!'

Unity is power, and when I reflect on the importance of it to the stability of all governments, I am astounded at the silly moves of persons and parties, to foment discord, in order to ride into power on the current of popular excitement; nor am I less surprised at the stretches of power, or restrictions of right, which too often appear as acts of legislators, to pave the way to some favourite political schemes, as destitute of intrinsic merit as a wolf's heart is of the milk of human kindness. A Frenchman would say, '*Prosque tout aimer richesses et pouvoir* ' (Almost all men like wealth and power).

" I must dwell on this subject longer than others, for nearly one hundred years ago, that golden patriot, Benjamin Franklin, drew up a plan of union for the then colonies of Great Britain, that *now* are such an independent nation, which, among many wise provisions for obedient children under their father's more rugged hand, proceeds thus:—' They have power to make laws, and lay and levy such general duties, imposts, or taxes, as to them shall appear most equal and just (considering the ability and other circumstances of the inhabitants in the several colonies), and such as may be collected with the least inconvenience to the people; rather discouraging luxury, than loading industry with unnecessary burdens.' Great Britain surely lacked the laudable humanity and fostering clemency to grant such a just plan of union—but the sentiment, remains, like the land that honoured its birth, as a pattern for wise men *to study the convenience of the people more than the comfort of the cabinet.*

" And one of the most noble fathers of our freedom and country's glory; great in war, great in peace, great in the estimation of the world, and great in the hearts of his countrymen,—the illustrious Washington,—said, in his first inaugural address to Congress:—' I hold the surest pledges that as, on one side, no local prejudices or attachments, no separate views or party animosities, will misdirect the comprehensive and equal eye which ought to watch over this great assemblage of communities and interest; so, on another, that the foundations of our national policy will be laid in the pure and immutable principles of private morality, and the pre-eminence of free government be exemplified by all the attributes which can win the affections of its citizens, and command the respect of the world.' Verily, here shines the virtue and the wisdom of a statesman in such lucid rays, that had every succeeding Congress followed the rich instruction, in all their deliberations and enactments, for the benefits and convenience of the whole community and the communities of which it is composed; no sound of a rebellion in South Carolina; no rupture in Rhode Island; no mob in Missouri, expelling her citizens by executive authority; corruption in the ballot-boxes; a border warfare between Ohio and Michigan; hard times and distress; outbreak upon outbreak in the principal cities ; murder, robbery, and defalcations, scarcity of money, and a thousand other difficulties, would have torn asunder the bonds of the Union; destroyed the confidence of man ; and left the great body of the people to mourn over misfortunes and poverty, brought on by corrupt legislation in an hour of corrupt vanity, for self-aggrandizement. The great Washington, soon after the foregoing faithful admonition for the common welfare of his nation, further advises Congress that, ' Among the many interesting objects which will engage your attention, that of providing for the common defence will merit particular regard.   To be prepared for war is one of the most effectual means of preserving peace.'   As the Italian would say, ' *Buono aviso*' (Good advice).

" The elder Adams, in his inaugural address, gives national pride such a grand turn of justification, that every honest citizen must look back upon the infancy of the United States with an approving smile, and rejoice that patriotism in the rulers, virtue in the people, and prosperity in the Union, once crowned the expectations of hope, unveiled the sophistry of the hypocrite, and silenced the folly of foes.   Mr. Adams said : ' If national pride is ever justifiable or excusable, it is when it springs not from *power* or *riches*, grandeur or glory, but from conviction of national innocence, information, and benevolence.'   There is no doubt such was actually the case with our young realm at the close of the last century : peace, prosperity, and union filled the country with religious toleration, temporal enjoyment, and virtuous enterprise ; and gradually, too, when the deadly winter of the ' Stamp Act,' the ' Tea Act, ' and other *close communion* acts of royalty had choked the growth of freedom of speech, liberty of the press, and liberty of conscience, did light, liberty, and loyalty flourish like the cedars of God.

" The respected and venerable Thomas Jefferson, in his inaugural address, made more than forty years ago, shows what a beautiful prospect an innocent, virtuous nation presents to the sage's eye, where there is a space for enterprise, hands for industry, heads for heroes, and hearts for moral greatness. He said : ' A rising nation, spread over a wide and fruitful land, traversing all the seas with the rich productions of their industry, engaged in commerce with nations who feel power and forget right, advancing rapidly to destinies beyond the reach of mortal eye : when I contemplate these transcendant objects, and see the honour, the happiness, and the hopes of this beloved country committed to the issue and the auspices of this day, I shrink from the contemplation, and humble myself before the magnitude of the undertaking.'   Such a prospect was truly soul-stirring to a good man; but ' since the fathers have fallen asleep,' wicked and designing men have unrobed the government of its glory, and the people, if not in dust and ashes, or in sackcloth, have to lament in poverty her departed greatness, while demagogues build fires in the north and south, east and west, to keep up their spirits *till it is better times ;* but year after year have left the people to *hope*, till the very name of *Congress* or *State Legislature* is as horrible to the sensitive friend of his country, as the house of ' Blue Beard ' is to children, or ' Crockett's ' Hell of London to meek men. When the people are secure and their rights properly respected, then the four main pillars of prosperity, viz.:—agriculture, manufactures, navigation, and commerce, need the fostering care of government; and in so goodly a country as ours, where the soil, the climate, the rivers, the lakes, and the sea coast; the productions, the timber, the minerals; and the inhabitants are so diversified, that a pleasing variety accommodates all tastes, trades, and calculations, it certainly is the highest point of subversion to protect the whole northern and southern, eastern and western, centre and circumference, of the realm, by a judicious tariff. It is an old saying and a true one, ' If you wish to be respected, respect yourselves.'

" I will adopt in part the language of Mr. Madison's inaugural address: ' To cherish peace and friendly intercourse with all nations, having correspondent dispositions ; to maintain sincere neutrality towards belligerent nations ; to prefer in all cases amicable discussion and reasonable accommodation of intrigues and foreign partialities, so degrading to all countries, and so baneful to free ones ; to foster a spirit of independence too just to invade the rights of others, too proud to surrender their own, too liberal to indulge unworthy prejudices ourselves, and too elevated not to look down upon them in others ; to hold the Union of the States as the basis of their peace and happiness; to support the Constitution, which is the cement of the Union, as in its limitations as in its authorities ; to respect the rights and authorities reserved to the States and to the people, as equally incorporated with, and essential to, the success of the general system ; to avoid the slightest interference with the rights of conscience, or the functions of religion, so wisely exempted from civil jurisdiction ; to preserve in their full energy the other salutary provisions in behalf of private and personal rights, and the freedom of the press : as far as intention aids in the fulfilment of duty, are consummations too big with benefits not to captivate the energies of all honest men to achieve them, when they can be brought to pass by reciprocation, friendly alliances, wise legislation, and honourable treaties.

" The government has once flourished under the guidance of trusty servants ; and the Hon. Mr. Monroe, in his day, while speaking of the Constitution, says :—' Our commerce has been wisely regulated with foreign nations, and between the States ; new States have been admitted into our Union ; our territory has been enlarged by fair and honourable treaty, and with great advantages to the original States ; the States respectively protected by the national government, under a mild paternal system, against foreign dangers, and enjoying within their separate spheres, by a wise partition of power, a just proportion of the sovereignty, have improved their police, extended their settlements, and attained a strength and maturity which are the best proofs of wholesome law well administered. And if we look to the condition of individuals, what a proud spectacle does it exhibit ? Who has been deprived of any right of person and property ? Who restrained from offering his vows in the mode he prefers to the Divine Author of his being ? It is well known that all these blessings have been enjoyed to their fullest extent; and I add, with peculiar satisfaction, that there has been no example of a capital punishment being inflicted on any one for the crime of high treason.' What a delightful picture of power, policy, and prosperity! Truly the wise proverb is just: '*Sedaukauh teromain goy, veh-kasade le-u-meem khahment*' (Righteousness exalteth a nation, but sin is a reproach to any people).

"But this is not all. The same honourable statesman, after having had about forty years' experience in the government, under the full tide of success-ful experiment, gives the following commendatory assurance of the efficiency of the *Magna Charta* to answer its great end and aim: *To protect the people in their rights.* 'Such, then, is the happy government under which we live; a government adequate to every purpose for which the social compact is framed; a government elective in all its branches, under which every citizen may, by his merit, obtain the highest trust recognised by the Constitution; which contains within it no cause of discord; none to put at variance one portion of the community with another: a government which protects every citizen in the full enjoyment of his rights, and is able to protect the nation against injustice from foreign powers.'

"Again, the younger Adams, in the silver age of our country's advance-ment to fame, in his inaugural address (1825), thus candidly declares the majesty of the youthful republic in its increasing greatness: 'The year of jubilee since the first formation of our Union has just elapsed—that of the Declaration of Independence is at hand. The consummation of both was effected by this Constitution. Since that period, a population of four millions has multiplied to twelve. A territory, bounded by the Mississippi, has been extended from sea to sea. New States have been admitted to the Union, in numbers nearly equal to those of the first confederation. Treaties of peace, amity, and commerce, have been concluded with the principal dominions of the earth. The people of other nations, the inhabitants of regions acquired, not by conquest, but by compact, have been united with us in the participation of our rights and duties, of our burdens and blessings. The forest has fallen by the axe of our woodsmen; the soil has been made to teem by the tillage of our farmers; our commerce has whitened every ocean. The dominion of man over physical nature has been extended by the invention of our artists; liberty and law have walked hand in hand. All the purposes of human association have been accomplished as effectively as under any other govern-ment on the globe, and at a cost little exceeding, in a whole generation, the expenditures of other nations in a single year.'

"In continuation of such noble sentiments, General Jackson, upon his ascension to the great chair of the chief magistracy, said, 'As long as our government is administered for the good of the people, and is regulated by their will; as long as it secures to us the rights of person and property, liberty of conscience, and of the press, it will be worth defending; and so long as it is worth defending, a patriotic militia will cover it with an impene-trable ægis.'

"General Jackson's administration may be denominated the *acme* of American glory, liberty, and prosperity, for the national debt, which in 1815, on account of the late war, was 125,000,000 dollars and lessened gradually,

was paid up in his golden day ; and preparations were made to distribute the
surplus revenue among the several States ; and that august patriot, to use his
own words in his farewell address, retired, leaving 'a great people prosperous
and happy, in the full enjoyment of liberty and peace, honoured and respected
by every nation of the world.'

"At the age, then, of sixty years, our blooming republic began to decline
under the withering touch of Martin Van Buren ! Disappointed ambition ;
thirst for power, pride, corruption, party spirit, faction, patronage, perquisites,
fame, tangling alliances, priestcraft, and spiritual wickedness in *high places*,
struck hands, and revelled in midnight splendour. Trouble, vexation, perplexity, and contention, mingled with hope, fear, and murmuring, rumbled
through the Union, and agitated the whole nation, as would an earthquake at
the centre of the earth, the world heaving the sea beyond its bounds, and
shaking the everlasting hills. So, in hopes of better times, while jealousy,
hypocritical pretensions, and pompous ambition, were luxuriating on the ill-
gotten spoils of the people, they rose in their majesty like a tornado, and
swept through the land, till General Harrison appeared as a star among the
storm for better weather.

"The calm came ; and the language of that venerable patriot, in his inaugural address, while descanting upon the merits of the constitution and its
framers, thus expressed himself :—' There were in it features which appeared
not to be in harmony with their ideas of a simple representative democracy or
republic ; and knowing the tendency of power to increase itself, particularly
when executed by a single individual, predictions were made that, at no very
remote period, the government would terminate in virtual monarchy. It
would not become me to say that the fears of these patriots have been already
realized. But, as I sincerely believe that the tendency of measures and of
men's opinions, for some years past, has been in that direction, it is, I conceive, strictly proper that I should take this occasion to repeat the assurances
I have hitherto given of my determination to arrest the progress of that
tendency, if it really exists, and restore the government to its pristine health
and vigour.' This good man died before he had the opportunity of applying
one balm to ease the pain of our groaning country ; and I am willing the
nation should be the judge whether General Harrison, in his exalted station,
upon the eve of his entrance into the world of spirits, *told the truth or not :*
with acting President Tyler's three years of perplexity and pseudo Whig
Democrat reign, to heal the breaches, or show the wounds, *secundum artum*
(according to art). Subsequent events, all things considered, Van Buren's
downfall, Harrison's exit, and Tyler's self-sufficient turn to the whole, go to
show, as a Chaldean might exclaim, ' *Beram etai elauh besmayauh gaulah rau-
zeen* ' (Certainly there is a God in heaven to reveal secrets).

"No honest man can doubt for a moment but the glory of American
liberty is on the wane, and that calamity and confusion will sooner or later
destroy the peace of the people. Speculators will urge a national bank as a
saviour of credit and comfort. A hireling pseudo priesthood will plausibly
push Abolition doctrines and doings, and 'human rights,' into Congress, and

into every other place where conquest smells of fame, or opposition swells to popularity. Democracy, Whiggery, and Cliquery, will attract their elements, and foment divisions among the people, to accomplish fancied schemes, and accumulate power, while poverty driven to despair, like hunger forcing its way through a wall, will break through the statutes of men, to save life, and mend the breach in prison glooms.

"A still higher grade, of what the 'nobility of the nations' call 'great men,' will dally with all rights, in order to smuggle a fortune at 'one fell swoop;' mortgage Texas, possess Oregon, and claim all the unsettled regions of the world for hunting and trapping; and should a humble, honest man, red, black, or white, exhibit a better title, these gentry have only to clothe the judge with richer ermine, and spangle the lawyer's fingers with finer rings, to have the judgment of his peers, and the honour of his lords as a pattern of honesty, virtue, and humanity, while the motto hangs on his nation's escutcheon, '*Every man has his price!*'

"Now, O people! turn unto the Lord and live; and reform this nation. Frustrate the designs of wicked men. Reduce Congress at least one half. Two senators from a State, and two members to a million of population, will do more business than the army that now occupy the halls of the National Legislature. Pay them two dollars and their board per diem (except Sundays); that is more than the farmer gets, and he lives honestly. Curtail the offices of government in pay, number, and power, for the Philistine lords have shorn our nation of its goodly locks in the lap of Delilah.

"Petition your State Legislature to pardon every convict in their several penitentiaries, blessing them as they go, and saying to them in the name of the Lord, *Go thy way and sin no more*. Advise your legislators, when they make laws for larceny, burglary, or any felony, to make the penalty applicable to work upon the roads, public works, or any place where the culprit can be taught more wisdom and more virtue, and become more enlightened. Rigour and seclusion will never do as much to reform the propensities of man, as reason and friendship. Murder only can claim confinement or death. Let the penitentiaries be turned into seminaries of learning, where intelligence, like the angels of heaven, would banish such fragments of barbarism. Imprisonment for debt is a meaner practice than the savage tolerates with all his ferocity; '*Amor vincit omnia*' (Love conquers all).

"Petition also, ye goodly inhabitants of the Slave States, your legislators to abolish slavery by the year 1850, or now, and save the Abolitionist from reproach and ruin, infamy and shame. Pray Congress to pay every man a reasonable price for his slaves, out of the surplus revenue arising from the sale of public lands, and from the deduction of pay from the members of Congress. Break off the shackles from the poor black man, and hire them to work like other human beings; for 'an hour of virtuous liberty on earth, is worth a whole eternity of bondage!' Abolish the practice in the army and navy of trying men by court-martial for desertion; if a soldier or marine runs away, send him his wages, with this instruction, that *his country will never trust him again; he has forfeited his honour*. Make HONOUR the standard with all men be sure that good is rendered for evil in all cases, and the whole nation, like a kingdom of kings and priests, will rise up with righteousness, and be respected as wise and worthy on earth, and as just and holy for heaven, by Jehovah, the author of perfection. More economy in the National and State Governments would make less taxes among the people; more equality through the cities, towns, and country, would make less distinction among the people; and more honesty and familiarity in societies, would make less hypocrisy and flattery in all branches of community; and open, frank, candid, decorum to all men, in this boasted land of liberty, would beget esteem, confidence, union, and love; and the neighbour from any State, or from any country, of whatever colour, clime, or tongue, could rejoice when he put his foot on the sacred soil of freedom, and exclaim, The very name of '*American*' is fraught with *friendship.* Oh, then, create confidence! restore freedom! break down slavery! banish imprisonment for debt, and be in love, fellowship, and peace, with all the world! Remember that honesty is not subject to law : the law was made for transgressors : wherefore, a Dutchman might exclaim, '*Ein shrlicher name ist besser als Reichthum*' (A good name is better than riches).

"For the accommodation of the people in every state and territory, let Congress show their wisdom by granting a national bank, with branches in each State and territory, where the capital stock shall be held by the nation for the mother bank; and by the States and territories for the branches : and whose officers and directors shall be elected yearly by the people, with wages at the rate of two dollars per day for services : which several banks shall never issue any more bills than the amount of capital stock in her vaults, and the interest. The nett gain of the mother bank shall be applied to the national revenue, and that of the branches to the States' and territories' revenues. And the bills shall be par throughout the nation, which will mercifully cure that fatal disorder known in cities as *brokerage*, and leave the people's money in their own pockets.

" Give every man his constitutional freedom, and the President full power to send an army to suppress mobs, and the States authority to repeal and impugn that relic of folly, which makes it necessary for the Governor of a State to make the demand of the President for troops, in cases of invasion or rebellion. The Governor himself may be a mobber, and, instead of being punished, as he should be, for murder and treason, he may destroy the very lives, rights, and property, he should protect. Like the good Samaritan, send every lawyer, as soon as he repents and obeys the ordinances of heaven, to preach the Gospel to the destitute, without purse or scrip, pouring in the oil and the wine: a learned priesthood is certainly more honourable than a '*hireling clergy.*'

" As to the contiguous territories to the United States, wisdom would direct no tangling alliance. Oregon belongs to this government honourably; and when we have the red man's consent, let the Union spread from the east to the west sea; and if Texas petitions Congress to be adopted among the sons of liberty, give her the right hand of fellowship; and refuse, no! the same friendly grip to Canada and Mexico; and when the right arm of freemen is stretched out in the character of a navy, for the protection of rights, commerce, and honour, let the iron eyes of power watch from Maine to Mexico, and from California to Columbia. Thus may union be strengthened, and foreign speculation prevented from opposing broadside to broadside.

" Seventy years have done much for this goodly land; they have burst the chains of oppression and monarchy, and multiplied its inhabitants from two to twenty millions; with a proportionate share of knowledge, keen enough to circumnavigate the globe, drain the lightning from the clouds, and cope with all the crowned heads of the world.

"Then why! oh, why! will a once flourishing people not arise, phœnix-like, over the cinders of Martin Van Buren's power; and over the sinking fragments and smoking ruins of other catamount politicians; and over the windfalls of Benton, Calhoun, Clay, Wright, and a caravan of equally unfortunate law doctors, and cheerfully help to spread a plaster, and bind up the *burnt, bleeding wounds* of a sore but blessed country? The southern people are hospitable and noble: they will help to rid so *free* a country of every vestige of slavery, whenever they are assured of an equivalent for their property. The country will be full of money and confidence, when a national bank of twenty millions, and a State bank in every State, with a million or more, gives a tone to monetary matters, and make a circulating medium as valuable in the purses of a whole community, as in the coffers of a speculating bank or broker.

" The people may have faults, but they never should be trifled with. I think Mr. Pitt's quotation, in the British Parliament, of Mr. Prior's couplet for the husband and wife, to apply to the course which the king and ministry of England should pursue to the then colonies, of the *now* United States, might be a genuine rule of action for some of the *breath made* men in high place to use towards the posterity of that noble daring people:

" ' Be to her faults a little blind;
Be to her virtues very kind.'

" We have had Democratic presidents, Whig presidents, a pseudo Democratic Whig president; and now it is time to have *a president of the United States;* and let the people of the whole Union, like the inflexible Romans, whenever they find a *promise* made by a candidate that is not *practised* as an officer, hurl the miserable sycophant from his exaltation, as God did Nebuchadnezzar, to crop the grass of the field, with a beast's heart among the cattle.

" Mr. Van Buren said in his inaugural address, that he went 'into the presidential chair the inflexible and uncompromising opponent of every attempt, on the part of Congress, to abolish slavery in the District of Columbia, against the wishes of the slave-holding States; and also with a determination equally decided to resist the slightest interference with it in the States where it exists.' Poor little Matty made his rhapsodical sweep with the fact before his eyes, that the State of New York, his native State, had abolished slavery without a struggle or a groan. Great God, how independent! From henceforth slavery is tolerated where it exists: constitution or no constitution; people or no people; right or wrong; *vox Matti, vox Diaboli* (the voice of Matty, the voice of the Devil), and, peradventure, his great ' sub-

Treasury' scheme was a piece of the same mind; but the man and his measures have such a striking resemblance to the anecdote of the Welchman and his cart-tongue, that, when the Constitution was so long that it allowed slavery at the capital of a free people, it could not be cut off; but when it was so short that it needed a *sub-Treasury* to save the funds of the nation, it *could be spliced!* Oh, granny, what a long tail our puss has got! As a Greek might say, '*Hysteron proteron*' (The cart before the horse). But his mighty whisk through the great national fire, for the presidential chesnuts, *burnt the locks of his glory with the blaze of his folly!*

"In the United States, the people are the government, and their united voice is the only sovereign that should rule; the only power that should be obeyed; and the only gentlemen that should be honoured, at home or abroad, on the land and on the sea. Wherefore, were I the President of the United States, by the voices of a virtuous people, I would honour the old paths of the venerated fathers of freedom; I would walk in the tracks of the illustrious patriots, who carried the ark of the government upon their shoulders with an eye single to the glory of the people; and when that people petitioned to abolish slavery in the Slave States, I would use all honourable means to have their prayers granted, and give liberty to the captive, by giving the southern gentleman a reasonable equivalent for his property, that the whole nation might be free indeed! When the people petitioned for a national bank, I would use my best endeavours to have their prayers assured, and establish one on national principles to save taxes, and make them the comptrollers of its ways and means; and when the people petitioned to possess the territory of Oregon, or any other contiguous territory, I would lend the influence of a chief magistrate to grant so reasonable a request, that they might extend the mighty efforts and enterprise of a free people from the east to the west sea, and make the wilderness blossom as the rose; and when the neighbouring realm petitioned to join the Union of the sons of liberty, my voice would be, *Come:* yea, come Texas; come Mexico; come Canada; and come all the world—let us be brethren; let us be one great family, and let there be universal peace. Abolish the cruel customs of prisons (except certain cases), penitentiaries, and court-martials for desertion, and let reason and friendship reign over the ruins of ignorance and barbarity; yea, I would, as the universal friend of man, open the prisons; open the eyes; open the ears; and open the hearts of all people, to behold and enjoy freedom, unadulterated freedom; and God, who once cleansed the violence of the earth with a flood, whose Son laid down his life for the salvation of all his Father gave him out of the world, and who has promised that he will come and purify the world again with fire in the last days, shall be supplicated by me for the good of all people.

"With the highest esteem,

"I am a friend of virtue,

"And of the people,

"Joseph Smith."

"*Nauvoo, Illinois, February 7th,* 1844."

Joseph was of course aware that his candidature was an act which had no other meaning than to please his disciples; and he therefore wrote to Mr. Clay, who was supposed to have a good chance of being elected to the Presidency, to know what course he would pursue towards the Mormons if he were successful.

The correspondence was characteristic of both parties. The letter of the "Prophet" was to the following effect:—

"Nauvoo, Illinois, Nov. 4th, 1843.

"HON. H. CLAY,—DEAR SIR,—As we understand you are a candidate for the Presidency at the next election, and as the Latter-Day Saints (sometimes called Mormons, who now constitute a numerous class in the school politic of this vast republic) have been robbed of an immense amount of property, and endured nameless sufferings by the State of Missouri, and from her borders have been driven by force of arms, contrary to our national covenants, and as in vain we have sought redress by all constitutional, legal, and honourable means, in her courts, her executive councils, and her legislative halls, and as we have petitioned Congress to take cognizance of our sufferings without effect, we have judged it wisdom to address you this communication, and solicit an immediate, specific, and candid reply to *What will be your rule of action relative to us as a people,* should fortune favour your ascension to the chief magistracy?

"Most respectfully, Sir, your friend, and the friend of peace, good order, and constitutional rights.

"JOSEPH SMITH,
"In behalf of the Church of Jesus Christ of Latter-Day Saints.

"Hon. H. Clay, Ashland, Kentucky."

The reply of Mr. Clay was guarded, and studiously courteous:—

"Ashland, Nov. 15th, 1843.

"DEAR SIR,—I have received your letter in behalf of the Church of Jesus Christ of Latter-Day Saints, stating that you understand that I am a candidate for the Presidency, and inquiring what would be my rule of action relative to you as a people, should I be elected.

"I am profoundly grateful for the numerous and strong expressions of the people in my behalf, as a candidate for President of the United States; but I do not so consider myself. That much depends upon future events, and upon my sense of duty.

"Should I be a candidate, I can enter into no engagements, make no promises, give no pledges, to any particular portion of the people of the United States. If I ever enter into that high office, I must go into it free and unfettered, with no guarantees but such as are to be drawn from my whole life, character, and conduct.

"It is not inconsistent with this declaration to say, that I have viewed with a lively interest the progress of the Latter-Day Saints; that I have

sympathized in their sufferings under injustice, as it appeared to me, which
has been inflicted upon them ; and that I think, in common with all other religious communities, they ought to enjoy the security and the protection of
the constitution and the laws.

" I am, with great respect,

" Your Friend and obedient Servant,

" H. CLAY."

" Joseph Smith, Esq."

Joseph was by no means satisfied with Mr. Clay's reply; and
after taking nearly six months to reflect, he wrote a long and angry
rejoinder, in which he insinuated that Mr. Clay was a blackleg
in politics, and used many other phrases by no means complimentary.
The letter is exceedingly amusing, and as it gives the opinions of
Joseph on the affairs of Christendom and of the world in general, and
affords a fair specimen of the shrewd but coarse talent of this singular
man, we reproduce it *in extenso :—*

" *Nauvoo, Illinois, May* 13*th,* 1844.

" SIR,—Your answer to my inquiry, ' What would be your rule of action
towards the Latter-Day Saints, should you be elected President of the United
States ?' has been under consideration since last November, in the fond expectation that you would give (for every honest citizen has a right to demand
it) to the country a manifesto of your views of the best method and means
which would secure to the people, *the whole people,* the most freedom, the most
happiness, the most union, the most wealth, the most fame, the most glory at
home, and the most honour abroad, at the least expense ; but I have waited
in vain. So far as you have made public declarations, they have been made,
like your answer to the above, soft to flatter, rather than solid to feed the
people. You seem to abandon all former policy which may have actuated
you in the discharge of a statesman's duty, when the vigour of intellect and
the force of virtue should have sought out an everlasting habitation for
liberty ; when, as a wise man, a true patriot, and a friend to mankind, you
should have resolved to ameliorate the awful condition of our *bleeding* country
by a mighty plan of wisdom, righteousness, justice, goodness, and mercy, that
would have brought back the golden days of our nation's youth, vigour, and
vivacity; when prosperity crowned the efforts of a youthful Republic, when the
gentle aspirations of the sons of liberty were, ' We are one.'

" In your answer to my questions, last fall, that peculiar tact of modern
politicians, declaring, ' *If you ever enter into that high office, you must go into
it free and unfettered, with no guarantee but such as are to be drawn from your
whole life, character, and conduct,*' so much resembles a lottery vendor's sign,
with the goddess of Good-luck sitting on the car of fortune, astraddle of the horn
of plenty, and driving the merry steeds of beatitude, without reins or bridle,
that I cannot help exclaiming, O frail man ! what have you done that will
exalt you ? Can anything be drawn from your *life, character,* or *conduct,* that is
worthy of being held up to the gaze of this nation as a model of *virtue, charity,*

and wisdom ? Are you not a lottery picture, with more than two blanks to a prize ? Leaving many things prior to your Ghent treaty, let the world look at that, and see where is the wisdom, honour, and patriotism, which ought to have characterized the plenipotentiary of the only free nation upon the face of the earth ? A quarter of a century's negotiation to obtain our rights on the north-eastern boundary, and the motley manner in which Oregon tries to shine as American territory, coupled with your presidential race and come-by-chance secretaryship, in 1825, all go to convince the friends of freedom, the golden patriots of Jeffersonian democracy, free trade and sailor's rights, and the protectors of person and property, that an honourable war is better than a dishonourable peace.

" But had you really wanted to have exhibited the wisdom, clemency, benevolence, and dignity of a great man, in this boasted republic, when fifteen thousand free citizens were exiled from their own homes, lands, and property, in the wonderful patriotic State of Missouri, and you then upon your oath and honour, occupying the exalted station of a senator of Congress, from the noble-hearted State of Kentucky, why did you not show the world your loyalty to law and order, by using all honourable means to restore the innocent to their rights and property ? Why, Sir, the more we search into your character and conduct, the more we must exclaim from holy writ, *The tree is known by its fruit.*

" Again, this is not all; rather than show yourself an honest man, by guaranteeing to the people what you will do in case you should be elected president, ' you can enter into no engagement, make no promises, and give no pledges,' as to what you will do. Well, it may be that some hot-headed partisan would take such nothingarianism upon trust, but sensible men, and even *ladies*, would think themselves insulted by such an evasion of coming events ! If a tempest is expected, why not prepare to meet it ; and in the language of the poet exclaim—

> " ' Then let the trial come, and witness thou
> If terror be upon me, if I shrink
> Or falter in my strength to meet the storm,
> When hardest it beset me.'

" True greatness never wavers ; but when the Missouri compromise was entered into by you, for the benefit of *slavery*, there was a mighty shrinkage of *western honour ;* and from that day, Sir, the sterling Yankee, the struggling Abolitionist, and the staunch Democrat, with a large number of the liberal-minded Whigs, have marked you as a *blackleg* in politics, begging for a chance to *shuffle* yourself into the presidential chair, where you might deal out the destinies of our beloved country for a *game* of *brag*, that would end in ' *Hark, from the tombs a doleful sound*.' Start not at this picture, for your ' whole life, character, and conduct,' have been spotted with deeds that cause a blush upon the face of a virtuous patriot. So you must be contented in your lot, while crime, cowardice, cupidity, or low cunning, have handed you down from the high tower of a statesman to the black hole of a gambler. A man that accepts a challenge, or fights a duel, is nothing more nor less than a mur-

J

derer, for holy writ declares that ' *whoso sheds man's blood, by man shall his blood be shed ;*' and when, in the renowned city of Washington, the notorious *Henry Clay* dropped from the summit of a senator to the sink of a scoundrel, to shoot at that chalk line of a Randolph, he not only disgraced his own fame, family, and friends, but he polluted the sanctum sanctorum of American glory ; and the kingly blackguards throughout the whole world are pointing the finger of scorn at the boasted ' asylum of the oppressed,' and hissing at American statesmen, as *gentlemen vagabonds and murderers*, holding the olive branch of peace in one hand and a pistol for death in the other ! Well might the Saviour rebuke the heads of this nation with *Wo unto you Scribes, Pharisees, Hypocrites*, for the United States Government and Congress, with a few honourable exceptions,˙ have gone the way of Cain, and must perish in their gainsayings, like Korah and his wicked host. And honest men of every clime, and the innocent, poor, and oppressed, as well as Heathens, Pagans, and Indians, everywhere, who could but hope that the tree of liberty would yield some precious fruit for the hungry human race, and shed some balmy leaves for the healing of nations, have long since given up all hopes of equal rights, of justice, and judgment, and of truth and virtue, when such polluted, vain, heaven-daring, bogus patriots, are forced or flung into the front rank of government, to guide the destinies of millions. Crape the heavens with weeds of woe, gird the earth with sackcloth, and let hell mutter one melody in commemoration of fallen splendour ! For the glory of America has departed, and God will set a flaming sword to guard the tree of liberty, while such minttithing Herods as Van Buren, Boggs, Benton, Calhoun, and Clay, are thrust out of the realms of virtue, as fit subjects for the kingdom of fallen greatness ; *vox reprobi, vox Diaboli !* In your late addresses to the people of South Carolina, where rebellion budded, but could not blossom, you ' renounced ultraism,' ' high tariff,' and almost banished your ' banking system,' for the more certain standard of ' public opinion.' This is all very well, and marks the intention of a politician, the calculations of a demagogue, and the allowance for leeings of a shrewd manager, just as truly as the weather-cock does the wind when it turns upon the spire. Hustings for the south, barbacues for the west, confidential letters for the north, and ' American system' for the east :

> " ' Lull-a-by baby upon the tree top,
> And when the wind blows the cradle will rock.'

"Suppose you should also, taking your ' whole life, character, and conduct,' into consideration, and, as many hands make light work, stir up the old ' Clay party,' the ' National Republican party,' ' High Protective Tariff party,' and the late ''Coon Skin party,' with all their parapheralia, *ultraism, ne plus ultraism, sine qua non*, which have grown with your growth, strengthened with your strength, and shrunk with your shrinkage, and ask the people of this enlightened Republic, what they think of your powers and policy as a statesman ; for verily it would seem, from all past remains of parties, politics, projects, and pictures, that you are the *Clay*, and the people the *potter;* and as some vessels are marred in the hands of the potter, the natural conclusion is, that *you are a vessel of dishonour.*

" You may complain that a close examination of your ' whole life, character, and conduct,' places you, as a Kentuckian would pleasantly term it, ' in a bad fix;' but, Sir, when the nation has sunk deeper and deeper in the mud at every turn of the great wheels of the Union, while you have acted as one of the principal drivers, it becomes the bounden duty of the whole community, as one man, to whisper you on every point of government, to uncover every act of your life, and inquire what mighty acts you have done to benefit the nation; how much you have tithed the mint to gratify your lust; and why the fragments of your raiment hang upon the thorns by the path, as signals *to beware.*

" But your *shrinkage* is truly wonderful! Not only your banking system, and high tariff project, have vanished from your mind, 'like the baseless fabric of a vision,' but the 'annexation of Texas ' has touched your pathetic sensibilities of national pride so acutely, that the poor Texians, your own *brethren,* may fall back into the ferocity of Mexico, or be sold at auction to British stock-jobbers, and all is well, for ' I,' the old senator from Kentucky, am fearful it would militate against my interest in the north, to enlarge the borders of the union in the south. Truly, ' a poor wise child is better than an old foolish king, who will be no longer admonished.' Who ever heard of a nation that had too much territory? Was it ever bad policy to make friends? Has any people ever become too good to do good? No, never; but the ambition and vanity of some men have flown away with their wisdom and judgment, and left a creaking *skeleton* to occupy the place of a noble *soul.*

" Why, Sir, the condition of the whole earth is lamentable. Texas dreads the teeth and toe nails of Mexico. Oregon has the rheumatism, brought on by a horrid exposure to the heat and cold of British and American trappers; Canada has caught a bad cold from extreme fatigue in the patriot war; South America has the headache, caused by bumps against the beams of Catholicity and Spanish sovereignty; Spain has the gripes from age and inquisition; France trembles and wastes under the effects of contagious diseases; England groans with the gout, and wiggles with wine; Italy and the German states are pale with the consumption; Prussia, Poland, and the little contiguous dynasties, duchies, and domains, have the mumps so severely, that ' the whole head is sick, and the whole heart is faint;' Russia has the cramp by lineage; Turkey has the numb palsy; Africa, from the curse of God, has lost the use of her limbs; China is ruined by the queen's evil, and the rest of Asia fearfully exposed to the small pox, the natural way from British pedlars; the islands of the sea are almost dead with the scurvy; the Indians are blind and lame; and the United States, which ought to be the good physician with ' balm from Gilead,' and an ' *asylum for the oppressed,*' has boosted, and is boosting up into the council chamber of the government, a clique of political gamblers, to play for the old clothes and old shoes of a sick world, and ' *no pledge, no promise, to any particular portion of the people*' that the rightful heirs will ever receive a cent of their Father's legacy ! Away with such self-important, self-aggrandizing, and self-willed demagogues ! Their friendship is colder than polar ice ; and their professions meaner than the damnation of hell.

"Oh, man! when such a great dilemma of the globe, such tremendous convulsions of kingdoms, shakes the earth from centre to circumference; when castles, prison-houses, and cells, raise a cry to God against the cruelty of man; when the mourning of the fatherless and 'the widow causes anguish in heaven; when the poor among all nations cry day and night for bread and a shelter from the heat and storm; and when the degraded black slave holds up his manacled hands to the great statesman of the United States, and sings:—

<blockquote>
"'O Liberty, where are thy charms
That sages have told me were sweet!'
</blockquote>

and when fifteen thousand free citizens of the high-blooded Republic of North America, are robbed and driven from one State to another without redress or redemption, it is not only time for a candidate for the presidency to *pledge* himself to execute judgment and justice in righteousness, law or no law, but it is his bounden duty, as a man, for the honour of a disgraced country, and for the salvation of a once virtuous people, to call for a union of all honest men, and appease the wrath of God, by acts of wisdom, holiness, and virtue! The fervent prayer of a righteous man availeth much.

"Perhaps you may think I go too far with my strictures and inuendos, because in your concluding paragraph you say:—'It is not inconsistent with your declarations to say, that you have viewed with a lively interest the progress of the Latter-Day Saints, that you have sympathized in their sufferings, under injustice, as it appeared to you, which has been inflicted upon them; and that you *think*, in common with all other religious communities, they ought to enjoy the security and protection of the constitution and the laws.' If words were not wind, and imagination not a vapour, such 'views' 'with a lively interest' might coax out a few Mormon votes; such 'sympathy' for their suffering under injustice might heal some of the sick, yet lingering amongst them; raise some of the dead, and recover some of their property, from Missouri; and finally, if thought was not a phantom, we might, in common with other religious communities, '*you think*,' *enjoy the security* and *protection of the constitution and laws*. But during ten years, while the Latter-Day Saints have bled, been robbed, driven from their own lands, paid oceans of money into the Treasury to pay your renowned self and others for legislating and *dealing* out equal rights and privileges to those *in common with all other religious communities*, they have waited and expected in vain! If you have possessed any patriotism, it has been veiled by your *popularity* for fear the Saints would fall in love with its charms. Blind charity and dumb justice never do much towards alleviating the wants of the needy, but straws show which way the wind blows. It is currently rumoured that your dernier resort for the Latter-Day Saints is to emigrate to Oregon or California. Such cruel humanity, such noble injustice, such honourable cowardice, such foolish wisdom, and such vicious virtue, could only emanate from Clay. After the Saints have been plundered of three or four millions of land and property, by the people and powers of the *sovereign* State of Missouri—after they have sought for redress and redemption from the county court to

Congress, and been denied through religious prejudice and sacerdotal dignity—after they have builded a city and two temples at an immense expense of labour and treasure—after they have increased from hundreds to hundreds of thousands—and after they have sent missionaries to the various nations of the earth, to gather Israel, according to the predictions of all the holy prophets since the world began—that great plenipotentiary, the renowned Secretary of State, the ignoble duellist, the gambling senator, and Whig candidate for the presidency, *Henry Clay*, the wise Kentucky lawyer, advises the Latter-Day Saints to go to Oregon, to obtain justice, and set up a government of their own. O ye crowned heads among all nations, is not Mr. Clay a wise man, and very patriotic! Why, great God! to transport 200,000 people through a vast prairie, over the Rocky Mountains, to Oregon, a distance of nearly 2,000 miles, would cost more than *four millions*, or should they go by Cape Horn, in ships to California, the cost would be more than *twenty millions!* and all this to save the United States from inheriting the disgrace of Missouri, for murdering and robbing the Saints with impunity! Benton and Van Buren, who make no secret to say, if they get into power they will carry out Boggs' exterminating plan, to rid the country of the Latter-Day Saints, are

‘ Little nipperkins of milk,’

compared to ‘Clay's great aqua fortis jars.’ Why, he is a real giant in humanity. Send the Mormons to Oregon, and free Missouri from debt and disgrace! Ah! Sir, let this doctrine go to and fro throughout the whole earth, that we, as Van Buren said, know your cause is just, but the United States government can do nothing for you, because it has no power; *you must go to Oregon, and get justice from the Indians!*

"I mourn for the depravity of the world; I despise the hypocrisy of Christendom; I hate the imbecility of American statesmen; I detest the shrinkage of candidates for office, from pledges and responsibility; I long for a day of righteousness, when He, ‘ whose right it is to reign, shall judge the poor, and reprove with equity for the meek of the earth,' and I pray God, who hath given our fathers a promise of a perfect government in the last days, to purify the hearts of the people, and hasten the welcome day.

"With the highest consideration for virtue and unadulterated freedom, I have the honour to be your obedient servant,

"JOSEPH SMITH."

"Hon. C. Clay, Ashland, Kentucky."

Joseph, in order to know the opinions of both candidates, sent to Mr. Calhoun a letter precisely similar to that which he had addressed to Mr. Clay. He received the following reply:—

"*Fort Hill, December 2nd*, 1843.

"SIR,—You ask me what would be my rule of action relative to the Mormons, or Latter-Day Saints, should I be elected President; to which I answer, that if I should be elected, I would strive to administer the government according to the constitution and the laws of the Union; and that, as they mak᛭ no distinction between citizens of different religious creeds, I should make none. As far as it depends on the executive department, all should have the full benefit of both, and none should be exempt from their operation.

"But, as you refer to the case of Missouri, candour compels me to repeat what I said to you at Washington, that, according to my views, the case does not come within the jurisdiction of the federal government, which is one of limited and specific powers.

"With respect, I am, &c.

"J. C. CALHOUN."

"Mr. Joseph Smith."

Joseph's rejoinder to this letter was in the following terms:—

"*Nauvoo, Illinois, January 2nd,* 1844.

"SIR,—Your reply to my letter of last November, concerning your rule of action towards the Latter-Day Saints, if elected President, is at hand; and that you and your friends of the same opinion relative to the matter in question may not be disappointed as to me, or my mind, upon so grave a subject, permit me, as a law-abiding man, as a well-wisher to the perpetuity of constitutional rights and liberty, and as a friend to the free worship of Almighty God by all, according to the dictates of every person's conscience, to say *I am surprised,* that a man, or men, in the highest stations of public life, should have made up such a fragile ' view' of a case, than which there is not one on the face of the globe fraught with so much consequence to the happiness of men in this world, or the world to come.   To be sure, the first paragraph of your letter appears very complacent and fair on a white sheet of paper, and who that is ambitious for greatness and power would not have said the same thing ?   Your oath would bind you to support the constitution and laws, and as all creeds and religions are alike tolerated, they must, of course, all be justified or condemned, according to merit or demerit; but why, tell me why, are all the principal men held up for public stations so *cautiously careful* not to publish to the world, that *they will judge a righteous judgment*—law or no law; for laws and opinions, like the vanes of steeples, change with the wind.   One Congress passes a law, and another repeals it ; and one statesman says that the Constitution means this, and another that: and who does not know that all may be wrong ?   The opinion and pledge, therefore, in the first paragraph of your reply to my question, like the forced steam from the engine of a steam-boat, makes the show of a bright cloud at first, but when it comes in contact with a purer atmosphere, dissolves to common air again.

"Your second paragraph leaves you naked before yourself, like a likeness in a mirror, when you say that, ' according to your *view*, the federal government is one of limited and specific powers,' and has no jurisdiction in the case of the Mormons.   So, then, a State can at any time expel any portion of her citizens with impunity, and, in the language of Mr. Van Buren, frosted over with your gracious ' *views of the case*,' ' though the cause is ever so just, government can do nothing for them, because it has no power.'

" Go on, then, Missouri, after another set of inhabitants (as the Latter-Day Saints did) have entered some two or three hundred thousand dollars' worth of land, and made extensive improvements thereon ; go on, then, I say, banish the occupants or owners, or kill them, as the mobbers did many of the Latter-Day Saints, and take their lands and property as a spoil ; and let the legislature, as in the case of the Mormons, appropriate a couple of hundred thousand dollars to pay the mob for doing the job ; for the renowned senator from South Carolina, Mr J. C. Calhoun, says the powers of the federal government are so *specific and limited that it has no jurisdiction of the case !* Oh, ye people who groan under the oppression of tyrants ; ye exiled Poles, who have felt the iron hand of Russian grasp ; ye poor and unfortunate among all nations, come to the 'asylum of the oppressed,' buy ye lands of the general government, pay in your money to the treasury to strengthen the army and the navy, worship God according to the dictates of your own consciences, pay in your taxes to support the great heads of a *glorious* nation ; but remember a ' *sovereign State !*' is so much more powerful than the United States, the parent government, that it can exile you at pleasure, mob you with impunity, confiscate your lands and property, have the legislature sanction it ; yea, even murder you, as an edict of an emperor, *and it does no wrong,* for the noble senator of South Carolina says the power of the federal government is *so limited and specific that it has no jurisdiction of the case !* What think ye of *imperium in imperio ?*

" Ye spirits of the blessed of all ages, hark ! Ye shades of departed statesmen, listen ! Abraham, Moses, Homer, Socrates, Solon, Solomon, and all that ever thought of right and wrong, look down from your exaltations, if you have any, for it is said in the midst of counsellors there *is safety ;* and when you have learned that fifteen thousand innocent citizens, after having purchased their lands of the United States, and paid for them, were expelled from a ' sovereign State' by order of the Governor at the point of the bayonet, their arms taken from them by the same authority, and their right of migration into said State denied under pain of imprisonment, whipping, robbing, mobbing, and even death, and no justice or recompense allowed ; and from the legislature, with the Governor at their head, down to the justice of the peace, with a bottle of whiskey in one hand and a bowie knife in the other, hear them all declare there is no justice for a Mormon in that State, and judge ye a righteous judgment, and tell me when the virtue of the States was stolen, where the honour of the general government lies hid, and what clothes a senator with wisdom ? Oh, nullifying Carolina ! Oh, little tempestuous Rhode Island ! wouldit not be well for the great men of the nation to read the fable of the *Partial Judge,* and when part of the free citizens of a State had been expelled contrary to the constitution, mobbed, robbed, plundered, and many murdered, instead of searching into the course taken with Joanna Southcott, Ann Lee, the French prophets, the Quakers of New England, and rebellious niggers in the slave States, to hear both sides, and then judge, rather than have the mortification to say, ' Oh, it is *my* bull that has killed *your* ox ; that alters the case ! I must inquire into it, *and if, and if ?*'

" If the general government has no power to reinstate expelled citizens
to their rights, there is a monstrous hypocrite fed and fostered from the hard
earnings of the people! A real ' bull beggar' upheld by sycophants; and
although you may wink to the priests to stigmatise, wheedle the drunkards
to swear, and raise the hue and cry of *Impostor, false prophet, God damn old
Joe Smith*, yet remember, if the Latter-Day Saints are not restored to all their
rights, and paid for all their losses, according to the known rules of justice
and judgment, reciprocation and common honesty among men, that God will
come out of his hiding-place and vex this nation with a sore vexation; yea,
the consuming wrath of an offended God shall smoke through the nation,
with as much distress and woe, as independence has blazed through with
pleasure and delight. Where is the strength of government? Where is the
patriotism of a Washington, a Warren, and Adams? and where is a spark from
the watch-fire of '76, by which one candle might be lit, that would glimmer
upon the confines of democracy? Well may it be said that one man is not
a State, nor one State the nation. In the days of General Jackson, when
France refused the first instalment for spoliations, there was power, force, and
honour enough to resent injustice and insult, and the money came; and shall
Missouri, filled with negro-drivers and white men-stealers, go ' unwhipped of
justice' for tenfold greater sins than France? No! verily no! While I
have powers of body and mind; while water runs and grass grows; while
virtue is lovely and vice hateful; and while a stone points out a sacred spot
where a fragment of American liberty once was, I or my posterity will plead
the cause of injured innocence, until Missouri makes atonement for all her
sins; or sinks disgraced, degraded, and damned to hell, ' where the worm
dieth not, and the fire is not quenched.'

" Why, Sir, the power not delegated to the United States, and the States
belong to the people, and Congress sent to do the people's business have all
the power; and shall fifteen thousand citizens groan in exile? Oh, vain men,
will ye not, if ye do not restore them to their rights and $2,000,000 worth of
property, relinquish to them (the Latter-Day Saints), as a body, their portion
of power that belongs to them according to the Constitution? Power has its
convenience as well as inconvenience. ' The world was not made for Cæsar
alone, but Titus too.'

" I will give you a parable: A certain lord had a vineyard in a goodly land,
which men laboured in at their pleasure; a few meek men also went and purchased with money from some of these chief men that laboured at pleasure,
a portion of land in the vineyard, at a very remote part of it, and began to
improve it, and to eat and drink the fruit thereof; when some vile persons,
who regarded not man, neither feared the lord of the vineyard, rose up suddenly and robbed these meek men, and drove them from their possessions,
killing many. This barbarous act made no small stir among the men in the
vineyard, and all that portion who were attached to that part of the vineyard
where the men were robbed, rose up in grand council with their chief man,
who had firstly ordered the deed to be done, and made a covenant not to pay
for the cruel deed, but to keep the spoil, and never let those meek men set

their feet on that soil again, neither recompense them for it.   Now these meek men, in their distress, wisely sought redress of those wicked men in every possible manner, and got none.   They then supplicated the chief men who held the vineyard at pleasure, and who had the power to sell and defend it, for redress and redemption, and those men, loving the fame and favour of the multitude more than the glory of the lord of the vineyard, answered, Your cause is just; but we can do nothing for you, because we have no power.   Now, when the lord of the vineyard saw that virtue and innocence was not regarded, and his vineyard occupied by wicked men, he sent men and took the possession of it to himself, and destroyed those unfaithful servants, and appointed them their portion among hypocrites.

"And let me say, that all men who say that Congress has no power to restore and defend the rights of her citizens, have not the love of the truth abiding in them.   Congress has power to protect the nation against foreign invasion and internal broil ; and whenever that body passes an act to maintain right with any power, or to restore right to any portion of her citizens, IT IS THE SUPREME LAW OF THE LAND, and should a State refuse submission, that State is guilty of *insurrection or rebellion*, and the President has as much power to repel it as Washington had to march against the ' whiskey boys of Pittsburg,' or General Jackson had to send an armed force to suppress the rebellion of South Carolina

"To close, I would admonish you, before you let your ' *candour compel*' you again to write upon a subject great as the salvation of man, consequential as the life of the Saviour, broad as the principles of eternal truth, and valuable as the jewels of eternity, to read in the 8th section and 1st article of the Constitution of the United States, the *first*, *fourteenth*, and *seventeenth* ' specific' and not very ' limited powers' of the federal government, what can be done to protect the lives, property, and rights of a virtuous people, when the administrators of the law, and law-makers, are unbought by bribes, uncorrupted by patronage, untempted by gold, unawed by fear, and uncontaminated by tangling alliances, even like Cæsar's wife, not *only unspotted*, *but unsuspected*, and God, who cooled the heat of a Nebuchadnezzar's furnace, or shut the mouths of lions for the honour of a Daniel, will raise your mind above the narrow notion, that the general government has no power, to the sublime idea that Congress, with the President as executor, is as almighty in its sphere, as Jehovah is in his.

"With great respect,

"I have the honour to be your obedient servant,

"JOSEPH SMITH."

"Hon. (' Mr. !') J. C. Calhoun, Fort Hill, S. C."

Joseph was evidently out of temper when he penned this epistle ; and the " Mr. !" within brackets was intended to remind Mr. Calhoun of his want of courtesy, in addressing a general, a mayor, a candidate for the Presidency, " a seer, a revelator, and a prophet," as simply " *Mr*. Joseph Smith."   But there was much truth, nevertheless, in the arguments he employed, and too much foundation for his angry denunciations of the State of Missouri.

But his correspondence with these and other persons formed only a small portion of the multifarious business that occupied the Prophet's attention at this period of his life. His history during the first five months of the year 1844—powerful as he was, and absolute lord, spiritual and temporal, of the little community of Nauvoo, a state within a state, and governed by its own peculiar laws—had its dark as well as its bright side. There was a drop of gall and bitterness in the cup of his prosperity. The persecution of his old enemies in Missouri, and of new enemies quite as bitter and unrelenting in his new home in Illinois, never for a moment relaxed.

Shortly prior to the announcement of his name as a candidate for the Presidency, he was on a visit with his family at a place called Dixon in Illinois. An action had previously been brought against him by some of the people of Jackson county, in Missouri, who had suffered a loss of property in the disturbances that preceded the expulsion of the Mormons from that State. As Dixon was on the frontier between Missouri and Illinois, two sheriff's officers of Missouri, named Reynolds and Wilson, resolved to seize the Prophet, and carry him for trial before the Missouri courts. They disguised themselves for that purpose, and knocking at night at the farm-house where he was residing, stated that they were Mormon elders from Nauvoo, desirous of an interview with the Prophet. They were incautiously admitted to the passage, when they immediately rushed upon Joseph, each with a loaded pistol in his hand, and swore "to shoot him dead" if he offered the slightest resistance. On his asking for their authority to arrest him, they showed their pistols, and said "those were their authorities." They refused to let him go into the room to bid farewell to his family, or even to get his hat, and forced him into a waggon. They struck him over the head and back with the butt ends of their pistols, and, as he alleged, "otherwise abused, insulted, and threatened him in the cruellest manner." He was retained in custody by these men for several weeks, but ultimately obtained his release on a writ of *habeas corpus*, and was sent back to Illinois. He thereupon commenced an action against them for false imprisonment, and for using unnecessary force and violence towards him. Though the case was clearly proved, he only obtained the small damages of forty dollars; and from first to last had to pay upwards of three thousand five hundred dollars for legal expenses.

The unfounded and vindictive accusation brought against him by ex-Governor Boggs was productive of still greater annoyance, and the authorities, legal and military, of Missouri, instigated by the people of Jackson county, demanded that the State of Illinois should deliver him up to take his trial on this charge before a Missouri jury! A requisition was actually drawn up to this effect. A letter from J. Arlington Bennett, counsellor-at-law, and who appears to be no other than our old friend "General" Bennett, the "right-hand man," was published in the New York papers at this time. It strongly advised the authorities of Missouri to leave Joseph Smith alone; and predicted, in a remarkable manner, the consequences that would follow the continued persecution of the Prophet and his people—the death of Joseph—the increase of the sect—and their establishment in a free and powerful State of their own beyond the Rocky Mountains.

"I do not believe," said the writer, "that Joseph Smith has done anything to injure ex-Governor Boggs of Missouri. The Governor, no doubt under strong feelings, may have thought and believed that Smith had preconcerted the plan for his assassination; but there is no legal evidence whatever of that fact. None by which an unprejudiced jury would convict any man;—yet to send this man into Missouri, under the present requisition, would be an act of great injustice, and his ruin would be certain. How could any man, against whom there is a bitter religious prejudice, escape ruin, being in the circumstances of Smith? Look at the history of past ages—see the force of fanaticism and bigotry in bringing to the stake some of the best of men; and in all these cases the persecutors had their pretexts, as well as in the case of the Mormon chief. Nothing follows its victim with such deadly aim as religious zeal, and therefore nothing should be so much guarded against by the civil power.

"Smith, I conceive, has just as good a right to establish a church, if he can do it, as Luther, Calvin, Wesley, Fox, or even King Henry the Eighth. All these chiefs in religion had their opponents, and their people their persecutors. Henry the Eighth was excommunicated, body and bones, soul and all, by his holiness the Pope; still the Church of England has lived as well as all the other sects. Just so will it be with the Mormons: they may kill one prophet, and confine in chains half his followers, but another will take his place, and the Mormons will still go a-head.

"One of their elders said to me, when conversing on this subject, that they were like a mustard plant, 'If you don't disturb, the seed will fall and multiply; and if you kick it about, you only give the seed more soil, and it will multiply the more.' Undertake to convince them that they are wrong, and that Smith is an impostor, and the answer is, laying the hand on the heart, ' I know in mine own soul that it is true, and want no better evidence. I feel happy in my faith, and why should I be disturbed?' Now, I cannot see but what this is the sentiment that governs all religiously-disposed persons, their object being heaven and happiness, no matter what their church or their creed. They, therefore, cannot be put down while the Constitution of the United States offers them protection in common with all other sects, and while they believe that their eternal salvation is at stake. From what I know of the people, I fully believe that all the really sincere Mormons would die sooner than abandon their faith and religion.

"General J. C. Bennett has stated that, to conquer the Mormon legion, it would require five to one against them, all things taken into consideration, and that they will die to a man sooner than give up their Prophet.

"Now, is the arrest of this man worth such a sacrifice of life as must necessarily follow an open war with his people? The loss of from one to three thousand lives will no doubt follow in an attempt to accomplish an object not, in the end, worth a button.

"Persecute them, and you are sure to multiply them. This is fully proved since the Missouri persecution, as, since that affair, they have increased one hundred fold.

"It is the best policy, both of Missouri and Illinois, to let them alone; for if they are driven farther west they may set up an independent government, under which they can worship the Almighty as may suit their taste. Indeed, I would recommend to the Prophet to pull up stakes, and take possession of the Oregon territory in his own right, and establish an independent empire. In one hundred years from this time, no nation on earth could conquer such a people. Let not the history of David be forgotten. If the Prophet Joseph would do this, millions would flock to his standard and join his cause. He could then make his own laws by the voice of revelation, and have them executed like the act of one man."

In addition to the troubles and difficulties springing from the persecution of his Missourian enemies, Joseph was exposed to vexations and dangers of a kind even more exasperating. He might, from the secure fortress of Nauvoo, and in firm reliance upon the legally-constituted tribunals of the United States, have set at defiance the malice of those who persecuted him upon religious grounds, or found a sufficient answer to those who, having suffered loss, desired to make him generally responsible for all the acts committed by his followers at a time which was actually one of civil warfare; but when, in addition to these troubles, he had to defend himself against false friends and domestic traitors in his own church and city, the accumulation of perplexity and sorrow was great indeed. Joseph, at this time, appears to have been quite as convinced of the divinity of his mission as the most credulous of his disciples. He dreamed dreams, and he saw visions; he imagined that what he spoke was spoken by the Almighty, and that in him was all authority in matters of religion. But there were men in the church who despised Joseph Smith as an impostor while pretending to believe in him, knaves who used Mormonism for their own purposes—either of sensuality or ambition—and who led him by their extravagant licentiousness into continual difficulty. Many of these persons pretended to have " revelations " quite as valid as those of Joseph, by which they were permitted to have as many wives as the patriarchs of old, provided they could afford to maintain them. Joseph would not tolerate this scandal, and every offender was forthwith excommunicated, and publicly declared to be cut off from the church. One man of this kind, named Higbee, gave him more trouble than all the rest, and involved him in vexatious law proceedings, which lasted for upwards of two years, and were only brought to a close in May, 1844. Higbee, it appears, had been publicly accused by Joseph of having seduced several women, and was cut off from the Mormon church in consequence. Whether the charge were or were not true, is now difficult, and perhaps not important, to discover; but Higbee sued Joseph before the Municipal Court of Nauvoo for slander and defamation, and laid his damages at five thousand dollars. At his suit, Joseph was arrested, and the case came before the Municipal Court, on a writ of habeas corpus, on the 6th of May. The aldermen of the city, all of them Mormons, sat on the bench to hear the case, and Sidney Rigdon acted as counsel for the Prophet. At this trial, several disclosures were made, which went to prove a most deplorable laxity of morals on the part of men who had once been members and officer-bearers of the church, and who had been " cut off for their adulteries, and handed over to Satan," by the Prophet and the other heads of the sect. The court, after hearing the evidence of Joseph and Hyrum Smith and others, decreed, *first*, that Joseph Smith should be discharged from arrest on the ground of the illegality of the writ and *secondly*, that Higbee's conduct having been fully shown to be infamous, and the suit to have been instituted through malice, private pique, and corruption, he was not entitled to his costs.

But Higbee was not the only person who had been expelled from the church who was concerned in these proceedings. The libertines and seducers of Nauvoo, foiled before the Municipal Court— of which Joseph himself as mayor of Nauvoo, and the leading " Saints" as aldermen of the city, were severally members *ex officio*—tried other means to excite a schism, and adopted the bold course of accusing Joseph himself of the very crimes with which he had charged Higbee. Among other stories which were circulated by this party was one which obtained great currency, and led to important and unforeseen

results.   It was asserted that one Dr. Foster, a Mormon, and member
of the Danite band, or society of the "Destroying Angels," organized
in Missouri for the defence of the "Saints," having been absent from
home, had suddenly returned without giving notice to his wife, and
found the carriage of the Prophet at the door.   Having been cut off
from the church, and having, it is alleged, had previous suspicions of
an improper intercourse between Joseph and his wife, he questioned
Mrs. Foster as soon as Smith took his departure, when the lady
confessed that Joseph had been endeavouring to persuade her to
become his "spiritual wife."   The Mormons then, and ever since, have
indignantly denied the truth of this particular charge ; and of all the
charges brought against Joseph as regards a plurality of wives—and in
especial reference to the "spiritual wife" doctrine—they allege what
appears from his whole career to be most probable, that he was at all
times most anxious to preserve the church free from taint, and to ex-
clude adulterers, seducers, and persons of immoral lives.   But as the
consequences of this charge against Joseph were so momentous to him
and to the whole Mormon people, and as Dr. Foster probably believed
that there was some foundation for his suspicions, it is necessary that
the statements of both sides should be given.   An affidavit was put
in upon the trial of Higbee's case, by a person of the name of Eaton,
to the effect, that Dr. Foster had stated "that during his absence from
home a carriage drove up to his door; that a person alighted; that
the carriage then drove off again; that this person went into the
house and told Mrs. Foster a great many things to prejudice her
mind against her husband; that he finally introduced and preached the
"spiritual wife" doctrine to her; that he made an attempt to seduce
her; that he then sat down to dine with Mrs. Foster and blessed the
victuals; that while so doing Dr. Foster suddenly returned; that
this person rose up and said, "How d'ye do?" in a very polite manner;
that he soon afterwards went away; that Dr. Foster then questioned
his wife as to what had passed, but she refused to tell; that he then
drew a pistol and threatened to shoot her, but that she still refused;
that he then gave her a double-barrelled pistol, and told her to defend
herself; that she then fainted away through fear and excitement, and
that when she came to herself again, she had confessed that the person
alluded to had endeavoured to convert her to the "spiritual wife" doctrine, and to seduce her."   It was evident that Joseph Smith was the
person signified, but not named in this document.   It was treated by
the Municipal Court as false and scandalous.   Higbee described to the
same witness his own ideas of the "spiritual wife" system.   He said
that "some of the elders had ten or twelve spiritual wives a-piece; that
they entered the names of the women in a large book which was kept

sealed at Hyrum Smith's; and that when an elder or other Mormon wanted to seduce a woman, he led her to see this book opened, where, if her name was found entered, she was told it was the will of heaven that she should submit, and she submitted accordingly." It is utterly incredible that Joseph Smith, who, great impostor as he was, never missed an opportunity to denounce seducers and adulterers as unfit to enter into his church, should have been concerned directly or indirectly in proceedings like these, though it is scarcely surprising that when such stories had been circulated by men whom the " Prophet" had thwarted or reprimanded, there should have been found some persons willing to credit them.

Dr. Foster, who may or who may not have fancied he had real grounds of suspicions against Joseph, lent himself to the designs of the excommunicated party, and, in conjunction with a person named Law, commenced the publication, in the city of Nauvoo itself, of a newspaper called the *Expositor*. In the first number they printed the affidavits of sixteen women, to the effect that Joseph Smith, Sidney Rigdon, and others, had endeavoured to convert them to the "spiritual wife" doctrine, and to seduce them under the plea of having had especial permission from Heaven. This was somewhat too daring, and Joseph Smith, in his capacity of Mayor of Nauvoo, immediately summoned the aldermen, councillors, and other members of the corporation to consider the publication. They unanimously declared it to be a public nuisance, and ordered the city marshal to " abate it forthwith." A body of the prophet's adherents, to the number of two hundred and upwards, sallied forth in obedience to this order, and proceeding to the office of the *Expositor*, speedily rased it to the ground. They then destroyed the presses, and made a bonfire of the papers and furniture. Foster and Law fled for their lives, and took refuge in Carthage, where they applied for a warrant against Joseph and Hyrum Smith, and sixteen other persons known to have aided and abetted in putting down the *Expositor* office. The warrant was granted and served upon the Mayor of Nauvoo. He refused to acknowledge its validity, and the constable who served it was marched out of Nauvoo by the city marshal. The authorities of the county could not suffer this affront to the law; and the militia were ordered out to support the county officer in arresting the two Smiths and their sixteen confederates. The Mormons in Nauvoo fortified the city, and determined to fight to the last extremity in support of the " Prophet." The brethren from all parts of the country hastened to give assistance. Illinois, like Missouri, divided itself into two great camps, the Mormons and the anti-Mormons, and the circumstances were so menacing that Mr. Ford, the Governor, took the field in person. In a proclamation to the people of Illinois, he stated that he had discovered that nothing but the utter destruction of the city of Nauvoo would satisfy the militia and troops under his command, and that if he marched into the city pretexts would not be wanting on their part for the commencement of slaughter. Anxious to spare the effusion of blood, he called upon the two Smiths to surrender peaceably, pledging his word and the honour of the State, that they should be protected. He also called upon the Mormons to surrender their public arms, and upon the Nauvoo legion to submit to the command of a State officer. The Mormons agreed to the terms, and Joseph and his brother surrendered to take their trial for the riot, and for the destruction of the office of the *Expositor*. The "Prophet" had a presentiment of evil, and said, as he surrendered, "I am going like a lamb to the slaughter, but I am calm as a summer's morning; I have a conscience void of offence, and shall die innocent." While in prison at Carthage, another writ was served upon him and Hyrum for high treason against the State of Illinois, on an information in which the principal witness was the Higbee already mentioned, and whose hostility to Joseph had not ended at the trial before the Court of Nauvoo. As the mob breathed vengeance against both prisoners, and as the militia very indecently sided with the people, and were not to be depended on in case of any violence being offered to the two Smiths, the Governor was requested by the citizens of Nauvoo and other Mormons to set a guard over the gaol. On the morning of the 26th of June, 1844, the Governor visited the prisoners, and pledged his word to protect them against the threatened violence. It now began to be rumoured among the mob that there would be no case against the Smiths on either of the charges brought against them, and that the Governor was anxious they should escape. A band of ruffians accordingly resolved that as "law could not reach them, powder and shot should." About six o'clock in the evening of the 27th, the small guard stationed at the gaol was overpowered by a band of nearly two hundred men, with blackened faces, who rushed into the prison where the unfortunate men were confined. They were at the time in consultation with two of their friends. The mob fired upon the whole four. Hyrum was shot first, and fell immediately, exclaiming, "I am a dead man." Joseph endeavoured to leap from the window, and was shot in the attempt, exclaiming, " O Lord, my God." They were both shot after they were dead, each receiving four balls. John Taylor, one of the two Mormons in the room, was seriously wounded, but afterwards recovered.

The following account of this cruel murder was given by Mr. Willard Richards, the second of the two Mormons who were present with Joseph and Hyrum in the prison, when the mob broke in upon them.

It appeared in the *Times and Seasons* of the following month, under the title of "Two Minutes in Gaol."

"Possibly the following events occupied near three minutes, but I think only about two, and have penned them for the gratification of many friends :—

"Carthage, June 27th, 1844.

"A shower of musket balls were thrown up the stairway against the door of the prison in the second story, followed by many rapid footsteps. While Generals Joseph and Hyrum Smith, Mr. Taylor, and myself, who were in the front chamber, closed the door of our room against the entry at the head of the stairs, and placed ourselves against it, there being no lock on the door, and no ketch that was useable ;—the door is a common panel—and as soon as we heard the feet at the stairs' head, a ball was sent through the door, which passed between us, and showed that our enemies were desperadoes, and we must change our position. General Joseph Smith, Mr. Taylor, and myself, sprang back to the front part of the room, and General Hyrum Smith retreated two-thirds across the chamber, directly in front of and facing the door. A ball was sent through the door, which hit Hyrum on the side of his nose, when he fell backwards, extended at length, without moving his feet. From the holes in his vest (the day was warm, and no one had a coat on but myself), pantaloons, drawers, and shirt, it appears evident that a ball must have been thrown from without, through the window, which entered his back on the right side, and passing through lodged against his watch, which was in his right vest pocket, completely pulverizing the crystal and face, tearing off the hands, and mashing the whole body of the watch, at the same instant the ball from the door entered his nose. As he struck the floor he exclaimed emphatically, '*I'm a dead man.*' Joseph looked towards him, and responded, '*O dear Brother Hyrum !*' and opening the door two or three inches with his left hand, dis-charged one barrel of a six shooter (pistol) at random in the entry from whence a ball grazed Hyrum's breast, and entering his throat, passed into his head, while other muskets were aimed at him, and some balls hit him. Joseph continued snapping his revolver, round the casing of the door into the space as before, three barrels of which missed fire, while Mr. Taylor, with a walking stick, stood by his side and knocked down the bayonets and muskets which were constantly discharging through the doorway, while I stood by him, ready to lend any assistance, with another stick, but could not come within striking distance without going directly before the muzzle of the guns. When the revolver failed we had no more fire-arms, and expecting an imme-diate rush of the mob, and the doorway full of muskets—half way in the room, and no hope but instant death from within, Mr. Taylor rushed into the window, which is some fifteen or twenty feet from the ground. When his body was nearly on a balance, a ball from the door within entered his leg, and a ball from without struck his watch, a patent lever, in his vest pocket, near the left breast, and smashed it in 'pie,' leaving the hands standing at 5 o'clock, 16 minutes, and 26 seconds—the force of which ball threw him back on the floor, and he rolled under the bed which stood by his side, where he

K

lay motionless, the mob from the door continuing to fire upon him, cutting away a piece of flesh from his left hip as large as a man's hand, and were hindered only by my knocking down their muzzles with a stick; while they continued to reach their guns into the room, probably left-handed, and aimed their discharge so far around as almost to reach us in the corner of the room to where we retreated and dodged, and then I re-commenced the attack with my stick again. Joseph attempted, as the last resort, to leap the same window from whence Mr. Taylor fell, when two balls pierced him from the door, and one entered his right breast from without, and he fell outward exclaiming, ' *O Lord, my God!*' As his feet went out of the window my head went in, the balls whistling all around. He fell on his left side a dead man. At this instant the cry was raised, ' *He's leaped the window*,' and the mob on the stairs and in the entry ran out. I withdrew from the window, thinking it of no use to leap out on a hundred bayonets, then around General Smith's body. Not satisfied with this, I again reached my head out of the window, and watched some seconds, to see if there were any signs of life, regardless of my own, determined to see the end of him I loved. Being fully satisfied that he was dead, with a hundred men near the body, and more coming round the corner of the gaol, and expecting a return to our room, I rushed towards the prison door, at the head of the stairs, and through the entry from whence the firing had proceeded, to learn if the doors into the prison were open. When near the entry, Mr. Taylor called out, ' *Take me.*' I pressed my way until I found all doors unbarred; returning instantly, caught Mr. Taylor under my arm, and rushed by the stairs into the dungeon, or inner prison, stretched him on the floor, and covered him with a bed, in such a manner as not likely to be perceived, expecting an immediate return of the mob. I said to Mr. Taylor, ' This is a hard case to lay you on the floor; but if your wounds are not fatal I want you to live to tell the story.' I expected to be shot the next moment, and stood before the door awaiting the onset.

"WILLARD RICHARDS."

An eye-witness of the murder, named Daniels, who was connected with neither the Mormons nor the mob, gave some additional particulars of the outrage in a small work published by himself, in the State of Illinois, in 1844. Daniels, it seems, was overtaken on the prairies on the afternoon of the murder by a band of settlers, all more or less disguised with blackened faces, &c., who communicated to him the object of their gathering, which was, to force the gaol at Carthage, and to assassinate Smith and his fellow-prisoners. They appealed to him to join the expedition; and on his refusal, compelled him, by threats, to accompany them to the scene, that he might not, by giving an alarm, betray their object to the authorities. His impression was, that when Smith fell from the window he was not dead, but merely stunned by the fall, and he states that one of the gang raised him up and placed him against a well, and that, while in this position, four others among the mob advanced to the front rank with loaded muskets, and fired at the " Prophet." From the circumstance that four bullets were afterwards found in his body, there would appear to be some ground for believing this to be the correct account of Smith's death, as each of these four men stood at so short a distance from him as to make it quite certain that every shot fired took effect.

Thus died this extraordinary personage. " In the short space of twenty years," says the account of his " Martyrdom" appended to the *Book of Doctrines and Covenants*, " he brought forth the *Book of Mormon*, which he translated by the gift and power of God, and was the means of publishing in two continents. He sent the fulness of the everlasting Gospel which it contained to the four quarters of the earth. He brought forth the revelations and commandments which compose the *Book of Doctrines and Covenants*, and many other wise documents and instructions for the benefit of the children of men. He gathered many thousands of the Latter-Day Saints, founded a great city, and left a fame and a name that cannot be slain. He lived great, and died great in the eyes of God and his people ; and like most of the Lord's anointed in ancient times, sealed his mission and his works with his own blood, and so did his own brother Hyrum. In life they were not divided, and in death they were not separated."

The *Christian Reflector*, a less friendly critic of his character and actions, thus spoke of his life and death :—

" It is but a few weeks since the death of Joe Smith was announced. His body now sleeps, and his spirit has gone to its reward. Various are the opinions of men concerning this singular personage ; but whatever may be the views of any in reference to his principles, objects, or moral character, all agree that he was one of the most remarkable men of the age. Not fifteen years have elapsed since a band, composed of six persons, was formed in Palmyra, New York, of which Joseph Smith, jun., was the presiding genius. Most of these were connected with the family of Smith the senior. They were notorious for breach of contracts, and the repudiation of their honest debts. All of them were addicted to vice. They obtained their living not by honourable labour, but by deceiving their neighbours with their marvellous tales of money-digging. Notwithstanding the low origin, poverty, and profligacy, of the members of that band of mountebanks, they have augmented their numbers till more than 100,000 persons are now numbered among the followers of the Mormon Prophet, and never were increasing so rapidly as at the time of his death. Born in the very lowest walks of life, reared in poverty, educated in vice, having no claims to even common intelligence, coarse and vulgar in deportment, the Prophet Smith succeeded in establishing a religious creed, the tenets of which have been taught throughout the length and breadth of America. The Prophet's virtues have been rehearsed and admired in Europe; the ministers of Nauvoo have even found a welcome in Asia; and Africa has listened to the grave sayings of the seer of Palmyra. The standard of the Latter-Day Saints has been reared on the banks of the Nile, and even the Holy Land has been entered by the emissaries of this wicked impostor.

"He founded a city in one of the most beautiful situations in the world, in a beautiful curve of the 'father of waters' of no mean pretensions, and in it he has collected a population of twenty-five thousand, from every part of the world. He planned the architecture of a magnificent temple, and reared its walls nearly fifty feet high, which, if completed, will be the most beautiful, most costly, and the most noble building in America.

"The acts of his life exhibit a character as incongruous as it is remarkable. If we can credit his own words, and the testimony of eye-witnesses, he was at the same time the vicegerent of God, and a tavern-keeper—a prophet of Jehovah, and a base libertine—a minister of the religion of peace, and a lieutenant-general—a ruler of tens of thousands, and a slave to all his own base, unbridled passions—a preacher of righteousness, and a profane swearer—a worshipper of Bacchus, mayor of a city, and a miserable bar-room fiddler—a judge upon the judicial bench, and an invader of the civil, social, and moral relations of men; and, notwithstanding these inconsistencies of character, there are not wanting thousands who are willing to stake their souls' eternal salvation upon his veracity. For aught we know, time and distance will embellish his life with some new and rare virtues, which his most intimate friends failed to discover while living with him.

"Reasoning from effect to cause, we must conclude that the Mormon Prophet was of no common genius: few are able to commence and carry out an imposition like his, so long, and to such an extent. And we see, in the history of his success, most striking proofs of the gullibility of a large portion of the human family. What may not men be induced to believe?"

Joseph Smith was indeed a remarkable man; and, in summing up his character, it is extremely difficult to decide, whether he were indeed the vulgar impostor which it has been the fashion to consider him, or whether he were a sincere fanatic who believed what he taught. But whether an impostor, who, for the purposes of his ambition, concocted the fraud of the *Book of Mormon*, or a fanatic who believed and promulgated a fraud originally concocted by some other person, it must be admitted that he displayed no little zeal and courage; that his tact was great, that his talents for governing men were of no mean order, and that, however glaring his deficiencies in early life may have been, he manifested, as he grew older, an ability both as an orator and a writer, which showed that he possessed strong natural gifts, only requiring cultivation to have raised him to a high reputation among better educated men. There are many incidents in his life which favour the supposition that he was guilty of a deliberate fraud in pretending to have revelations from heaven, and in palming off upon the world his new Bible; but, at the same time, there is much in his later career which seems to prove that he really believed what he asserted—that he imagined himself to be in reality what he pretended—the chosen medium to convey a new Gospel to the world—the inspired of heaven, the dreamer of divine dreams, and the companion of angels. If he were an impostor, deliberately and coolly inventing, and pertinaciously propagating a falsehood, there is this much to be said, that never was an impostor more cruelly punished than he was, from the first moment of his appearance as a prophet to the last. Joseph Smith, in consequence of his pretensions to be a seer and prophet of God, lived a life of continual misery and persecution. He endured every kind of hardship, contumely, and suffering. He was derided, assaulted, and imprisoned. His life was one long scene of peril and distress, scarcely brightened by the brief beam of comparative repose which he enjoyed in his own city of Nauvoo. In the contempt showered upon his head his whole family shared. Father and mother, and brothers, wife, and friends, were alike involved in the ignominy of his pretensions, and the sufferings that resulted. He lived for fourteen years amid vindictive enemies, who never missed an opportunity to vilify, to harass, and to destroy him; and he died at last an untimely and miserable death, involving in his fate a brother to whom he was tenderly attached. If anything can tend to encourage the supposition that Joseph Smith was a sincere enthusiast, maddened with religious frenzies, as many have been before and will be after him—and that he had strong and invincible faith in his own high pretensions and divine mission, it is the probability that unless supported by such feelings, he would have renounced the unprofitable and ungrateful task, and sought refuge from persecution and misery in private life and honourable industry. But whether knave or lunatic, whether a liar or a true man, it cannot be denied that he was one of the most extraordinary persons of his time, a man of rude genius, who accomplished a much greater work than he knew; and whose name, whatever he may have been whilst living, will take its place among the notabilities of the world.

The perpetrators of the shameful murder of the two brothers were never discovered. Several persons were arrested on suspicion, but

there was not sufficient proof to convict them, and possibly no rea-
efforts were made to bring them to justice. The event was greatly
deplored. The sincerest opponents of Mormonism were those who
were most grieved at it. Joseph Smith murdered was a greater
prophet than Joseph Smith alive; and it was predicted, both by
friends and foes, that, however rapid the progress of the sect might
have been in past times, it would be still more rapid when fanaticism
might point to the martyrs of the faith — when the faults of the
Prophet would be buried in the oblivion of the tomb, and when his
virtues would be enhanced by the remembrance of his unhappy fate.
The prediction was verified; but not, however, until the Mormons had
passed through another long period of persecution and suffering.

JOSEPH SMITH.
(From a Sketch by M. Didier.)

JOHN TAYLOR.

CHAPTER VII.

THE news of the death of Joseph, and of his brother, was announced
to the Prophet's widow, in a letter signed by John Taylor and Willard
Richards, the two " Saints" who were present in the prison at the time
of the catastrophe, and by Samuel H. Smith,* a younger brother of
the murdered men. This letter, written in great haste, implored the
citizens of Nauvoo " to be still—and to know that God still reigned
over the world." It entreated them not to rush out of the city to
attack Carthage, " but to stay at home, and be prepared for an on-
slaught of the Missouri mobbers." It added that the people of
Handcock county were greatly excited, fearing that the Mormons

---

* Samuel H. Smith died in less than five weeks after the assassination of his brothers;
the Mormons say of a broken heart. He is also claimed as one of the martyrs of the faith.

would come and take vengeance, but that the writers had pledged
their words that no reprisals should be made. To this letter were
appended two short postscripts. The first bore the signature of
Thomas Ford, Governor and Commander-in-Chief of Illinois, and
recommended the Mormons to defend themselves until protection could
be furnished. The second postscript bore the signature of M. R.
Deming, Brigadier-General of the army of Illinois, acting under the
Governor, and was addressed to Mr. Orson Spencer, one of the twelve
apostles of the Mormons, and urged him and the citizens of Nauvoo to
deliberate earnestly, "as prudence might obviate material destruction." It added that the writer was at "his private residence when
the horrible crime was committed, and that it would be condemned
by three-fourths of the people of Missouri."

Early on the following morning the Nauvoo Legion was called out
and addressed by Mr. Phelps, the editor of the Mormon paper, and
other leading members of the community, who severally urged the
legion and citizens to be peaceable. The legion remained under arms
from ten in the morning until three in the afternoon, awaiting the
arrival of the bodies of Joseph and Hyrum. "About three o'clock," says
the *Times and Seasons*, published in Nauvoo three days afterwards,
"the bodies were met by a great assemblage of people, east of the
Temple, under the direction of the City Marshal, Samuel H. Smith,
the brother of the deceased, Dr. Richards, and Mr. Hamilton of Carthage. The waggons in which the bodies were conveyed were guarded
by three men. A procession was formed behind them, consisting of
the City Council, the staff of the Lieutenant-General, the Major-
General, and the Brigadier-General, of the Nauvoo Legion, the commanders, officers, and men, and the citizens of Nauvoo, to the number
of from eight to ten thousand." These followed the bodies to the
Mansion House, "amid the most solemn lamentations and wailings
that ever ascended into the ears of the Lord God of Hosts to be re-
venged of their enemies!" An oration was pronounced over the bodies
by Dr. Richards, and addresses were also delivered by four other
Mormons, in which the multitude were strongly urged to remain
peaceable. "That vast assemblage, with one united voice," said the
Times and Seasons, "resolved to trust to the law for justice for such a
high-handed assassination, and if that failed, to call upon God to
avenge them of their wrongs. Oh, widows and orphans!" it concluded,
"Oh, Americans, weep! The glory of freedom has departed!"

As the conduct of the Governor was much impugned in this
melancholy transaction, Mr. Ford deemed it necessary to issue the
following address to the people of Illinois in explanation of his conduct:—

"I desire to make a brief but true statement of the recent disgraceful affair at Carthage, in regard to the Smiths, so far as circumstances have come to my knowledge. The Smiths, Joseph and Hyrum, have been assassinated in gaol, by whom it is not known, but will be ascertained. I pledged myself for their safety; and upon the assurance of that pledge, they surrendered as prisoners. The Mormons surrendered the public arms in their possession; and the Nauvoo Legion submitted to the command of Captain Singleton, of Brown county, deputed for that purpose by me. All these things were required to satisfy the old citizens of Handcock that the Mormons were peaceably disposed, and to allay jealousy and excitement in their minds. It appears, however, that the compliance of the Mormons with every requisition made upon them, failed of that purpose. The pledge of security to the Smiths was not given upon my individual responsibility. Before I gave it, I obtained a pledge of honour by a unanimous vote from the officers and men under my command, to sustain me in performing it. If the assassination of the Smiths was committed by any portion of these, they have added treachery to murder, and have done all they could to disgrace the State and sully the public honour.

"On the morning of the day the deed was committed, we had proposed to march the army under my command into Nauvoo. I had, however, discovered on the evening before, that nothing but the utter destruction of the city would satisfy a portion of the troops; and that, if we marched into the city, pretexts would not be wanting for commencing hostilities. The Mormons had done everything required, or which ought to have been required of them. Offensive operations on our part would have been as unjust and disgraceful as they would have been impolitic in the present critical season of the year, the harvest, and the crops. For these reasons, I decided, in a council of officers, to disband the army, except three companies, two of which were reserved as a guard for the gaol. With the other company I marched into Nauvoo, to address the inhabitants there, and tell them what they might expect in case they designedly or imprudently provoked a war. I performed this duty, as I think, plainty and emphatically, and then set out to return to Carthage. When I had marched about three miles, a messenger informed me of the occurrences at Carthage. I hastened on to that place. The guard, it is said, did their duty, but were overpowered. Many of the inhabitants of Carthage had fled with their families. Others were preparing to go. I apprehended danger to the settlements from the sudden fury and passion of the Mormons, and sanctioned their movements in this respect.

"General Deming volunteered to remain with a few troops to observe the progress of events, to defend property against small numbers, and with orders to retreat if menaced by a superior force. I decided to proceed immediately to Quincy, to prepare a force sufficient to suppress disorders, in case it should ensue from the foregoing transactions or from any other cause. I have hopes that the Mormons will make no further difficulties. In this I may be mistaken. The other party may not be satisfied. They may recommence aggression. I have determined to preserve the peace against all breakers of the same, at all hazards. I think present circumstances warrant the precaution of having competent force at my disposal in readiness to march at a moment's warning. My position at Quincy will enable me to get the earliest intelligence, and to communicate orders with greater celerity.

"I have decided to issue the following general orders:—

"*Head Quarters, Quincy, June* 29, 1844.

"It is ordered that the commandants of regiments in the counties of Adams, Marquette, Pike, Brown, Schuyler, Morgan, Scott, Cass, Fulton, and M'Donough, and the regiments composing General Stapp's brigade, will call their respective regiments and battalions together immediately upon the receipt of this order, and proceed by voluntary enlistment to enrol as many men as can be armed in their respective regiments. They will make arrangements for a campaign of twelve days, and will provide themselves with arms, ammunition, and provisions accordingly, and hold themselves in readiness immediately to march upon the receipt of further orders.

"The independent companies of riflemen, infantry, cavalry, and artillery, in the above named counties, and in the county of Sangamon, will hold themselves in readiness in like manner.

"THOMAS FORD,

"Governor and Commander-in-Chief."

Governor Ford, who appears to have been greatly apprehensive that the Mormons would rise, *en masse*, to revenge the death of Joseph, dispatched, on the third day after the murder, two officers of the army of Illinois to Nauvoo, to ascertain the disposition of the citizens, "and whether any of them proposed in any manner to revenge themselves, and to report what threats had been used." They were also directed to proceed to the town of Warsaw, where the anti-Mormon militia had mustered in great strength, and to ascertain whether they meditated any attack upon Nauvoo—whether any of the people from the neighbouring States of Missouri and Iowa were among them—and to forbid any interference in the name of the State of Illinois, under the highest penalties of the law. These officers, on their arrival at Nauvoo, communicated to the members of the municipality a copy of the instructions they had received. A meeting of the City Council was immediately summoned to consider the matter. A string of resolutions was unanimously passed, to the effect that the Mormons as a body would endeavour to promote the peace and welfare of the county of Handcock, and the State of Illinois generally, by rigidly sustaining the laws, as long as the Governor would support them in the exercise of their constitutional rights. That as they had surrendered the public arms with which they had been entrusted, they solicited the Governor to disarm their opponents in like manner; that the Saints would reprobate the taking of private vengeance on the murderers of General Joseph Smith and General Hyrum Smith; that the City Council pledged itself on behalf of the whole body of citizens, that no aggressions should be made by them on the people of the adjoining country; and furthermore, that it highly approved of the pacific course taken by the Governor to allay excitement, and restore peace among the people of Illinois. A public meeting was then held on the great square, at which the Governor's emissaries attended, and addressed the people in the same conciliatory spirit, the multitude responding by one loud "Amen!"

On the same afternoon, an address to the Mormons in Nauvoo was issued by a committee of the "Saints:"—

"TO THE CHURCH OF JESUS CHRIST OF LATTER-DAY SAINTS.

"Deeply impressed for the welfare of all, while mourning the great loss of President *Joseph Smith*, our 'prophet and seer,' and President *Hyrum Smith*, our 'patriarch,' we have considered the occasion demanded of us a word of consolation. As has been the case in all ages, these saints have fallen martyrs for the truth's sake, and their escape from the persecution of a wicked world, in blood to bliss, only strengthens our faith, and confirms our religion as pure and holy. We, therefore, as servants of the Most High God, having the Bible, Book of Mormon, and the Book of Doctrine and Covenants, together with thousands of witnesses for Jesus Christ, would beseech the Latter-Day Saints in Nauvoo, and elsewhere, to hold fast to the faith that has been delivered to them in the last days, abiding in the perfect law of the Gospel. Be peaceable, quiet citizens, doing the works of righteousness, and as soon as the 'Twelve' and other authorities can assemble, or a majority of them, the onward course to the great gathering of Israel, and the final consummation of the dispensation of the fulness of times, will be pointed out, so that the murder of Abel, the assassination of hundreds, the righteous blood of all the holy prophets, from Abel to Joseph, sprinkled with the best blood of the Son of God, as the crimson sign of remission, only carries conviction to the business and bosoms of all flesh, that the cause is just, and will continue. And blessed are they that hold out faithful to the end, while apostates, consenting to the shedding of innocent blood, have no forgiveness in this world, nor in the world to come. Union is peace, brethren, and eternal life is the greatest gift of God. Rejoice, then, that you are found worthy to live and die for God. Men may kill the body, but they *cannot* hurt the soul, and wisdom shall be justified of her children. Amen.   "W. W. PHELPS.

W. RICHARDS.
JOHN TAYLOR."

"*July* 1, 1844."

A second address to the "Saints" in all parts of the world was issued a fortnight afterwards:—

"TO THE SAINTS ABROAD.

"DEAR BRETHREN,—On hearing of the martyrdom of our beloved Prophet and patriarch, you will doubtless need a word of advice and comfort, and look for it from our hands. We would say, therefore, first of all, be still, and know that the Lord is God, and that he will fulfil all things in his own due time, and not one jot or tittle of all his purposes and promises shall fail. *Remember*, REMEMBER that the priesthood, and the keys of power, are held in eternity as well as in time; and therefore the servants of God who pass the veil of death, are prepared to enter upon a greater and more effectual work, in the speedy accomplishment of the restoration of all things spoken of by his holy prophets.

" Remember that all the prophets and saints who have existed since the world began, are engaged in this holy work, and are yet in the vineyard, as well as the labourers of the eleventh hour, and are all pledged to establish the kingdom of God on the earth, and to give judgment unto the saints. Therefore, none can hinder the rolling on of the eternal purposes of the Great Jehovah. And we have now every reason to believe that the fulfilment of His great purposes is much nearer than we had supposed, and that not many years hence we shall see the kingdom of God coming with power and great glory to our deliverance.

" As to our country and nation, we have more reason to weep for them than for those they have murdered ; for they are destroying themselves and their institutions, and there is no remedy ; and as to feelings of revenge, let them not have place for one moment in our bosoms, for God's vengeance will speedily consume to that degree that we would fain be hid away, and not endure the sight.

" Let us, then, humble ourselves under the mighty hand of God, and endeavour to put away all our sins and imperfections as a people, and as individuals, and to call upon the Lord with the spirit of grace and supplication, and wait patiently on him, until he shall direct our way.

" Let no vain and foolish plans, or imaginations, scatter us abroad, and divide us asunder as a people, to seek to save our lives at the expense of truth and principle, but rather let us live or die together, and in the enjoyment of society and union. Therefore, we say, let us haste to fulfil the commandments which God has already given us. Yea, let us haste to *build the temple of our God*, and to GATHER together thereunto, our silver and our gold with us, unto the name of the Lord ; and then we may expect that he will teach us of his ways, and we will walk in his paths.

" We would further say, that in consequence of the great rains which have deluged the western country, and also in consequence of persecution and excitement, there has been but little done here, either in farming or building this season; therefore there is but little employment, and but little means of subsistence at the command of the Saints in this region—therefore let the Saints abroad, and others who feel for our calamities and wish to sustain us, come on with their money and means without delay, and purchase lots and farms, and build buildings, and employ hands, as well as to pay their tithings into the Temple, and their donations to the poor.

" We wish it distinctly understood abroad, that we greatly need the assistance of every lover of humanity, whether members of the church or otherwise, both in influence and in contributions for our aid, succour, and support.

Therefore, if they feel for us, now is the time to show their liberality and patriotism, towards a poor and persecuted, but honest and industrious people.

" Let the elders who remain abroad, continue to preach the Gospel in its purity and fulness, and to bear testimony of the truth of these things which have been revealed for the salvation of this generation.

> " P. P. Pratt.
> Willard Richards.
> John Taylor.
> W. W. Phelps."

" *Nauvoo, July* 15, 1844."

To re-assure the Mormon people, many of whom began to be apprehensive that the whole organization of the sect had fallen to pieces since the death of the Prophet, a more solemn address was issued in the name of the Twelve Apostles. This document urged the " Saints" to come from all parts of the Union, and of the world, to Nauvoo, to build up the Temple of the Lord; reminded them that the " Prophet Joseph," though removed from this world, " still held the keys of this last dispensation," and always would, in time and in eternity, and recommended them to abstain from all politics, voting, or president-making, and direct their whole attention to the affairs, social and religious, of the Mormon ody. This document was signed by Brigham Young, President of the Twelve Apostles, a man who was destined to play a most impor tant part in the future history of Mormonism. It ran as follows:—

" AN EPISTLE OF THE TWELVE,

" *To the Church of Jesus Christ of Latter-Day Saints, in Nauvoo and all the world,*
GREETING.

" Beloved Brethren—Forasmuch as the Saints have been called to suffer deep affliction and persecution, and also to mourn the loss of our beloved Prophet and also our Patriarch, who have suffered a cruel martyrdom for the testimony of Jesus, having voluntarily yielded themselves to cruel murderers who had sworn to take their lives, and thus, like good shepherds, have laid down their lives for the sheep, therefore it becomes necessary for us to address you at this time on several important subjects.

" You are now without a Prophet present with you in the flesh to guide you; but you are not without Apostles, who hold the keys of power to seal on earth that which shall be sealed in heaven, and to preside over all the affairs of the church in all the world; being still under the direction of the same God, and being dictated by the same Spirit, having the same manifestations of the Holy Ghost to dictate all the affairs of the church in all the world, to build up the kingdom upon the foundation that the Prophet Joseph has laid, who still holds the keys of this last dispensation, and will hold them to all eternity, as a king and priest unto the Most High God, ministering in heaven, on earth, or among the spirits of the departed dead, as seemeth good to Him who sent him.

"Let no man presume for a moment that his place will be filled by another; for, *remember he stands in his own place*, and always will; and the Twelve Apostles of this dispensation stand in their own place, and always will, both in time and in eternity, to minister, preside, and regulate the affairs of the whole church.

"How vain are the imaginations of the children of men, to presume for a moment that the slaughter of one, two, or a hundred of the leaders of this church could destroy an organization so perfect in itself and so harmoniously arranged, that it will stand while one member of it is left alive upon the earth. Brethren, be not alarmed, for if the Twelve should be taken away, still there are powers and offices in existence which will bear the kingdom of God triumphantly victorious in all the world. This church may have prophets many, and apostles many, but they are all to stand in due time in their proper organization, under the direction of those who hold the keys.

"On the subject of the gathering, let it be distinctly understood that the City of Nauvoo and the Temple of our Lord are to continue to be built up according to the pattern which has been commenced, and which has progressed with such rapidity thus far.

"The city must be built up and supported by the gathering of those who have capital, and are willing to lay it out for the erection of every branch of industry and manufacture, which is necessary for the employment and support of the poor, or of those who depend wholly on their labour; while farmers who have capital must come on and purchase farms in the adjoining country, and improve and cultivate the same. In this way all may enjoy plenty, and our infant city may grow and flourish, and be strengthened an hundred fold; and unless this is done, it is impossible for the gathering to progress, because those who have no other dependence cannot live together without industry and employment.

"Therefore, let capitalists hasten here; and they may be assured we have nerves, sinews, fingers, skill, and ingenuity, sufficient in our midst to carry on all the necessary branches of industry.

"The Temple must be completed by a regular system of tithing, according to the commandments of the Lord, which he has given as a law unto this church, by the mouth of his servant Joseph.

"Therefore, as soon as the Twelve have proceeded to a full and complete organization of the branches abroad, let every member proceed immediately to tithe himself, or herself, a tenth of all their property and money, and pay it into the hands of the Twelve; or into the hands of such bishops as have been, or shall be, appointed by them to receive the same, for the building of the Temple or the support of the priesthood, according to the Scriptures, and the revelations of God. And then let them continue to pay in a tenth of their income from that time forth, for this is a law unto this church as much binding on their conscience as any other law or ordinance. And let this law or ordinance be henceforth taught to all who present themselves for admission into this church, that they may know the sacrfiice and tithing which the Lord requires, and perform it; or else not curse the church with a mock membership, as many have done heretofore. This will furnish a steady public fund for all sacred purposes, and save the leaders from constant debt and embarrassment, and the members can then employ the remainder of their capital in every branch of enterprise, industry, and charity, as seemeth them good; only holding themselves in readiness to be advised in such manner as shall be for the good of themselves and the whole society; and thus all things can move in harmony, and for the general benefit and satisfaction of all concerned.

" The United States and adjoining provinces will be immediately organized by the Twelve into proper districts, in a similar manner as they have already done in England and Scotland, and high priests will be appointed over each district, to preside over the same, and to call quarterly conferences for the regulation and representation of the branches included in the same, and for the furtherance of the Gospel; and also to take measures for a yearly representation in a general conference. This will save the trouble and confusion of the running to and fro of elders; detect false doctrine and false teachers, and make every elder abroad accountable to the conference in which he may happen to labour. Bishops will also be appointed in the larger branches, to attend to the management of the temporal funds, such as tithings, and funds for the poor, according to the revelations of God, and to be judges in Israel.

"The Gospel, in its fulness and purity, must now roll forth through every neighbourhood of this wide-spread country, and to all the world; and millions will awake to its truths and obey its precepts; and the kingdoms of this world will become the kingdoms of our Lord and of his Christ.

" As rulers and people have taken council together against the Lord, and against his anointed, and have murdered him who would have reformed and saved the nation, it is not wisdom for the Saints to have anything to do with politics, voting, or president-making, at present. None of the candidates who are now before the public for that high office have manifested any disposition or intention to redress wrong or restore right, liberty, or law ; and, therefore, wo unto him who gives countenance to corruption, or partakes of murder, robbery, or other cruel deeds. Let us, then, stand aloof from all their corrupt men and measures, and wait, at least, till a man is found, who, if elected, will carry out the enlarged principles, universal freedom, and equal rights and protection, expressed in the views of our beloved prophet and martyr, General Joseph Smith.

" We do not, however, offer this political advice as binding on the consciences of others. We are perfectly willing that every member of this church should use their own freedom in all political matters ; but we give it as our own rule of action, and for the benefit of those who may choose to profit by it.

" Now, dear brethren, to conclude our present communication, we would exhort you in the name of the Lord Jesus Christ, to be humble and faithful before God and before all the people, and give no occasion for any man to speak evil of you ; but preach the Gospel in its simplicity and purity, and practise righteousness, and seek to establish the influence of truth, peace, and love,

among mankind, and in so doing, the Lord will bless you, and make you a blessing to all people.

"You may expect to hear from us again.

"BRIGHAM YOUNG,

"President of the Twelve."

"*Nauvoo, August* 15*th*, 1844."

No sooner had the Smiths been removed from the way of his long-
concealed but violent ambition, than Sidney Rigdon strove to vault
into the vacant place of the deceased "Prophet." Sidney, however,
miscalculated his power and influence. Joseph had long been
mistrustful of him. Sidney knew too much, and Joseph, without
quarrelling with him, had kept him at arm's length. The mistrust of
the Prophet was shared by the principal Mormons, and his "spiritual
wife" doctrine had alienated from him the confidence of many who
had once looked upon him as a founder of the faith, and a pillar of
the church. After the death of Joseph, Sidney Rigdon had a
"revelation," commanding the Saints to withdraw from their enemies,
and leave Nauvoo, and establish themselves in Pittsburg, Pennsylvania.
This "revelation" contradicted the "revelations" of Joseph, which
asserted positively that Jackson county was to be the final home of
the people; and the "Saints," under the guidance of Brigham
Young, who had his own views to serve, treated Sidney's "revelations" as the unwarrantable innovations of a man who "lied before
the Lord," and sought the destruction of his Saints. He was summoned
to answer for his misdeeds before the high quorum of the priesthood.
The trial commenced before the "Twelve Apostles,"* and the High
Council of the Church, on the 15th of September, about ten weeks after
the death of Joseph. Rigdon refused to appear; but evidence against
him was given in his absence, some of which was not a little curious and
suggestive. The business of the day began by the singing of a hymn
by the choir, and the delivery of a prayer by Orson Hyde. Brigham
Young then delivered a long address to the apostles and council, in
which he boldly spoke of the dissensions that had arisen, and called
upon those who had anything to say, to declare themselves openly.

---

* The Twelve Apostles are thus described in a letter from W. W. Phelps, addressed to
the editor of the *New York Prophet*, a small journal established at this time to promulgate
the views of the sect in the commercial metropolis of the Union :—" I know the Twelve,
and they know me. Their names are Brigham Young, the Lion of the Lord; Heber C.
Kimball, the Herald of Grace; Parley P. Pratt, the Archer of Paradise; Orson Hyde, the
Olive Branch of Israel; Willard Richards, the Keeper of the Rolls; John Taylor, the
Champion of Right; William Smith, the Patriarchal Staff of Jacob; Wilfred Woodruff,
the Banner of the Gospel; George A. Smith, the Entablature of Truth; Orson Pratt, the
Guage of Philosophy; John E. Page, the Sun Dial; and Lyman Wight, the Wild Ram of
the Mountains. They are good men; the best the Lord can find. They will do the will
of God, and the Saints know it."

" Those who wish," said he, " to tarry in Nauvoo, to build up the city and the temple, and carry out the message and revelation of our martyred Prophet, let them speak. We wish to know who they are. Those who are for Joseph and Hyrum, for the Book of Mormon, for the Book of Doctrines and Covenants, for the temple and Joseph's measures, and for the Twelve Apostles, all these being one party, let them manifest their principles openly and boldly. If they are of the opposite party, let them speak with the same freedom. If they are for Sidney Rigdon, and believe he is the man to be the First President and leader of this people, let them manifest it boldly ! Those who decline going either way, but secretly slander the character of Joseph and the Twelve, we withdraw our fellowship from them. If there be not more than ten men who hang on to the truth, to Joseph, and to the Temple, and who are willing to do right in all things, let me be one of the number. If there be but ten left, to have their lives threatened by mobs, because they will do right ;—and build up the Temple, let me be one to be martyred for the truth ! I have travelled for years in the midst of poverty and tribulation, and that, too, with blood in my shoes, month after month, year after year, to sustain and preach this Gospel, and to build up this kingdom, and God forbid that I should now turn round, and seek to destroy that which I have been building up."

After this eloquent exordium, Brigham Young proceeded to give evidence against Rigdon, stating that he refused to appear, thinking it would be better for him ; that he pretended to be sick, but was no more sick than he, Brigham Young, was at that moment ; that Rigdon, without authority, was acting as if he were the legal successor of Joseph Smith, and ordaining men " to be prophets, priests, and kings ;" that when accused of doing this, he equivocated and denied. " I saw," said Brigham, " the disposition of Elder Rigdon to equivocate, and I determined to know the whole secret. I said to him again, ' Elder Rigdon, did you not ordain these men at a meeting last night ?' He replied, ' Yes, I suppose I did.' I then asked Brother Rigdon by what authority *he* ordained prophets, priests, and kings? To which, with a very significant air, he replied—' Oh, I know all about that !' " Elder Orson Hyde, another of the Twelve, gave similar evidence, to the effect that Rigdon had admitted " that he was going to feel the minds of the branches, and then of the people of Nauvoo, until he got strong enough to make a party ; and that if he found he could raise influence to divide the Church, he would do so." When we (Hyde and others) demanded his license for ordaining men to be prophets, priests, and kings, he said, " I did not receive it from you, and shall not give it up to you." He also threatened " to turn traitor, saying, ' Inasmuch as you have demanded my license, I shall feel it my duty to publish all your secret meetings, and all the secret works of this Church in the public journals,'—intimating that this would bring the mob upon us." Amasa Lyman, another apostle, was the third of Rigdon's accusers. He said, "that it was plain Elder Sidney Rigdon had had a spirit as corrupt as hell, for the last four or five years." He added, " We have never heard of Sidney getting a revelation from heaven, but as soon as Brother Joseph has been removed, he can manufacture one, to allure the people and destroy them. After having given his testimony to the world (in support of the divine authority of the *Book of Mormon*, and its miraculous translation by Joseph), he finds fault with God because he happened to get into gaol in Missouri, and because he was poor. This is the man," continued Amasa Lyman, " who can get such wonderful revelations!" John Taylor corroborated all this evidence, and strengthened all these assertions against Rigdon, adding his belief " that this man's mind was enveloped in darkness; that he was ignorant and blinded by the Devil, and incompetent to fulfil the work which he had undertaken ;" and concluding, that in his opinion, "the men who had murdered Joseph and Hyrum, wicked as they were, were not one hundredth part so wicked and so guilty as the men who sowed dissensions in the Church—the Fosters, the Laws, the Higbees, and others, who were the instigators, the aiders, and the abettors, of murder." Elder Heber Kimball explained that the martyred Joseph had for many years been aware that Rigdon was unsafe, and not to be trusted ; and reminded the assembly, that a year previously, Joseph had said, at the annual conference, that " he should carry Rigdon no more : if the Church wanted to carry him, it might. but he should not ;" and that he had formally deprived him of all power and authority, appointing Elder Amasa Lyman in his stead.

On the second day of these proceedings, Brigham Young again rose, and inveighed against Rigdon in the following terms, which are curious as tending to prove Rigdon's complicity in the original fraud by which the *Book of Mormon* was palmed off upon the credulous as a divine revelation : " Brother Sidney says he will tell all our secrets," exclaimed Brigham Young : "but I would say, Oh, don't, Brother Sidney ! don't tell our secrets—oh, don't ! But if he tells our secrets, we will tell his. Tit for tat. He has had long visions in Pittsburgh, revealing to him wonderful iniquity among the Saints. Now, if he knows of so much iniquity, and has got such wonderful power, why don't he purge it out? He professes to have the keys of David. Wonderful power! and wonderful revelation ! And so he will publish our iniquity ! Oh, dear Brother Sidney, don't publish our iniquity ! Pray don't ! If Sidney Rigdon undertakes to publish all our secrets, as he says, he will lie the first jump he takes ! If he knew of all our iniquity, why did he not publish it sooner? If there is so much iniquity in the Church, Elder Rigdon, and you have known of it so long, you are a black-hearted wretch not to have published it sooner. If there is *not* this iniquity, you are a black-hearted wretch for endeavouring to bring a mob upon us, to murder innocent men, women, and children! Any man that says the Twelve are ' bogus makers,' adulterers, or wicked men, is a liar; and all who say such things shall have the fate of liars, where there is weeping and gnashing of teeth. Who is there that has seen us do such things? No man. The spirit that I am of tramples such slanderous wickedness under my feet." He concluded by expressing his firm conviction, that Rigdon was the prime cause of all the troubles of the Saints in Missouri and in Illinois, and that to suffer him to remain in the Church was to court destruction.

A few voices were raised in favour of Rigdon, but they had little to say. The feeling of the Mormons generally was against him; for it was felt that if he had done nothing else to injure the sect, the " spiritual wife " doctrine was alone sufficient to make him a dangerous ally. The evidence having been concluded, Mr. Phelps, the editor of the *Times and Seasons*, moved that " Sidney Rigdon be cut off from the Church, and handed over to the buffetings of Satan until he should repent." About ten hands out of several hundreds were held up in favour of Rigdon; upon which he was formally excommunicated by Brigham Young, "who," says the report, " delivered him over to the buffetings of Satan in the name of the Lord; and all the people said, ' Amen!'" It was then moved, seconded, and unanimously carried, that the ten persons who had held up their hands for Sidney Rigdon should be suspended from their fellowship with the Church, until brought to trial before the High Council. To this an amendment was immediately added, that all who should hereafter advocate Rigdon's principles should also be suspended. This, like the original resolution, was carried by acclamation, and thus terminated these very curious proceedings.

Brigham Young succeeded to the Presidency of the Church. Sidney Rigdon, unlike Orson Hyde, Oliver Cowdery, Martin Harris, and some others originally connected with Joseph Smith, who either seceded, proved traitors, or were excommunicated and cut off from the Church, has never been re-admitted, or sought re-admittance into the Mormon body. He has stood aloof, and founded a small church of his own; and, what is probably of more importance to the Mormons, he has held his tongue. As regards the polity of the Mormons, it has been fortunate for them that in a time of peril and perplexity, they were not induced to entrust themselves to his guidance. Under Brigham Young, and his able management, they speedily assumed a high position, not simply as religionists, but as citizens of the United States. Under Sidney Rigdon, it is probable the sect would have gone to pieces altogether.

The Missourians and anti-Mormons slightly relaxed in their hostility after the death of the Prophet and his brother, and for a twelvemonth affairs went on more quietly in the city of Nauvoo. Brigham Young, having relieved himself of the rivalry of Sidney Rigdon, carried on with vigour the building of the Temple and the Nauvoo House; in order to fulfil the "revelation," and prove to the Gentiles, not only the divinity of Joseph Smith's mission, but the power, wealth, and perseverance of his disciples.

The "Saints" were in great spirits. Persecution had made converts for them in many quarters; and those who had farms in New York and Pennsylvania, sold them and came to Nauvoo, or exchanged their land in those States for land in Illinois. Mr. Phelps, in a letter to the New York journal—*The Prophet*, gave a description of the city and Temple of Nauvoo, and the state of the Church at this time, which is almost the only record that has been preserved of the fortunes of the sect at this period of their history :—

" I shall not," he said, " describe the localities of Nauvoo now, because I shall not have room ; but as to the facilities, tranquillities, and virtues of the city, they are not equalled on the globe. The Saints, since Sidney, the great ' anti-Christ' of the last days, and his ' sons of Sceva,' have left Nauvoo, together with some other Simon Maguses, or foolish virgins, and wicked men who had crept in to revel on the bliss of Jehovah, have gone also, have enjoyed peace, union, and harmony.

" I speak advisedly when I say that Nauvoo is the best place in the world. No vice is meant to be tolerated; no grog-shops allowed; nor would we have any trouble, if it were not for our lenity in suffering the world, as I shall call them, to come in, and trade, and enjoy our society, as they say: which thing has made us the only trouble of late. These pretended friends too frequently, like old Balaam's girls when let 'in among the young men of Israel, find admirers, and break the ordinances of the city, and then 'Phineas's javelin' touches the heart·

" The Temple is up as high as the caps of the pilasters, and it looks majestic, and especially to me, when I know that the tithing, ' the mites of the poor,' thus speaks of the glory of God. All the description that is necessary to give you now is, that this splendid model of Mormon grandeur exhibits thirty hewn stone pilasters, which cost about three thousand dollars a-piece. The base is a crescent new moon ; the capitols, near fifty feet high; the sun, with a human face in bold relief, about two and a half feet broad, ornamented with rays of light and waves, surmounted by two hands holding two trumpets. It is always too much trouble to describe an unfinished building. The inside work is now going forward as fast as possible. When the whole structure is completed, it will cost some five or six hundred thousand dollars; and, as Captain Brown of Tobosco, near the ruins of Palenque, said, 'It will look the nearest like the splendid remains of antiquity in central America of anything he had seen, though not half so large.'

" The temple is erected from white limestone, wrought in a superior style; is one hundred and twenty-eight by eighty-three feet square; near sixty feet high; two stories in the clear, and two half stories in the recesses over the arches; four tiers of windows, two Gothic and two round. The two great stories will each have two pulpits, one at each end, to accommodate the Melchizidek and Aaronic priesthoods, graded into four rising seats—the first for the president of the elders and his two counsellors, the second for the president of the high priesthood and his two counsellors, the third for the Melchizidek president and his two counsellors, and the fourth for the president of the whole church and his two counsellors. This highest seat is where the Scribes and Pharisees used to crowd in ' to Moses' seat.' The Aaronic pulpit at the other end is the same.

" The fount in the basement story is for the baptism of the living, for health, for remission of sin, and for the salvation of the dead, as was the case in Solomon's temple, and all temples that God commands to be built. You know I am no Gentile, and, of course, do not believe that a monastery, cathedral, chapel, or meeting-house, erected by the notions and calculations of men, has any more sanction from God than any common house in Babylon.

" The steeple of our temple will be high enough to answer for a tower—between one hundred and two hundred feet high. But I have said enough about the Temple; when finished it will show more wealth, more art, more science, more revelation, more splendour, and more God, than all the rest of the world, and that will make it a Mormon temple:—' God and liberty,' patterned somewhat after the order of our forefathers, which were after the order of eternity.

" The other public buildings in Nauvoo, besides the Temple, are the Seventies' Hall, the Masonic Hall, and Concert Hall, all spacious, and well calculated for their designated purposes.

" There is no licensed grocery to sell or give away liquors of any kind in the city; drunkards are scarce; the probable number of inhabitants is 14,000, of whom nine-tenths are Mormons."

Among the more zealous Mormons, it became the fashion at this time to disuse the word Nauvoo, and to call the place the Holy City, or the City of Joseph. When the "capstone" of the Temple was laid in its place, their joy broke out in a manner which highly exasperated the people of the neighbouring counties. The first low rumblings of a new and violent persecution began to be heard. The old sores had never thoroughly healed; and the joy of the Mormons on the completion of their temple, which vented itself in vain-glorious boasts of the partial fulfilment of prophecies,—which would not be thoroughly fulfilled until the whole land was theirs, and none but a Mormon permitted to remain within it, from the Rocky Mountains to the Atlantic, —were not of a nature to allay any previously existing jealousy or ill-feeling. Quarrels occasionally took place between the Saints and their neighbours in Handcock county. The Mormons, when insulted, had not always the patience to forbear from retaliation; and among men who habitually bore arms to protect themselves, it is not surprising that the conflicts should not in all cases have been confined to words. Skirmish succeeded skirmish, until it became once more necessary to call out the militia for the preservation of the peace. Regular battles ensued, blood was shed, lives were lost, and the exasperation of both parties was raised even beyond its former height.

The *Times and Seasons* of the 15th of January, 1845, announced to the Saints in all parts of the world that the inhabitants of various parts of Illinois as well as of Missouri, were accumulating charges of every kind against the Mormons with the view of sweeping them into irretrievable ruin. Dr. Foster, in his newspaper, the *Expositor*, continued with the usual virulence of a friend converted into an enemy, to spread abroad defamatory reports against the " Apostles " and the leading Saints, which were copied, commented upon, and exaggerated by all the anti-Mormon press throughout the Union, and especially by the journals in the more immediate vicinity. The old cry of expulsion was raised, as the only means of restoring peace. A meeting of the Town Council of Nauvoo was held on the 13th of January, to consider these reports and the threatened expulsion of the Saints; and a meeting of the citizens in general was held on the day following with the same object. A few extracts from the resolutions passed at these assemblies will show the extent of the charges brought against the Mormon people, and the manner in which their leaders resolved to meet them. An address issued by D. Spencer, the successor of Joseph Smith in the mayoralty of Nauvoo, and countersigned by Willard Richards, the Recorder, one of the Twelve Apostles, stated " that while the Mormons were peaceable and loyal to the constitution and laws of their country, and were ever willing to join hands, with their honest virtues and patriotism, in the repressing of crime and the punishment of real criminals, they left their enemies to judge whether it would not be better to make Nauvoo one universal burial-ground, rather than suffer themselves to be driven from their lawful homes by such high-handed oppression. And it might yet become a question," they added, " to be decided by the community whether the Mormons, after having seen their best men murdered without redress, would quietly allow their enemies to wrench from them the last shreds of their constitutional liberties ; or whether they would not make their city a vast sepulchre, and be buried under its ruins in the defence of their rights." From the string of resolutions appended to this document, it appears that the crimes laid to the charge of the Mormons were, that they had organized a regular system of horse and cattle stealing, and other plunder throughout the State ; that Nauvoo had become a grand receptacle of stolen goods ; that every coiner, forger, robber, and even murderer found a safe refuge from justice within its walls; and that the Town Council allowed no legal process of any kind to be served within the limits of their jurisdiction. The resolutions admitted that many criminals had fled for refuge to Nauvoo under the mistaken notion that they would be screened from justice by the Mormons; but alleged that these criminals were not and never had been Mormons; that they had been induced to take this course by the false reports of the anti-Mormon press; and that in every case they had been delivered up to justice when demanded. The Town Council also pledged itself to use every means in its power to root such characters out of the city, and deputed fifty delegates to proceed to all the principal towns and districts in the neighbourhood, to inform the people of the falsehood of the accusations brought against the Saints, and to demand the aid of all the well-disposed to rid the country of the thieves and blackguards that swarmed into it. A conciliatory message from Governor Ford, published shortly afterwards, expressed his belief that the charges against the Mormons as a body were utterly unfounded; and that there was no more crime in the city of Nauvoo than in any other of a corresponding size and amount of population ; and called upon the inhabitants, whether Mormons or anti-Mormons, to preserve the peace and strictly respect the laws. From January to October, 1845, the Mormons "lived a life of'sturt and strife." Every man's hand was against them ; and not only riots, but regular pitched battles took place. The Governor was called upon to interfere actively; and a meeting of delegates from the nine counties surrounding Nauvoo was convened ; at which it was asserted by all the speakers that there would be no peace for Illinois as long as the Mormons remained within its boundaries. The delegates pledged themselves to support each other to the last extremity in expelling them forcibly, if they could not otherwise

be induced to go. The painful circumstances in which the Saints at
Nauvoo found themselves, and the history of the persecution which
they suffered, and which no doubt they brought upon themselves by
their assumption of superior holiness, and by their boasts, daily and
hourly repeated, that they would, by Divine permission and aid,
drive out all who were not of their Church, were detailed in an Official Letter to the Saints, under the date of the 1st of November, 1845.
This document ran as follows:—

"After we had began to realize the abundance of one of the most
fruitful seasons known for a long time, and while many hundreds of
Saints were labouring with excessive and unwearied diligence to finish
the Temple, and rear the Nauvoo House, suddenly, in the forepart of
September, the mob commenced burning the houses and grain of the
Saints in the south part of Handcock county. Though efforts were
made by the Sheriff to stay the torch of the incendiary, and parry off
the deluge of arson, still a 'fire and sword' party continued the work
of destruction for about a week, laying in ashes nearly two hundred
buildings, and much grain. Nor is this all; as it was in the sickly
season, many feeble persons, thrown out into the scorching rays of
the sun, or wet with the dampening dews of the evening, *died*, being
persecuted to death in a CHRISTIAN land of law and order; and while
they were fleeing and dying, the mob, embracing doctors, lawyers,
statesmen, *Christians* of various denominations, with the military from
colonels down, were busily engaged in filching or plundering, taking
furniture, cattle, and grain. In the midst of this horrid revelry,
having failed to procure aid among the 'old citizens,' the Sheriff
summoned a sufficient posse to stay the 'fire shower of ruin,' but not
until some of the offenders had paid for the aggression with their
lives.

"This, however, was not the end of the matter. Satan sits in the
hearts of the people to rule for evil, and the surrounding counties
began to fear that law, religion, and equal rights, in the hands of the
Latter-Day Saints, would feel after iniquity, or terrify their neighbours to larger acts of 'reserved rights,' and so they began to open a
larger field of woe. To cut this matter short, they urged the necessity (to stop the effusion of blood) to expel the Church, or, as they call
them, *the Mormons*, from the United States, 'peaceably, if they could,
and forcibly if they must,' unless they would transport themselves by
next spring. Taking into consideration the great value of life, and
the blessings of peace, a proposition, upon certain specified conditions,
was made to a committee of Quincy, and which it was supposed, from
the actions of conventions, was accepted. But we are sorry to say
that the continued depredations of the mob, and the acts of a few

individuals, have greatly lessened the confidence of every friend of law, honour, and humanity, in everything promised by the committees and conventions, though we have already made great advances towards fitting for a move next spring.

" A few troops stationed in the county have not entirely kept the mob at bay, several buildings having been burnt in the month of October.

" We shall, however, make every exertion on our part, as we have always done, to preserve the law and our engagements sacred, and leave the event with God, for he is sure.

" It may not be amiss to say, that the continued abuses, persecutions, murders, and robberies, practised upon us, by a horde of land pirates, with impunity in a *Christian* republic, and land of liberty (while the institutions of justice have either been too *weak* to afford us protection or redress, or else they too have been a little remiss), have brought us to the solemn conclusion that our exit from the United States is the only alternative by which we can enjoy our share of the elements which our Heavenly Father created free for all.

" We then can shake the dust from our garments, suffering wrong rather than do wrong, leaving this nation *alone in her glory*, while the residue of the world points the finger of scorn, till the indignation and consumption decreed makes a full end.

" In our patience we will possess our souls, and work out a more exceeding and eternal weight of glory, preparing, by withdrawing the power and priesthood from the Gentiles, for the great consolation of Israel, when the wilderness shall blossom as the rose, and Babylon fall like a millstone cast into the sea. The just shall live by faith ; but the folly of fools will perish with their bodies of corruption : then shall the righteous shine. Amen."

After a series of struggles and negotiations, and a regular siege of the city of Nauvoo by the anti-Mormons, of which no authentic account yet appears to have been published, with the exception of the short and interesting summary by Colonel Kane, to be referred to hereafter, the Saints agreed to leave Illinois in the spring of 1846, or as " soon as grass grew and water ran ;" provided that, in the interval, they should not be molested, and that they should be allowed time and opportunity to sell their farms and properties, and remove beyond the limits of civilization.

A circular of the High Council to the members of the Church throughout the world, which was published on the 20th of January, 1846, announced that the Mormons of Nauvoo had resolved to seek a home beyond the Rocky Mountains. The document is too curious in itself, and too remarkable in the history of the sect, to be omitted :—

" BELOVED BRETHREN AND FRIENDS,—We, the members of the High Council of the Church, by the voice of all her authorities, have unitedly and unanimously agreed, and embrace this opportunity to inform you, that we intend to set out into the Western country from this place, some time in the early part of the month of March, a company of pioneers, consisting mostly of young, hardy men, with some families. These are destined to be furnished with an ample outfit; taking with them a printing press, farming utensils of all kinds, with mill irons and bolting cloths, seeds of all kinds, grain, &c.

" The object of this early move is, to put in a spring crop, to build houses, and to prepare for the reception of families who will start so soon as grass shall be sufficiently grown to sustain teams and stock. Our pioneers are instructed to proceed West till they find a good place to make a crop, in some good valley in the neighbourhood of the Rocky Mountains, where they will infringe upon no one, and be not likely to be infringed upon. Here we will make a resting place, until we can determine a place for a permanent location. In the event of the President's recommendation to build block houses and stockade forts on the route to Oregon becoming a law, we have encouragements of having that work to do; and under our peculiar circumstances, we can do it with less expense to the Government than any other people. We also further declare, for the satisfaction of some who have concluded that our grievances have alienated us from our country, that our patriotism has not been overcome by fire—by sword—by daylight nor by midnight assassinations, which we have endured, neither have they alienated us from the institutions of our country. Should hostilities arise between the Government of the United States and any other power, in relation to the right of possessing the territory of Oregon, we are on hand to sustain the claim of the United States' Government to that country. It is geographically ours; and of right, no foreign power should hold dominion there; and if our services are required to prevent it, those services will be cheerfully rendered according to our ability. We feel the injuries that we have sustained, and are not insensible of the wrongs we have suffered. Still we are Americans; and should our country be invaded, we hope to do, at least, as much as did the conscientious Quaker who took his passage on board a merchant ship, and was attacked by pirates. The pirate boarded the merchantman, and one of the enemies' men fell into the water between the two vessels, but seized a rope that was hung over, and was pulling himself up on board the merchantman. The conscientious Quaker saw this, and though he did not like to fight, he took his jack-knife, and quickly moved to the scene, saying to the pirate, ' If thee wants that piece of rope I will help thee to it.' He cut the rope asunder— the pirate fell—and a watery grave was his resting-place.

" Much of our property will be left in the hands of competent agents for sale at a low rate, for teams, for goods, and for cash. The funds arising from the sale of property will be applied to the removal of families from time to time as fast as consistent, and it now remains to be proven whether those of our families and friends who are necessarily left behind for a season to obtain an outfit, through the sale of property, shall be mobbed, burnt, and driven away by force. Does any American want the honour of doing it? or will Americans suffer such acts to be done, and the disgrace of them to rest on their character under existing circumstances? If they will, let the world know it. But we do not believe they will.

" We agreed to leave the country for the sake of peace, upon the condition that no more vexatious prosecutions be instituted against us. In good faith have we laboured to fulfil this engagement. Governor Ford has also done his duty to further our wishes in this respect. But there are some who are unwilling that we should have an existence anywhere. But our destinies are in the hands of God, and so also is theirs.

" We venture to say that our brethren have made no counterfeit money; and if any miller has received fifteen hundred dollars base coin in a week from us, let him testify. If any land agent of the General Government has received waggon-loads of base coin from us in payment for lands, let him say so; or if he has received any at all from us, let him tell it. Those witnesses against us have spun a long yarn; but if our brethren had never used an influence against them to break them up, and to cause them to leave our city, after having satisfied themselves that they were engaged in the very business of which they accuse us, their revenge might never have been roused to father upon us their own illegitimate and bogus productions.

" We have never tied a black strap round any person's neck, neither have we cut their bowels out, nor fed any to the 'Cat-fish.' The systematic order of stealing, of which these grave witnesses speak, must certainly be original with them. Such a plan could never originate with any person, except some one who wished to fan the flames of death or destruction around us. The very dregs of malice and revenge are mingled in the statements of those witnesses alluded to by the *Sangamo Journal*. We should think that every man of sense might see this. In fact, many editors do see it, and they have our thanks for speaking of it.

" We have now stated our feelings, our wishes, and our intentions; and by them we are willing to abide; and such editors as are willing that we should live and not die, and have a being on the earth while Heaven is pleased to lengthen out our days, are respectfully requested to publish this article. And men who wish to buy property very cheap, to benefit themselves, and are willing to benefit us, are invited to call and look; and our prayer shall ever be, that justice and judgment, mercy and truth, may be exalted, not only in our own land, but throughout the world, and the will of God be done on earth as it is done in heaven.

" Done in Council at the City of Nauvoo, on the 20th day of January 1846.

" SAMUEL BENT.	" NEWEL KNIGHT.
JAMES ALLRED.	LEWIS D. WILSON.
GEORGE W. HARRIS.	EZRA T. BENSON.
WILLIAM HUNTINGTON.	DAVID FULLMER.
HENRY G. SHERWOOD.	THOMAS GROVER.
ALPHEUS CUTLER.	AARON JOHNSON."

The first companies of the Mormons commenced crossing the Mississippi on the 3rd February, 1846. They amounted to 1,600 men, women, and children, and passed the river on the ice. They continued to leave in detachments, or companies of similar magnitude, until July and August, travelling by ox-teams towards California, then almost unknown, and quite unpeopled by the Anglo-Saxon race.

The anti-Mormons asserted that the intention of the Saints was to excite the Indians against the commonwealth, and that they would return at the head of a multitude of the Red Skins to take vengeance upon the white people for the indignities they had suffered. Nothing appears to have been further from the intentions of the Mormons. Their sole object was to plant their Church in some fertile and hitherto undiscovered spot, where they might worship God in their own fashion, unmolested by any other sect of Christians. The war against Mexico was then raging, and, to test the loyalty of the Mormons, it was suggested by their foes that a demand should be made upon them to raise five hundred men for the service of the country. The Mormons obeyed, and five hundred of their best men enrolled themselves under the command of General Kearney, and marched 2,400 miles with the armies of the United States. At the conclusion of the Mexican war, they were disbanded in Upper California. The Mormons allege that it was one of this band who, in working at a mill, first discovered the golden treasures of California; and the " Saints" are said to have succeeded in amassing large quantities of the precious metal before the secret was made generally known to the " Gentiles."

But faith was not kept with the Mormons who remained in Nauvoo. Although they had agreed to leave in detachments, they were not allowed the necessary time to dispose of their property; and, in September, 1846, the city was besieged by their enemies, upon the pretence, that they did not intend to fulfil the stipulations made with the people and authorities of Illinois. After a three days' bombardment, the last remnant was finally driven out by fire and sword. The details will be found in the following chapter.

CHAPTER VIII.

THE "Great Salt Lake Valley" was
ultimately fixed upon as the halting-
place and future home of the sect; and
thither the successive detachments of
Mormons had directed their steps.
Whilst one party went overland to Upper California, another party chartered

MORMON CARAVAN CROSSING THE ROCKY MOUNTAINS.

the ship Brooklyn, at New York, and sailed round to the Pacific, by Cape Horn. This party was amongst the earliest of the arrivals in California, and its members were exceedingly fortunate at the "diggings," and amassed large quantities of gold.

But the great bulk of the Mormons proceeded overland to the Valley of the Great Salt Lake; a remarkable pilgrimage, which has not been paralleled in the history of mankind since Moses led the Israelites from Egypt. The distance to be traversed was enormous— the perils of the way were great—the whole circumstances were highly interesting and peculiar, and the zeal and courage of the sect were as remarkable as their faith. It is fortunate that a record of these events of the Mormon exodus was kept by a person who knew how to use his eyes, his understanding, and his pen; and that he has been induced to give it to the world. The following narrative of Colonel Kane, who accompanied the Mormons from Nauvoo to the Salt Lake, has all the interest of a romance. It was originally delivered as a lecture before the Historical Society of Pennsylvania, and is here reproduced from the American edition:—

A few years ago (said Colonel Kane), ascending the Upper Mississippi in the autumn when its waters were low, I was compelled to travel by land past the region of the Rapids. My road lay through the Half-Breed Tract, a fine section of Iowa, which the unsettled state of its land-titles had appropriated as a sanctuary for coiners, horse thieves, and other outlaws. I had left my steamer at Keokuk, at the foot of the Lower Fall, to hire a carriage, and to contend for some fragments of a dirty meal with the swarming flies, the only scavengers of the locality. From this place to where the deep water of the river returns, my eye wearied to see everywhere sordid, vagabond, and idle settlers; and a country marred, without being improved, by their careless hands.

I was descending the last hill-side upon my journey, when a landscape in delightful contrast broke upon my view. Half encircled by a bend of the river, a beautiful city lay glittering in the fresh morning sun; its bright new dwellings, set in cool green gardens, ranging up around a stately dome-shaped hill, which was crowned by a noble marble edifice, whose high tapering spire was radiant with white and gold. The city appeared to cover several miles; and beyond it, in the background, there rolled off a fair country, chequered by the careful lines of fruitful husbandry. The unmistakeable marks of industry, enterprise, and educated wealth everywhere, made the scene one of singular and most striking beauty.

It was a natural impulse to visit this inviting region. I procured a skiff, and rowing across the river, landed at the chief wharf of the

city. No one met me there. I looked, and saw no one. I could hear
no one move; though the quiet everywhere was such that I heard
the flies buzz, and the water-ripples break against the shallow of the
beach. I walked through the solitary streets. The town lay as in a
dream, under some deadening spell of loneliness, from which I almost
feared to wake it; for plainly it had not slept long. There was no
grass growing up in the paved ways; rains had not entirely washed
away the prints of dusty footsteps.

Yet I went about unchecked. I went into empty workshops,
rope-walks, and smithies. The spinner's wheel was idle; the carpenter
had gone from his work-bench and shavings, his unfinished sash and
casing. Fresh bark was in the tanner's vat, and the fresh-chopped
lightwood stood piled against the baker's oven. The blacksmith's
shop was cold; but his coal heap, and ladling pool, and crooked water
horn, were all there, as if he had just gone off for a holiday. No
work-people anywhere looked to know my errand. If I went into
the gardens, clinking the wicket-latch loudly after me, to pull the
marygolds, heart's-ease, and lady-slippers, and draw a drink with the
water-sodden well-bucket and its noisy chain; or, knocking off with
my stick the tall heavy-headed dahlias and sun-flowers, hunted over
the beds for cucumbers and love-apples—no one called out to me from
any opened window, or dog sprang forward to bark an alarm. I
could have supposed the people hidden in the houses, but the doors
were unfastened; and when at last I timidly entered them, I found
dead ashes white upon the hearths, and had to tread a-tiptoe, as if
walking down the aisle of a country church, to avoid rousing irre-
verent echoes from the naked floors.

On the outskirts of the town was the city graveyard; but there was
no record of plague there, nor did it in anywise differ much from other
Protestant American cemeteries. Some of the mounds were not long
sodded; some of the stones were newly set, their dates recent, and
their black inscriptions glossy in the mason's hardly dried lettering
ink. Beyond the graveyard, out in the fields, I saw, in one spot hard
by where the fruited boughs of a young orchard had been roughly torn
down, the still smouldering remains of a barbecue fire, that had been
constructed of rails from the fencing round it. It was the latest sign
of life there. Fields upon fields of heavy-headed yellow grain lay
rotting ungathered upon the ground. No one was at hand to take
in their rich harvest. As far as the eye could reach, they stretched
away—they sleeping too in the hazy air of autumn.

Only two portions of the city seemed to suggest the import of
this mysterious solitude. On the southern suburb, the houses looking
out upon the country showed, by their splintered wood-work, and
walls battered to the foundation, that they had lately been the mark

of a destructive cannonade. And in and around the splendid Temple, which had been the chief object of my admiration, armed men were barracked, surrounded by their stacks of musketry and pieces of heavy ordnance. These challenged me to render an account of myself, and why I had had the temerity to cross the water without a written permit from a leader of their band.

Though these men were generally more or less under the influence of ardent spirits, after I had explained myself as a passing stranger, they seemed anxious to gain my good opinion. They told the story of the Dead City : that it had been a notable manufacturing and commercial mart, sheltering over 20,000 persons ; that they had waged war with its inhabitants for several years, and had been finally successful only a few days before my visit, in an action fought in front of the ruined suburb ; after which, they had driven them forth at the point of the sword. The defence, they said, had been obstinate, but gave way on the third day's bombardment. They boasted greatly of their prowess, especially in this battle, as they called it ; but I discovered they were not of one mind as to certain of the exploits that had distinguished it ; one of which, as I remember, was, that they had slain a father and his son, a boy of fifteen, not long residents of the fated city, whom they admitted to have borne a character without reproach.

They also conducted me inside the massive sculptured walls of the curious Temple, in which they said the banished inhabitants were accustomed to celebrate the mystic rites of an unhallowed worship. They particularly pointed out to me certain features of the building, which, having been the peculiar objects of a former superstitious regard, they had, as matter of duty, sedulously defiled and defaced. The reputed sites of certain shrines they had thus particularly noticed ; and various sheltered chambers, in one of which was a deep well, constructed, they believed, with a dreadful design. Beside these, they led me to see a large and deep chiselled marble vase or basin, supported upon twelve oxen, also of marble, and of the size of life, of which they told some romantic stories. They said the deluded persons, most of whom were emigrants from a great distance, believed their Deity countenanced their reception here of a baptism of regeneration, as proxies for whomsoever they held in warm affection in the countries from which they had come. That here parents ' went into the water' for their lost children, children for their parents, widows for their spouses, and young persons for their lovers ; that thus the Great Vase came to be for them associated with all dear and distant memories, and was therefore the object, of all others in the building, to which they attached the greatest degree of idolatrous affection. On this account, the victors had so diligently desecrated it, as to render the apartment in which it was contained too noisome to abide in.

They permitted me also to ascend into the steeple, to see where it had been lightning-struck on the Sabbath before ; and to look out, east and south, on wasted farms like those I had seen near the city, extending till they were lost in the distance. Here, in the face of the pure day, close to the scar of the Divine wrath left by the thunderbolt, were fragments of food, cruises of liquor, and broken drinking vessels, with a brass drum and a steam-boat signal bell, of which I afterwards learned the use with pain.

It was after nightfall, when I was ready to cross the river on my return. The wind had freshened since the sunset, and the water beating roughly into my little boat, I hedged higher up the stream than the point I had left in the morning, and landed where a faint glimmering light invited me to steer.

Here, among the dock and rushes, sheltered only by the darkness, without roof between them and sky, I came upon a crowd of several hundred human creatures, whom my movements roused from uneasy slumber upon the ground.

Passing these on my way to the light, I found it came from a tallow candle in a paper funnel shade, such as is used by street venders of apples and pea-nuts, and which, flaming and guttering away in the bleak air off the water, shone flickeringly on the emaciated features of a man in the last stage of a bilious remittent fever. They had done their best for him. Over his head was something like a tent, made of a sheet or two, and he rested on a but partially ripped open old straw mattress, with a hair sofa cushion under his head for a pillow. His gaping jaw and glazing eye told how short a time he would monopolize these luxuries; though a seemingly bewildered and excited person, who might have been his wife, seemed to find hope in occasionally forcing him to swallow awkwardly, sips of the tepid river water, from a burned and battered bitter-smelling tin coffee-pot. Those who knew better had furnished the apothecary he needed ; a toothless old bald-head, whose manner had the repulsive dullness of a man familiar with death scenes. He, so long as I remained, mumbled in his patient's ear a monotonous and melancholy prayer, between the pauses of which I heard the hiccup and sobbing of two little girls, who were sitting up on a piece of drift-wood outside.

Dreadful, indeed, was the suffering of these forsaken beings ; bowed and cramped by cold and sunburn, alternating as each weary day and night dragged on, they were, almost all of them, the crippled victims of disease. They were there because they had no homes, nor hospital, nor poor-house, nor friends to offer them any. They could not satisfy the feeble cravings of their sick : they had not bread to quiet the fractious hunger-cries of their children. Mothers and babes,

M

daughters and grand-parents, all of them alike, were bivouacked in tatters, wanting even covering to comfort those whom the sick shiver of fever was searching to the marrow.

These were Mormons, in Lee county, Iowa, in the fourth week of the month of September, in the year of our Lord 1846. The city —it was Nauvoo, Illinois. The Mormons were the owners of that city, and the smiling country around. And those who had stopped their ploughs, who had silenced their hammers, their axes, their shuttles, and their workshop wheels; those who had put out their fires, who had eaten their food, spoiled their orchards, and trampled under foot their thousands of acres of unharvested bread; these were the keepers of their dwellings, the carousers in their temple, whose drunken riot insulted the ears of the dying.

I think it was as I turned from the wretched nightwatch of which I have spoken, that I first listened to the sounds of revel of a party of the guard within the city. Above the distant hum of the voices of many, occasionally rose distinct the loud oath-tainted exclamation, and the falsely intonated scrap of vulgar song: but lest this requiem should go unheeded, every now and then, when their boisterous orgies strove to attain a sort of ecstatic climax, a cruel spirit of insulting frolic carried some of them up into the high belfry of the Temple steeple, and there, with the wicked childishness of inebriates, they whooped, and shrieked, and beat the drum that I had seen, and rang in charivaric unison their loud-tongued steam-boat bell.

They were, all told, not more than six hundred and forty persons who were thus lying on the river flats. But the Mormons in Nauvoo and its dependencies had been numbered the year before at over twenty thousand. Where were they ? They had last been seen, carrying in mournful train their sick and wounded, halt and blind, to disappear behind the western horizon, pursuing the phantom of another home. Hardly anything else was known of them : and people asked with curiosity, 'What had been their fate—what their fortunes ?'

Since the expulsion of the Mormons to the present date, I have been intimately conversant with the details of their history. But I shall invite your attention most particularly to an account of what happened to them during their first year in the wilderness; because at this time more than any other, being lost to public view, they were the subjects of fable and misconception. Happily it was during this period I myself moved with them ; and earned, at dear price, as some among you are aware, my right to speak with authority of thm and their character, their trials, achievements, and intentions.

The party encountered by me at the river shore were the last of the Mormons that left the city. They had all of them engaged, the year before, that they would vacate their homes, and seek some other place of refuge. It had been the condition of a truce between them and their assailants; and as an earnest of their good faith, the chief elders, and some others of obnoxious standing, with their families, were to set out for the West in the spring of 1846. It had been stipulated in return, that the rest of the Mormons might remain behind in the peaceful enjoyment of the Illinois abode, until their leaders, with their exploring party, could, with all diligence, select for them a new place of settlement beyond the Rocky Mountains, in California, or elsewhere, and until they had opportunity to dispose, to the best advantage, of the property which they were then to leave.

Some renewed symptoms of hostile feeling had, however, determined the pioneer party to begin their work before the spring. It was, of course, anticipated that this would be a perilous service; but it was regarded as a matter of self-denying duty. The ardour and emulation of many, particularly the devout and the young, were stimulated by the difficulties it involved, and the ranks of the party were therefore filled up with volunteers from among the most effective and responsible members of the sect. They began their march in mid-winter; and by the beginning of February, nearly all of them were on the road, many of the waggons having crossed the Mississipp' on the ice.

Under the most favouring circumstances, an expedition of this sort, undertaken at such a season of the year, could scarcely fail to be disastrous. But the pioneer company had set out in haste, and were very imperfectly supplied with necessaries. The cold was intense. They moved in the teeth of keen-edged north-west winds, such as sweep down the Iowa Peninsula from the ice-bound regions of the timber-shaded Slave Lake and Lake of the Woods; on the Bald Prairie there, nothing above the dead grass breaks their free course over the hard rolled hills. Even along the scattered water-courses, where they broke the thick ice to give their cattle drink, the annual autumn fires had left little wood of value. The party, therefore, often wanted for good camp fires, the first luxury of all travellers; but, to men insufficiently furnished with tents and other appliances of shelter, almost an essential to life. After days of fatigue, their nights were often past in restless efforts to save themselves from freezing. Their stock of food, also, proved inadequate; and as their systems became impoverished, their suffering from cold increased.

Sickened with catarrhal affections, manacled by the fetters of dreadfully acute rheumatisms, some contrived for a while to get over the shortening day's march, and drag along some others. But the sign of an impaired circulation soon began to show itself in the liability of all to be dreadfully frost-bitten. The hardiest and strongest became helplessly crippled. About the same time, the strength of their beasts of draught began to fail. The small supply of provender they could carry with them had given out. The winter-bleached prairie straw proved devoid of nourishment; and they could only keep them from starving by seeking for the browse, as it is called, a green bark, and tender buds, and branches of the cotton-wood, and other stinted growths of the hollows.

To return to Nauvoo was apparently the only escape; but this would have been to give occasion for fresh mistrust, and so to bring new trouble to those they had left there behind them. They resolved at least to hold their ground, and to advance as they might, were it only by limping through the deep snows a few slow miles a day. They found a sort of comfort in comparing themselves to the exiles of Siberia, and sought cheerfulness in earnest prayers for the spring—longed for as morning by the tossing sick.

The spring came at last. It overtook them in the Sac and Fox country, still on the naked prairie, not yet half way over the trail they were following between the Mississippi and Missouri rivers. But it brought its own share of troubles with it. The months with which it opened proved nearly as trying as the worst of winter.

The snow and sleet and rain which fell, as it appeared to them, without intermission, made the road over the rich prairie soil as impassable as one vast bog of heavy black mud. Sometimes they would fasten the horses and oxen of four or five waggons to one, and attempt to get a-head in this way, taking turns; but at the close of a day of hard toil for themselves and their cattle, they would find themselves a quarter or half a-mile from the place they left in the morning. The heavy rains raised all the water-courses: the most trifling streams were impassable. Wood fit for bridging was often not to be had, and in such cases the only resource was to halt for the freshets to subside—a matter in the case of the headwaters of the Clariton, for instance, of over three weeks' delay.

These were dreary waitings upon Providence. The most spirited and sturdy murmured most at their forced inactivity. And even the women, whose heroic spirits had been proof against the lowest thermometric fall, confessed their tempers fluctuated with the ceaseless variations of the barometer. They complained, too, that the health of their children suffered more. It was the fact, that the open winds of March and April brought with them more mortal sickness than the sharpest freezing weather.

The frequent burials made the hardiest sicken. On the solder's march it is matter of discipline, that after the rattle of musketry over his comrade's grave, he shall tramp it to the music of some careless tune in a lively quick-step. But, in the Mormon camp, the companion who lay ill and gave up the ghost within view of all, all saw as he stretched a corpse, and all attended to his last resting-place. It was a sorrow, too, of itself to simple-hearted people, the deficient pomps of their imperfect style of funeral. The general hopefulness of human —including Mormon—nature, was well illustrated by the fact, that the most provident were found unfurnished with undertaker's articles; so that bereaved affection was driven to the most melancholy makeshifts.

The best expedient generally was to cut down a log of some eight or nine feet long, and slitting it longitudinally, strip off its dark bark in two half cylinders. These, placed around the body of the deceased and bound firmly together with withes made of the alburnum, formed a rough sort of tubular coffin which surviving relations and friends, with a little show of black crape, could follow with its enclosure to the hole, or bit of ditch, dug to receive it in the wet ground of the prairie. They grieved to lower it down so poorly clad, and in such an unheeded grave. It was hard—was it right, thus hurriedly to plunge it in one of the undistinguishable waves of the great land-sea, and leave it behind them there, under the cold north rain, abandoned to be forgotten? They had no tombstones; nor could they find rocks to pile the monumental cairn. So, when they had filled up the grave, and over it prayed a *miserère* prayer, and tried to sing a hopeful psalm, their last office was to seek out landmarks, or call in the surveyor to help them to determine the bearings of valley bends, headlands, or forks and angles of constant streams, by which its position should in the future, be remembered and recognised. The name of the beloved person, his age, the date of his death, and these marks were all registered with care. This party was then ready to move on. Such graves mark all the line of the first year of the Mormon travel—dispiriting milestones to failing stragglers in the rear.

It is an error to estimate largely the number of Mormons dead of starvation, strictly speaking. Want developed disease, and made them sink under fatigue, and maladies that would otherwise have proved trifling. But only those died of it outright who fell in out-of-the-way places, that the hand of brotherhood could not reach. Among the rest no such thing as plenty was known, while any went an hungered. If but a part of a group was supplied with provision, the only result was, that the whole went on the half or quarter ration, according to the sufficiency that there was among them ; and this so ungrudgingly and

contentedly, that, till some crisis of trial to their strength, they were
themselves unaware that their health was sinking, and their vital
force impaired. Hale young men gave up their own provided food
and shelter to the old and helpless, and walked their way back to
parts of the frontier States, chiefly Missouri and Iowa, where they
were not recognised, and hired themselves out for wages, to purchase
more. Others were sent there to exchange for meal and flour, or
wheat and corn, the table and bed furniture, and other last resources
of personal property which a few had still retained.

In a kindred spirit of paternal forecast, others laid out great
farms in the wilds, and planted in them the grain saved for their own
bread, that there might be harvests for those who should follow them.
Two of these, in the Sac and Fox country, and beyond it, Garden
Grove and Mount Pisgah, included within their fences above two
miles of land a-piece, carefully planted in grain, with a hamlet of
comfortable log-cabins in the neighbourhood of each.

Through all this, the pioneers found redeeming comfort in the
thought, that their own suffering was the price of humanity to their
friends at home. But the arrival of spring proved this a delusion.
Before the warm weather had made the earth dry enough for easy
travel, messengers came in from Nauvoo to overtake the party, with
fear-exaggerated tales of outrage, and to urge the chief men to hurry
back to the city, that they might give counsel and assistance there.
The enemy had only waited till the emigrants were supposed to be
gone on their road too far to return to interfere with them, and then
renewed their aggressions.

The Mormons outside Nauvoo were indeed hard pressed; but
inside the city they maintained themselves very well for three or four
months longer.

Strange to say, the chief part of this respite was devoted to
completing the structure of their quaintly devised but beautiful Temple. Since the dispersion of Jewry, probably, history affords us no
parallel to the attachment of the Mormons for this edifice. Every
architectural element, every most fantastic emblem it embodied, was
associated for them with some cherished feature of their religion. Its
erection had been enjoined upon them as a most sacred duty : they
were proud of the honour upon their city, when it grew up in its
splendour to become the chief object of the admiration of strangers
upon the Upper Mississippi. Besides, they had built it as a labour of
love : they could count up to half a million the value of their tithings
and free-will offerings laid upon it. Hardly a Mormon woman who had
not given up to it some trinket or pin-money ; the lowest Mormon
man had at least served the tenth of his year upon its walls ; and the

coarsest artizan could turn to it with something of the ennobling attachment of an artist for his fair creation. Therefore, though their enemies drove on them ruthlessly, they succeeded in parrying the last sword thrust till they had completed even the guilding of the angel and trumpet on the summit of its lofty spire. As a closing work, they placed on the entablature of the front, like a baptismal mark on the forehead—

THE HOUSE OF THE LORD :

BUILT BY THE CHURCH OF JESUS CHRIST OF LATTER-DAY SAINTS.

HOLINESS TO THE LORD!

Then, at high noon, under the bright sunshine of May, the next only after its completion, they consecrated it to divine service. There was a carefully studied ceremonial for the occasion. It was said the high elders of the sect travelled furtively from the Camp of Israel in the Wilderness ; and throwing off ingenious disguises, appeared in their own robes of holy office, to give it splendour.

For that one day the Temple stood resplendent in all its typical glories of sun, moon, and stars, and other abounding figured and lettered signs, hieroglyphs, and symbols : but that day only. The sacred rites of consecration ended, the work of removing the sacrosancta proceeded with the rapidity of magic. It went on through the night; and when the morning of the next day dawned, all the ornaments and furniture, everything that could provoke a sneer, had been carried off; and, except some fixtures that would not bear removal, the building was dismantled to the bare walls.*

* This building, so dear to the Mormons, is no longer in existence : " On Monday, the 19th November, 1848," says the *Nauvoo Patriot*, " our citizens were awakened by the alarm of fire, which, when first discovered, was bursting out through the spire of the Temple, near the small door that opened from the east side to the roof, on the main building. The fire was seen first about three o'clock in the morning, and not until it had taken such hold of the timbers and roof as to make useless any effort to extinguish it. The materials of the inside were so dry, and the fire spread so rapidly, that a few minutes were sufficient to wrap this famed edifice in a sheet of flame.

" It was evidently the work of an incendiary. There had been, on the evening previous, a meeting in the lower room; but no person was in the upper part, where the fire was first discovered. Who it was, and what could have been his motives, we have now no idea. Some feeling, infinitely more unenviable than that of the individual who put the torch to the beautiful Ephesian structure of old, must have possessed him. To destroy a work of art, at once the most elegant in its construction and the most renowned in its celebrity of any in the whole West, would, we should think, require a mind of more than ordinary depravity ; and we feel assured that no one in this community could have been so lost to every sense of justice, and every consideration of interest, as to become the author of the deed. Admit that it was a monument of folly and of evil, yet it was, to say the least of it, a splendid and a harmless one.

" Its loss, no doubt, will be more forcibly felt by the people of this place than any other ; because even the most dreamy will hardly think of soon seeing another such ornament, and because it was on the eve of changing hands, and being converted into a commodious

It was this day saw the departure of the last elders, and the largest band that moved in one company together. The people of Iowa have told me, that from morning to night they passed westward like an endless procession. They did not seem greatly out of heart, they said; but at the top of every hill, before they disappeared, they were seen to be looking back, like banished Moors, on their abandoned homes, and the far seen Temple and its glittering spire.

After this consecration, which was construed to indicate an insincerity on the part of the Mormons as to their stipulated departure, or at least a hope of return, their foes set upon them with renewed bitterness. As many fled as were at all prepared; but by the very fact of their so decreasing the already diminished forces of the city's defenders, they encouraged the enemy to greater boldness. It soon became apparent that nothing short of an immediate emigration could save the remnant.

From this time onward the energies of those already on the road were engrossed by the duty of providing for the fugitives who came crowding in after them. At a last general meeting of the sect in Nauvoo, there had been passed an unanimous resolve, that they would sustain one another, whatever their circumstances, upon the march; and this, though made in view of no such appalling exigency, they now with one accord set themselves together to carry out.

building of useful education, such as the West greatly needs, and such as no one ought to be envious of."

" In May 1850, another calamity occurred to the devoted City of Nauvoo: at that time occupied by a colony of Icarians, who had emigrated thither from Paris, under the superintendence of M. Cabet.

"The dreadful tornado of May 27th," says the *Handcock Patriot*, "which invaded the City of Nauvoo and neighbouring places, has been for us, Icarians, (little accustomed to such revolutions in the atmosphere), a spectacle of frightful sublimity, and also a source of mortal anguish, on account of the disasters and catastrophes which have resulted from it, to the inhabitants of this county, and to us.

"The Temple, which we were preparing so actively and resolutely to rebuild; the Temple which we hoped to cover this year; and in which we were to settle our refectories, our halls of reunion, and our schools; that gigantic monument has become the first victim of the tornado.

" How many projects are buried under those heaps of rubbish! How much outlay and days of hard labour has been lost to us! It was for that magnificent edifice to again give a soul to that great body, that one of our agents in the north pineries has just bought all the great beams necessary for its rebuilding; it is for it, that we were adding a saw machine to the mill, and establishing a vast shed, to shelter our labourers; in a word, it was for it that all our efforts and strength have been employed; and now, one gale of the tempest brings to naught all our endeavours; has violently ended what incendiary had begun in October 1848, and what *union fraternity* tried to repair in 1850. We resign without murmuring to that catastrophe.

"There now remains nothing of the gigantic work of the Mormons, except the west face, strongly united by its sides to another wall in the interior part, and surmounted by an arch; between the two walls at the north and south are the two towers or seat of the staircases."

Here begins the touching period of Mormon history ; on which, but that it is for me a hackneyed subject, I should be glad to dwell, were it only for the proof it has afforded of the strictly material value to communities of an active common faith, and its happy illustrations of the power of the spirit of Christian fraternity to relieve the deepest of human suffering. I may assume that it has already fully claimed the public sympathy.

Delayed thus by their own wants, and by their exertions to provide for the wants of others, it was not till the month of June that the advance of the emigrant companies arrived at the Missouri.

This body, I remember, I had to join there, ascending the river for the purpose from Fort Leavenworth, which was at that time our frontier post. The fort was the interesting rendezvous of the army of the West, and the head-quarters of its gallant chief, Stephen F. Kearney, whose guest and friend I account it my honour to have been. Many as were the reports daily received at the garrison from all portions of the Indian territory, it was a significant fact how little authentic intelligence was to be obtained concerning the Mormons. Even the region in which they were to be sought after, was a question not attempted to be designated with accuracy, except by what are very often called in the West, " Mormon stories," none of which bore any sifting. One of these averred, that a party of Mormons in spangled crimson robes of office, headed by one in black velvet and silver, had been teaching a Jewish pow-wow to the medicine men of the Sauks and Foxes. Another averred that they were going about in buffalo robe short frocks, imitative of the costume of Saint John, preaching baptism and the instance of the kingdom of heaven among the Ioways. To believe one report, ammunition and whiskey had been received by Indian braves at the hands of an elder with a flowing white beard, who spoke Indian, he alleged, because he had the gift of tongues, this, as far north as the country of the Yankton Sioux. According to another, yet which professed to be derived officially from at least one Indian sub-agent, the Mormons had distributed the scarlet uniforms of H. B. M.'s servants among the Pottawatamies, and had carried into the country twelve pieces of brass cannon, which were counted by a traveller as they were rafted across the East Fork of Grand River, one of the northern tributaries of the Missouri. The narrators of these pleasant stories were at variance as to the position of the Mormons, by a couple of hundred leagues ; but they harmonized in the warning, that to seek certain of the leading camps would be to meet the treatment of a spy.

Almost at the outset of my journey from Fort Leavenworth, while yet upon the edge of the Indian border, I had the good fortune to fall in with a couple of thin-necked sallow persons, in patchwork pantaloons, conducting northward waggon loads of Indian corn, which they had obtained, according to their own account, in barter from a squatter for some silver spoons and a feather bed. Their character was disclosed by their eager request of a bite from my wallet; in default of which, after a somewhat superfluous scriptural grace, they made an imperfect lunch before me off the softer of their corn ears, eating the grains as horses do, from the cob. I took their advice to follow up the Missouri; somewhere not far from which, in the Pottawatamie country, they were sure I would encounter one of their advancing companies.

I had bad weather on the road. Excessive heats, varied only by repeated drenching thunder squalls, knocked up my horse, my only travelling companion; and otherwise added to the ordinary hardships of a kind of life to which I was as yet little accustomed. I suffered a sense of discomfort, therefore, amounting to physical nostalgia, and was, in fact, wearied to death of the staring silence of the prairie, before I came upon the objects of my search.

They were collected a little distance above the Pottawatamie agency. The hills of the "High Prairie" crowding in upon the river at this point, and overhanging it, appear of an unusual and commanding elevation. They are called the Council Bluffs, a name given them with another meaning, but well illustrated by the picturesque congress of their high and mighty summits. To the south of them, a rich alluvial flat of considerable width follows down the Missouri, some eight miles, to where it is lost from view at a turn, which forms the site of the Indian town of Point aux Poules. Across the river from this spot the hills recur again, but are skirted at their base by as much low ground as suffices for a landing.

This landing, and the large flat or bottom on the east side of the river, were crowded with covered carts and waggons; and each one of the Council Bluff hills opposite was crowned with its own great camp, gay with bright white canvass, and alive with the busy stir of swarming occupants. In the clear blue morning air, the smoke streamed up from more than a thousand cooking fires. Countless roads and by-paths checkered all manner of geometric figures on the hill sides. Herd boys were dozing upon the slopes; sheep and horses, cows and oxen, were feeding around them, and other herds in the luxuriant meadow of the then swollen river. From a single point I counted four thousand head of cattle in view at one time. As I approached the camps, it seemed to me the children there were to prove still more numerous. Along a little creek I had to cross were women in greater force than *blanchisseuses* upon the Seine, washing and rinsing all manner of white muslins, red flannels, and parti-coloured calicoes, and hanging them to bleach upon a greater area of grass and bushes than we can display in all our Washington Square.

Hastening by these, I saluted a group of noisy boys, whose purely vernacular cries had for me an invincible home-savouring attraction. It was one of them, a bright faced lad, who, hurrying on his jacket and trowsers, fresh from bathing in the creek, first assured me I was at my right destination. He was a mere child; but he told me of his own accord where I had best go seek my welcome, and took my horse's bridle to help me pass a morass, the bridge over which he alleged to be unsafe.

There was something joyous for me in my free rambles about this vast body of pilgrims. I could range the wild country wherever I listed, under safeguard of their moving host. Not only in the main camp s was all stir and life, but in every direction, it seemed to me, I could follow "Mormon Roads," and find them beaten hard, and even dusty, by the tread and wear of the cattle and vehicles of emigrants labouring over them. By day, I would overtake and pass, one after another, what amounted to an army train of them; and at night, if I encamped at the places where the timber and running water were found together, I was almost sure to be within call of some camp or other, or at least within sight of its watch-fires. Wherever I was compelled to tarry I was certain to find shelter and hospitality, scant, indeed, but never stinted, and always honest and kind. After a recent unavoidable association with the border inhabitants of Western Missouri and Iowa, the vile scum which our own society, to apply the words of an admirable gentleman and eminent divine, "like the great ocean washes upon its frontier shores," I can scarcely describe the gratification I felt in associating again with persons who were almost all of Eastern American origin—persons of refined and cleanly habits and decent language—and in observing their peculiar and interesting mode of life; while every day seemed to bring with it its own especial incidents, fruitful in the illustration of habits and character.

It was during the period of which I have just spoken, that the Mormon battalion of five hundred and twenty men was recruited and marched for the Pacific coast.

At the commencement of the Mexican war, the President considered it desirable to march a body of reliable infantry to California at as early a period as practicable, and the known hardihood and habits of discipline of the Mormons were supposed peculiarly to fit them for this service. As California was supposed also to be their ultimate destination, the long march might cost them less than other citizens. They were accordingly invited to furnish a battalion of volunteers early in the month of July.

The call could hardly have been more inconveniently timed. The young, and those who could best have been spared, were then away from the main body, either with pioneer companies in the van, or, their faith unannounced, seeking work and food about the north-western settlements, to support them till the return of the season for commencing emigration. The force was, therefore, to be recruited from among fathers of families, and others, whose presence it was most desirable to retain.

There were some, too, who could not view the invitation without jealousy. They had twice been persuaded by (State) Government authorities in Illinois and Missouri, to give up their arms on some special appeals to their patriotic confidence, and had then been left to the malice of their enemies. And now they were asked, in the midst of the Indian country, to surrender over five hundred of their best men for a war march of thousands of miles to California, without the hope of return till after the conquest of that country. Could they view such a proposition with favour?

But the feeling of country triumphed. The Union had never wronged them : " You shall have your battalion at once. if it has to be a class of our elders," said one, himself a ruling elder. A central " mass meeting" for council, some harangues at the more remotely scattered camps, an American flag brought out from a storehouse of things rescued, and hoisted to the top of a tree mast, and in three days the force was reported, mustered, organized, and ready to march.

There was no sentimental affectation at their leave-taking. The afternoon before was appropriated to a farewell ball ; and a more merry dancing rout I have never seen, though the company went without refreshments, and their ball-room was of the most primitive. It was the custom, whenever the larger camps rested for a few days together, to make great arbours, or boweries, as they called them, of poles and brush and wattling, as places of shelter for their meetings of devotion or conference. In one of these, where the ground had been trodden firm and hard by the worshippers of the popular Father Taylor's precinct, was gathered now the mirth and beauty of the Mormon Israel.

If anything told the Mormons had been bred to other lives, it was the appearance of the women, as they assembled here. Before their flight, they had sold their watches and trinkets as the most available resource for raising ready money; and hence, like their partners, who wore waistcoats cut with useless watch-pockets, they, although their ears were pierced and bore the loop-marks of rejected pendants, were without ear-rings, finger-rings, chains, or brooches.

Except such ornaments, however, they lacked nothing most becoming the attire of decorous maidens. The neatly darned white stocking, and clean bright petticoat, the artistically clear-starched collar and chemisette, the something faded, only because too well washed, lawn or gingham gown, that fitted modishly to the waist of its pretty wearer—these, if any of them spoke of poverty, spoke of a poverty that had known its better days.

With the rest attended the Elders of the Church within call, including nearly all the chiefs of the High Council, with their wives and children. They, the gravest and most trouble-worn, seemed the most anxious of any to be first to throw off the burden of heavy thoughts. Their leading off the dancing in a great double cotillion was the signal bade the festivity commence. To the canto of debonnair violins, the cheer of horns, the jingle of sleigh-bells, and the jovial snoring of the tambourine, they did dance! None of your minuets or other mortuary processions of gentles in etiquette, tight shoes, and pinching gloves, but the spirited and scientific displays of our venerated and merry grandparents, who were not above following the fiddle to the Fox-Chase Inn or Gardens of Gray's Ferry. French fours, Copenhagen jigs, Virginia reels, and the like forgotten figures, executed with the spirit of people too happy to be slow, or bashful, or constrained. Light hearts, lithe figures, and light feet, had it their own way from an early hour till after the sun had dipped behind the sharp sky line of the Omaha hills. Silence was then called, and a well-cultivated mezzo-soprano voice, belonging to a young lady with fair face and dark eyes, gave, with quartette accompaniment, a little song, the notes of which I have been unsuccessful in repeated efforts to obtain since,—a version of the text, touching to all earthly wanderers:—

" By the rivers of Babylon we sat down and wept:
We wept when we remember Zion."

There was danger of some expression of feeling when the song was over, for it had begun to draw tears; but breaking the quiet with his hard voice, an Elder asked the blessing of Heaven on all who, with purity of heart, and brotherhood of spirit, had mingled in that society, and then all dispersed, hastening to cover from the falling dews. All, I remember, but some splendid Indians, who, in cardinal scarlet blankets and feathered leggings, had been making foreground figures for the dancing rings, like those in Mr. West's picture of our Philadelphia Treaty, and staring their inability to comprehend the wonderful performances. These loitered to the last, as if unwilling to seek their abject homes.

Well as I knew the peculiar fondness of the Mormons for music,

their orchestra in service on this occasion astonished me by its numbers and fine drill. The story was, that an eloquent Mormon missionary had converted its members in a body at an English town, a
stronghold of the sect, and that they took up their trumpets, trom-
bones, drums, and hautboys together, and followed him to America.

When the refugees from Nauvoo were hastening to part with
their table-ware, jewellery, and almost every other fragment of metal
wealth they possessed that was not iron, they had never a thought of
giving up the instruments of this favourite band. And when the
battalion was enlisted, though high inducements were offered some of
the performers to accompany it, they all refused. Their fortunes
went with the Camp of the Tabernacle. They had led the Farewell
Service in the Nauvoo Temple. Their office now was to guide the
monster choruses and Sunday hymns; and like the trumpets of silver
made of a whole piece " for the calling of the assembly, and for the
journeying of the camps," to knoll the people in to church. Some of
their wind instruments, indeed, were uncommonly full and pure-
toned, and in that clear dry air could be heard to a great distance. It
had the strangest effect in the world, to listen to their sweet music
winding over the uninhabited country. Something in the style of a
Moravian death-tone blown at day-break, but altogether unique. It
might be when you were hunting a ford over the Great Platte, the
dreariest of all wild rivers, perplexed among the far-reaching sand-
bars and curlew shallows of its shifting bed :—the wind rising would
bring you the first faint thought of a melody ; and, as you listened,
borne down upon the gust that swept past you a cloud of the dry
sifted sands, you recognised it—perhaps a home-loved theme of Henry
Proch or Mendelssohn. Mendelssohn Bartholdy, away there in the
Indian Marches !

The battalion gone, the host again moved on. The tents, which
had gathered on the hill summits, like white birds hesitating to venture on the long flight over the river, were struck one after another,
and the dwellers in them and their waggons, and their cattle, hastened
down to cross it at a ferry in the valley, which they made ply night
and day. A little beyond the landing, they formed their companies,
and made their preparations for the last and longest stage of their
journey. It was a more serious matter to cross the mountains then
than now, that the thirst of our people for the gold of California has
made the region between them and their desire such literally trodden
ground.

Thanks to this wonderful movement, I may dismiss an effort to
describe the incidents of emigrant life upon the Plains, presuming that
you have been made more than familiar with them already, by the

many repeated descriptions of which they have been the subject.
The desert march, the ford, the quicksand, the Indian battle, the bison
chase, the prairie fire :—the adventures of the Mormons comprised
every variety of these varieties ; but I could not hope to invest them
with the interest of novelty.   The character of their every-day life, its
routine and conduct, alone offered any exclusive or marked peculiarity.
Their romantic devotional observances, and their admirable concert
of purpose and action, met the eye at once.   After these, the stranger
was most struck, perhaps, by the strict order of march, the uncon-
fused closing up to meet attack, the skilful securing of the cattle upon
the halt, the system with which the watches were set at night to
guard them and the lines of *corral* —with other similar circumstances
indicative of the maintenance of a high state of discipline.   Every ten
of their waggons was under the care of a captain.   This captain of ten,

MORMON TABERNACLE CAMP.

as they termed him, obeyed a captain of fifty ; who, in turn, obeyed
his captain of a hundred, or directly a member of what they call the
High Council of the Church.   All these were responsible and determined men, approved of by the people for their courage, discretion,
and experience.   So well recognised were the results of this organiza-

tion, that bands of hostile Indians have passed by comparative small
parties of Mormons, to attack much larger, but less compact bodies of
other emigrants.

The most striking feature, however, of the Mormon emigration,
was undoubtedly their formation of the Tabernacle Camps, and temporary Stakes, or Settlements, which renewed, in the sleeping soli-
tudes everywhere along their road, the cheering signs of intelligent
and hopeful life.

I will make this remark plainer by describing to you one of these
camps, with the daily routine of its inhabitants. I select at random,
for my purpose, a large camp upon the delta between the Nebraska
and Missouri, in the territory disputed between the Omaha and Otto
and Missouri Indians. It remained pitched here for nearly two
months, during which period I resided in it.

It was situated near the Petit Papillon, or Little Butterfly
River, and upon some finely-rounded hills that encircle a favourite cool
spring. On each of these a square was marked out; and the waggons,
as they arrived, took their positions along its four sides in double
rows, so as to leave a roomy street or passage-way between them.
The tents were disposed also in rows, at intervals, between the waggons.
The cattle were folded in high-fenced yards outside. The quadrangle
inside was left vacant for the sake of ventilation, and the streets,
covered in with leafy arbour work, and kept scrupulously clean,
formed a shaded cloister walk. This was the place of exercise for
slowly-recovering invalids, the day-home of the infants, and the evening promenade of all.

From the first formation of the camp, all its inhabitants were
constantly and laboriously occupied. Many of them were highly
educated mechanics, and seemed only to need a day's anticipated rest
to engage them at the forge, loom, or turning-lathe, upon some needed
chore of work. A Mormon gunsmith is the inventor of the excellent
repeating rifle, that loads by slides instead of cylinders ; and one of the
neatest finished fire-arms I have ever seen was of this kind, wrought
from scraps of old iron, and inlaid with the silver of a couple of half
dollars, under a hot July sun, in a spot where the average height of
the grass was above the workman's shoulders. I have seen a cobbler,
after the halt of his party on the march, hunting along the river
bank for a lap-stone, in the twilight, that he might finish a famous
boot-sole by the camp fire ; and I have had a piece of cloth, the wool
of which was sheared, and dyed, and spun, and woven, during a progress over three hundred miles.

Their more interesting occupations, however, were those growing out of their peculiar circumstances and position. The chiefs were

seldom without some curious affair on hand to settle with the restless Indians; while the immense labour and responsibility of the conduct of their unwieldy moving army, and the commissariat of its hundreds of famishing poor, also devolved upon them. They had good men they called Bishops, whose special office it was to look up the cases of extremest suffering, and their relief parties were out night and day to scour over every trail.

At this time, say two months before the final expulsion from Nauvoo, there were already, along three hundred miles of the road between that city and our Papillon Camp, over two thousand emigrating waggons, besides a large number of nondescript turn-outs, the motley make-shifts of poverty, from the unsuitably heavy-cart, that lumbered on mysteriously, with its sick driver hidden under its counterpane cover, to the crazy two-wheeled trundle, such as our own poor employ for the conveyance of their slop-barrels, this pulled along, it may be, by a little dry, dogged heifer, and rigged up only to drag some such light weight as a baby, a sack of meal, or a pack of clothes and bedding.

Some of them were in distress from losses upon the way. A strong trait of the Mormons was their kindness to their brute dependents, and particularly to their beasts of draught. They gave them the holiday of the Sabbath whenever it came round. I believe they would have washed them with old wine, after the example of the emigrant Carthaginians, had they had any. Still, in the Slave-coast heats, under which the animals had to move, they sometimes foundered. Sometimes, too, they strayed off in the night, or were mired in morasses, or oftener were stolen by Indians, who found market covert for such plunder among the horse-thief whites of the frontier. But the great mass of these pilgrims of the desert was made up of poor folks, who had fled in destitution from Nauvoo, and been refused a resting-place by the people of Iowa.

It is difficult fully to understand the state of helplessness in which some of these would arrive, after accomplishing a journey of such extent, under circumstances of so much privation and peril. The fact was, they seemed to believe that all their trouble would be at an end if they could only come up with their comrades at the great camps. For this they calculated their resources, among which their power of endurance was by much the largest and most reliable item, and they were not disappointed if they arrived with these utterly exhausted.

I remember a signal instance of this at the Papillon Camp:

It was that of a joyous-hearted clever fellow, whose songs and fiddle-tunes were the life and delight of Nauvoo in its merry days. I forget his story, and how exactly it fell about, that, after a Mormon's

N

full peck of troubles, he started after us, with his wife and little ones, from some "lying-down place" in the Indian country, where he had contended with an attack of a serious malady. He was just convalescent, and the fatigue of marching on foot again, with a child on his back, speedily brought on a relapse. But his anxiety to reach a place where he could expect to meet friends with shelter and food, was such that he only pressed on the harder, Probably for more than a week of the dog-star weather, he laboured on under a high fever, walking every day till he was entirely exhausted.

His limbs failed him then; but his courage holding out, he got into his covered cart, on top of its freight of baggage, and made them drive him on while he lay down. They could hardly believe how ill he was, he talked on so cheerfully: "I'm nothing on earth ailing but home-sick. I'm cured the very minute I get to camp and see the brethren."

Not being able thus to watch his course, he lost his way, and had to regain it through a wretched tract of low meadow-prairie, where there were no trees to break the noon, no water but what was ague-sweet or brackish. By the time he got back to the trail of the high prairie, he was, in his own phrase, pretty far gone. Yet he was resolute in his purpose as ever, and to a party he fell in with avowed his intention to be cured at the camp, "and nowhere else." He even jested with them, comparing his jolting couch to a summer cot in a white-washed cock-loft. "But I'll make them take me down," he said, "and give me a dip in the river when I get there. All I care for is to see the brethren."

His determined bearing rallied the spirits of his travelling household, and they kept on their way till he was within a few hours' journey of the camp. He entered on his last day's journey with the energy of increased hope.

I remember that day well, for in the evening I mounted a tired horse to go a short errand, and in mere pity, had to turn back before I had walked him a couple of hundred yards. Nothing seemed to draw life from the languid air but the clouds of gnats and stinging midges; and long after sun-down, it was so hot that the sheep lay on their stomachs panting, and the cattle strove to lap wind like hard-fagged hunting-dogs. In camp, I had spent the day in watching the invalids, and the rest hunting the shade under the waggon-bodies, and veering about them like the shadows round the sun-dial. I know I thought myself wretched enough to be of their company.

Poor Merryman had all that heat to bear, with the mere pretence of an awning to screen out the sun from his close muslin cock-loft.

He did not fail till somewhere hard upon noon. He then began to grow restless, to know accurately the distance travelled. He made them give him water, too, much more frequently; and when they stopped for this purpose, asked a number of obscure questions. A little after this he discovered himself that a film had come over his eyes. He confessed that this was discouraging, but said with stubborn resignation, that if denied to see the brethren, he still should hear the sound of their voices.

After this, which was when he was hardly three miles from our camp, he lay very quiet, as if husbanding his strength; but when he had made, as is thought, a full mile further, being interrogated by the woman that was driving, whether she should stop, he answered her, as she avers, " No, no; go on !"

The anecdote ends badly. They brought him in dead, I think about five o'clock in the afternoon. He had on his clean clothes, as he had dressed himself in the morning, looking forward to his arrival.

Beside the common duty of guiding and assisting these unfortunates, the companies in the van united in providing the highway for the entire body of emigrants. The Mormons have laid out for themselves a road through the Indian Territory, over four hundred leagues in length, with substantial well-built bridges, fit for the passage of heavy artillery, over all the streams, except a few great rivers where they have established permanent ferries. The nearest unfinished bridging to the Papillon Camp was that of the Corne à Cerf, or Elk-horn, a tributary of the Platte, distant may be a couple of hours' march. Here, in what seemed to be an incredibly short space of time, there rose the seven great piers and abutments of a bridge, such as might challenge honours for the entire public-spirited population of Lower Virginia. The party detailed to the task worked in the broiling sun, in water beyond depth, and up to their necks, as if engaged in the perpetration of some pointed and delightful practical joke. The chief sport lay in floating along with the logs, cut from the overhanging timber up the stream, guiding them till they reached their destination, and then plunging them under water in the precise spot where they were to be secured. This the laughing engineers would execute with the agility of happy, diving ducks.

Our nearest ferry was that over the Missouri. Nearly opposite Pull Point, or Point aux Poules, a trading post of the American Fur Company, and village of the Pottawatamies, they had gained a favourable crossing by making a deep cut for the road through the steep right bank. And here, without intermission, their flat-bottomed scows plied, crowded with the waggons, and cows, and sheep, and

children, and furniture of the emigrants, who, in waiting their turn,
made the woods around smoke with their crowding camp fires. But
no such good fortune as a gratuitous passage awaited the heavy
cattle, of whom, with the others, no less than thirty thousand were
at this time on their way westward; these were made to earn it by
swimming.

FORMATION OF A BRIDGE.

A heavy freshet had at this time swollen the river to a width, as
I should judge, of something like a mile and a half, and dashed past
its fierce current, rushing, gurgling, and eddying, as if thrown from
a mill-race, or *scriptural* fountain of the deep. Its aspect did not
invite the oxen to their duty, and the labour was to force them to it.
They were gathered in little troops upon the shore, and driven forward till they lost their footing. As they turned their heads to
return, they encountered the combined opposition of a clamorous crowd
of bystanders, vieing with each other in the pungent administration
of inhospitable affront. Then rose their hubbub; their geeing and
woing, and hawing; their yelling, and yelping, and screaming; their

CATTLE FORDING THE MISSOURI.

hooting, and hissing, and pelting. The
rearmost steers would hesitate to brave such
a rebuff; halting they would impede the
return of the outermost; they all would
waver; wavering for a moment, the curren
would sweep them together downward. At
this juncture a fearless youngster, climbing
upon some brave bull in the front rank, would
urge him boldly forth into the stream; the
rest then surely followed; a few moments
saw them struggling in mid current; a few more, and they
were safely landed on the opposite shore. The driver's was
the sought after post of honour here; and sometimes, when repeated
failures have urged them to emulation, I have seen the youths, in
stepping from back to back of the struggling monsters, or swimming
in among their battling hoofs, display feats of address and hardihood,
that would have made Franconi's or the Madrid bull-ring vibrate with
bravos of applause. But in the hours after hours that I have watched
this sport at the ferry side, I never heard an oath, or the language
of quarrel, or knew it provoke the least sign of ill feeling.

After the sorrowful word was given out to halt, and make preparations for winter, a chief labour became the making hay; and with
everyday dawn brigades of mowers would take up the march to their
positions in chosen meadows, a prettier sight than a charge of cavalry,
as they laid their swarths, whole companies of scythes abreast. Before this time the manliest, as well as most general daily labour, was
the herding of the cattle; the only wealth of the Mormons, and more

and more cherished by them, with the increasing pastoral character of their lives. A camp could not be pitched in any spot without soon exhausting the freshness of the pasture around it; and it became an ever recurring task to guide the cattle, in unbroken droves, to the nearest places where it was still fresh and fattening. Sometimes it was necessary to go farther, to distant ranges which were known as

MORMON MOWERS.

feeding grounds of the buffalo. About these there were sure to prowl parties of thievish Indians; and each drove therefore had its escort of mounted men and boys, who learned self-reliance and heroism, while on night guard alone, among the silent hills. But generally the cattle were driven from the camp at the dawn of morning, and brought back thousands together in the evening, to be picketed in the great corral or enclosure, where beeves, bulls, cows, and oxen, with the horses, mules, hogs, calves, sheep, and human beings, could all look together upon the red watch-fires, with the feeling of security, when aroused by the Indian stampede, or the howlings of the prairie wolves at moonrise.

When they set about building their winter houses, too, the Mormons went into quite considerable timbering operations, and performed desperate feats of carpentry. They did not come ornamental gentlemen or raw apprentices, to extemporize new versions of Robinson Crusoe. It was a comfort to notice the readiness with which they turned their hands to wood-craft; some of them, though I believe these had generally been bred carpenters, wheel-wrights, or more particularly boat-builders, quite outdoing the most notable *royageurs* in the use of the axe. One of these would fell a tree, strip off its bark, cut and split up the trunk in piles of plank, scantling, or shingles; make posts, and pins, and pales—everything wanted almost, of the branches; and treat his toil from first to last with more sportive flourish than a school-boy whittling his shingle.

Inside the camp, the chief labours were assigned to the women. From the moment, when after the halt, the lines had been laid, the spring-wells dug out, and the ovens and fire-places built, though the men still assumed to set the guards and enforce the regulations of police, the Empire of the Tented Town was with the better sex. They were the chief comforters of the severest sufferers, the kind nurses who gave them in their sickness those dear attentions with which pauperism is hardly poor, and which the greatest wealth often fails to buy; and they were a nation of most wonderful managers. They could hardly be called housewives in etymological strictness; but it was plain that they had once been such, and most distinguished ones. Their art availed them in their changed affairs. With almost their entire culinary material, limited to the milk of their cows, some store of meal or flour, and a very few condiments, they brought their thousand and one receipts into play with a success that outdid for their families the miracle of the Hebrew widow's cruise. They learned to make butter on a march by the dashing of the waggon, and so nicely to calculate the working of barm in the jolting heats, that as soon after the halt as an oven could be dug in the hill-side and heated, their well-kneaded loaf was ready for baking, and produced good leavened bread for supper. I have no doubt the appetizing zest, their humble lore succeeded in imparting to diet which was both simple and meagre, availed materially for the health as well as the comfort of the people.

But the first duty of the Mormon women was, through all change of place and fortune, to keep alive the altar fire of home. Whatever their manifold labours for the day, it was their effort to complete them against the sacred hour of evening fall; for, by that time, all the out-workers, scouts, ferrymen, or bridgemen, road-makers, herdsmen, or hay-makers, had finished their tasks, and come in to their rest; and before the last smoke of the supper-fire curled up, reddening in the glow of sunset, a hundred chimes of cattle bells announced their looked-for approach across the open hills, and the women went out to meet them at the camp gates, and with their children in their laps sat by them at the cherished family meal, and talked over the events of the well-spent day.

But every day closed, as every day began, with an invocation of the Divine favour; without which, indeed, no Mormon seemed to dare to lay him down to rest. With the first shining of the stars, laughter and loud talking hushed, the neighbour went his way, you heard the last hymn sung, and then the thousand-voiced murmur of prayer was heard like bubbling water falling down the hills.

There was no austerity, however, about the religion of Mormonism. Their fasting and penance, it is no jest to say, was altogether involuntary; they made no merit of that; They kept the Sabbath with considerable strictness; they were too close copyists of the wanderers of Israel in other respects not to have learned, like them, the value of this most admirable of the Egypto-Mosaic institutions. But the rest of the week their religion was independent of ritual observance. They had the sort of strong stomached faith that is still found embalmed in sheltered spots of Catholic Italy and Spain, with the spirit of the believing or dark ages. It was altogether too strongly felt to be dependent on intellectual ingenuity or careful caution of the ridiculous. It mixed itself up fearlessly with the common transactions of their every-day life, and only to give them liveliness and colour.

If any passages of life bear better than others a double interpretation, they are the adventures of travel and of the field. What old persons call discomforts and discouraging mishaps, are the very elements to the young and sanguine, of what they are willing to term fun. The Mormons took the young and hopeful side. They could make sport and frolic of their trials, and often turn right sharp suffering into right round laughter against themselves. I certainly heard more jests and Joe Millers while in this Papillon camp than I am likely to hear in all the remainder of my days.

This, too, was at a time of serious affliction. Besides the ordinary suffering from insufficient food and shelter, distressing and mortal sickness, exacerbated, if not originated by these causes, was greatly prevalent.

In the camp nearest us on the west, which was that of the bridging party near the Corne, the number of its inhabitants being small enough to invite computation, I found, as early as the 31st of July, that 37 per cent. of its inhabitants were down with the fever, and a sort of strange scorbutic disease, frequently fatal, which they named the Black Canker. The camps to the east of us, which were all on the eastern side of the Missouri, were yet worse fated.

The climate of the entire upper " Misery Bottom," as they term it, is, during a considerable part of summer and autumn, singularly pestiferous. Its rich soil, which is to a depth far beyond the reach of the plough as flat as the earth of kitchen garden, or compost heap, is annually the force-bed of a vegetation as rank as that of the tropics.

To render its fatal fertility the greater, it is everywhere freely watered by springs and creeks, and larger streams, that flow into it from both sides. In the season of drought, when the sun enters Virgo, these dry down till they run impure as open sewers, exposing to the day foul broad flats, mere quagmires of black dirt, stretching along for miles, unvaried, except by the limbs of half-buried carrion, tree trunks, or by occasional yellow pools of what the children call frog spawn: all together steaming up thick vapours redolent of the savour of death.

The same is the habit of the Great River. In the beginning of August, its shores hardly could contain the millions of forest logs, and tens of billions of gallons of turbid water that came rushing down together from its mountain head-gates. But before the month was out, the freshet had all passed by ; the river diminished one half, threaded feebly southward through the centre of the valley, and the mud of its channel, baked and creased, made a wide tile pavement between the choking crowd of reeds and sedgy grasses, and wet stalked weeds, and growths of marsh meadow flowers, the garden homes at this tainted season of venom, crazy snakes, and the fresher ooze by the water's edge, which stank in the sun like a naked muscle shoal.

Then the plague raged. I have no means of ascertaining the mortality of the Indians who inhabited the Bottom. In 1845, the year previous, which was not more unhealthy, they lost one-ninth of their number in about two months. The Mormons were scourged severely. The exceeding mortality among some of them was no doubt in the main attributable to the low state to which their systems had been brought by long-continued endurance of want and hardship. It is to be remembered also that they were the first turners up of the prairie sod, and that this of itself made them liable to the sickness of new countries. It was where their agricultural operations had been most considerable, and in situations on the left bank of the river, where the prevalent south-west winds wafted to them the miasmata of its shores, that disease was most rife.

In some of these, the fever prevailed to such an extent that hardly any escaped it. They let their cows go unmilked ; they wanted for voices to raise the psalm of Sundays ; the few who were able to keep their feet, went about among the tents and waggons with food and water, like nurses through the wards of an infirmary. Here, at one time, the digging got behind hand ; burials were slow ; and you might see women sit in the open tents keeping the flies off their dead children, some time after decomposition had set in.

In our own camp, for a part of August and September, things wore an unpleasant aspect enough. Its situation was one much praised for its comparative salubrity ; but perhaps on this account the number of cases of fever among us was increased by the hurrying arrival from other localities of parties in whom the virus leaven of disease was fermented by forced travel.

But I am excused sufficiently the attempt to get up for your entertainment here any circumstantial picture of horrors, by the fact, that at the most interesting season, I was incapacitated for nice observation by an attack of fever—mine was what they call the congestive—that it required the utmost use of all my faculties to recover from. I still kept my tent in the camp line; but, for as much as a month, had very small notion of what went on among my neighbours. I recollect overhearing a lamentation over some dear baby, that its mother no doubt thought the destroying angel should have been specially instructed to spare.

I wish, too, for my own sake, I could forget how imperfectly, one day, I mourned the decease of a poor Saint, who, by clamour, rendered his vicinity troublesome. He no doubt endured great pain; for he groaned shockingly till death came to his relief. He interfered with my own hard gained slumbers, and I was glad when death did relieve him.

Before my attack, I was fond of conversing with an amiable old man, I think English born, who, having then recently buried his only daughter and grandson, used to be seen sitting out before his tent, resting his sorrowful forehead on his hands, joined over a smooth white oak staff. I missed him when I got about again; probably he had been my moaning neighbour.

So, too, having been much exercised in my dreams at this time, by the vision of dismal processions, such as might have been formed by the union in line of all the forlornest and ugliest of the struggling fugitives from Nauvoo, I happen to recall, as I write, that I had some knowledge somewhere of one of our new comers, for whom the nightmare revived, and repeated without intermission, the torment of his trying journey. As he lay feeding life with long drawn breaths, he muttered, " Where 's next water ? Team—give out ! Hot, hot—God, it 's hot: Stop the waggon—stop the waggon—stop, stop the waggon ! " They woke him ;—to his own content—but I believe returning sleep ever renewed his distressing visions, till the sounder slumber came on from which no earthly hand or voice could rouse him : into which, I hope, he did not carry them.

In a half dreamy way, I remember, or think I remember, a crowd of phantoms like these. I recall but one fact, however, going far in proof of a considerable mortality. Earlier in the season, while going westward with the intention of passing the Rocky Mountains that summer, I had opened with the assistance of Mormon spades and sho-

vels, a large mound on a commanding elevation, the tomb of a warrior of the ancient race ; and continuing on my way, had left a deep
trench excavated entirely through it. Returning fever-struck to the
Papillon Camp, I found it planted close by this spot. It was just
forming as I arrived ; the first waggon, if I mistake not, having but
a day or two halted into place. My first airing upon my convales-
cence took me to the mound, which, probably to save digging, had
been re-adapted to its original purpose. In this brief interval, they
had filled the trench with bodies, and furrowed the ground with
graves around it, like the ploughing of a field.

The lengthened sojourn of the Mormons in this insalubrious region,
was imposed upon them by circumstances which I must now ad-
vert to.

Though the season was late when they first crossed the Missouri,
some of them moved forward with great hopefulness, full of the notion
of viewing and choosing their new homes that year. But the van
had only reached Grand Island and the Pawnee villages, when they
were overtaken by more ill news from Nauvoo. Before the summer
closed, their enemies set upon the last remnant of those who were
left behind in Illinois. They were a few lingerers, who could not be
persuaded but there might yet be time for them to gather up their
worldly goods before removing, some weakly mothers and their infants,
a few delicate young girls, and many cripples and bereaved and sick
people. These had remained under shelter, according to the Mormon
statement at least, by virtue of an express covenant in their behalf.
If there was such a covenant, it was broken. A vindictive war was
waged upon them, from which the weakest fled in scattered parties,
leaving the rest to make a reluctant and almost ludicrously unavailing
defence till the 17th day of September, when one thousand six hundred and twenty-five troops entered Nauvoo, and drove all forth who
had not retreated before that time.

Like the wounded birds of a flock fired into toward nightfall, they
came straggling on with faltering steps, many of them without bag or
baggage, beast or barrow, all asking shelter or burial, and forcing a
fresh repartition of the already divided rations of their friends. It
was plain now that every energy must be taxed to prevent the entire
expedition from perishing. Further emigration for the time was out
out of the question, and the whole people prepared themselves for
encountering another winter on the prairie.

Happily for the main body, they found themselves at this juncture
among Indians, who were amicably disposed. The lands on both
sides of the Missouri in particular were owned by the Pottawatamies
and Omahas, two tribes whom unjust treatment by our United States,

had the effect of rendering most auspiciously hospitable to strangers whom they regarded as persecuted like themselves.

The Pottawatamies, on the eastern side, are a nation from whom the United States bought some years ago a number of hundred thoutand acres of the finest lands they have every brought into market. Whatever the bargain was, the sellers were not content with it; the people saying, their leaders were cheated, made drunk, bribed, and all manner of naughty things besides. No doubt this was quite as much of a libel on the fair fame of this particular Indian treaty, as such stories generally are; for the land to which the tribe was removed in pursuance of it, was admirably adapted to enforce habits of civilized thrift. It was smooth prairie, wanting in timber, and of course in game; and the humane and philanthropic might rejoice therefore that necessity would soon indoctrinate its inhabitants into the practice of agriculture. An impracticable few, who may have thought these advantages more than compensated by the insalubrity of their allotted resting-place, fled to the extreme wilds, where they could find deer and woods, and rocks, and running water, and where, I believe, they are roaming to this day. The remainder, being what the political vocabulary designates on such occasions as Friendly Indians, were driven—marched is the word—galley-slaves are marched thus to Barcelona and Toulon—marched from the Mississippi to the Missouri, and planted there. Discontented and unhappy, they had hardly begun to form an attachment for this new soil, when they were persuaded to change it for their present *Fever Patch*, upon the Kaw or Kansas River. They were under this second sentence of transportation when the Mormons arrived among them.

They were pleased with the Mormons. They would have been pleased with any whites who would not cheat them, nor sell them whiskey, nor whip them for their poor gipsy habits, nor bear themselves indecently toward their women, many of whom, among the Pottawatamies, especially those of nearly unmixed French descent, are singularly comely, and some of them educated. But all Indians have something like a sentiment of reverence for the insane, and admire those who sacrifice, without apparent motive, their worldly welfare to the triumph of an idea. They understand the meaning of what they call a great vow, and think it the duty of the right-minded to lighten the votary's penance under it. To this feeling they united the sympathy of fellow-sufferers for those who could talk to them of their own Illinois, and tell the story how from it they also had been ruthlessly expelled.

Their hospitality was sincere, almost delicate. Fanny Le Clerc, the spoiled child of the great brave, Pied Riche, interpreter of the

Nation, would have the pale-face, Miss Devine, learn duetts with her to the guitar; and the daughter of substantial Joseph La Framboise, the interpreter of the United States,—she died of the fever that summer,—welcomed all the nicest young Mormon Kitties and Lizzies, and Jennies and Susans, to a coffee-feast at her father's house, which was probably the best cabin in the river village. They made the Mormons at home there and elsewhere. Upon all their lands they formally gave them leave to tarry just so long as should suit their own good pleasure.

The affair, of course, furnished material for a solemn council. Under the auspices of an officer of the United States, their chiefs were summoned, in the form befitting great occasions, to meet in the dirty yard of one Mr. P. A. Sarpy's log trading house, at their village. They came in grand toilet, moving in their fantastic attire with so much aplomb and genteel measure, that the stranger found it difficult not to believe them high-born gentlemen, attending a costumed ball. Their aristocratically thin legs, of which they displayed fully the usual Indian proportion, aided this illusion. There is something too, at all times, very mock-Indian in the theatrical French millinery tie of the Pottawatamie turban; while it is next to impossible for a sober white man, at first sight, to believe that the red, green, black, blue and yellow cosmetics, with which he sees such grave personages so variously dotted, diapered, cancelled and arabesqued, are worn by them in any mood but one of the deepest and most desperate quizzing. From the time of their first squat upon the ground, to the final breaking up of the council circle, they sustained their characters with equal self-possession and address.

I will not take it upon myself to describe their order of ceremonies. Indeed, I ought not, since I have never been able to view the habits and customs of our Aborigines in any other light than that of a reluctant and sorrowful subject of jest. Besides, in this instance, the displays of pow-wow and eloquence were both probably moderated by the conduct of the entire transaction on temperance principles. I therefore content myself with observing, generally, that the proceedings were such as every way became the grandeur of the parties interested, and the magnitude of the interests involved. When the Red Men had indulged to satiety in tobacco smoke from their peace-pipes, and in what they love still better, their peculiar metaphoric rhodomontade, which, beginning with the celestial bodies, and coursing downwards over the grandest sublunary objects, always managed to alight at last on their Grand Father Polk, and the tenderness for him of his affectionate coloured children. All the solemn funny fellows present, who played the part of chiefs, signed formal articles of convention with their unpronounceable names.

The renowned chief, Pied Riche — he was surnamed Le Clerc on account of his remarkable scholarship,—then rose, and said :—

" MY MORMON BRETHREN,—The Pottawatamie came sad and tired into this unhealthy Missouri Bottom, not many years back, when he was taken from his beautiful country beyond the Mississippi, which had abundant game, and timber, and clear water everywhere. Now you are driven away the same from your lodges and lands there, and the graves of your people. So we have both suffered. We must help one another, and the Great Spirit will help us both. You are now free to cut and use all the wood you may wish. You can make all your improvements, and live on any part of our actual land not occupied by us. Because one suffers, and does not deserve it, it is no reason he shall suffer always, I say. We may live to see all right yet. However, if we do not, our children will.—*Bon jour*."

And thus ended the pageant. I give this speech as a morsel of real Indian. It was recited to me after the treaty by the Pottawatamie orator in French, which language he spoke with elegance. *Bon jour* is the French, Indian, and English hail and farewell of the Pottawatamies.

The other entertainers of the Mormons at this time, the Omahas, or Mahaws, are one of the union tribes of the Grand Prairie. Their Great Father, the United States, has found it inconvenient to protect so remote a dependency against the overpowering league of the Dahcotahs or Sioux, and has judged it dangerous, at the same time, to allow them to protect themselves, by entering into a confederation with others. Under the pressure of this paternal embarrassment and restraint, it has therefore happened most naturally, that this tribe, once a powerful and valued ally of ours, has been reduced to a band of little more than a hundred families; and these, a few years more will entirely extinguish. When I was among them, they were so ill fed, that their protruding high cheek bones gave them the air of a tribe of consumptives. The buffalo had left them, and no good ranges lay within several hundred miles reach. Hardly any other game found cover on their land. What little there was they were short of ammunition to kill. Their annuity from the United States was trifling. They made next to nothing at thieving. They had planted some corn in their awkward Indian fashion, but through fear of ambush dared not venture out to harvest it. A chief resource for them the winter previous had been the spoliation of their neighbours, the Prairie Field Mice.

These interesting little people, more industrious and thrifty than the Mahaws, garner up in the neat little cellars of their underground homes, the small seeds or beans of the wood pea vine, which are black and hard, but quite nutritious. Gathering them one by one,

a single mouse will thus collect as much as half a pint, which before
the cold weather sets in he piles away in a dry and frost proof exca-
vation, cleverly thatched and covered in.   The Omaha animal, who,
like enough, may have idled during all the season the mouse was
amassing his toilsome treasure, finds this subterranean granary to give
out a certain peculiar cavernous vibration, when briskly tapped upon
above the ground.   He wanders about, therefore, striking with a wand
in hopeful spots ; and as soon as he hears the hollow sound he knows,
unearths the little retired capitalist, along with his winter's hope.
Mouse wakes up from his nap to starve, and Mahaw swallows several
relishing mouthfuls.

But the mouse has his revenge in the powerful Sioux, who wages
against his wretched red brother an almost bootless but exterminating
warfare.   He robs him of his poor human peltry.   One of my friends
was offered for sale a Sioux scalp of Omaha, " with grey hair nearly
as long as a white horse's tail."

The pauper Omahas were ready to solicit as a favour the residence
of white protectors among them.   The Mormons harvested and stored
away for them their crops of maize ; with all their own poverty, they
spared them food enough besides, from time to time, to save them from
absolutely starving; and their entrenched camp, to the north of the
Omaha villages, served as a sort of breakwater between them and the
destroying rush of the Sioux.

This was the Head Quarters of the Mormon Camps of Israel.   The
miles of rich prairie enclosed and sowed with the grain they could
contrive to spare, and the houses, stacks, and cattle shelters, had the
seeming of an entire county, with its people and improvements transplanted there unbroken.   On a pretty plateau, overlooking the river,
they built more than seven hundred houses in a single town, neatly
laid out with highways and byways, and fortified with breast-work,
stockade, and blockhouses.   It had, too, its place of worhip, " Tabernacle of the Congregation," and various large workshops, and mills
and factories, provided with water power.

They had no camp or settlement of equal size in the Pottowatamie
country.   There was less to apprehend here from Indian invasion ;
and the people scattered themselves, therefore, along the rivers and
streams, and in the timber-groves, wherever they found inviting localities for farming operations.   In this way many of them acquired
what have since proved to be valuable pre-emption rights.

Upon the Pottowatamie lands, scattered through the border regions
of Missouri and Iowa, in the Sauk and Fox country, a few among the
Ioways, among the Poncahs in a great company upon the banks of the
L'Eau qui Coule, or Running Water River, and at the Omaha winter-

quarters;—the Mormons sustained themselves through the heavy winter of 1846-1847. It was the severest of their trials; and if I aimed at rhetorical effect, I would be bound to offer you a minute narrative of its progress, as a sort of climax to my history. But I have, I think, given you enough of the Mormon's sorrows. We are all of us content to sympathize with a certain extent of suffering; but very few can bear the recurring yet scarcely varied narrative of another's distress without something of impatience. The world is full of griefs, and we cannot afford to extend too large a share of our charity, or even our commiseration in a single quarter.

This winter was the turning-point of the Mormon fortunes: those who lived through it were spared to witness the gradual return of better times; and they now liken it to the passing of a dreary night, since which they have watched the coming of a steadily brightening day.

Before the grass-growth of 1847, a body of one hundred and forty-three picked men, with seventy waggons, drawn by their best horses, left the Omaha quarters under the command of the members of the High Council who had wintered there. They carried with them little but seed and farming implements, their aim being to plant spring crops at their ultimate destination. They relied on their rifles to give them food, but rarely left their road in search of game. They made long daily marches, and moved with as much rapidity as possible.

PASS OF THE STANDING ROCK.

Against the season when ordinary emigration passes the Missouri, they were already through the South Pass; and a couple of short days' travel beyond it, entered upon the more arduous portion of their journey. It lay, in earnest, through the Rocky Mountains. They turned Fremont's Peak, Long's Peak, the Twins, and other King summits, but had to force their way over other mountains of the rugged Utah range, sometimes following the stony bed of torrents, the head waters of some of the mightiest rivers of our continent, and sometimes literally cutting their road through heavy and ragged timber. They arrived at the grand basin of the Great Salt Lake much exhausted, but without losing a man, and in time to plant for a partial autumn harvest.

Another party started after these pioneers, from the Omaha winter quarters, in the summer. They had 566 waggons, and carried large quantities of grain, which they were able to put in the ground before it froze.

The same season also, these were joined by a part of the Battalion, and other members of the Church, who came eastward from California and the Sandwich Islands. Together, they fortified themselves strongly with sunbrick wall and blockhouses, and living safely through the winter, were able to tend crops that yielded ample provision for the ensuing year.

In 1848, nearly all the remaining members of the Church left the Missouri country in a succession of powerful bands, invigorated and enriched by their abundant harvests there; and that year so fully established their Commonwealth of the New Covenant, the future State of Deseret.

I may not undertake to describe to you, in a single lecture, the geography of Deseret, and its great basin. Were I to consider the face of the country, its military position, or its climate, and its natural productions, each head, I am confident, would claim more time than you have now to spare me; for Deseret is emphatically a new country; new in its own characteristic features, newer still in its bringing together within its limits the most inconsistent peculiarities of other countries. I cannot aptly compare it to any. Descend from the mountains, where you have the scenery and climate of Switzerland, to seek the sky of your choice among the many climates of Italy, and you may find welling out of the same hills the freezing springs of Mexico and the hot springs of Iceland, both together coursing their way to the Salt Sea of Palestine, in the plain below. The pages of Malte Brun provide me with a less truthful parallel to it than those which describe the happy Valley of Rasselas, or the Continent of Balnibarbi.

Let me, then, press on with my history, during the few minutes that remain for me.

Only two events have occurred to menace seriously the establishment at Deseret : the first threatened to destroy its crops, the other to break it up altogether.

The shores of the Salt Lake are infested by a sort of insect pest, which claims a vile resemblance to the locust of the Syrian Dead Sea. Wingless, dumpy, black, swollen-headed, with bulging eyes in cases like goggles, mounted upon legs of steel wire and clock spring, and with a general personal appearance that justified the Mormons in comparing him to a cross of the spider and the buffalo, the Deseret cricket comes down from the mountains at a certain season of the year, in voracious and desolating myriads. It was just at this season that the first crops of the new settlers were in the full glory of their youthful green. The assailants could not be repulsed. The Mormons, after their fashion, prayed and fought, and fought and prayed, but to no purpose; the " Black Philistines " mowed their way even with the ground, leaving it as if touched with an acid, or burnt by fire.

But an unlooked for ally came to the rescue. Vast armies of bright birds, before strangers to the valley, hastened across the lake from some unknown quarter, and gorged themselves upon the well-fatted enemy. They were snow-white, with little heads, and clear, dark eyes, and little feet, and long wings, that arched in flight " like an angel's." At first the Mormons thought they were new enemies to plague them; but when they found them hostile only to the locusts, they were careful not to molest them in their friendly office ; and to this end declared a heavy fine against all who should kill or annoy them with fire-arms. The gulls soon grew to be tame as the poultry, and the delighted little children learned to call them their pigeons. They disappeared every evening beyond the lake ; but, returning with sunrise, continued their welcome visitings till the crickets were all exterminated.

This curious incident recurred the following year, with this variation, that, in 1849, the gulls came earlier, and saved the wheat crops from all harm whatever.

A severer trial than the visit of the cricket locusts threatened Deseret, in the discovery of the gold of California. It was due to a party of the Mormon Battalion recruited on the Missouri, who, on their way home, found employment at New Helvetia. They were digging a mill race there, and threw up the gold dust with their shovels. You all know the crazy fever that broke out as soon as this was announced. It infected every one through California. Where the gold was discovered, at Sutter's and around, the standing grain was left uncut ; whites, Indians, and mustees, all set them to gathering gold, every other labour forsaken, as if the first comers could rob the casket of all that it contained. The disbanded soldiers came to the valley; they showed their poor companions pieces of the yellow treasure they had gained; and the cry was raised, "To California! To the Gold of Ophir, our brethren have discovered! To California!"

Some of you have, perhaps, come across the half ironic instructions of the heads of the Church to the faithful outside the Valley:—

"THE TRUE USE OF GOLD is for paving streets, covering houses, and making culinary dishes; and when the Saints shall have preached the Gospel, raised grain, and built up cities enough, the Lord will open up the way for a supply of gold, to the perfect satisfaction of his people. Until then, let them not be over-anxious, for the treasures of the earth are in the Lord's storehouse, and he will open the doors thereof when and where he pleases."

The enlightened virtue of their rulers saved the people and the fortunes of Deseret. A few only went away—and they were asked in kindness never to return. The rest remained to be healthy and happy, to "raise grain and build up cities."

The history of the Mormons has ever since been the unbroken record of the most wonderful prosperity. It has looked as though the elements of fortune, obedient to a law of natural re-action, were struggling to compensate to them their undue share of suffering. They may be pardoned for deeming it miraculous. But, in truth, the economist accounts for it all, who explains to us the speedy recuperation of cities, laid in ruin by flood, fire, and earthquake. During its years of trial, Mormon labour has subsisted on insufficient capital, and under many trials, but it *has* subsisted, and survives them now, as intelligent and powerful as ever it was at Nauvoo; with this difference, that it has in the meantime been educated to habits of unmatched thrift, energy, and endurance, and has been transplanted to a situation where it is in every respect more productive. Moreover, during all the period of their journey, while some have gained by practice in handicraft, and the experience of repeated essays at their various halting-places, the minds of all have been busy framing designs and planning the improvements they have since found opportunity to execute.

The territory of the Mormons is unequalled as a stock-raising country. The finest pastures of Lombardy are not more estimable than those on the east side of the Utah Lake and Jordan River. We find here that cereal anomaly, the Bunch grass. In May, when the other grasses push, this fine plant dries upon its stalk, and becomes a light yellow straw, full of flavour and nourishment. It continues thus, through what are the dry months of the climate, till January,

and then starts with a vigorous growth, like that of our own winter wheat in April, which keep on till the return of another
May. Whether as straw or grass, the cattle fatten on it the year
round. The numerous little dells and sheltered spots that are found
in the mountains, are excellent sheep-walks; it is said that the wool
which is grown upon them is of an unusually fine pile and soft tex-
ture. Hogs fatten on a succulent bulb or tuber, called the Seacoe, or
Seegose Root, which I hope will soon be naturalized with us. It is
highly esteemed as a table vegetable by Mormons and Indians, and I
remark that they are cultivating it with interest at the French Garden of Plants. The emigrant poultry have taken the best care of
each other, only needing liberty to provide themselves with every
other blessing.

The Mormons have also been singularly happy in their Indian relations. They have not made the common mistake of supposing savages
insensible to courtesy of demeanour; but, being taught by their religion to regard them all as decayed brethren, have always treated the
silly, wicked souls with kind-hearted civility. Though their outlay
for tobacco, wampum, and vermillion has been of the very smallest,
yet they have never failed to purchase what goodwill they have
wanted.

Hence it happens that in their Land of Promise they are on the best
of terms with all the Canaanites, and Hittites, and Hivites, and Amorites,
and Gergashites, and Perizzites, and Jebusites, within its borders;
while they "maintain their cherished relations of amity with the rest
of mankind," who, in their case, include a sort of latest remnant of the
primeval primates, called the Root Diggers. The Diggers, who in
stature, strength, and general personal appearance, may be likened to
a society of old negro women, are only to be dreaded for their exceeding ugliness. The tribes that rob and murder in war, and otherwise
live more like white men, are however numerous all around them.

Fortunately, upon the marauding expeditions, and in matters that
affect their freebooting relations generally, they all obey the great
war-chief of the tribe called the Utahs, in the heart of whose proper
territory the Mormon settlements are comprehended.

If accounts are true, the Utahs are brave fellows. They differ
obviously from the deceased nations, to whose estates we have taken
it upon ourselves to administer. They ride strong, well-limbed Spanish horses, not ponies; bear well cut rifles, not shot-guns, across their
saddle-bows, and are not without some idea of military discipline.
They carry their forays far into the Mexican States, laying the nha-
bitants under contribution, and taking captive persons of condition,
whom they hold to ransom. They are, as yet at least, little given to

drink; some of them manifest considerable desire to acquire useful knowledge; and they are attached to their own infidel notions of religion, making long journeys to the ancient cities of the Colorado, to worship among the ruined temples there. The Soldan of these red Paynims, too, their great war chief, is not without his knightly graces. According to some of the Mormons, he is the paragon of Indians. His name, translated to diminish its excellence as an exercise in Prosody, is Walker. He is a fine figure of a man, in the prime of life. He excels in various manly exercises, is a crack shot, a rough rider, and a great judge of horse flesh.

He is besides very clever, in our sense of the word. He is a peculiarly eloquent master of the graceful alphabet of pantomime, which stranger tribes employ to communicate with one another. He has picked up some English, and is familiar with Spanish and several Indian tongues. He rather affects the fine gentleman. When it is his pleasure to extend his riding excursions into Mexico, to inflict or threaten outrage, or to receive the instalments of his black mail salary, he will take offence if the poor people there fail to kill their fattest beeves, and adopt other measures to show him obsequious and distinguished attention. He has more than one black-eyed mistress there, acco ding to his own account, to whom he makes love in her own language. His dress is a full suit of the richest broadcloth, generally brown, cut in European fashion, with a shining beaver hat, and fine cambric shirt. To these he adds his own gaudy Indian trimmings, and in this way contrives, they say, to look superbly, when he rides at the head of his troop, whose richly caparisoned horses, with their embroidered saddles and harness, shine and tinkle as they prance under the weight of gay metal ornaments.

With all his wild-cat fierceness, Walker is perfectly velvet-pawed to the Mormons. There is a queer story about his being influenced in their favour by a dream. It is the fact, that from the first he has received the Mormon exiles into his kingdom with a generosity that, in its limited sphere, transcends that of the Grand Monarch to the English Jacobites. He rejoices to give them the information they want about the character of the country under his rule, advises with them as to the advantages of particular localities, and wherever they choose to make their settlements, guarantees them personal safety, and immunity from depredation.

From the first, therefore, the Mormons have had little or nothing to do in Deseret, but attend to their mechanical and strictly agricultural pursuits. They have made several successful settlements; the farthest north, at what they term Brownsville, is above forty miles; and the farthest south, in a valley called the Sanpeech, two hundred miles from that first formed. A duplicate of the Lake Tiberias, or Genesareth. empties its waters into the innocent Dead Sea of Deseret, by a fine river, to which the Mormons have given the name—it was impossible to give it any other—of the Western Jordan.

It was on the right bank of the stream, at a choice spot upon a rich table land, traversed by a great company of exhaustless streams falling from the highlands, that the Pioneer band of Mormons, coming out of the mountains in the night, pitched their first camp in the Valley, and consecrated the ground. Curiously enough, this very spot proved the most favourable site for their chief settlement, and after exploring the whole country, they have founded on it their city of the New Hierusalem. Its houses are spread to command as much as possible the farms, which are laid out in wards or cantons, with a common fence to each ward. The farms in wheat already cover a space greater than the district of Columbia, over all of which they have completed the canals, and other arrangements, for bountiful irrigation, after the manner of the cultivators of the East. The houses are distributed over an area nearly as great as the City of New York.

They have little thought as yet of luxury in their public buildings; but they will soon have nearly completed a large common public store-many house and granary, and a great sized public bath-house. One of the wonderful thermal springs of the valley, a white sulphur water, of the temperature of 102° Fahrenheit, with a head "the thickness of a man's body," they have already brought into the town for this purpose; and all have learned the habit of indulging in it. They have besides a yellow brick meeting-house, one hundred feet by sixty, in which they gather on Sundays and in the week-day evenings; but this is only a temporary structure. They have reserved a summit level in the heart of the city, for the site of a Temple far superior to that of Nauvoo, which, in the days of their future wealth and power, is to be the landmark of the Basin, and goal of future pilgrims.

They mean to seek no other resting-place. After pitching camps enough to exhaust many times over the chapter of names in 33rd Numbers, they have at last come to their Promised Land, and, "behold, it is a good land and large, and flowing with milk and honey;" and here again for them, as at Nauvoo, the forge smokes and the anvil rings, and whirring wheels go round. Again has returned the merry sport of childhood, and the evening quiet of old age, and again dear house-pet flowers bloom in garden plots round happy homes.

It is to these homes, in the heart of our American Alps, like the holy people of the Grand Saint Bernard, they hold out their welcome to the passing traveller. Some of you have probably seen, in the St.

Louis papers, the repeated votes of thanks to them of companies of emigrants to California. These are often reduced to great straits after passing Fort-Laramie, and turn aside to seek the Salt Lake Colony in pitiable plights of fatigue and destitution. The road, after leaving the Oregon trace, is one of increasing difficulty; and when the last mountain has been crossed, passes along the bottom of a deep Canon, whose scenery is of an almost terrific gloom. It is a defile that I trust no Mormon Martin Hofer of this Western Tyrol will be called to consecrate to liberty with blood. At every turn, the overhanging cliffs threaten to break down upon the little torrent river that has worn its way at their base. Indeed, the narrow ravine is so serrated by this stream, that the road crosses it from one side to the other, something like forty times in the last five miles. At the end of the ravine, the emigrant comes abruptly out of the dark pass into the lighted valley, on an even bench or terrace of its upper table land. No wonder if he loses his self-control here. A ravishing panoramic landscape opens out below him, blue, and green, and gold, and pearl; a great sea with hilly islands, rivers, a lake, and broad sheets of grassy plain, all set, as in a silver-chased cup, within mountains whose peaks of perpetual snow are burnished by a dazzling sun. It is less these, however, than the fore-ground of old country farms, with their stacks, and thatchings, and stock, and the central city, smoking from its chimneys, and swarming with working inhabitants, that tries the men of fatigue broken nerves. The "Californeys" scream, they sing, they give three cheers, and do not count them; a few have prayed more swear, some fall on their faces, and cry outright. News arrived a few days since from a poor townsman of ours, a journeyman saddler, that used to work up Market Street beyond Broad, by name Gillian, who sought the Valley, his cattle given out, and himself broke down and half heart-broken. The recluse Mormons fed and housed him and his party, and he made his way through to the gold diggings with restored health and strength. To Gillian's credit for manhood, should perhaps be cited his own allegation, that he first whistled through his fingers various popular nocturnal, street, circus, and theatre calls; but it is certain that, when my tidings speak of him, which was when he was afterwards hospitably entreated by a Mormon, whom he knew ten years ago as one of our Chester county farmers, he was completely dissolved into something not far from the hysterics, and wept on till the tears ran down his dusty beard.

Several hundred emigrants, in more or less distress, received gratuitous assistance last year from the Mormons.

Their community must go on thriving. They are to be the chief workers and contractors upon "Whitney's Railroad," or whatever scheme is to unite the Atlantic and Pacific by way of the South Pass; and their valley must be its central station. They have already raised a "Perpetual Fund" for "the final fulfilment of the covenant made by the Saints in the Temple at Nauvoo," which "is not to cease till all the poor are brought to the Valley." All the poor still lingering behind, will be brought there; so at an early period, will the fifty thousand communicants, the Church already numbers in Great Britain, with all the other "increase among the Gentiles." Their place of rendezvous will be upon what were formerly the Pottawatamie lands. The interests of the stake have been admirably cared for. It now comprises the thriving counties of "Fremont" and "Pottawatamie," in which the Mormons still number a majority of the inhabitants. Their chief town is growing rapidly, already boasting over three thousand inhabitants, with nineteen large merchants' stores, the mail lines and five regular steam-packets running to it, and other western evidences of prosperity; besides a fine Music Hall and public buildings, and the printing establishment of a very ably edited newspaper, *The Frontier Guardian.*

It is probably the best station on the Missouri for commencing the overland journey to Oregon and California; as travellers can follow directly from it the Mormon road, which, in addition to other advantages, proves to be more salubrious than those to the south of it. Large numbers are expected to arrive at this point from England during the present spring, on their way to the Salt Lake. They will repay their welcome; for every working person gained to the hive of their "Honey State" counts as added wealth. So far, the Mormons write in congratulation, that they have not among them "a single loafer, rich or poor, idle gentleman, or lazy vagabond." They are no communists; but their experience has taught them the gain of joint-stock to capital, and combination to labour,—perhaps something more; for I remark they have recently made arrangements "to classify their mechanics," which is probably a step in the right direction. They will be successful manufacturers, for their vigorous land-locked industry cannot be tampered with by protection. They have no gold—they have not hunted for it; but they have found wealth of other valuable minerals: rock-salt enough to do the curing of the world,—"We'll salt the Union for you," they write, "if you can't preserve it in any other way;" perhaps coal; excellent ores of iron everywhere. They are near enough, however, to the Californian Sierra to be the chief quartermasters of its miners; and they will dig their own gold in their unlimited fields of admirably fertile land. I should only invite your incredulity, and the disgust of the Horticultural Society, by giving you certain measurements of mammoth beets, turnips, pumpkins, and garden vegetables, in my possession. In that country where stock thrives care-free,—where a poor man's thirty-two potatoes saved can return him eighteen bushels, and two and a-half bushels of wheat sown yield three hundred and fifty bushels in a season,—or where an average crop of wheat on irrigated lands is fifty bushels to the acre; the farmer's part is hardly to be despised. Certainly it will not be under a continuance of the present prices-current of the region, wheat at four dollars the bushel, and flour twelve dollars the cwt., with a ready market.

The recent letters from Deseret interest me in one thing more. They are eloquent in describing the anniversary of the Pioneers' arrival in the Valley. It was the 24th of July; and they have ordained that that day shall be commemmorated in future, like our 21st of December, as their Forefathers' Day. The noble Walker attended as an invited guest, with two hundred of his best-dressed mounted cavaliers, who stalked their guns, and took up their places at the ceremonies and banquet, with the quiet precision of soldiers marched to mass. The Great Band was there, too, that had helped their humble hymns through all the wanderings of the wilderness. Through the many trying marches of 1846,—through the fierce winter ordeal that followed, and the long journey after over plain and mountain,—it had gone unbroken, without the loss of any of its members. As they set out from England, and as they set out from Illinois, so they all came into the Valley together, and together sounded the first glad notes of triumph when the Salt Lake City was founded. It was their right to lead the psalm of praise. Anthem, song and dance,—all the innocent and thankful frolic of the day owed them its chief zest. "They never were in finer key." The people felt their sorrows ended. FAR WEST, their old settlement in Missouri, and NAUVOO; with their wealth and ease, like "Pithom and Ramses, treasure cities built for Pharaoh," went awhile forgotten. Less than four years had restored them every comfort that they needed. Their entertainment, the contribution of all, I have no doubt was really sumptuous. It was spread on broad buffet tables, about fourteen hundred feet in length, at which they took their seats by turns, while they kept them heaped with ornamented delicacies, "butter of kine, and milk, with fat of lambs, with the fat of kidneys of wheat;" "and the cucumbers, and the melons, and the leeks, and the onions, and the garlic, and the remembered fish, which we did eat in Egypt freely." They seem unable to dilate with too much pride upon the show it made.

"To behold the tables," says one that I quote from literally, "to behold them filling the Bowery and all adjoining grounds, loaded with all luxuries of the fields and gardens, and nearly all the varieties that any vegetable market in the world could produce, and to see the seats around those tables filled and refilled by a people who had been deprived of those luxuries for years by the cruel hand of oppression, and freely offering seats to every stranger within their borders,—and this, too, in the Valley of the Mountains, over a thousand miles from civilization, where, two years before, naught was to be found save the wild root of the prairie and the mountain cricket; was a theme of unbounded thanksgiving and praise to the Giver of all Good, as the dawning of a day when the Children of the Kingdom can sit under their own vines and fig-trees, and inhabit their own houses, having none to make them afraid.   May the time be hastened when the scattered Israel may partake of such like banquets from the gardens of Joseph !"

PASS IN THE SIERRA NEVADA,
(Near the Great Salt Lake Valley.)

THE GREAT SALT LAKE CITY.

CHAPTER IX.

THE narrative of Colonel Kane, which has been impugned by many
persons in America as giving too favourable an account of the Mormons, relates to the most important incident in the history of the sect.
We have reproduced it *in extenso*, not only for its interest, but
because it is the only consecutive account of the exodus of the
Mormons, from Nauvoo to the Valley of the Salt Lake, which

has been given to the world. Colonel Kane, in a postscript to his pamphlet, reiterates the truth of all he has stated, and bears a cordial testimony to the virtues of the men with whom he made the long and painful journey through the wilderness   Having now traced the rise and progress of this extraordinary religion, of which the chief incidents have been enacted in America, we enter upon a new portion of our subject, and proceed to show what the Mormons have accomplished in the Great Salt Lake Valley, the means they have adopted to gather the "Saints" into that place from all parts of the world, and the developments, both social and doctrinal, which have resulted since the Church has been under the guidance of Brigham Young and Orson Pratt.

Prior to the arrival of the several detachments of the Mormon people at the Salt Lake, the following general epistle from the council of the Twelve Apostles was addressed "to the Saints throughout the earth," from Council Bluffs, the half-way station of the long overland journey to California:—

"BELOVED BRETHREN,—At no period since the organization of the Church, on the 6th of April, 1830, have the Saints been so extensively scattered, and their means of receiving information from the proper source so limited, as since their expulsion from Illinois; and the time has now arrived when it will be profitable for you to receive, by our epistle, such information and instruction as the Father hath in store, and which he has made manifest by his Spirit.

" Knowing the designs of our enemies, we left Nauvoo in February, 1846, with a large pioneer company, for the purpose of finding a place where the Saints might gather and dwell in peace.   The season was very unfavourable; and the repeated and excessive rains, and scarcity of provisions, retarded our progress, and compelled us to leave a portion of the camp in the wilderness, at a place we called Garden Grove, composed of an enclosure for an extensive farm and sixteen houses, the fruits of our labour; and soon after, from similar causes, we located another place, called Mount Pisgah, leaving another portion of the camp; and after searching the route, making the road and bridges over a multitude of streams, for more than three hundred miles, mostly on lands then occupied by the Pottawatamie Indians, and since vacated in favour of the United States, lying on the south and west, and included within the boundary of Iowa, we arrived near Council Bluffs, on the Missouri River, during the latter part of June, where we were met by Captain J. Allen, from Fort Leavenworth, soliciting us to enlist five hundred men into the service of the United States. To this call of our country we promptly responded; and before the middle of July more than five hundred of the Brethren were embodied in the ' Mormon Battalion,' and on their march for California, by way of Fort Leavenworth, under command of Lieut.-Colonel J. Allen, leaving hundreds of waggons, teams, and families, destitute of protectors and guardians, on the open prairie, in a savage country, far from the abodes of civilized life, and farther still from any place where they might hope to locate.

" Our camp, although aware of a cold northern winter approaching, with all attendant evils,—famine, risk of life in an unhealthy climate, Indian depredations, and everything of a like nature that would tend to make life gloomy, —responded to this call of the President with all the alacrity that is due from children to a parent; and when the strength of our camp had taken its departure in the battalion, the aged, the infirm, the widow, and the fatherless that remained, full of hope and buoyant with faith, determined to prosecute their journey : a small portion of which went as far west as the Pawnee Mission, where, finding it too late to pass the mountains, they turned aside to winter on the bank of the Missouri, at the mouth of the Running Water, about two hundred and fifty miles north-west of the Missouri settlements ; while the far more extensive and feeble numbers located at this place, called by us Winter Quarters, where upwards of seven hundred houses were built in the short space of about three months ; while the great majority located on Pottawatamie lands. In July there were more than two thousand emigrating waggons between this and Nauvoo.

" In September 1846, an infuriated mob, clad in all the horrors of war, fell on the Saints who had still remained at Nauvoo for want of means to remove, murdered some, and drove the remainder across the Mississippi into Iowa, where, destitute of houses, tents, clothing, or money, they received temporary assistance from some benevolent souls in Quincy, St Louis, and other places, whose name will ever be remembered with gratitude. But at that period the Saints were obliged to scatter to the north, south, east, and west, wherever they could find shelter and procure employment. And hard as it was to write it, it must ever remain a truth on the page of history, that while the flower of Israel's camp were sustaining the wing of the American eagle by their influence and arms in a foreign country, their brothers, sisters, fathers, mothers, and children, were driven by mob violence from a free and independent State of the same national republic, and were compelled to flee from the fire, the sword, the musket, and the cannon's mouth, as from the demon of death. From that time to this the Latter-day Saints have been roaming without home from Canada to New Orleans, from the Atlantic to the Pacific Ocean, and have taken up their abode in foreign lands. Their property in Handcock county, Illinois, was little or no better than confiscated. Many of their houses were burned by the mob, and they were obliged to leave most of those that remained without sale, and those who bargained sold almost for a song ; for the influence of their enemies was to cause such a diminution in property, that from a handsome estate was seldom realized enough to remove the family comfortably away; and thousands have since been wandering to and fro, destitute, afflicted, and distressed for the common necessaries of life, or unable to endure, have sickened and died by hundreds, while the temple of the Lord is left solitary in the midst of our enemies, an enduring monument of the diligence and integrity of the Saints.

" Lieut.-Colonel Allen died at Fort Leavenworth, much lamented by the

'Mormon Battalion,' who proceeded *en route* by way of Santa Fe, from whence a small portion, who were sick, returned to Pueblo to winter; while the remainder continued their march, mostly on half rations, or meat without salt, making new roads, digging deep wells in the desert, levelling mountains, performing severe labours, and undergoing the utmost fatigue and hardship ever endured by infantry, as reported by Colonel Cooke, their commanding officer, and arrived in California, in the neighbourhood of San Diego, with the loss of very few men.

" Soon after the battalion left the Bluffs, three of our Council took their departure for England, where they spent the winter, preaching and setting in order all things pertaining to the Church, and returned to this place in the spring of 1847, as did also the camp from Running Water for provisions.

" On April 14, the remainder of the Council, in company of one hundred and forty- three pioneers, left this place in search of a location, and making a new road, a majority of more than one thousand miles westward, arrived at the Great Basin in the latter part of July, where we found a beautiful valley of some twenty by thirty miles in extent, with a lofty range of mountains on the east, capped with perpetual snow, and a beautiful line of mountains on the west, watered with daily showers; the Utah Lake on the south, hid by a range of hills; north-west extending as far as the eye can reach, interspersed with lofty islands, and a continuation of the valley; or opening on the north, extending along the eastern shore about sixty miles to the mouth of Bear River. The soil of the valley appeared good, but will require irrigation to promote vegetation, though there are many small streams emptying in from the mountains, and the Western Jordan (Utah Outlet) passes through from south to north. The climate is warm, dry, and healthy ; good salt abounds at the lake ; warm, hot, and cold springs are common ; mill sites excellent; but the valley is destitute of timber. The box, the fir, the pine, the sugar-maple, &c. may be found on the mountains sufficient for immediate consumption, or until more can grow.

" In this valley we located a site for a city, to be called the Great Salt Lake City, of the Great Basin, North America ; and, for the convenience of the Saints, instituted and located the Great Basin Post-office at this point. The city is surveyed in blocks of ten acres, eight lots to a block, with streets eight rods wide, crossing at right angles. One block is reserved for a temple, and several more in different parts of the city for public grounds.

" Soon after our arrival in the valley, we were joined by that portion of the battalion who had been stationed at Pueblo, and a small camp of the Saints from Mississippi, who had wintered at the same place, who united with the pioneers in ploughing, planting, and sowing near 100 acres, with a great variety of seeds, and in laying the foundation of a row of houses around a ten-acre block, and nearly completing the same on one side. Materials for brick and stone buildings are abundant.

" After tarrying four or five weeks, most of the pioneers commenced their return, nearly destitute of provision, accompanied by a part of the battalion, who were quite destitute, except a very small quantity of beef, which was soon exhausted. The company had to depend for their subsistence on wild beasts, such as buffalo, deer, antelope, &c., which most of the way were very scarce, and many obtained were exceedingly poor and unwholesome. Between the Green and Sweetwater Rivers, we met 566 waggons of the emigrating Saints on their way to the valley, at our last encampment with whom we had fifty horses and mules stolen by the Indians ; and a few days after we were attacked by a large war party of Sioux, who drove off many of our horses, but most of these we recovered. Our route was by Fort Bridger, the South Pass, Fort John (Loraine), and from thence on the north bank of the Platte, to Winter Quarters, where we arrived on the 31st of October, all well ; having performed this long and tedious journey, with ox as well as horse teams, and with little food except wild flesh, without losing a single man, although many were sick when they left in the spring, inasmuch as they were unable to walk until we had travelled more than one half of the outward distance.

" On the 11th instant, fifteen of the battalion arrived from California, with a pilot from the valley, having suffered much on their return from cold and hunger, with no provisions part of the way but a little horse-flesh of the worst kind. From these Brethren we received intelligence that the battalion was discharged in California in July, agreeably to the time of their enlistment; that a portion of the battalion, constituting a company, under Captain Davis, had re-enlisted to sustain a military post in California ; that many had commenced labour to procure means to return ; that a small portion had come on to the Great Salt Lake City, where they found the emigrants which we passed in the mountains alive and in good health and spirits, except three deaths ; and that some of the battalion, who had left the valley with them, had stopped on the Sweetwater, searching for buffalo, who with others, in all about thirty, arrived here on the 18th instant, penniless and destitute, having suffered much from cold and hunger, subsisting on their worn-out mules and horses.

" All who possibly could went to the valley this season ; and the Saints now in this vicinity have had to depend on their own resources in labour for their sustenance, which, on account of the absence of those engaged in the Government service, the sickness that has prevailed in camp, and the destruction of the cattle by the Indians, consists mostly of corn, with a few garden vegetables.

" The Saints in this vicinity are bearing their privations in meekness and patience, and making all their exertions to their removal westward. Their hearts and all their labours are towards the setting sun, for they desire to be so far removed from those who have been their oppressors, that there shall be an everlasting barrier between them and future persecution ; and although, as a people, we have been driven from state to state, and although Joseph and Hyrum, our Prophet and Patriarch, were murdered in cold blood, while in Government duress, and under the immediate control, inspection, and supervision of the Governor and Government offices, we know, and feel assured, that there are many honest, noble, and patriotic souls now living under that government, and under other similar governments in the sister states of the great confederacy, who would loathe the shedding of innocent blood, and were it in their power, would wipe the stain from the nation.

" If such would clear their garments in the public eye and before God, they must speak out; they must proclaim to the world their innocence, and their hatred and detestation of such atrocious and unheard-of acts. But with this we have nothing to do; only we love honesty and right wherever we find them; the cause is between them, their country, and their God: and we again re-iterate what we have often said, and what we have ever shown by our conduct, that, notwithstanding all our privations and sufferings, we are more ready than any portion of the community to sustain the constitutional institutions of our mother country, and will do the utmost for them if permitted; and we say to all Saints throughout the earth, Be submissive to the law that protects you in your person, rights, and property, in whatever nation or kingdom you are; and suffer wrong rather than do wrong. This we have ever done, and mean still to continue to do. We anticipate, as soon as circumstances will permit, to petition for a territorial government in the Great Basin.

" In compliance with the wishes of the sub-agents, we expect to vacate the Omaha lands in the spring. Thus, brethren, we have given you a brief idea of what has transpired among us since we left Nauvoo; the present situation of the Saints in this vicinity; and of our feelings and views in general, as prepa-ratory to the reply which we are about to give to the cry of the Saints from all quarters, What shall we do?

" Gather yourselves together speedily, near to this place, on the east side of the Missouri River, and, if possible, be ready to start from hence by the 1st of May next, or as soon as grass is sufficiently grown, and go to the Great Salt Lake City, with bread-stuff sufficient to sustain you until you can raise grain the following season. Let the Saints who have been driven and scat-tered from Nauvoo, and all others in the Western States, gather immediately to the east bank of the river, bringing with them all the young stock, of various kinds, they possibly can: and let all the Saints in the United States and Canada gather to the same place, by the first spring navigation, or as soon as they can, bringing their money, goods, and effects with them; and, so far as they can consistently, gather young stock by the way, which is much needed here, and will be ready sale. And when here, let all who can, go directly over the mountains; and those who cannot, let them go immediately to work at making improvements, raising grain and stock, on the lands recently va-cated by the Pottawatamie Indians, and owned by the United States, and by industry they can soon gather sufficient means to prosecute their journey. In a year or two their young cattle will grow into teams; by interchange of labour they can raise their own grain and provisions, and build their own waggons; and by sale of their improvements to citizens who will gladly come and occupy, they can replenish their clothing, and thus speedily and comfort-ably procure an outfit. All Saints who are coming on this route will do well to furnish themselves with woollen or winter, instead of summer clothing, generally, as they will be exposed to many chilling blasts before they pass the mountain heights.

" We have named the Pottawatamie lands as the best place for the Brethren to assemble on the route, because the journey is so very long, that they must have a stopping-place, and this is the nearest point to their final destination, which makes it not only desirable, but necessary; and, as it is a wilderness country, it will not infringe on the rights and privileges of any one: and yet it is so near Western Missouri, that a few days' travel will give them an opportunity of trade, if necessity requires, and this is the best general rendezvous that now presents, without intruding on the rights of others.

"To the Saints in England, Scotland, Ireland, Wales, and adjacent islands and countries, we say, Emigrate as speedily as possible to this vicinity, looking to, and following the counsel of, the Presidency at Liverpool ; shipping to New Orleans, and from thence direct to Council Bluffs, which will save much expense. Those who have but little means, and little or no labour, will soon exhaust that means if they remain where they are ; therefore, it is wisdom that they remove without delay ; for here is land, on which, by their labour, they can speedily better their condition for their further journey. And to all Saints in any country bordering upon the Atlantic we would say, Pursue the same course ; come immediately and prepare to go west : bringing with you all kinds of choice seeds of grain, vegetables, fruits, shrubbery, trees, and vines, everything that will please the eye, gladden the heart, or cheer the soul of man, that grows upon the face of the whole earth , also the best stock of beast, bird, and fowl of every kind ; also the best tools of every description, and machinery for spinning, or weaving, and dressing cotton, wool, flax, and silk, &c. &c., or models and descriptions of the same, by which they can construct them ; and the same in relation to all kinds of farming utensils and husbandry, such as corn shellers, grain threshers and cleaners, smut machines, mills, and every implement and article within their knowledge that shall tend to promote the comfort, health, happiness, or prosperity of any people. So far as it can be consistently done, bring models and drafts, and let the machinery be built where it is used, which will save great expense in transportation, particularly in heavy machinery, and tools and implements generally.

"The Brethren must recollect that from this point they pass through a savage country, and their safety depends on good fire-arms and plenty of ammunition ; and then they may have their teams run off in open day-light, as we have had, unless they shall watch closely and continually.

"The Presidents of the various branches will cause this epistle to be read to those under their counsel, and give such instruction in accordance therewith as the Spirit shall dictate ; teaching them to live by every principle of righteousness, walk humbly before God, doing his will in all things, that they may have his Spirit to lead them and assist them speedily to the gathering place of his Saints.

"Let the Seventies, High Priests, Elders, Priests, Teachers, and Deacons report themselves immediately on their arrival at the Bluffs to the presidency of their respective quorum if present, and if not, to the presidency or council of the place, that their names may be registered with their quorum, and that they may be known among their Brethren.

"It is the duty of all parents to train up their children in the way they should go, instructing them in every correct principle so fast as they are capable of receiving, and setting an example worthy of imitation: for the Lord holds parents responsible for the conduct of their children until they arrive at the years of accountability before him; and the parents will have to answer for all misdemeanors arising through their neglect. Mothers should teach their little ones to pray as soon as they are able to talk. Presiding Elders should be particular to instruct parents concerning their duty, and Teachers and Deacons should see that they do it.

"It is very desirable that all the Saints should improve every opportunity of securing at least a copy of every valuable treatise on education, every book, map, chart, or diagram that may contain interesting, useful, and attractive matter, to gain the attention of children, and cause them to love to learn to read; and also every historical, mathematical, philosophical, geographical, geological, astronomical, scientific, practical, and all other variety of useful and interesting writings, maps, &c., to present to the general Church Recorder when they shall arrive at their destination—from which important and interesting matter may be gleaned to compile the most valuable works on every science and subject, for the benefit of the rising generation.

"We have a printing-press; and any who can take good printing or writing paper to the Valley, will be blessing themselves and the Church. We also want all kinds of mathematical and philosophical instruments, together with all rare specimens of natural curiosities and works of art that can be gathered and brought to the Valley, where, and from which, the rising generation can receive instruction; and if the Saints will be diligent in these matters, we will soon have the best, the most useful, and attractive museum on the earth.

"Let every Elder keep a journal, and gather historical facts concerning the Church or world, with specific dates, and present the same to the Historian; also let the presiding officer of every emigrating company, immediately on arrival, see that his clerk presents the Recorder with a perfect list of the names of every soul, the number of waggons, teams, and every living thing in his camp; and let the Saints organize at, and travel from, the Pottawatamie district, according to the pattern which will there be given them.

"Since the murder of President Joseph Smith, many false prophets and false teachers have arisen, and tried to deceive many, during which time we have mostly tarried with the body of the Church, or been seeking a new location, leaving those prophets and teachers to run their race undisturbed, who have died natural deaths or committed suicide; and we now, having it in contemplation soon to re-organize the Church according to the original pattern, with a First Presidency and Patriarch, feel that it will be the privilege of the Twelve, ere long, to spread abroad among the nations, not to hinder the gathering, but to preach the Gospel, and push the people—the honest in heart—together from the four quarters of the earth.

"The Saints in Western California who choose are at liberty to remain, and all who may hereafter arrive on the western coast may exercise their privilege of tarrying in that vicinity or of coming to head-quarters.

"The Saints in the Society and other Islands of the Pacific Ocean are at liberty to tarry where they are for the time being, or until further notice; and we will send them more Elders as soon as we can. But if a few of their young or middle-aged intelligent brethren wish to visit us at the Basin, we bid them God speed, and shall be happy to see them.

" The Saints in Australia, China, and the East Indies generally, will do well to ship to the most convenient port in the United States, and from thence make to this point, and pursue the same course as do others ; or, if they find it more convenient, they may ship to Western California.

" We wish the travelling Elders throughout the world to remember the revelations of the *Doctrine and Covenants*, and say nought to this generation but repentance ; and if men have faith to repent, lead them into the waters o baptism, lay your hands upon them for the reception of the Holy Ghost, confirm them in the Church of Jesus Christ of Latter-Day Saints, comfort their hearts, teach them the principles of righteousness and uprightness between man and man, administer to them bread and wine, in the remembrance of the death of Jesus Christ; and if they want further information, tell them to flee to Zion. There the servants of God will be ready to wait upon them, and teach them all things that pertain to salvation ; and anything beyond this in your teaching cometh of evil : for it is not required at your hands, but leadeth you into snares and temptations, which tendeth to condemnation. Should any ask, Where is Zion ? tell them in America ; and if any ask, What is Zion ? tell them the pure in heart.

" It is the duty of the rich Saints everywhere to assist the poor, according to their ability, to gather ; and if they choose, with a covenant and promise that the poor thus helped, shall repay as soon as they are able. It is also the duty of the rich, those who have the intelligence and the means, to come home forthwith and establish factories and all kinds of machinery that will tend to give employment to the poor, and produce those articles which are necessary for the comfort, convenience, health, and happiness of the people ; and no one need to be at a loss concerning his duty in these matters, if he will walk so humbly before God as to keep the small still whisperings of the Holy Ghost within him continually.

" Let all Saints who love God more than their own dear selves—and none else are Saints—gather without delay to the place appointed, bringing their gold, their silver, their copper, their zinc, their tin, and brass, and iron, and choice steel, and ivory, and precious stones; their curiosities of science, of art, of nature, and everything in their possession or within their reach, to build in strength and stability, to beautify, to adorn, to embellish, to delight, and to cast a fragrance over, the house of the Lord ; with sweet instruments of music and melody, and songs, and fragrance, and sweet odours, and beautiful colours : whether it be in precious jewels, or minerals, or choice ores, or in wisdom and knowledge or understanding, manifested in carved work or curious workmanship of the box, the fir, and pine tree, or anything that ever was, or is, or is to be, for the exaltation, glory, honour, and salvation of the living and the dead, for time and for all eternity. Come, then, walking in righteousness before God, and your labour shall be accepted ; and kings will be your nursing fathers, and queens will be your nursing mothers, and the glory of the whole earth shall be yours, in connection with all those who shall keep the commandments of God; or else the Bible, those ancient prophets who prophesied from generation to generation, and which the present generation profess to believe, must fail; for the time has come for the Saints to go up to the mountains of the Lord's house, and help to establish it upon the tops of the mountains; and the name of the Lord will be there, and the glory of the Lord will be there, and the excellency of the Lord will be there, and the honour of the Lord will be there, and the exaltation of his Saints will be there, and they will be held as in the hollow of his hand, and be hid as in the cleft of the rock when the overflowing scourge of Jehovah shall go through to depopulate the earth and lay waste the nations because of their wickedness, and cleanse the land from pollution and blood.

"We are at peace with all nations, with all kingdoms, with all powers, with all governments, with all authorities under the whole heavens, except the kingdom and power of darkness, which are from beneath, and are ready to stretch forth our arms to the four quarters of the globe, extending salvation to every honest soul; for our mission in the Gospel of Jesus Christ is from sea to sea, and from the river to the ends of the earth; and the blessing of the Lord is upon us: and when every other arm shall fail, the power of the Almighty will be manifest in our behalf; for we ask nothing but what is right, we want nothing but what is right, and God has said that our strength shall be equal to our day: and we invite all presidents, and emperors, and kings, and princes, and nobles, and governors, and rulers, and judges, and all nations, kindreds, tongues, and people under the whole heavens, to come and help us to build a house to the name of the God of Jacob,—a place of peace, a city of rest, a habitation for the oppressed of every clime, even for those that love their neighbour as they do themselves, and who are willing to do, God being our helper; and we will help every one that will help to sustain good and wholesome laws for the protection of virtue and punishment of vice.

"The kingdom which we are establishing is not of this world, but is the kingdom of the great God. It is the fruits of righteousness, of peace, of salvation to every soul that will receive it, from Adam down to his latest posterity. Our good will is towards all men, and we desire their salvation in time and eternity; and we will do them good as far as God will give us the power, and men will permit us the privilege: and we will harm no man; but if men will rise against the power of the Almighty, to overthrow his cause, let them know assuredly that they are running on the bosses of Jehovah's buckler, and, as God lives, they will be overthrown.

"Come, then, ye Saints; come, then, ye honourable men of the earth; come, then, ye wise, ye learned, ye rich, ye noble, according to the riches, and wisdom, and knowledge of the great Jehovah; from all nations, and kindreds, and kingdoms, and tongues, and people, and dialects on the face of the whole earth, and join the standard of Emmanuel, and help us to build up the kingdom of God, and establish the principles of truth, life, and salvation, and you shall receive your reward among the sanctified, when the Lord Jesus Christ cometh to make up his jewels; and no power on earth or in hell can prevail against you.

" The kingdom of God consists in correct principles; and it mattereth not what a man's religious faith is, whether he be a Presbyterian, or a Methodist, or a Baptist, or a Latter-Day Saint or ' Mormon,' or a Campbellite, or a Catholic, or Episcopalian, or Mahometan, or even Pagan, or anything else. If he will bow the knee, and with his tongue confess that Jesus is the Christ, and will support good and wholesome laws for the regulation of society, we hail him as a brother, and will stand by him as he stands by us in these things; for every man's religious faith is a matter between his own soul and his God alone. But if he shall deny the Jesus, if he shall curse God, if he shall indulge in debauchery and drunkenness and crime, if he shall lie and swear and steal, if he shall take the name of the great God in vain, and commit all manner of abominations, he shall have no place in our midst; for we have long sought to find a people that will work righteousness, that will distribute justice equally, that will acknowledge God in all their ways, that will regard those sacred laws and ordinances which are recorded in that sacred book called the Bible, which we verily believe, and which we proclaim to the ends of the earth.

" We ask no pre-eminence, we want no pre-eminence; but where God has us, there we will stand, and that is, to be one with our brethren ; and our brethren are those that keep the commandments of God, that do the will of our Father who is in heaven ; and by them we stand, and with them we will dwell in time and in eternity.

" Come, then, ye Saints of Latter Day, and all ye great and small, wise and foolish, rich and poor, noble and ignoble, exalted and persecuted, rulers and ruled of the earth, who love virtue and hate vice, and help us to do this work which the Lord hath required at our hands ; and inasmuch as the glory of the latter house shall exceed that of the former, your reward shall be an hundredfold, and your rest shall be glorious. Our universal motto is, ' Peace with God, and good will to all men.' "

For the first twelvemonth of their residence in the Salt Lake Valley, as has already been described by Colonel Kane, the Mormons had sufficient to occupy themselves in clearing their farms, and in establishing their relations with their new neighbours, the Utah Indians. Their next care was to organize themselves, not only as a religious community, but as a State claiming admission into the American Union. For this purpose a constitution was drawn up and promulgated.

The preamble, which is as follows, shows the geographical position and limits of the proposed Mormon State :—

" THE CONSTITUTION OF THE NEW STATE OF DESERET.

" Whereas a large number of the Citizens of the United States, before and since the treaty of peace with the Republic of Mexico, emigrated to and settled in that portion of the territory of the United States lying west of the Rocky Mountains, and in the great interior basin of Upper California ; and

" Whereas, by reason of said treaty, all civil organization originating from the Republic of Mexico became abrogated ; and

" Whereas, the Congress of the United States has failed to provide a form of civil government for the territory so acquired, or any portion thereof ; and

" Whereas civil government and laws are necessary for the security, peace, and prosperity of society ; and

" Whereas, it is a fundamental principle in all the Republican governments, that all political power is inherent in the people ; and governments instituted for their protection, security, and benefit, should emanate from the same—

" Therefore, your Committee beg leave to recommend the adoption of the following constitution, until the Congress of the United States shall otherwise provide for the government of the territory hereinafter named and described.

" We, the people, grateful to the Supreme Being for the blessings hitherto enjoyed, and feeling our dependence on Him for a continuation of those blessings, do ordain and establish a free and independent government, by the name of the State of Deseret ; including all the territory of the United States within the following boundaries, to wit :—commencing at the 33rd degree of north latitude, where it crosses the 108th degree of longitude, west of Greenwich ; thence running south and west to the northern boundary of Mexico ; thence west to, and down the main channel of the Gila River, on the northern line of Mexico, and on the northern boundary of Lower California to the Pacific Ocean ; thence along the coast north-westerly to 118 degrees 30 minutes of west longitude ; thence north to where said line intersects the dividing ridge of the Sierra Nevada mountains ; thence north along the summit of the Sierra Nevada mountains to the dividing range of mountains that separates the waters flowing into the Columbia River—from the waters running into the Great Basin ; thence easterly, along the dividing range of mountains that separates said waters flowing into the Columbia River on the north from the waters flowing into the Great Basin on the south, to the summit of the Wind River chain of mountains ; thence south-east and south, by the dividing range of mountains that separate the waters flowing into the Gulf of Mexico from the waters flowing into the Gulf of California ; to the place of beginning, as set forth in a map drawn by Charles Preuss, and published by order of the Senate of the United States, in 1848,'' &c.

It appears, however, that the general Government of the United States has not seen fit to accord to the Mormons the exact boundaries which they desire—that it ignores the name of Deseret, and prefers that of Utah—and is anxious to deprive the Mormons of the coast line claimed in this document, and to shut them up in the table-land among the mountains. Accordingly, in the first section of the bill passed by Congress we find it enacted that the new territory is " bounded on the west by the State of California ; on the north by the territory of Oregon ; and on the east and south by the dividing ridge which separates the waters flowing into the Great Basin from those flowing into the Colorada River and the Gulf of California."

By the same bill, a territorial government for Utah was appointed; and in October, 1850, the President of the United States, with the advice and consent of the Senate, nominated Mr. Brigham Young to be its Governor, and six other persons to the subordinate offices of Secretary, Chief Justice, Associate Justice, Attorney-General, and States-Marshal. Out of these seven, four are members of the Mormon Church.

"The spot on which the Mormons are now settled," says the *Cincinnatti Atlas*, "is, geographically, one of the most interesting in the Western World. There is no other just like it, that we recollect, on the globe. Look at the map a little east of the Great Salt Lake,

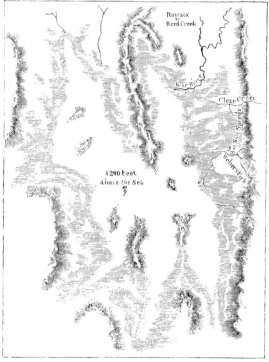

PLAN OF THE GREAT SALT LAKE.

and just south of the South-west Pass, and you will see in the northeast corner of California the summit level of the waters which flow on the North American continent. It must be four thousand feet,

perhaps more, above the level of the Atlantic. In this sequestered
corner, in a vale hidden among mountains and lakes, are the Mormons; and there rise the mighty rivers, than which no continent has
greater. Within a stone's throw almost of one another lie the head
springs of the Sweetwater and Green Rivers. The former flows
into the Platte River; that into the Missouri, and that into the
Mississippi, and that into the Gulf of Mexico, and becomes a part of
the Gulf Stream, laving the shores of distant lands. The latter, the
Green River, flows into the Colorado, the Colorado into the Gulf of
California, and is mingled with the Pacific. The one flows more than
two thousand five hundred miles, the other more than one thousand
five hundred. These flow into tropical regions. Just north of the
same spot are the head streams of Snake River, which flows into the
Columbia, near latitude 46°, after a course of one thousand miles.
Just south are the sources of the Rio Grande, which, after winding
one thousand seven hundred miles, finds the Gulf of Mexico. It is a
remarkable point in the earth's surface where the Mormons are; and,
locked in by mountains and lakes, they will probably remain, and
constitute a new and peculiar colony."

After having drawn up a constitution, declaring Deseret a free
and not a slave State, and trusting to the chances of politics and political parties to fix their exact boundaries, the next thing to be accomplished by their leaders was to gather their people together. Before
a "territory" under the protection of the United States Government can
claim admission into the Union as a State, its population must amount
to sixty thousand; and to bring their number to this point has been
the great work in which the Mormon leaders have been incessantly
occupied since 1848.

Several emissaries or "Apostles" of the sect were despatched to
Europe at the commencement of 1850, to "gather" the European
Saints to the New Zion. Not the least remarkable circumstances in
Mormon history are the faith and zeal of their missionaries. They
start without money, or, as they express it, "without purse and scrip,"
and trust to Providence for their subsistence, feeling assured that "He
who provideth for the sparrows will provide for them." Some have
proceeded to Germany, to Italy, to France, to Norway, and to Russia,
in total ignorance of the languages of those countries, but trusting to
pick up by the way sufficient knowledge to answer their purpose.
Little success, however, has attended them upon the Continent. The
strongholds of the sect are in England, Wales, and Scotland; fully
thirty thousand people in Great Britain are members of their Church,
and there is not a considerable town in which they have not a congregation.

At the Mormon conferences held throughout the British Isles, in June, 1850, the number of Mormons in England and Scotland was reported at 27,863,—of whom there were in London, 2,529; in Manchester, 2,787; in Liverpool, 1,018; in Glasgow, 1,846; in Sheffield, 1,929; in Edinburgh, 1,331; in Birmingham, 1,909; and in Wales, 4,342. The report of June, 1851, showed a still further increase; and detailed some particulars of the growth of the sect, which we present in the words of that document:—

" In 1837, one year before the Saints reached Nauvoo, Elders K. C. Kimball and Orson Hyde, together with several others, landed at Liverpool, friendless and destitute. They separated, and went forth preaching into the towns on either side. Preston first heard and obeyed the principles of truth. In eight months, seven hundred members met in conference in that town, rejoicing in the power and privilege of the Gospel. In a very short time, several counties, among which were Yorkshire, Cheshire, Lancashire, Stafford, Gloucester, Worcester, and Hereford, had heard and received the servants of God. Thus the Church increased; so that, in 1840, after three years' labour, the general conference reported 3,626 members, and 383 in the priesthood, making in all 4,019 Saints. But such triumphant success was not confined to England. Scotland enjoyed a portion; and Ireland was also made to rejoice; and Wales testified by her thousands how the Church had progressed in that province. In Scotland, the blood-cemented pyramid of bigotry and superstition had been triumphantly attacked, although sustained by the proverbial wariness of the Scotch. The conference established in Edinburgh, notwithstanding that hundreds had removed and hundreds more emigrated, still represented more than 1,500 members. Glasgow was also proclaimed, and over 2,063 members were now revelling in the enjoyment of the spirit of truth. In 1851, more than 3,530 had obeyed the mandates of Heaven, and thousands had besides emigrated to the gathering place of the Saints. As to Ireland, it was not until 1850 that Dublin had heard the principles of truth; he was, however, glad to say that a small branch had been established in that city. In Wales, their success was still more great and glorious. In 1851, the number of Saints in the principality was 4,848, including officers. The statistics of January last showed there were, altogether, in the United Kingdom, 42 conferences, 602 branches, 22 seventies, 12 high priests, 1,761 elders, 1,590 priests, 1,226 teachers, 682 deacons, and 25,454 members, making a total of 30,747 Saints. During the last fourteen years, more than 50,000 had been baptized in England, of which nearly 17,000 had emigrated from her shores to Zion."

We gather from other sources that for the two years prior to the death of Joseph Smith, thirteen vessels, wholly engaged by the Mormons for the emigration of their people, quitted Liverpool for New Orleans,—the largest number proceeding by one vessel being three hundred and fourteen, and the smallest sixty. During the year 1850, the Mormon emigration amounted to nearly two thousand five hundred. Being desirous to know something of the class of persons who emigrate under Mormon auspices to establish themselves in the Salt Lake City, and to ascertain from what parts of the country their ranks were principally recruited, the writer made inquiries at the office in Liverpool of Messrs. Pilkington and Wilson, the shipping-agents for the New Orleans packets. The principal manager of this branch of their business, who is thus thrown into frequent intercourse with the Mormons, furnished the following statement :—

"With regard to 'Mormon' Emigration, and the class of persons of which it is composed, they are principally farmers and mechanics, with some few clerks, surgeons, &c. They are generally intelligent and well-behaved, and many of them are highly respectable. Since the 1st of October—when, according to the new act, a note of the trades, professions, and avocations of emigrants, was first required to be taken by the emigration officer—until March in the present year, the follow-

EMIGRANTS GOING ON BOARD

ing seems to be the numbers of each who have gone out in our ships, as far as I can ascertain. I find in our books the names of sixteen miners, twenty engineers, nineteen farmers, one hundred and eight labourers, ten joiners, twenty-five power-loom weavers, fifteen shoemakers, twelve smiths, nineteen tailors, eight watchmakers, twenty-five stone-masons, five butchers, four bakers, four potters, ten painters, seven shipwrights, four iron-moulders, three basketmakers, five dyers, five ropers, four paper-makers, four glass-cutters, five nailors, five saddlers, six sawyers, four gunmakers, &c. These emigrants generally take with them the implements necessary to pursue their occupation in the Salt Lake Valley; and it is no unusual thing to perceive (previous to the ship leaving the dock) a watchmaker with his tools spread out upon his box, busy examining and repairing the watches of the 'brethren,' or a cutler displaying to his fellow-passengers samples of his handicraft which he is bringing out with him. Of course the stock thus taken out is small, when placed in the scale with the speculations of commercial men; but, judging from the enormous quantity of boxes generally taken by these people, in the aggregate it is large indeed. Many of these families have four, five, or six boxes, bound and hooped with iron, marked, 'Not wanted on the passage,' and which are stowed down in the ship's hold; these all contain implements of husbandry or trade. I have seen, with Mormons on board ship, a piano placed before one berth, and opposite the very next, a travelling cutler's machine for grinding knives, &c. Indeed it is a general complaint with captains, that the quantity of luggage put on board with Mormons quite takes them by surprise, and often sinks the ships upwards of an inch deeper in the water than they would otherwise have allowed her to go. Their provisions are always supplied by their agent here, of the very best description, and more than ample; for while the law requires that a certain quantity shall be put on board for each passenger, the Mormon superior puts, in all cases, twenty pounds per head above this quantity, and, in addition, a supply of butter and cheese. Everything is good. The bread always is good, frequently better than that used by the ship. The surplus provisions are given to the passengers on their arrival at New Orleans, and distributed by their superiors to each family in proportion to its numbers. As to the localities from which they come, the majority are from the manufacturing districts—Birmingham, Sheffield, the Potteries, &c. Scotland and Wales have also dispatched a large quantity. When the Scotch or Welsh determine on going, it is generally in large companies. It may perhaps be worthy of remark, that no Irish 'Saints' have yet made their appearance. The Mormons have the greatest objections against going in any ship carrying other passengers than

themselves; and when such is the case, they invariably stipulate that
a partition shall be erected across the ship's lower decks, so as to separate them from all other passengers.

THE FAREWELL.

"The means taken by this people for the preservation of order and
cleanliness on board are admirable, and worthy of imitation. Their
first act, on arrival here, is to hold a general meeting, at which they
appoint a 'president of the company,' and 'six committee-men.'
The president exercises a complete superintendence over everything
connected with the passengers; he allots the berths, settles disputes,
attends to all wants, complaints, or inquiries, whether for or by the
passengers; advises each how to proceed the most economically, whether in purchasing provisions, bedding, or other articles; and he being
in constant communication with the superiors here, the people are
thus safely guarded from the hands of 'Man-catchers' and all others
of the many who frequent our quays, and whose profession it is to
entrap and prey upon the unwary stranger. The duty of the committee-men is to assist in getting the luggage on board, and to make
a proper arrangement in the ship, &c. They also stand sentinel alter-
nately at the hatchway day and night, during the period the ship
remains in dock, to prevent the intrusion of strangers. To show how
effectually this is done, I may just mention that while in *every* ship

taking the general class of emigrants, persons are found concealed on board, or ' stow-aways,' *in no instance* has such been the case in a ship wholly laden with Mormons. To those acquainted with the slovenly and dirty arrangements of emigrants on shipboard, those of the Mormons, for the preservation of decency and morality, will appear deserving of the highest commendation. Each berth, or at least a great majority of the berths, has its little curtain spread before it, so as to prevent the inmates from being seen, and also to enable them to dress and undress behind it. In allotting the berths, the members of each family are placed in the berths next each other; and in case the passengers are from different parts—say from England and Scotland—the Scotch are berthed on one side of the ship, the English on the other. The duties of the president and committee do not cease after the ship leaves dock, but are continued during the whole voyage. The president still exercises his superintendence over the general conduct of the passengers, the delivery of provisions, water, &c. The committee act at sea as police. Three of them take each side of the between decks, and see that every person is in bed by eight o'clock in the evening, and in the morning that every passenger is up, the beds made, and the rubbish swept together, hauled up in buckets, and thrown overboard before seven o'clock. It is remarkable the implicit obedience which is paid by the passengers to those whom they thus elect over them; their slightest word is law,

SCENE BETWEEN DECKS.

always respected, and cheerfully obeyed; in their social intercourse they address each other as 'brother' and 'sister;' and with regard to their care of the things entrusted to their charge, I have been told by an American captain who carried them, that having delivered to their committee a quantity of water which he had told them was to serve for three days, he found at the end of the third day a fourth day's supply left; whereas had he given it into the charge of one of his sailors for distribution, it would not have lasted the three days.

NEW ORLEANS.

From my knowledge of the emigration at present going on from Liverpool, I can truly say that it would, indeed, be not only conducive to the comfort and health, but would absolutely save the lives of many who now die on shipboard, could the same rules for cleanliness, order, &c., be introduced amongst the general class of emigrants who leave this port for America."

The following particulars respecting the route of the emigrants after their arrival at New Orleans will conclude this part of the subject. After remaining a few days in New Orleans, the emigrants start in companies, sometimes of two or three hundred or more, to St. Louis, by steamboat on the Mississippi. The distance is 1,300 miles. The next stage, also by steamboat, is a distance of 800 miles from St.

ST. L   S.

Louis, to the settlements of Council Bluffs, already mentioned. Here they either remain to fatten their young cattle on the prairies, or squat upon the rich lands until they are ready to go forward to the Great Salt Lake City. The distance from Council Bluffs to their final destination is 1,030 miles. The emigrants travel in ox-teams, and their large caravans present a singular spectacle. These waggons are sometimes drawn by as many as six or eight oxen, and there are frequently 600 waggons in the procession. Each is so arranged as to comprise a bed-room and sitting-room. They dine on the road-side, giving their cattle, in the meantime, an hour's grazing in the prairies. They take three months to complete the journey from New Orleans to the Salt Lake City, and being supplied with necessary provisions purchased at St. Louis, they trust for their luxuries to the occasional proceeds of the chase, in pursuing which the male emigrants amuse themselves on the way. They trade with the Indians as they go, exchanging fire-arms and ammunition for buffalo robes and peltries. *

* We learn, as these sheets are passing through the press, that the Mormon emigration will for the future be conducted across the Isthmus of Panama, or round by Cape Horn.

MORMON CARAVAN CROSSING THE PRAIRIES.

The Mormons established a perpetual emigration fund in 1849.
the nature and objects of which were stated in an epistle from Brigham Young to Mr. Orson Pratt, at that time their emigration agent
in Liverpool :—

"Great Salt Lake City, Oct. 14, 1849.

" DEAR BROTHER,—You will learn from our General Epistle the principal
events occurring with us, but we have thought proper to write you, more particularly in relation to some matters of general interest, in an especial manner,
the perpetual emigration fund for the poor Saints. This fund, we wish all to
understand, is perpetual, and in order to be kept good, will need constant ac-
cessions. To further this end, we expect all who are benefited by its operations will be willing to reimburse that amount as soon as they are able,
facilities for which will very soon after their arrival here present themselves
in the shape of public works; donations will also continue to be taken from
all parts of the world, and expended for the gathering of the poor Saints. This
is no Joint Stock Company arrangement, but free donations. Your office in
Liverpool is the place of deposit for all funds received, either for this or the
tithing funds, for all Europe, and you will not pay out, only upon our order,
and to such persons as we shall direct. We wish to have machinery of all
kinds introduced in these valleys as soon as practicable. If you commence
operations now, before you can get men to engage in the business, the material
for cotton and woollen factories will be produced. Our settlements another

season will extend over the rim of the basin, where we can raise the cotton, the sugar cane, rice, &c. Therefore, if you can find those who will engage in manufacturing cloth for this market in the Valley, we want you should let these cotton factory proprietors, operatives, and all, with all the necessary fixtures, come to this place. We have a carrying company started, who will accommodate all emigrants to this place with passage and freight from Missouri River; they need not be obliged under this arrangement to buy oxen and waggons when they arrive there, and can be immediately transported through the entire route. We have considered it policy for us to collect tithing in money, instead of labour, as heretofore, therefore we employ constant hands upon our public works, and pay them the money, or such things as they need for themselves and families. We, therefore, have appointed Joseph L. Heywood and Edwin D. Woolley, our agents, to go east and purchase such things as we need to supply our public works with, such as are necessary, such as glass, nails, paint, &c., and furnish workmen; these agents will probably call upon you from Boston for funds—if they should, you will send them accordingly. It is distinctly understood that these arrangements are entirely disconnected with the Perpetual Emigrating Fund; that is sacred to its proper use in gathering the poor Saints. Our true policy is, to do our own work, make our own goods as soon as possible; therefore, do all you can to further the emigration of artisans and mechanics of all kinds; also continue to collect tithing.

" Our beloved Brother Franklin D. Richards, who is appointed to go on a mission to England, will co-operate with you, and give you more particular items, policy, &c.

"With sentiments of the highest esteem, love, and kindness, we remain your brethren in the new and everlasting covenant.

" BRIGHAM YOUNG.

" P. S. We want a company of woollen manufacturers to come with machinery, and take our wool from the sheep, and convert it into the best clothes —and the wool is ready. We want a company of cotton manufacturers, who will convert cotton into cloth and calico, &c., and we will raise the cotton before the machinery can be ready. We want a company of potters. We need them. The clay is ready, and dishes wanted. Send a company of each, if possible, next spring. Silk manufacturers and all others will follow in rapid succession. We want some men to start a furnace forthwith; the coal, iron, and moulders are waiting.

B. Y.

It will be seen, from the foregoing statements, that the Mormons have made a great movement in advance since the death of Joseph Smith. California has been their golden land, and the source of their present prosperity and hope in the future.

" When the Saints were about leaving Nauvoo," says an epistle in the *Millennial Star*, " Heber C. Kimball prophesied that in five years they would be better off than at this time. Little more than three

Q

years have elapsed when we behold the poor exiled Mormons in flourishing circumstances, counting among their riches a thousand hills and
valleys, situate in the most remarkable, interesting, and auspicious
portion of the globe; having the fountains of rivers that must speedily
command the commerce of the world, in the midst of their territories.
Thus the banishment of the Church has become her freedom, the
greatest boon her opponents could confer, and the glad signal for her
to arise and shine. Forcibly ejected from the mother country on her
arrival at the age of puberty, and thrown back upon her own unaided
resources, the development of her wonderful constitution, capabilities,
and organization, strike the whole world with astonishment and admiration; they who have plundered, robbed, and driven her into the
wilderness, and thought she was dead, now turn their eyes, and discover to their great surprise that she lives, and nobly aspires to power,
honour, might, majesty, glory, and dominion. She has triumphed
over every form of persecution and every species of cruelty. Under
circumstances the most extraordinary and discouraging, she has
proved herself not a whit behind the very first and foremost in all the
characteristics necessary to constitute a great people. She has earned
a title to a fair name and place amongst the nations. Yes, Zion is
firmly established in the strongholds of the land. Riches unknown
are at her disposal. And it is to be hoped that her oppressors will
rejoice over her no more; and that no weapon formed against her
shall prosper. Every one is aware of the impracticability of subduing
a brave people, entrenched in the fastnesses of the mountains. A
nation of mountaineers is not easily subjected. Even our enemies
begin to acknowledge the manifest natural advantages and rising
importance of the peculiar locality of the city 'sought out,' and are not
backward in foretelling the proud and enviable station we must shortly
occupy. They look to her for support, and think of calculating on
her assistance, whom they have driven to the last extremity.

" All things work together for good. When an iron highway
shall be cast up in the desert, not only will the flight of the righteous
be greatly facilitated, but the kings, nobles, and rulers of the earth,
with the great men, will flock to the city of refuge, painfully aware
that in Zion alone will be found peace and safety. The signs of the
times augur an unparalleled growth for the city in the midst of the
everlasting hills."

The following additional particulars, with reference to the Great
Salt Lake City, are of interest :—

" The Nauvoo Legion," says a general epistle to the Saints, signed
by Brigham Young, and dated on the 12th of October last, "has been
reorganized in the Valley, and it would have been a source of joy to

the Saints throughout the earth, could they have witnessed its movements on the day of its great parade; to see a whole army of mighty men in martial array, ground their arms, not by command, but simply by request, repair to the temple block, and with pick and spade open the foundation for a place of worship, and erect the pilasters, beams, and roof, so that we now have a commodious edifice, one hundred feet by sixty, with brick walls, where we assemble with the Saints from Sabbath to Sabbath, and almost every evening in the week, to teach, counsel, and devise ways and means for the prosperity of the kingdom of God; and we feel thankful that we have a better house or bowery for public worship the coming winter, than we have heretofore had any winter in this dispensation.

" Thousands of emigrants from the States to the gold mines have passed through our city this season, leaving large quantities of domestic clothing, waggons, &c., in exchange for horses and mules, which exchange has been a mutual blessing to both parties.

" The direct emigration of the Saints to this place will be some five or six hundred waggons this season; besides, many who came in search of gold, have heard the Gospel for the first time, and will go no further, having believed and been baptized.

" On the 28th September, fourteen or fifteen of the brethren arrived from the gold country, some of whom were very comfortably supplied with the precious metal, and others, who had been sick, came as destitute as they went on the ship Brooklyn in 1846. That there is plenty of gold in Western California is beyond doubt, but the valley of the Sacramento is an unhealthy place, and the Saints can be better employed in raising grain, and building houses in this vicinity, than digging for gold in the Sacramento, unless they are counselled so to do.

" The grain crops in the valley have been good this season; wheat, barley, oats, rye, and peas, more particularly. The late corn and buckwheat, and some lesser grains and vegetables, have been materially injured by the recent frosts; and some early corn in Brownsville, forty miles north, a month since; and the buckwheat was severely damaged by hail at the Utah settlement, sixty miles south, about three weeks since; but we have great occasion for thanksgiving to Him who giveth the increase, that he has blest our labours, so that with prudence we shall have a comfortable supply for ourselves, and our brethren on the way, who may be in need, until another harvest; but we feel the need of more labourers, for more efficient help, and multiplied means of farming and building at this place. We want men. Brethren, come from the States, from the nations, come! and help us to build and grow, until we can say, 'Enough—the valleys of Ephraim are full.' "

The following letter from a Mormon to his father in England, gives some additional particulars of the city, and the journey overland from New York:—

City of the Great Salt Lake, Rocky Mountains, Oct., 1849.

"MY DEAR FATHER,—I scarcely know how to commence the chequered history of my journey from New York, but will endeavour to give you a very abbreviated account, reserving my journal until we again meet, which happiness will, I trust, yet be permitted to us. We started twenty-four in number, on 10th of March, armed and equipped for a long and toilsome journey. During the first part, having the advantage of hotels, we were very merry, and enjoyed ourselves amazingly; but this was not to last long, as we had yet to experience the toils of a camp life. We travelled some 1,000 miles upon the

CAVE IN ROCK ON THE OHIO.

Mississippi and Ohio rivers, in American steamers, a mode of transit I am by no means partial to, as I was in a fever of apprehension the whole time, the accidents on these rivers being innumerable. They arise from 'snags' (pieces of timber sticking up in the muddy waters), from fire, collision, and bursting of the thin boilers, which are placed under the saloon. This part of our travel was, however, accomplished, with only the loss of a few goods; and in the early part of May our mules were purchased, and we were ready for a start across the prairie. Our party had four waggons, each drawn by eight mules; and, in addition, we rode upon these combinations of all that is stupid, spiteful, and obstinate. For some little time I enjoyed the change—the novelty of this predatory mode of life. At day-break we left our tents, were soon busy around the camp fire, preparing breakfast. Our stores did not admit of much variety; coffee, bacon, and hard biscuit, forming the staple of our provisions. The weather soon became oppressively hot, the thermometer rising to 100° and 110°. This was rendered very trying by the entire absence of shade upon this ocean of land; indeed, these vast plains closely resemble in atmospheric phenomena, and in the appearance of the ground, the dry bed of some mighty sea. The heat, with the quality of our food, soon produced bilious fever, and before our journey thus far was accomplished, half our number had suffered from this complaint. We were much mistaken in believing the route a healthy one, the road being marked with the graves of victims to the California fever. Turning over the leaves of my journal, I find the following account of a night in the prairie, and only one of many similar :—*June* 19 : We had not been an hour in our tents before one of the dreadful storms swept over us; the horizon was of the deepest purple, illumed occasionally by flashes of forked lightning, the accompanying rain resembling, at the distance at which we stood, a rugged cloud descending to the earth. I cannot describe the startling effect of the thunder—each clap resembling some immense cannon, shaking the very earth. I have a full perception of the sublimity and grandeur of these storms, but cannot attempt an adequate description. When the storm reached the tent it was blown over, and we were left to seek shelter in the best way we could. I dragged my coverings under a waggon, but soon found I was lying in a pool of water, with saturated blankets. I then crawled into a waggon, and in a cramped position, bitten horribly by mosquitoes, I passed an emphatically miserable night.

"About the middle of June I was taken ill, and, with slight interruptions, continued so till we reached this 'city.' You will perhaps imagine that, being so styled, it resembles an English city; but it is only in prospect. The houses are either of logs, or built of mud bricks, called 'dobies,' and, but in a few instances, are not larger than one or two rooms; but time will accomplish much for this energetic and faithful people. Each house stands in an acre and a quarter of garden ground, eight lots in a block, forming squares. The streets, which are wide, are to be lined with trees, with a canal, for the purpose of irrigation, running through the centre. As our waggon entered this beautiful valley, with the long absent comforts of a home in prospect, I experienced a considerable change for the better; and when, to my surprise and gratitude, I met a pious, kind, and intelligent artist, and a countryman also, who took me, emaciated, sick, and dirty, to his humble home, my happiness seemed completed. You must, from their own works, read the history of the Mormonites, and you will then learn how this despised people have been persecuted and driven from place to place, until they have at length found a haven in the all but inaccessible valley of the Rocky Mountains, where are gathered together, almost from every nation, some 10,000 of those who felt happy in sacrificing all that the world holds dear for the sake of their faith ; and after struggling with innumerable diffi-culties and hardships, are building their temple in the wilderness, and are rapidly increasing both in spiritual and temporal wealth, having a Church organized according to the New Testament pattern, and endeavouring to live by every word that proceedeth from the mouth of the Lord.   The land here is most fruitful—I am told it produces 80 bushels of wheat to the acre ; and vines, delicious melons, with other fruits and vegetables, grow in profusion. A city lot—that is, one acre and a quarter—may be purchased at one dollar fifty cents, and would produce food sufficient for my wants the whole year. No man with ordinary intelligence can be poor in such a place ; and then, glorious privilege ! he can be free from the harassments and perplexities which continually destroy the peace of those who live in an artificial state of society.

"When recruited, in order to accomplish the remaining 600 miles, the distance that still intervened between the city and California, the waggons were sold, and ten of our number started for their original destination, through mountains covered with snow, with a prospect of being slain by Indians, or of feeding either upon their mules or each other.   The other thirteen re-mained, earned their living in different ways until later in the season, and have since started upon a southern route of 1,600 miles, for the gold mines, leaving me still too unwell to accompany them."

A correspondent of the *New York Tribune*, writing under the date of July 8, 1849, gives the following account of the state of affairs at the new Mormon city :—

" The company of gold-diggers which I have the honour to com-mand, arrived here on the 3rd instant, and judge our feelings when, after some twelve hundred miles of travel through an uncultivated desert, and the last one hundred miles of the distance through and among lofty mountains, and narrow and difficult ravines, we found ourselves suddenly, and almost unexpectedly, in a comparative para-dise.

" We descended the last mountain by a passage excessively steep and abrupt, and continued our gradual descent through a narrow *canon* for five or six miles, when, suddenly emerging from the pass, an ex-tensive and cultivated valley opened before us, at the same instant that we caught a glimpse of the distant bosom of the Great Salt Lake, which lay expanded before us to the westward, at the distance of some twenty miles.

" Descending the table land which bordered the valley, extensive herds of cattle, horses, and sheep, were grazing in every direction, reminding us of that home and civilization from which we had so widely departed—for as yet the fields and houses were in the distance. Passing over some miles of pasture land, we at length found ourselves in a broad and fenced street, extending westward in a straight line for several miles. Houses of wood or sun-dried brick were thickly clustered in the vale before us, some thousands in number, and occupying a spot about as large as the city of New York. The whole space for miles, excepting the streets and houses, was in a high state of cultivation. Fields of yellow wheat stood waiting for the harvest, and Indian corn, potatoes, oats, flax, and all kinds of garden vegetables, were growing in profusion, and seemed about in the same state of forwardness as in the same latitude in the States.

"At first sight of all these signs of cultivation in the wilderness, we were transported with wonder and pleasure. Some wept, some gave three cheers, some laughed, and some ran and fairly danced for joy—while all felt inexpressibly happy to find themselves once more amid scenes which mark the progress of advancing civilization. We passed on amid scenes like these, expecting every moment to come to some commercial centre, some business point in this great metropolis of the mountains; but we were disappointed. No hotel, signpost, cake and beer shop, barber pole, market-house, grocery, provision, dry goods, or hardware store distinguished one part of the town from another, not even a bakery or mechanic's sign was anywhere discernible.

"Here, then, was something new: an entire people reduced to a level, and all living by their labour—all cultivating the earth, or following some branch of physical industry. At first I thought it was an experiment, an order of things established purposely to carry out the principles of ' Socialism' or ' Mormonism.' In short, I thought it very much like Owenism personified. However, on inquiry, I found that a combination of seemingly unavoidable circumstances had produced this singular state of affairs. There were no hotels, because there had been no travel; no barbers' shops, because every one chose to shave himself, and no one had time to shave his neighbour; no stores, because they had no goods to sell, nor time to traffic; no centre of business, because all were too busy to make a centre.

"There was abundance of mechanic's shops, of dressmakers, milliners, and tailors, &c.; but they needed no sign, nor had they time to paint or erect one, for they were crowded with business. Beside their several trades, all must cultivate the land, or die; for the country was new, and no cultivation but their own within a thousand miles. Every one had his lot, and built on it; every one cultivated it, and perhaps a small farm in the distance.

"And the strangest of all was, that this great city, extending over several square miles, had been erected, and every house and fence made, within nine or ten months of the time of our arrival; while at the same time, good bridges were erected over the principal streams, and the country settlements extended nearly one hundred miles up and down the valley.

"This territory, state, or, as some term it, 'Mormon Empire,' may justly be considered as one of the greatest prodigies of our time, and, in comparison with its age, the most gigantic of all republics in existence; being only its second year since the first seed of cultivation was planted, or the first civilized habitation commenced. If these people were such thieves and robbers as their enemies represented them in the States, I must think they have greatly reformed in point of industry since coming to the mountains.

"I this day attended worship with them in the open air. Some thousands of well dressed, intelligent-looking people assembled; some on foot, some in carriages, and on horseback. Many were neatly, and even fashionably clad. The beauty and neatness of the ladies reminded me of some of our best congregations in New York. They had a choir of both sexes, who performed extremely well, accompanied by a band who played well on almost every musical instrument of modern invention. Peals of the most sweet, sacred, and solemn music filled the air, after which, a solemn prayer was offered by Mr. Grant (a Latter-Day Saint), of Philadelphia. Then followed various business advertisements, read by the clerk. Among these I remember a call of the seventeenth ward, by its presiding bishop, to some business meeting; a call for a meeting of the thirty-second quorum of the seventy; and a meeting of the officers of the second cohort of the military legion, &c., &c.

"After this, came a lengthy discourse from Mr. Brigham Young, president of the society, partaking somewhat of politics, much of religion and philosophy, and a little on the subject of gold, showing the wealth, strength, and glory of England, growing out of her coal mines, iron, and industry; and the weakness, corruption, and degradation of Spanish America, Spain, &c., growing out of her gold, silver, &c., and her idle habits.

"Every one seemed interested and pleased with his remarks, and all appeared to be contented to stay at home and pursue a persevering industry, although mountains of gold were near them. The able speaker painted in lively colours the ruin which would be brought upon the United States by gold, and boldly predicted that they would be overthrown because they had killed the prophets, stoned and rejected those who were sent to call them to repentance, and finally plundered and driven the Church of the Saints from their midst, and burned and desolated their city and temple. He said God had a reckoning with that people, and gold would be the instrument of their overthrow. The constitutions and laws were good—in fact, the best in the world; but the administrators were corrupt, and the laws and constitutions were not carried out. Therefore they must fall. He further observed, that the people here would petition to be organized into a territory under that same government, notwithstanding its abuses, and that, if granted, they would stand by the constitution and laws of the United States; while at the same time he denounced their corruption and abuses.

"But, said the speaker, we ask no odds of them, whether they grant us our petition or not! We never will ask any odds of a nation who has driven us from our homes. If they grant us our rights, well; if not, well; they can do no more than they have done. They, and ourselves, and all men, are in the hands of the great God, who will govern all things for good, and all will be right, and work together for good to them that serve God.

" Such, in part, was the discourse to which we listened in the strongholds of the mountains. The Mormons are not dead, nor is their spirit broken. And, if I mistake not, there is a noble, daring, stern, and democratic spirit swelling in their bosoms, which will people these mountains with a race of independent men, and influence the destiny of our country and the world for a hundred generations. In their religion they seem charitable, devoted, and sincere; in their politics, bold, daring, and determined; in their domestic circle, quiet, affectionate, and happy; while in industry, skill, and intelligence, they have few equals, and no superiors on the earth.

" I had many strange feelings while contemplating this new civilization growing up so suddenly in the wilderness. I almost wished I could awake from my golden dream, and find it but a dream; while I pursued my domestic duties as quiet, as happy, and contented as this strange people."

A more recent correspondent of a New York newspaper also describes the rising condition of the Great Salt Lake City :—

" It is now three years since the Mormons arrived in Salt Lake Valley, and their progress in laying out a city, buildings, fencing farms, raising crops, &c., is truly wonderful to behold; and is but another striking demonstration of the indefatigable enterprise, industry, and perseverance, of the Anglo-Saxon race.

" The city is laid out into about twenty different wards, and covers an area of three square miles. It already contains about one thousand houses, nearly one story and a half high, built of *adobe*, or sunburnt brick. A fine stream of cold water rushes down from the mountains, which is distributed in ditches through every street in the city, through the gardens, and to the doors of the dwellings, where it is used for culinary and other purposes. The ground whereon the

city is built is sloping, which affords a great fall for the water, the
current through the ditches running at the rate of about 'four knots
an hour,' and keeps up a continual supply of fresh water from the
mountains. The valley where the city stands is quite 'handsome,'
running east and west. The city is situate about three miles from the
Timpanagos Mountains on the east, within five of the Utah outlet on
the south-east, and within twenty miles from a range of mountains on
the south, and within twenty-two miles of the Great Salt Lake. Its
population is about five thousand, that of the valley ten thousand, exclusive of the city. The Mormons are now building a neat stone
State House, two stories high, and its dimensions are forty by ninety
feet. Most of the city is fenced, every half square mile being under
one enclosure, almost every foot of the ground (except where the
house stands) being occupied in grain and vegetables. There are
several stores kept here. Mechanics of different trades are busily
engaged. The Mormons, take them as a body, I truly believe are a
most industrious people, and, I confess, as intelligent as any I have
met with, either in the east or the west. It is true they are a little
fanatical about their religious views, which is not at all strange when
compared with the majority of religious denominations in the east.
But let no man be deceived in his estimation of the people who have
settled here. Any people who have the courage to travel over plains,
rivers, and mountains, for twelve hundred miles, such probably as cannot be travelled over in any other part of the world, to settle in a region
which scarcely ever received the tread of any but the wild savage and
beasts who roam the wilderness, must be possessed of indomitable
energy which is but rarely met with.

"Brigham Young, the president of the Mormon Church here (and
to whom I had a letter of introduction), is a man about forty years of
age, of light complexion, ordinary height, but rather corpulent. He
exercises a vast influence among the Mormons, probably more than
any other man, and I think stands nearly in the same position as their
Saint, Joseph Smith. He is a man of considerable intelligence, and I
think has seen a good deal of the world. The greatest fault I can find
with his preaching is, that he is almost too egotistical. Instead of
taking a text from the Good Book, and if possible showing that the
Book of Mormon is the true road, he confines himself altogether to
giving accounts of their persecuted Church in bygone days, and in
'showing up' its present enemies. I have heard him preach twice,
and have had several private conversations with him. In private,
he is very sociable and talkative, joking and laughing as heartily as
anybody."

The latest traveller through the Great Salt Lake Valley, who has published an account of his journey, is Mr. William Kelly, the author of *Excursions in California*. In this very entertaining work he thus describes his first view of the New Mormon City:—

" Instead of a charming valley beautifully diversified with wood and water, there was a bald, level plain, extending over to the base of the Utah range on the other side, without bush or bramble to cast a shade from the scorching rays of a flaming sun, that blazed with a twofold intensity, reflected by the lofty ranges by which the plain is bounded. Some miles to the north lay the Great Salt Lake, glistening in radiance like a sheet of crystals, in strange contrast with the dark and sombre Utah range that stretch along its western shores. At first the city was not visible, but on passing over a piece of table land the new capital of the Mormons became revealed—not, I must admit, with any very striking effect, for it was too young as yet to boast the stately ornaments of spire and dome, which first attract the eye of the anxious traveller. We saw from here, with great distinctness, the plan of the place, which had nothing novel or peculiar about it, laid out in very wide, regular streets, radiating from a large space in the centre, where there appeared the basement and tall scaffolding-poles of an immense building in progress of erection. The houses were far apart, each being allotted a space for gardens and enclosure, which caused it to cover a very large space of ground.

" We were soon discovered coming down the slope, and as we entered the precincts of the town, the inhabitants came to the front of their houses, but showed no disposition to open an acquaintance account, believing us to be an exclusively American caravan. So soon, however, as they were undeceived, they came about us in great numbers, inquiring what we had to dispose of. They were neat and well clad, their children tidy, the rosy glow of health and robustness mantling on the cheeks of all, while the softer tints of female loveliness prevailed to a degree that goes far to prove those " Latter-Day Saints " have very correct notions of angelic perfectability. We politely declined several courteous offers of gratuitous lodging, selecting our quarters in a luxuriant meadow at the north end of the city ; but had not our tents well pitched, when we had loads of presents—butter, milk, small cheeses, eggs, and vegetables, which we received reluctantly, not having any equivalent returns to make, except in money, which they altogether declined ; in fact, the only thing we had in superabundance was preserved apples and peaches, a portion of which we presented to one of the elders, who gave a delightful party in the evening, at which all our folk were present. We found a very large and joyous throng assembled ; the house turned inside out to make more room on the occasion, with gaiety, unembarrassed by ceremony,

animating the whole, making me almost fancy I was spending the
evening amongst the crowded haunts of the old world, instead of a
sequestered valley, lying between the Utah and Timpanagos Mountains.   After tea was served,

> " ' There were the sounds of dancing feet
> Mingling with the tones of music sweet."

or, as Dermot MacFig would say,

> " ' We shook a loose toe,
> While he humoured the bow."

Keeping it up to a late hour, perfectly enraptured with the Mormon
ladies, and Mormon hospitality.

"I was not aware before that polygamy was sanctioned by their
creed, beyond a species of ethereal Platonism which accorded to its
especial saints chosen partners, called 'spiritual wives;' but I now
found that these, contrary to one's ordinary notions of spiritualism,
gave birth to cherubs and unfledged angels.   When our party arrived
we were introduced to a staid, matronly-looking lady as Mrs. ****,
and as we proceeded up the room, to a blooming young creature, a
fitting mother for a celestial progeny, as the other Mrs. ****, without
any worldly or spiritual distinction whatsoever.   At first, I thought
it a misconception; but inquiry confirmed the fact of there being two
mistresses in the same establishment, both with terrestrial habits and
duties to perform, which I found afterwards to be the case in other
instances, where the parties could lay no claim to any particular
saintliness.

"On Saturday morning, we had a very early levee at our tents, with
fresh milk, butter, fowls and eggs, and a light waggon in attendance,
with a side of beef, a carcase of mutton, and a veal,—all of superior
quality; the latter articles for sale professionally, but certainly on
most moderate terms,—the prime joints not averaging over one penny
per pound.   The other matters we were forced to accept, and gave to
the donors what we could afford of coffee, sugar, and tobacco, which
were not to be had in the city for the last two months.   In addition
to those timely presents, we got all our washing done in the very best
style of art.   After breakfast we went out returning visits, and were
most graciously received in every quarter.   The houses are small,
principally of brick, built up only as temporary abodes, until the more
urgent and important matter of inclosure and cultivation are attended
to; but I never saw anything to surpass the ingenuity of arrangement
with which they are fitted up, and the scrupulous cleanliness with
which they are kept.   There were tradesmen and artizans of all descriptions, but no regular stores or workshops, except forges.   Still,

from the shoeing of a waggon to the mending of a watch, there was no difficulty experienced in getting it done, as cheap and as well put out of hand as in any other city in America. Notwithstanding the oppressive temperature, they were all hard at work at their trades, and abroad in the fields, weeding, moulding, and irrigating; and it certainly speaks volumes for their energy and industry, to see the quantity of land they have fenced in, and the breadth under cultivation, considering the very short time since they had founded the settlement in 1847. There was ample promise of an abundant harvest, in magnificent crops of wheat, maize, potatoes, and every description of garden vegetable, all of which require irrigation, as there is little or no rain in this region, a salt-lake shower being estimated at a drop to each inhabitant. They have numerous herds of the finest cattle, droves of excellent sheep, with horses and mules enough and to spare; but very few pigs, persons having them being obliged to keep them chained, as the fences are not close enough to prevent them damaging the crops. However, they have legions of superior poultry, so that they live in the most plentiful manner possible. We exchanged and purchased some mules and horses on very favourable terms, knowing we would stand in need of strong teams in crossing the Sierra Nevada.

"On Sunday morning early we went to the hot springs, a mile beyond the town, where the authorities were erecting a handsome and commodious building, and had a glorious bath, in sulphur water, at a temperature just as high as could be comfortably endured, drinking, too, of the stream as it gushed from the hill-side in a thick volume, being told it possessed certain medicinal properties of which we all stood in need. The Mormons made a boast of their good health, and attribute it to bathing in those springs, many that I met declaring they came to the Valley perfect cripples, and were restored to their health and agility by frequenting them.

"After bathing, we dressed in our best attire, and prepared to attend the Mormon service, held for the present in the large space adjoining the intended temple, which is only just above the foundations, but will be a structure of stupendous proportions; and, if finished according to the plan, of surpassing elegance. I went early, and found a rostrum in front of which there were rows of stools and chairs for the townfolk; those from the country, who arrived in great numbers, in light waggons, sitting on chairs, took up their stations in their vehicles in the background, after unharnessing the horses. There was a very large and most respectable congregation; the ladies attired in rich and becoming costumes, each with parasols; and I hope I may say, without any imputation of profanity, a more bewitching assemblage of the sex it has rarely been my lot to look upon. Before the

religious ceremony commenced, five men mounted the rostrum, who
were, as I learned, the weekly committee of inspection. The chair-
man read his general report of the prospects and proceedings of the
colony, and then read a list of those deserving of particular commendation for their superior husbandry, the extent of their fencing,
and other improvements, which was followed by the black list, enu-
rating the idle, slothful, and unimproving portion of the community,
who were held up to reprobation; and threatened, in default of certain
tasks allotted them being finished at the next visit, to be deprived of
their lots, and expelled the community. The reading of these lists
produced an evident sensation, and, I am satisfied, stimulate the
industrious to extra exertion, and goad the lazy to work in self-
defence. This over, another, " the gentleman in black," got up, and,
without any form of service or prefatory prayer, read aloud a text
from the Book of Mormon, and commenced a sermon, or discourse,
de multis rebus et quibusdam aliis, taking a fling at the various other
religions, showing them up by invidious comparison with the creed of
the Valley. He then pointed out the way to arrive at Mormon sanctity, in which there was nothing objectionable as laid down, and
exhorted the congregation, not only as they valued their salvation,
but their crops, to so demean themselves, and endeavour to propitiate
the favour and indulgence of the Supreme Being, calling to mind that,
in the year of righteousness (last year) he sent sea-gulls, a bird never
before known to visit the valley, to devour the crickets, who would
otherwise, from their numbers, have annihilated all vegetation.*

" He then adverted to the barbarous treatment they received at the
hands of the Americans, forgetting to avow his charitable forgiveness,
and expressed a belief that their avarice would yet induce them to
covet their possessions in Salt Sake; but he entertained a hope that
the Mormons by that time would be strong enough to guard and
maintain their rights and independence. He talked of the gold of
California, which he said was discovered by Mormon energy, but they
freely abandoned it to American cupidity, as they (the Mormons) did
not desire such worldly aggrandizement.

"The affairs of Church and State here go strictly hand in hand, the
elders of the Church being the magistrates and functionaries in all
civil and criminal matters, the framers of the law and chancellors of
the exchequer, with whom it is expected that every member of the
community will lodge whatever wealth they may acquire beyond
their immediate wants, taking treasury notes of acknowledgment.

---

* It is surprising the Mormons, who are, as a class, a most astute and reasoning
people, can be gulled and gammoned after this fashion, for sea-gulls are met all across
the plains, and were seen in the Valley the first time Colonel Fremont visited it, in 1845,
two years before the Mormons thought of settling there.

" There are no written laws among them ; but trespasses, outrages, and such matters, are taken cognizance of by the elders, and adjudicated on summarily, according to conscience, fines and public flogging being the punishments most in vogue. The authorities have a mint, from which they issue gold coin only ; it is plain, but massive, without any alloy,

" There are, as far as I could hear or judge, about 5,000 inhabitants in the town, and 7,000 more in the settlements, which extend forty miles each way—north to the Weber, and south towards Utah Lake. The valley, at its greatest width, is not over fifteen miles, and I think seven would be a fair average. Its soil is a rich black loam, and is watered, besides the Jordan, which flows through its centre from Utah to Salt Lake, by innumerable springs of good water, and streamlets flowing from the snowy mountains ; but it has a naked bleak look for want of timber, which renders the effects of the sun next thing to unbearable. The city is situated on the south-east end of the lake, about nine miles from its shores."

Brigham Young, in a paragraph previously quoted, talks magniloquently of gold as being only fit for the paving of streets and the roofing of houses ; but it appears that the sect has been so successful at the diggings of California, as well as at the more profitable diggings of the soil of a grain and fruit produce country, that they have put aside $3\frac{1}{2}$ tons, or 94,080 ounces, of gold, gathered in California, for the purpose of " gathering" the poor Saints from England and other parts of Europe, as well as from the remote districts of the American Union, into the Great Salt Lake Valley. At £4 an ounce, this would amount to £376,320. It is possible that they may have exaggerated their resources in this respect. The gold coinage of their new State of Deseret has been already struck. The five-dollar pieces are of pure Californian gold, without alloy, and somewhat smaller, but much heavier, than a sovereign. The reverse bears the inscription, " Holiness to the Lord," surmounting the eye of Jehovah, and a cap somewhat like a mitre, both very rudely executed. The obverse bears two hands joined, and the words, " Five dollars." The two and a half dollar pieces are precisely similar.

MORMON GOLD COIN.

CEREMONY OF CONFIRMATION.

CHAPTER X.

MORMONISM—ITS PRESENT STATE, AND SOCIAL, POLITICAL, AND RELIGIOUS ASPECT.

IN tracing the history of the rise and progress of Mormonism, and detailing the varied fortunes of the founders and leaders of the new faith, as well as of the large community who have recognised Joseph Smith as the prophet of God, and his Book of Mormon as a new Bible, we have necessarily omitted to notice many controversial points, in order that the continuity of the narrative might not be broken. Having concluded this portion of the work, we proceed to the consideration of the present state of Mormonism, and to the arguments by which its divinity is asserted by the men who believe in it.

The discovery of the Book of Mormon is connected, by the believers in it, with certain Scripture doctrines and prophecies concerning the Latter Days. Hence, indeed, the designation of the sect, as the Church of the Latter-Day Saints. Here, we have to admire the cleverness of the case which they have contrived to make out for themselves. The wonder is, that so much plausible evidence should be collectible in support of the most transparent pious fraud ever attempted to be palmed off on the credulity of mankind. However, so it is; and it is " writ down in our duty " to say a few words on this curious point.

In treating of this subject, in his pamphlet on the Divine Authenticity of the Book of Mormon, Mr. Orson Pratt, by far the ablest writer whom Mormonism has produced, commences by a triumphant recapitulation of the means by which he has reduced his opponents to the necessity of asserting a mere negation in defence of their disbelief. Secure in the strength of his affirmative position, he characteristically defies " all the powers of priestcraft, editors, and the infernal regions combined," to disprove his " vast amount of most incontestible evidences," by which it has been " abundantly " testified that " the Book of Mormon has been confirmed by the voice of the Lord, by the ministry of angels, by heavenly visions, or by the miraculous gifts and powers of the Holy Ghosts, unto tens of thousands of witnesses." Nay, he boldly declares that " if any one will follow the steps of demonstration which he has pointed out, he will know with the same certainty that it is a revelation from God, that a geometrician has when he follows the rules of demonstration in relation to any particular problem."

Such being the state of the argument, Mr. Orson Pratt professes to feel that he need call no further witnesses; but nevertheless, for the sake of completeness, he summons the prophets into court. He takes the last first. St. John on Patmos (Revelations, xiv. 6, 7, 8), and his vision of an angel " having the everlasting Gospel to preach unto them that dwell on the earth," in the latter days, which, of course, is none other than the all-needed New Revelation contained in the " Book of Mormon," with the restoration of the Gospel priesthood, its gifts, powers, and blessings. Hitherto the world has had a history (in the New Testament) of the Gospel, but not its enjoyment. That the angel was to preach his Everlasting Gospel " to every nation, kindred, tongue, and people," shows that they were to be previously destitute of it, as they have been practically. Now, the " Book of Mormon " contains the Everlasting Gospel in all its fulness; moreover, it has been revealed to the inhabitants of earth by " an angel." Q. E. D.

COROLLARY.—" The only people that do testify that the Gospel has been restored to the earth by an angel are the Latter-Day Saints; therefore, if the Gospel is restored, the Latter-Day Saints are the only people to whom it is restored; all others testify that it has not

R

been restored to them. If the only people who do testify to the restoration of the Gospel by an angel be impostors, then all nations must still be in darkness, without the Gospel, and without a Christian Church, and must remain so until the angel is sent in fulfilment of John's prediction."

Again. The Church of the Latter-Day Saints is none other than the Stone foretold by Daniel to smite the Image upon its feet of iron and clay. The [Mormon] proof follows :—

" The nations of modern Europe, including England and the Gentile nations of America, compose the legs, and feet, and toes, of the image, while the other portions of the Image will be found mostly among the Asiatic nations. The geographical position of the image is from east to west ; its head is found in Asia, and its toes in Europe and America. When the kingdom of God is set up, it must be somewhere near the western extremity of this great image, for the toes and feet are first broken by it, and afterwards all the other portions, from which we learn that its advancement is from west to east. The progress of the kingdoms of the world has been from east to west ; the progress of the kingdom of God is from west to east, in a retrograde direction. This stone, according to Daniel (ii. 45), is to be ' CUT OUT OF THE MOUNTAIN WITHOUT HANDS,' 'Cut out of the mountain,' signifies its location before any part of the image is broken. The present location of the Latter-Day Church is in the valleys among the *Rocky Mountains ;* this appears to be its appropriate position, according to prophecy. The stone is to be ' cut out *without hands :*' this signifies that it is a kingdom, not formed by the will of man, but by the will of God ; human wisdom has no hand in its formation ; it is ' the God of Heaven ' that sets it up, and by him it will be sustained and never be destroyed, nor broken to pieces, nor left to other people.

" The kingdoms of the world made war upon the saints of the former-day kingdom, and prevailed against them, and overcame them, and rooted them out of the earth, so that the kingdom no longer existed among the nations ; not so with the Latter-Day kingdom ; for it will prevail against the kingdoms of the world, until they shall, as Daniel says, ' become like the chaff of the summer thrashing-floors : and the wind carry them away, that no place shall be found for them ; and the stone that smote the image shall become a great mountain, and fill the whole earth' (Daniel, ii. 35). And then shall the kingdom and dominion, and the greatness of the kingdom under the whole heaven, be given to the people of the saints of the Most High, whose kingdom is an everlasting kingdom, and all dominions shall serve and obey him' (Daniel, vii. 27). The events predicted by Daniel are the same as the events predicted by John ; Daniel says a kingdom shall be set up : John tells us by what means, namely, through the ever-lasting Gospel, revealed by an angel. Daniel says, when the kingdom of God is set up, that the kingdoms of the world shall be broken in pieces : John says, that when the everlasting Gospel has been restored and preached to the nations, that then is 'the hour of God's judgment' —the downfall of Babylon. Both of these writers beheld the same great events, but described them in different language. That which was predicted by those two inspired men is now being fulfilled. The angel has appeared—the Gospel is restored—the kingdom is set up—its location is among the mountains, and shortly the balance of these predictions will also be fulfilled to the very letter, and not one jot or tittle shall fail, until the earth shall rest from wickedness, and 'the kingdoms of this world become the kingdoms of our God and his Christ.'"

But the great proof of all, according to the believers in Joseph Smith and his book, is derived from the 29th chapter of Isaiah, and his prophecy concerning Ariel therein contained, particularly the latter part of the second verse—"And IT shall be unto me as Ariel."* Taking advantage of the current translation, which seems to compare by the word " it," some other place to Ariel, the Mormon writer contends that another nation than Jerusalem, suffering similar judgments is intended. The rest of the argument must be taken in Mr. Orson Pratt's own words : —

" In the three following verses, the Lord describes more fully the second event ; he says, 'And I will camp against thee round about, and will lay siege against thee with a mount, and I will raise forts against thee. And thou shalt be brought down, *and shalt speak out of the ground, and thy speech shall be low out of the dust, and thy voice shall be as of one that hath a familiar spirit, out of the ground, and thy speech shall whisper out of the dust.* Moreover, the multitude of thy strangers shall be like small dust, and the multitude of the terrible ones shall be as chaff that passeth away ; yea, it shall be at an instant suddenly.' These predictions of Isaiah could not refer to Ariel, or Jerusalem, because their speech has not been 'out of the ground,' or 'low out of the dust,' but it refers to the remnant of Joseph who were destroyed in America upwards of fourteen hundred years ago. The Book of Mormon describes their downfall, and truly it was great and terrible. At the crucifixion of Christ, 'the multitude of their terrible-ones,' as Isaiah predicted, ' became as chaff that passed away.' and it took place, as he further predicts, ' at an instant suddenly.' Many of their great and magnificent cities were destroyed by fire, others by earthquakes, others by being sunk and buried in the depths of the

* It is believed that the correct translation of the passage is "And it shall indeed be an Ariel (a stout lion) to me," a play upon the name.

earth. This sudden destruction came upon them because they had stoned and killed the prophets sent among them. Between three and four hundred years after Christ, they again fell into great wickedness, and the principal nation fell in battle. Forts were raised in all parts of the land, the remains of which may be seen at the present day. Millions of the people perished in battle, and they suffered just as the Lord foretold by Isaiah, " And I will camp against thee round about, and will lay siege against thee with a mount, and I will raise forts against thee, and thou shalt be brought down, and shalt speak out of the ground,' &c. This remnant of Joseph in their distress and destruction, became unto the Lord AS Ariel. As the Roman Army lay siege to Ariel, and brought upon her great distress and sorrow, so did the contending nations of ancient America bring upon each other the most direful scenes of blood and carnage. Therefore the Lord could, with the greatest propriety, when speaking in reference to this event, declare that ' It shall be unto me as Ariel.' "

' One of the most marvellous things connected with this prediction is, that after the nation should be brought down, they should ' speak out of the ground.' This is mentioned or repeated four times in the same verse. Never was a prophecy more truly fulfilled than this, in the coming forth of the Book of Mormon. Joseph Smith took that sacred history " out of the ground." It is the voice of the ancient prophets of America speaking ' out of the ground.' Their speech ' is low out of the dust ;' it speaks in a most familiar manner of the doings of bygone ages ; it is the voice of those who slumber in the dust. It is the voice of prophets speaking from the dead, crying repentance in the ears of the living. In what manner could a nation, after they were brought down and destroyed, ' speak out of the ground ?' Could their dead bodies, or their dust, or their ashes speak ? Verily, no : they can only speak by their writings, or their books that they wrote while living. Their voice, or speech, or words, can only ' speak out of the ground,' or whisper out of the dust,' by their books or writings being discovered. Therefore, Isaiah further says, in the eleventh and twelfth verses, ' And the vision of all is become unto you as the words of a book that is sealed, which men deliver to one that is learned, saying, read this, I pray thee ; and he saith, I cannot, for it is sealed ; and the book is delivered to him that is not learned, saying, read this, I pray thee; and he saith, I am not learned.'

" After obtaining the Book of Mormon through the ministry of the angel ' out of the ground,' Mr. Smith transcribed some of the original characters upon paper, and sent them by the hands of Martin Harris, a farmer, to the city of New York, where they were presented to Professor Anthon, a man deeply learned in both ancient and modern languages. Mr. Harris very anxiously requested the learned professor to read it, but he replied that he could not. None of the learned have as yet been able to decipher the characters and hieroglyphics which are found among the ancient ruins, in almost every part of America. The written language of ancient America is a sealed language to this generation."

The story is then told of Professor Anthon's considering the application made to him as "a hoax," and particularly because of the "singular medley" presented by the alleged letters, which were arranged in columns like the Chinese mode of writing. In this it would now appear that Professor Anthon judged too hastily. Some American glyphs discovered by Professor Rafinesque, and of which fac-similes were given in his Asiatic Journal for 1832, (two years after the publication of the Book of Mormon), agree very much with the description of the specimen as shown to him by the Mormon emissary. Thus, we are told by Professor Rafinesque that "the glyphs of Otolum are written from top to bottom, like the Chinese, or from side to side, indifferently, like the Egyptian and the Demotic Lybian. Although the most common way of writing the groups is in rows, and each group separated, yet we find some formed, as it were, in oblong squares or tablets, like those of Egypt." The glyphs found by the Professor in Mexico, were arranged in columns, being forty-six in number. These the learned professor denominates "the elements of the glyphs of Otolum," and he supposes that by the combination of these elements, words and sentences were formed, constituting the written language of the ancient nations of that vast continent. By an inspection of the fac-simile of these forty-six elementary glyphs, we find all the particulars which Professor Anthon ascribes to the characters, which, he says Martin Harris, a "plain looking countryman" presented to him. The "Greek, Hebrew, and all sorts of letters," inverted and in different positions, "with sundry delineations of half-moons," planets, suns, "and other natural objects," are found among these forty-six elements. This "plain-looking countryman," according to Professor Anthon's testimony, got, says Mr. Orson Pratt, "some three or four years the start of Professor Rafinesque, and presented him with the genuine elementary glyphs years before the Atlantic Journal made them public; and what is still more remarkable, 'the characters,' Professor Anthon says, 'were arranged in columns, like the Chinese mode of writing,' which exactly corresponds with what Professor Rafinesque testifies, as quoted above, in relation to the glyphs of Otolum. We see nothing in Professer Anthon's statement that proves the characters presented to him to be a 'hoax,' as he terms it; unless, indeed, he considers their exact resemblance to the glyphs of Otolum, and their being arranged in the right kind of columns, is a 'hoax.' But, as Joseph Smi h was an unlearned young man, living in the country, where he had not access to the writings and discoveries of antiquarians, he would be entirely incapable of forging the true and genuine glyphs of ancient America; therefore we consider this testimony of Professor Anthon, coming as it does from an avowed enemy of the Book of Mormon to be a great collateral evidence in its favour. Professor Rafinesque says, as we have already quoted, that 'the glyphs of Otolum are written from top to bottom, like the *Chinese*, or from side to side, indifferently, like the *Egyptian*.' Now the most of the Book of Mormon was written from side to side, like the Egyptian. Indeed, it was written in the ancient Egyptian, reformed by the remnant of the tribe of Joseph."

Other glyphs have since been found, as we learn from the following statement which appeared in the *Times and Seasons:*—

"On the 16th of April, 1843, a respectable merchant, by the name of Robert Wiley, commenced digging in a large mound near this place; he excavated to the depth of ten feet, and came to rock. About that time the rain began to fall, and he abandoned the work. On the 23rd, he and quite a number of the citizens, with myself, repaired to the mound, and after making ample opening, we found plenty of rock, the most of which appeared as though it had been strongly burned; and after removing full two feet of said rock, we found plenty of charcoal and ashes, also human bones, that appeared as though they had been burned; and near the eciphalon a bundle was found that consisted of Six Plates of Brass, of a bell shape, each having a hole near the small end, and a ring through them all, and clasped with two clasps. The ring and clasps appeared to be iron, very much oxidated: the plates first appeared to be copper, and had the appearance of being covered with characters. It was agreed by the company that I should cleanse the plates. Accordingly, I took them to my house, washed them with soap and water, and a woollen cloth; but finding them not yet cleansed, I treated them with dilute sulphuric acid, which made them perfectly clean, on which it appeared that they were completely covered with characters, that none, as yet, have been able to read. Wishing that the world might know the hidden things as fast as they come to light, I was induced to state the facts, hoping that you would give them an insertion in your excellent paper, for we all feel anxious to know the true meaning of the plates; and publishing the facts might lead to the true translation. They were found, I judge, more than twelve feet below the surface of the top of the mound.

"I am, most respectfully, a citizen of Kinderhook,

"W. P. HARRIS, M.D."

The following certificate was forwarded for publication at the same time:

"We, citizens of Kinderhook, whose names are annexed, do certify and declare, that on the 23rd of April, 1843, while excavating a large mound in this vicinity Mr. Wiley took from said mound *six brass plates*, of a bell shape, covered with ancient characters. Said plates were very much oxidated. The bands and rings on said plates mouldered into dust on a slight pressure.

" Robert Wiley.   G. W. F. Ward.   Fayette Grubb.
George Dickenson.   J. R. Sharp.   W. P. Harris.
W. Longnecker.   Ira S. Curtis.   W. Fugate."

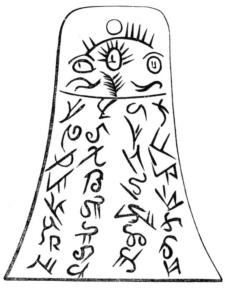

ANCIENT GLYPH.

Of one of the last glyphs we are enabled to present an engraved copy which will allow the reader to judge of their character for himself. We have now to do with the manner in which the Mormons apply the supposed possession of some such plates as these by Joseph Smith to Isaiah's prophecy respecting Ariel, as interpreted by the Latter-Day Saints in their own favour. We therefore proceed with Mr. Orson Pratt's statement :—

" Isaiah says, as we have already quoted, that ' the vision of all is become unto you as the words of a book that is sealed, which men deliver to one that is learned, saying, read this, I pray thee ; and he saith, I cannot for it is sealed.' Mark this prediction ; the Book itself was not to be delivered to the learned, but only ' the WORDS of a

Book ;' this was literally fulfilled in the event which has already been
described, as clearly testified of, not only by the 'plain-looking countryman,' namely, Martin Harris, but by the learned Professor Anthon
himself.

"But Isaiah informs us, in the next verse (12), that the book itself
shall be delivered to the unlearned. He says, 'And the book is delivered to him that is not learned, saying, read this, I pray thee; and
he saith, I am not learned." This was fulfilled when the angel of the
Lord delivered the Book into the hands of Mr. Smith; though unlearned
in every language but his own mother tongue, yet he was commanded
to read or translate the Book. Feeling his own incapacity to read
such a book, he said to the Lord, in the words of Isaiah, 'I am not
learned.' When he made this excuse, the Lord answered him in
the words of Isaiah, next verses (13, 14), 'Wherefore, the Lord said,
forasmuch as this people draw near me with their mouth, and with
their lips do honour me, but have removed their heart far from me, and
their fear toward me is taught by the precept of men; therefore, behold, I will proceed to do a marvellous work among this people, even
a marvellous work and a wonder; for the wisdom of their wise men
shall perish, and the understanding of their prudent men shall be hid.'
What words could better pourtray the powerless apostate condition of
modern Christendom than this description? and what words could be
more descriptive of the 'marvellous work and a wonder,' than to say,
that, the wisdom of their wise men shall perish, and the understanding of their prudent men shall be hid?' What could be more marvellous and wonderful, than for the Lord to cause an unlearned youth
to read or translate a book which the wisdom of the most wise and
learned could not read? Surely the Lord's ways are not as our ways,
and his thoughts are not as our thoughts; for the wisdom of the world
is foolishness in the sight of God; he bringeth forth by his power the
hidden things of his wisdom through the meek, the simple, and the
unlearned, while he rejecteth the wisdom and learning of men, because
of their pride and highmindedness."

To us it is clear that the reply,—" I cannot, for it is sealed," fully
proves that the Prophet meant that the book itself, not the words
only, were delivered to the learned. But we are not here showing
the truth or the contrary of the Mormon argument, but its ingenuity,
which, sometimes, is best shown where it is the most evidently false.
Besides, we must not pause on the way, and the subject is not exhausted. Hear, then, again, Mr. Orson Pratt, the "learned apostle"
of Mormonism :—

"Isaiah, in the ninth and tenth verses, has given a further description of the condition of all the nations, addressing himself to them, he

exclaims, 'Stay yourselves and wonder; cry ye out, and cry: they are drunken, but not with wine; they stagger, but not with strong drink; for the Lord hath poured out upon you the spirit of deep sleep, and hath closed your eyes: the prophets and your rulers, the seers hath he covered, and the vision of all is become unto you as the words of a Book that is sealed,' &c. Here we perceive the dark and benighted condition of the multitude of all the nations; at the time 'the words of the Book' should 'speak out of the ground' 'the spirit of deep sleep' was to be poured out upon them; they were to be drunken and stagger, but not with wine nor with strong drink; the prophets and seers were to be covered from them; and 'the vision of all,' that is, the revelations of all the holy prophets and seers, contained either in the Bible or any other place, were to become as the words of the sealed Book of Mormon. If they understood 'the vision of all' who have spoken in past ages by the spirit of prophecy, they would not be 'drunken,' nor 'stagger,' nor be in a 'deep sleep,' but all nations are drunken with the wine of the wrath of the fornication of great Babylon; they see not, neither do they understand the judgments which are about to befall them. As the learned Professor Anthon could not read the 'the words of the Book' presented to him because it was a sealed book—a language not understood by the learned—so with 'the multitude of all the nations' in regard to 'the vision of all the prophets and seers;' they are covered; they are not understood any more than the words of the sealed Book were understood by the learned. When the events of Scripture prophecy are so clearly fulfilled before their eyes, they will not even then perceive it; when the wisdom of the wise and learned perishes, and a 'marvellous work, and a wonder is performed, in causing the unlearned to read the Book, the nations will not take it to heart; though, as Isaiah says, they will 'stay themselves and wonder,' and 'cry out and cry,' because of the Book which 'speaks out of the ground;' yet, because they are drunken with every species of wickedness and abominations, and because they 'draw near to the Lord with their mouths and with their lips, while their hearts are removed far from him, and because they are taught by the precepts of men they will reject it, and in so doing, they will reject the Lord's great and last warning message to man, and bring upon themselves swift destruction. Because they despise so great a work, they 'shall be visited,' as Isaiah says, 'with storm and tempest,' and 'earthquakes,' and 'the flame of devouring fire.'

"As another evidence that the Book of which Isaiah speaks, was to come forth in the latter times, he says, in the seventeenth verse, 'Is it not yet a very little while, and Lebanon shall be turned into a fruitful field, and the fruitful field shall be esteemed as the forest ? Eighteenth verse: 'And in that day shall the deaf hear the words of the Book, and the eyes of the blind shall see out of obscurity, and out of darkness.' This Book could not mean the New Testament, for when that was written, it was about the time that Lebanon was to be forsaken by the Jews, and become a desolation, a forest or wilderness, for many generations. 'Upon the land of my people shall come up thorns and briers' (Isaiah, xxxii. 13). Hence, the land of Palestine, which includes Lebanon, was, when the New Testament was written, about to be cursed. But immediately after the unlearned should read the Book, 'Lebanon shall be turned into a fruitful field, and the fruitful field shall be esteemed as the forest.' The Book, therefore, that Isaiah prophecies of, is to come forth just before the great day of the restoration of Israel to their own lands ; at which time Lebanon, and all the land of Canaan, is again to be blessed, while the fruitful field, occupied by the nations of the Gentiles, 'will be esteemed as a forest;' the multitude of the nations of the Gentiles are to perish, and their lands, which are now like a fruitful field, are to be left desolate of inhabitants, and become as Lebanon has been for many generations past ; while Lebanon shall again be occupied by Israel, and be turned into a fruitful field.' These great events could not take place until the Lord should first bring forth a book out of the ground.

"'And, in that day, shall the deaf hear the words of the Book.' This has already been literally fulfilled. Those who were so deaf that they could not hear the loudest sound, have had their ears opened to hear the glorious and most precious words of the Book of Mormon, and it has been done by the power of God and not of man. 'And the eyes of the blind shall see out of obscurity and out of darkness.' This has also been literally fulfilled. as abundantly testified of in the fifth number of this series. 'The meek also shall increase their joy in the Lord.' Now, during the long night of darkness, there have been some humble meek persons, who have had a degree of light ; but as the Church of Christ had fled from the earth, there was no one that had authority to baptize or administer the ordinances of the Gospel to those meek persons; therefore, their joy was very imperfect : but Isaiah says, when the Book is revealed, 'the meek shall increase their joy in the Lord.' This is what the Book is calculated to produce ; for by its contents the meek learn that the time is at hand for them to inherit the earth, according to the blessing of our Saviour on the mount: 'Blessed are the meek, for they shall inherit the earth.' This will be fulfilled after all the wicked natons are destroyed. 'And the poor among men shall rejoice in the Holy One of Israel.' This also is promised as a result of the revelation of the Book, and the means by which it is to be effected is by a general overthrow of the wicked ; as, says Isaiah, 'For the terrible one is brought to nought, and the scorner is consumed, and all that watch for iniquity are cut off; that make a man an offender for a word, and lay a snare for him that reproveth in the gate, and turn aside the just for a thing of nought.' O how plainly it is declared that judgment was soon to fall upon all the wicked after the appearance of this Book—this marvellous work and a wonder ! And O how plainly it is also declared that the deaf, the blind, the meek, and the poor among men were to be greatly benefited by the Book ! "

But the prophetic argument of the Mormons has wider ramifications. Not alone Isaiah, but Ezekiel, is produced as a witness :—

" We have already shown from Isaiah that the house of Jacob never could be restored, until God should bring forth a *Book*, and that, too, ' out of the ground;' and, until the deaf should hear the words of it. It will next be shown from the testimony of Ezekiel, that the Book which is to perform so great a work for Israel, was really and truly to be a record of Joseph. Ezekiel says (xxxvii.), ' The Word of the Lord came again unto me, saying, Moreover, thou son of man, take thee one stick, and write upon it, for Judah, and for the children of Israel, his companions; then take another stick, and write upon it, for Joseph the stick of Ephraim, and for all the house of Israel, his companions: and join them one to another into one stick, and they shall become one in thine hand. And when the children of thy people shall speak unto thee, saying, wilt thou not show us what thou meanest by these ? Say unto them, Thus saith the Lord God, Behold, I will take the stick of Joseph which *is* (shall be) in the hand of Ephraim, and the tribes of Israel his fellows, and will put them with him, even with the stick of Judah, and make them one stick, and they shall be one in mine hand. And the sticks whereon thou writest shall be in thine hand before their eyes.

" It was customary in ancient days to write upon parchment, and roll the same upon *sticks*, and such reading-sticks or *rolls* were called *books*. All the prophecies of Jeremiah, from the days of Josiah down to the fourth year of Jehoikim were written in one of these ROLLS (Jeremiah, xxxvi. 1, 2). This ' roll ' of the writings of Jeremiah, is called a ' book ' in the 8th, 10th, 11th, and 13th verses : hence, the terms *roll* and *book* are synonymous. If, then, a reading-stick or roll, containing writings, is called a 'book,' we can all understand the meaning of the word of the Lord to Ezekiel : it was a clear and beautiful representation of the union of two books in the hand of the Lord. Ezekiel was commanded first, to *write* upon one stick, '*for Judah and for the children of Israel his companions.*' This was a representation of the Bible, which is the record of Judah. ' *Then take another stick, and write upon it, for Joseph, the stick of Ephraim, and for all the house of Israel his companions.*' This was a representation of the Book of Mormon, which is the record of Joseph written in ancient America. ' *And join them one to another into one stick, and they shall become one in thine hand.*' This was a representation of the union of the records of the two nations. In the interpretation of the meaning of the two sticks, the Lord says that He himself ' *will take the stick of Joseph*' and put it ' *with the stick of Judah.*' Therefore, we learn by this that the stick of Joseph was not found united with the stick of Judah by accident, but it was a work which the Lord himself should perform. Hence, he further says, ' *They shall be one in mine hand.*' Therefore, the two writings becoming one in Ezekiel's hand, was a most beautiful representation of the two writings which should become one in the Lord's hand.

" Having learned by Ezekiel that the Lord God will take the stick of Joseph, and put it with the stick of Judah, and make them one in his hand; let us next inquire, what events are to follow the union of these two writings. The Lord further declares, 'And the stick whereon thou writest shall be in thine hand before their eyes. And say unto them, Thus saith the Lord God, Behold, I will take the children of Israel from among the heathen, whither they be gone, and will gather them on every side, and bring them into their own land, and I will make them one nation in the land upon the mountains of Israel; and one king shall be king to them all; and they shall be no more two nations, neither shall they be divided into two kingdoms any more at all: neither shall they defile themselves any more with their idols, nor with their detestable things, nor with any of their transgressions; but I will save them out of all their dwelling places, wherein they have sinned, and will cleanse them: so shall they be my people, and I will be their God.' We learn from this, that the great object the Lord has in view, in bringing forth the book of Joseph, and uniting it with the Bible, is to gather Israel never more to be scattered. Thus we see that both Isaiah and Ezekiel have spoken of the same great and marvellous events; one declares that the house of Jacob should never again ' wax pale ' or ' be made ashamed ' in the day that a certain book should make its appearance; the other declares, that the whole house of Israel should be restored to their own lands, and should never again be divided into two nations, in the day that the Lord should put the writings of Joseph with the writings of Judah. Take the testimony of Isaiah and Ezekiel in connection with the testimony of Moses, concerning the ' precious things of heaven,' which should be given on the land of Joseph, and join this with the testimony of John concerning the restoration of the Gospel by an angel, and the testimony of Daniel concerning the stone cut from the mountain without hands, representing the latter-day kingdom of God, and we have, by a combination of all these testimonies, prophetic evidences of the divine authenticity of the Book of Mormon, which should convince the most incredulous, and destroy Atheism out of existence."

Such is the argument of the great Mormon Apostle! After all, however, it is designed exclusively for the profane. He himself needs it not ; he has higher, more immediate evidence.—This !

' And I now bear my humble testimony to all the nations of the earth, who shall read this series of pamphlets, that the Book of Mormon is a divine revelation, for the voice of the Lord hath declared it unto me."

But we must proceed, however, with our abstract of the theology of the Mormons, as it has grown out of and upon the Book of Mormon, as invented by Joseph Smith ; and as it has been developed by the acuter men, such as Orson Pratt, who succeeded him in the management of the sect.

For the last fourteen hundred years, according to the persuasion of the Mormon, the Church has been in a state of suspended animation. Mr. Orson Pratt, too, would prove the allegation out of the mouths of Christian controversialists themselves. "We believe," he states, in " Remarkable Visions, No 6," " That there has been a general and awful apostacy from the religion of the New Testament, so that all the known world have been left for centuries without the Church of Christ among them ; without a priesthood authorized of God to administer ordinances ; that every one of the churches has perverted the gospel; some in one way, and some in another. For instance, almost every church has done away ' immersion for remission of sins.' Those few who have practised it for remission of sins, have done away the ordinance of the ' laying on of hands ' upon baptized believers for the gift of the Holy Ghost. Again, the few who have practised the last ordinance have perverted the first, or have done away the ancient gifts, powers, and blessings, which flow from the Holy Spirit, or have said to inspired apostles and prophets, we have no need of you in the body in these days. Those few, again, who have believed in, and contended for, the miraculous gifts and powers of the Holy Spirit, have perverted the ordinances or done them away. Thus all the churches preach false doctrines and pervert the gospel, and instead of having authority from God to administer its ordinances they are under the curse of God for perverting it."

In corroboration of these views, we are reminded that Protestants

ORSON PRATT.

charge on the churches of Rome and Greece the sin of apostacy, and
Roman Catholics have charged with heresy all reformed churches ;—
mutual recriminations which involve the predicated period of fourteen hundred years in the charge brought against it by the Mormon
prophet. Mr. Pratt, indeed, in his " Divine Authenticity of the
Book of Mormon," boldly declares, that " the whole Romish, Greek,
and Protestant ministry, from the Pope down, through every grade of
office, are as destitute of authority from God, as the Devil and his
angels." And this state of things, (he says,) was prophesied by Paul, in
the memorable words, that " the day of Christ shall not come, except
there come a falling away first," and by other apostles in many texts
of Scripture. The Mormons admit that the churches which have
existed from the first century " have all had a form of godliness, while
denying the power; and they yet stand in the same predicament."

" Such," says Mr. Pratt, in the work just alluded to, " such was to
be the religion of the latter ages, as prophetically described by the
ancient apostles; and such is the religion of the Papal, Greek, and
Protestant churches of the nineteenth century. The predictions were
uttered eighteen centuries ago, and modern Christendom exhibits a

most perfect fulfilment. Instead of having apostles, prophets, and other inspired men in the church now, receiving visions, dreams, revelations, ministry of angels, and prophecies for the calling of officers, and for the government of the church,—they have a wicked, corrupt, uninspired pope, or uninspired archbishops bishops, clergymen, &c., who have a great variety of corrupt forms of Godliness, but utterly, deny the gift of revelation, and every other miraculous power which always characterised Christ's Church. These man-made, powerless, hypocritical false teachers, ' make merchandise of the people,' by preaching for large salaries, amounting in many instances to tens of thousands of pounds sterling annually. They and their deluded followers are reprobate concerning the faith once delivered to the Saints. The faith which once quenched the violence of fire, stopped the mouths of lions, divided waters, and controlled the powers of nature, is discarded as unnecessary. The faith that inspired men with the gift of revelation—that opened the heavens and laid hold on mysteries that were not lawful to be uttered—that unfolded the visions of the past and future—and that called down the angels of heaven to eat and drink with men on earth,—is denied as being attainable in this age. The sound doctrine taught by the apostles which put mankind in the possession of these glorious gifts and powers cannot now be endured. The doctrines, commands, fables, traditions, and creeds, of uninspired men, are now substituted in the place of direct inspiration from God. ' They are ever learning, but are never able to come to the knowledge of the truth.' Guess work, conjecture, opinion, and, perhaps, in some instances, a belief in regard to the truth, are all that they attain to, while a knowledge they do not obtain, because they deny new revelation the only means of obtaining it. This great multitude of false teachers who have found their way into all nations, deceiving millions, ' resist the truth,' contend against the miraculous powers of the gospel, and reject inspired men, as ' Jannes and Jambres'—the magicians, did Moses; but ' their folly shall be made manifest unto all men, as their's also was;' yea, all nations shall see the righteous judgments which shall speedily be executed upon them, for they shall, like Pharaoh's host, perish quickly from the earth."

Pursuing this course of logic, in connexion with the evidence of history Mr. Orson Pratt argues that it is neither unscriptural nor unreasonable to expect more revelation; and that, in fact, more revelation is necessary. This, however, is an argument in behalf of modern visions and prophecyings, and but little in favour of the Book of Mormon, which, like the Scriptures in general, deals with the past, not with the present. And this, as we have before remarked, is the main proposition about which the Mormon advocate is solicitous. That proposition he uses both negatively and affirmatively. Negatively, as against all churches preceding his own :—e. g.

" As the Church of England and other Protestants do not profess to have received any new commission by revelation, but, on the contrary, require their followers to reject everything of the kind, it may be asked, how did they get their authority? It will be replied, that they received it from Wickliffe, Cranmer, Luther, Calvin, and various other dissenters from the Papal Church. But where did those dissenters get theirs from? They answer, from the Roman Catholics. But the Catholics excommunicated them as heretics; and surely if they had power to impart authority, they had power to take it away. Therefore, if the Romish Church had any authority, the Protestants, being excommunicated, can hold none from that source. But if the Catholics hold authority, they must be the true church, and consequently the Protestants must be apostates; but, on the other hand, if the Catholics are not the true church, they can have no authority themselves, and therefore could not impart any to others. Now the Church of England states in one of her homilies. ' *that laity and clergy, learned and unlearned, men and women, and children of all ages, sects, and degrees, of* WHOLE CHRISTENDOM, *have been at once buried in* THE MOST ABOMINABLE IDOLATRY. (*a most dreadful thing to think,) and that for the* SPACE OF EIGHT HUNDRED YEARS OR MORE.' Wesley in his 94th sermon states the same in substance; he says, ' The real cause why the extraordinary gifts of the Holy Ghost were no longer to be found in the Christian Church, was, *because the Christians were turned heathens again, and had only a dead form left.*' If, then, the ' whole of Christendom,' without one exception, have been ' buried in the most abominable idolatry for upwards of eight hundred years,' as the Church of England declares, and if they, because they are destitute of the gifts, are not even now Christians, but heathens as Wesley asserts, we ask where the authority was during the eight hundred years, and where is it now? Surely God would not recognise ' the most abominable idolators,' as holding authority ; if so, the authority of the worshippers of Juggernaut must be as valid as that of idolatrous Christendom. But the idolatry of ' the whole of Christendom' must have been more corrupt, according to the Church of England, than that of other idolaters; for they call it ' *the most abominable idolatry,*' and most positively declare that there was no exception of either clergy or laity—of either man, woman, or child— all were buried in it. This being the case, (and we feel no disposition to dispute it,) there could have been no possible channel on the whole earth through which authority could have been transferred from the apostles to our day. Therefore, as Wesley says, all Christendom are, sure enough, ' *heathens*,' having no more authority nor power than the idolatrous pagans. If, then, the ' whole of Christendom' have been without authority and power ' for eight hundred years and upwards,' we ask, when was the authority restored? how was it restored? and to what man or people was it restored? It could not have been restored to the papal churches, for they do not profess that any such restoration has been made to them; it could not have been restored to the Church of England and other Protestants, for they do not admit of any later revelation than the New Testament; consequently their own admissions prove most clearly that the whole of Christendom are without an authorised ministry; therefore it is indispensably necessary that more revelation should be given to restore the authority to the earth and call men to the ministry again, as in ancient days"

The Mormon writer uses the same proposition affirmatively as justifying the creation and ordination of official persons in the new church of Latter-Day Saints. Revelation, he says, is also necessary to point out their duties. " Without continued revelation the officers of the church can do nothing." "The apostles, and Jesus Christ himself, were under the same necessity in their time." Peter himself was one " of those visionary characters so much despised by modern religionists.'

So far the philosophical historian may recognise in these Mormon doctrines the spirit of reaction against that ultra Protestant opposition to mysticism of which Luther set the example. We therefore cannot do better than sum up the entire argument in the words of its clever though mistaken advocate.

" New revelation is the very life and soul of the religion of heaven, —that it is indispensably necessary for the calling of all officers in the church,—that without it, the officers can never be instructed in the various duties of their callings,—that where the spirit of revelation does not exist, the church cannot be comforted and taught in all wisdom and knowledge,—cannot be properly reproved and chastened according to the mind of God,—cannot obtain promise, for themselves, but are dependent upon the promises made through the ancients. Without new revelation the people are like a blind man groping his way in total darkness, not knowing the dangers that beset his path. Without prophets and revelators, darkness hangs over the future,— no city, people, or nation, understand what awaits them. Without new revelation, no people know of the approaching earthquake—of the deadly plague—of the terrible war—of the withering famine—and of the fearful judgments of the Almighty which hang over their devoted heads. When the voice of living prophets and apostles are no longer heard in the land—there is an end of perfecting and edifying

s

the saints—there is a speedy end to the ' work of the ministry '—there is an end to the obtaining of that knowledge so necessary to eternal life—there is an end to all that is great, and grand, and glorious, pertaining to the religion of heaven—there is an end to the very existence of the church of Christ on the earth—there is an end to salvation in the celestial kingdom.

From this statement, the dogma that " the Bible and tradition, without further revelation, are an insufficient guide," naturally follows as a corollary. Some of the illustrations of this insufficiency are pregnant of suggestion. For instance, has the following any connexion with the spiritual wife doctrine, which, notwitstanding many denials, we are bound, on the authority of Mr. Kelly and many other persons, to believe to be practised by at least some of the Mormons.

" There are many things practised by both Romish and Protestant churches which the Scriptures do not clearly reveal, therefore they must both of them consider that the Scriptures are not a sufficient guide. We are informed in Scripture that marriage is ordained of God, but we are not informed in Scripture who has the right to officiate in this ceremony. Who can tell from the New Testament anything about the order to be observed in relation to this subject? We read that " what God hath joined together let no man put asunder?" but through what particular office does God join together the sexes in matrimony? Can laymen officiate? Can those out of the church officiate? Can a woman officiate? Can the parties join themselves together in matrimony, in the name of the Lord? Who can answer these questions from the Bible alone? No one. The Bible does not guide the church in this important ordinance."

Similar questions are asked in the same manner as to all other ordinances of the church, baptism, confirmation, the Eucharist, ordination, &c, with similar result. The writer then condescends to be jocose; and asks,

" Furthermore, where in the Bible does it say that the king and people of England ought to revolt from the Romish Church, and form a church of their own by act of parliament? If the Bible were a sufficient guide, why was an act of parliament necessary as another guide to form the English Church? If the Bible were a sufficient guide, why was another book made, called the ' Book of Common Prayer,' and the people compelled to give heed to it under pain of banishment, and even death itself? If the articles of religion, contained in the New Testament were a sufficient guide, why were ' Thirty Nine Articles' more, enforced upon the people by acts of parliament, and the people butchered and murdered because they could not conscientiously comply with them? It is certain that this newly-formed-parliament-made church considered the Bible to be very deficient as a guide, or they never would have resorted to such blood-thirsty murderous measures to establish other books in addition to the Bible.

" Again, what part of the Bible has established the salaries of the different officers of the church ? If it be necessary that preachers should have wages, how much shall it be ? How much more shall an apostle get than a prophet ? If a bishop get from ten to twenty thousand pounds for one year's preaching, how much should an inspired apostle or prophet get ? or how much should some of the lower officers have ? the New Testament does not tell us the amount of wages religious hirelings should have, therefore, if it be important to know, the Bible is an insufficient guide. It says, however, that apostles should ' take neither purse nor script,' but it leaves us entirely in the dark, as to how much bishops, arch-bishops, and other officers should have. Would it not be a wise plan for an act of parliament to increase their wages a little, lest they suffer ? We see plainly that the Bible is not a sufficient guide in many, very many points, as the doings of the whole Protestant world most plainly declare."

Practical as all these questions are, and enforced with talent and eloquence not to be despised by any candid writer, they leave the divine authenticity of the Book of Mormon much where they found it. Accordingly, no attempt is made by Mr. Orson Pratt, to argue that question, by reference to internal evidence either of that book or of the Bible, or to support either by tradition or argument, but only by testimony. And that testimony is the story of the angel and the discovery of the buried plates already related. We are to accept the testimony of Joseph Smith and his witnesses ; the Mormons will give us no other. For the rest, they resort to every species of forensic recrimination.

This mode of argument is open to much suspicion. It indicates a bad cause. It is a plea in extenuation, not a proof of non guiltiness. It is the justification of one pious fraud by the allegation of another. To a considerable extent, however, the justification has succeeded, and we are presented with a new church claiming immediate revelation with its specific doctrines, officers, and orders.

These, for the most part, are to be found in another Mormon book, already frequently mentioned, and of which the full title is as follows :

" The Book of Doctrine and Covenants, of the Church of Jesus Christ of Latter-Day Saints, selected from the Revelations of God, by Joseph Smith, President. Liverpool : Orson Pratt.*

* This and the other numerous controversial tracts of the Mormons may be obtained at their Depôt, 35, Jewin Street, Aldersgate Street, London.

This work commences with seven lectures on the subject of faith,
said originally to have been delivered before a class of the elders, in
Kirtland, Ohio; and certainly marked by considerable acumen. On
this point Mr. Bowes, the author of a pamphlet entitled " Mormonism Exposed," and a public debater against the Saints in the manufacturing districts of England, has not been fortunate in attacking
their theology. He charges them with ignorance of the word faith
--he has only proved his own. Faith he says, is crediting testimony,
and asks, "What testimony God had to credit?"—and therefore
concludes that faith is not an attribute of God but of believers. Mr.
Bowes has here confounded speculative belief with practical faith.
With the Mormons, on the contrary, " faith is the principle of power,"
both human and divine. "The principle of power," say they, "which
existed in the bosom of God, by which the worlds were framed, was
faith; and it is by reason of this principle of power existing in the
Deity, that all created things exist; so that all things in heaven, on
earth, or under the earth, exist by reason of faith as it existed in
Him." It is to the credit of the Mormons that, considering faith in its
practical aspects, they have brought it to bear on the actual business
of life, and used it as the corner-stone of the social edifice, though rejected by other builders of churches and of states.

It is because the Mormons accept faith as a practical impulse
rather than as a speculative acquiescence, that they regard the living
prophet with even more esteem than his prophecy, and derive the
authenticity of the book rather from the institution of the church,
than found the church upon the book. They sympathise more
strongly with the Roman Catholic view in relation to the Bible than
with the Protestant. The church to both is the living witness
and interpreter of the dead letter in old documents. With them,
there still exists fellowship between God and man; with them,
the being of the former is testified by immediate inspiration;
and the believing recipient is, as of old, " the temple of the Holy
Ghost."

Now, other and more generally esteemed men than Joseph Smith
—men whom the world has accepted as philosophers, have yearned,
in these latter days, to supply the void which they felt to exist as a
want in modern Christendom. Luther's reformation in Europe was
directly opposed to the mystical spirit which lies concealed in the
bosom of all religious communities, and which, though the great re-
former sought to extinguish it, continues still unquenched to the
present time, and, as his biography proves, was not absent in his
deeper moods from his own mental operations. The Chillingworth
doctrine of " the Bible, and the Bible alone being the religion of

Protestants," had a tendency to substitute for the idolatry of the priest the idolatry of the book; and, indeed, it was a favourite tenet, and, strange as it may appear, the boast of the orthodox, that " there was no vision in the land." The time for miraculous communication was passed for ever. The great American sage, Mr. Emerson, felt the burthen of the Protestant yoke in this particular; and, in one of his lectures, declares that its teaching is equivalent to an admission that " God is dead," in respect to the human race at the present time. Now this is a conclusion against which the thinking man will reasonably revolt. Nor is much education required to perceive its fallacy. The self instructed man would be one of the first to perceive it. No wonder, then, that in some part of the Christian world, there should be a Joseph Smith, who would be deeply affected with such perception; and, pursuing the practical tendencies of a working-man, should seek to carry out its results in connexion with the actual conditions and relations of the social state, collectively and individually.

To accomplish such an end, the first thing to be done is, to destroy the Bibliolatry that impedes it. The infidel sought to do this by invalidating the Scriptures; but modern sages have proposed, on the other hand, to invest the whole range of literature with Divine sanctions, and to accept poets and philosophers as everywhere and always inspired. Joseph Smith adopted a more compact method. He set up a second Bible to partake the honours of the first; and having thus divided the homage, and thereby weakened the idolatry, he prepared the way for the acceptance of new pretensions. A third Bible was now possible, which should record the origin, progress, and full establishment of a new dispensation entrusted to his own personal conduct as a prophet.

The lecturer " on Faith " in the Book of Doctrine proceeds to ask, " Who cannot see, then, that salvation is the effect of faith? for, as we have previously observed, all the heavenly beings work by this principle; and it is because they are able so to do that they are saved, for nothing but this could save them. And this is the lesson which the God of heaven, by the mouth of all his holy prophets, has been endeavouring to teach to the world. Hence we are told, that without faith it is impossible to please God; and that salvation is of faith, that it might be by grace, to the end the promise might be sure to all the seed. Romans iv. 16. And that Israel, who followed after the law of righteousness, has not attained to the law of righteousness. Wherefore? Because they sought it not by faith, but as it were by the works of the law; for they stumbled at that stumbling stone. Romans ix. 32. And Jesus said unto the man who

brought his son to him, to get the devil who tormented him cast out,
' If thou canst believe, all things are possible to him that believeth.'
Mark ix. 23. These, with a multitude of other scriptures which
might be quoted, plainly set forth the light in which the Saviour, as
well as the Former-Day Saints, viewed the plan of salvation. That
it was a system of faith—it begins with faith, and continues by
faith; and every blessing which is obtained in relation to it, is the
effect of faith, whether it pertains to this life or that which is to
come. To this all the revelations of God bear witness. If there
were children of promise, they were the effects of faith, not even the
Saviour of the world excepted. ' Blessed is she that believeth,'
said Elizabeth to Mary, when she went to visit her, ' for there shall
be a performance of the things which were told her of the Lord.'
Luke i. 45. Nor was the birth of John the Baptist the less a matter
of faith; for in order that his father Zacharias might believe, he was
struck dumb. And through the whole history of the scheme of life
and salvation, it is a matter of faith : every man received according
to his faith—according as his faith was, so were his blessings and
privileges; and nothing was withheld from him when his faith was
sufficient to receive it. He could stop the mouths of lions, quench
the violence of fire, escape the edge of the sword, wax valiant in
fight, and put to flight the armies of the aliens; women could, by
their faith, receive their dead children to life again ; in a word, there
was nothing impossible with them who had faith. All things were
in subjection to the Former-Day Saints, according as their faith was.
By their faith they could obtain heavenly visions, the ministering of
angels, have knowledge of the spirits of just men made perfect, of the
general assembly and church of the first born, whose names are
written in heaven, of God the judge of all, of Jesus the Mediator of
the new covenant, and become familiar with the third heavens, see
and hear things which were not only unutterable, but were unlawful
to utter."

These lectures are followed by sections entitled, " Doctrines and
Commandments," which are given as from " the Lord, to his servants of the Church of Jesus Christ of Latter-Day Saints." In the
second section the origin of the church is thus dated.

" 1. The rise of the church of Christ in these last days, being one
thousand eight hundred and thirty years since the coming of our
Lord and Saviour Jesus Christ in the flesh, it being regularly organized and established agreeably to the laws of our country, by the
will and commandments of God, in the fourth month, and on the
sixth day of the month which is called April ; which commandments
were given to Joseph Smith jun., who was called of God, and or-

dained an apostle of Jesus Christ, to be the first elder of this church; and to Oliver Cowdery, who was also called of God, an apostle of Jesus Christ to be the second elder of this church, and ordained under his hand; and this according to the grace of our Lord and Saviour Jesus Christ, to whom be all glory, both now and for ever. Amen.

" 2. After it was truly manifested unto this first elder that he had received a remission of his sins, he was entangled again in the vanities of the world; but after repenting, and humbling himself sincerely, through faith, God ministered unto him by an holy angel, whose countenance was as lightning, and whose garments were pure and white above all other whiteness; and gave unto him commandments which inspired him; and gave him power from on high, by the means which were before prepared, to translate the Book of Mormon, which contains a record of a fallen people, and the fulness of the gospel of Jesus Christ to the Gentiles and to the Jews also, which was given by inspiration, and is confirmed to others by the ministering of angels, and is declared unto the world by them, proving to the world that the Holy Scriptures are true, and that God does inspire men and call them to his holy work in this age and generation, as well as in generations of old, thereby showing that he is the same God yesterday, to-day, and for ever. Amen."

We are then instructed in those particulars in which it was above stated the Scriptures are an insufficient guide.

" 7. *And again, by way of commandment to the church concerning the manner of baptism.*—All those who humble themselves before God, and desire to be baptized and come forth with broken hearts and contrite spirits, and witness before the church that they have truly repented of all their sins, and are willing to take upon them the name of Jesus Christ, having a determination to serve him to the end, and truly manifest by their works that they have received of the spirit of Christ unto the remission of their sins, shall be received by baptism into his church.

" 8. *The duty of the elders, priests, teachers, deacons, and members of the church of Christ.*—An apostle is an elder, and it is his calling to baptize and to ordain other elders, priests, teachers, and deacons, and to administer bread and wine—the emblems of the flesh and blood of Christ—and to confirm those who are baptized into the church, by the laying on of hands for the baptism of fire and the Holy Ghost, according to the Scriptures; and to teach, expound, exhort, baptize, and watch over the church; and to confirm the church by the laying on of the hands, and the giving of the Holy Ghost, and to take the lead of all meetings.

" 9. The elders are to conduct the meetings as they are led by the Holy Ghost, according to the commandments and revelations of God.

" 10. The priests' duty is to preach, teach, expound, exhort, and baptize, and administer the sacrament, and visit the house of each member, and exhort them to pray vocally and in secret, and attend to all family duties; and he may also ordain other priests, teachers, and deacons. And he is to take the lead of meetings when there is no elder present; but when there is an elder present, he is only to preach, teach, expound, exhort, and baptize, and visit the house of each member, exhorting them to pray vocally and in secret, and attend to all family duties. In all these duties the priest is to assist the elder if occasion requires.

" 11. The teacher's duty is to watch over the church always, and be with and strengthen them, and see that there is no iniquity in the church—neither hardness with each other—neither lying, back biting, nor evil speaking; and see that the church meet together often, and also see that all the members do their duty; and he is to take the lead of meetings in the absence of the elder priest—and is to be assisted always, in all his duties in the church, by the deacons, if occasion requires; but neither teachers nor deacons have authority to baptize, administer the sacrament, or lay on hands; they are, however, to warn, expound, exhort, and teach and invite all to come unto Christ.

" 12. Every elder, priest, teacher, or deacon, is to be ordained according to the gifts and callings of God unto him; and he is to be ordained by the power of the Holy Ghost, which is in the one who ordains him.

" 13. The several elders, composing this church of Christ are to meet in conference once in three months, or from time to time as said conferences shall direct or appoint; and said conferences are to do whatever church business is necessary to be done at the time.

" 14. The elders are to receive their licenses from other elders, by vote of the church to which they belong, or from the conferences.

" 15. Each priest, teacher, or deacon, who is ordained by a priest may take a certificate from him at the time, which certificate, when presented to an elder, shall entitle him to a license, which shall authorize him to perform the duties of his calling, or he may receive it from a conference.

" 16. No person is to be ordained to any office in this church, where there is a regularly organised branch of the same, without the vote of that church; but the presiding elders, travelling bishops, high counsellors, high priests, and elders, may have the privilege of ordaining, where there is no branch of the church that a vote may be called.

"17. Every president of the high priesthood, (or presiding elder,) bishop, high counsellor, and high priest, is to be ordained by the direction of a high council or general conference.

"18. *The duty of the members after they are received by baptism.*—The elders or priests are to have a sufficient time to expound all things concerning the church of Christ to their understanding, previous to their partaking of the sacrament and being confirmed by the laying on of the hands of the elders, so that all things may be done in order. And the members shall manifest before the church, and also before the elders, by a godly walk and conversation, that they are worthy of it, that there may be works and faith agreeable to the Holy Scriptures—walking in holiness before the Lord.

CEREMONY OF BAPTISM.

" 19. Every member of the Church of Christ having children, is to bring them unto the elders before the church, who are to lay their hands upon them in the name of Jesus Christ, and bless them in his name.

" 20. No one can be received into the church of Christ, unless he has arrived unto the years of accountability before God, and is capable of repentance.

" 21. Baptism is to be administered in the following manner unto all those who repent:—The person who is called of God, and has authority from Jesus Christ to baptize, shall go down into the water with the person who has presented him or herself for baptism, and shall say, calling him or her by name—Having been commissioned of Jesus Christ, I baptize you in the name of the Father, and of the Son, and of the Holy Ghost. Amen. Then shall he immerse him or her in the water, and come forth again out of the water.

" 22. It is expedient that the church meet together often, to partake of bread and wine in remembrance of the Lord Jesus; and the elder or priest shall administer it; and after this manner shall he administer it—he shall kneel with the church and call upon the Father in solemn prayer, saying—O God, the eternal Father, we ask thee in the name of thy son, Jesus Christ, to bless and sanctify this bread to the souls of all those who partake of it, that they may eat in remembrance of the body of thy Son, and witness unto thee O God, the eternal Father, that they are willing to take upon them the name of thy Son, and always remember him and keep his commandments which he has given them, that they may always have his spirit to be with them. Amen.

" 23. The manner of administering the wine. He shall take the cup also, and say—O God, the eternal Father, we ask thee in the name of thy Son Jesus Christ, to bless and sanctify this wine to the souls of all those who drink of it, that they may do it in remembrance of the blood of thy Son, which was shed for them; that they may witness unto thee O God, the eternal Father; that they do always remember him, that they may have his spirit to be with them. Amen."

In section III. we are presented with still more important matter.

" 1. There are, in the Church, two priesthoods, namely, the Melchizidek, and the Aaronic, including the Levitical priesthood. Why the first is called the Melchizidek priesthood, is because Melchizidek was such a great high priest. Before his day it was called *the holy priesthood, after the order of the Son of God;* but out of respect or reverence to the name of the Supreme Being, to avoid the too frequent repetition of his name, they, the church, in ancient days, called that priesthood after Melchizidek, or the Melchizidek priesthood.

" 2. All other authorities or offices in the Church are appendages to this priesthood; but there are two divisions or grand heads—one in the Melchizidek priesthood, and the other in the Aaronic, or Levitical priesthood.

" 3. The office of an elder comes under the priesthood of Melchizidek. The Melchizidek priesthood holds the right of presidency, and has power and authority over all the offices in the church in all ages of the world, to administer in spiritual things.

" 4. The presidency of the high priesthood, after the order of Melchizidek, have a right to officiate in all the offices in the church.

" 5. High priests after the order of the Melchizidek priesthood, have a right to officiate in their own standing, under the direction of the presidency, in administering spiritual things; and also in the office of an elder, priest (of the Levitical order), teacher, deacon, and member.

" 6. An elder has a right to officiate in his stead when the high priest is not present.

" 7. The high priest and elder are to administer in spiritual things, agreeably to the covenants and commandments of the church; and they have a right to officiate in all these offices of the church when there are no higher authorities present.'

" 8. The second priesthood is called the priesthood of Aaron, because it was conferred upon Aaron and his seed, throughout all their generations. Why it is called the lesser priesthood, is because it is an appendage to the greater or the Melchizidek priesthood, and has power in administering outward ordinances. The bishopric is the presidency of this priesthood, and holds the keys or authority of the same. No man has a legal right to this office, to hold the keys of this priesthood, except he be a literal descendant of Aaron. But as a high priest of the Melchizidek priesthood has authority to officiate in all the lesser offices, he may officiate in the office of bishop when no literal descendant of Aaron can be found, provided he is called and set apart and ordained unto this power by the hands of the presidency of the Melchizidek priesthood.

" 9. The power and authority of the higher or Melchizidek priesthood, is to hold the keys of all the spiritual blessings of the church— to have the privilege of receiving the mysteries of the kingdom of heaven—to have the heavens opened unto them—to commune with the general assembly and church of the first-born, and to enjoy the communion and presence of God the Father, and Jesus the Mediator of the new covenant.

" 10. The power and authority of the lesser or Aaronic priesthood, is to hold the keys of the ministering of angels, and to administer, in outward ordinances, the letter of the gospel—the baptism of repentance for the remission of sins, agreeably to the covenants and commandments.

" 11. Of necessity there are presidents, or presiding offices growing out of, or appointed of or from among those who are ordained to the several offices in these two priesthoods. Of the Melchizidek priesthood, three presiding high priests, chosen by the body, appointed and ordained to that office, and upheld by the confidence, faith, and prayer of the church, form a quorum of the presidency of the church. The twelve travelling counsellors are called to be the twelve apostles, or especial witnesses of the name of Christ in all the world ; thus differing from other officers in the church in the duties of their calling. And they form a quorum, equal in authority and power to the three presidents previously mentioned. The seventy are also called to preach the gospel, and to be especial witnesses unto the Gentiles and in all the world. Thus differing from other officers in the church in the duties of their calling ; and they form a quorum equal in authority to that of the twelve especial witnesses or apostles just named. And every decision made by either of these quorums, must be by the unanimous voice of the same ; that is, every member in each quorum must be agreed to its decisions, in order to make their decisions of the same power or validity one with the other. (A majority may form a quorum, when circumstances render it impossible to be otherwise.) Unless this is the case, their decisions are not entitled to the same blessings which the decisions of a quorum of three presidents were anciently, who were ordained after the order of Melchizidek, and were righteous and holy men. The decisions of these quorums, or either of them, are to be made in all righteousness, in holiness and lowliness of heart, meekness and long-suffering, and in faith, and virtue, and knowledge, temperance, patience, godliness, brotherly kindness, and charity ; because the promise is, if these things abound in them, they shall not be unfruitful in the knowledge of the Lord. And in case that any decision of these quorums is made in unrighteousness, it may be brought before a general assembly of the several quorums, which constitute the spiritual authorities of the church, otherwise there can be no appeal from their decision.

" 12. The twelve are a travelling presiding high council, to officiate in the name of the Lord, under the direction of the presidency of the church, agreeably to the institution of heaven ; to build up the church, and regulate all the affairs of the same in all nations; first unto the Gentiles, and secondly unto the Jews.

" 13. The seventy are to act in the name of the Lord, under the direction of the twelve or the travelling high council, in building up the church and regulating all the affairs of the same in all nations—first unto the Gentiles, and then unto the Jews; the twelve being sent out, holding the keys, to open the door by the proclamation of the gospel of Jesus Christ—and first unto the Gentiles and then unto the Jews.

" 14. The standing high councils, at the stakes of Sion, form a quorum, equal in authority, in the affairs of the church, in all their decisions, to the quorum of the presidency, or to the travelling high council.

" 15. The high council in Zion, forms a quorum equal in authority, in the affairs of the church, in all their decisions, to the councils of the twelve at the stakes of Zion.

" 16. It is the duty of the travelling high council to call upon the seventy, when they need assistance, to fill the several calls for preach-ing and administering the gospel, instead of any others.

" 17. It is the duty of the twelve, in all large branches of the church, to ordain evangelical ministers. as they shall be designated unto them by revelation.

" 18. The order of this priesthood was confirmed to be handed down from father to son, and rightly belongs to the literal descend-ants of the chosen seed, to whom the promises were made. This order was instituted in the days of Adam, and came down by lineage in the following manner:—

" 19. From Adam to Seth, who was ordained by Adam at the age of 69 years, and was blessed by him three years previous to his (Adam's) death, and received the promise of God by his father. that his posterity should be the chosen of the Lord and that they should be unreserved unto the end of the earth, because he (Seth) was a per-fect man, and his likeness was the express likeness of his father's, in-somuch that he seemed to be like unto his father in all things, and could be distinguished from him only by his age.

" 20. Enos was ordained at the age of 134 years and four months, by the hand of Adam.

" 21. God called upon Cainan in the wilderness, in the fortieth year of his age, and he met Adam in journeying to the place Shedolamak. He was 87 years old when he received his ordination.

" 22. Mahalaleel was 496 years and seven days old when he was ordained by the hand of Adam, who also blessed him.

" 23. Jared was 200 years old when he was ordained under the hand of Adam, who also blessed him.

" 24 Enoch was 25 years old when he was ordained under the hand of Adam, and he was 65 and Adam blessed him. And he saw the Lord, and he walked with him, and was before his face continually; and he walked with God 365 years, making him 430 years old when he was translated.

"25. Methuselah was 100 years old when he was ordained under the hand of Adam.

"26. Lamech was 32 years old when he was ordained under the hand of Seth.

"27. Noah was 10 years old when he was ordained under the hand of Methuselah.

"28. Three years previous to the death of Adam, he called Seth, Enos, Cainan, Mahalaleel, Jared, Enoch and Methuselah, who were all high priests, with the residue of his posterity who were righteous, into the valley of Adam-ondiahman, and there bestowed upon them his last blessing. And the Lord appeared unto them, and they rose up and blessed Adam, and called him Michael, the Prince, the Archangel. And the Lord Administered comfort unto Adam, and said unto him, I have set thee to be at the head—a multitude of nations shall come of thee, and thou art a prince over them for ever.

"29. And Adam stood up in the midst of the congregation, and notwithstanding he was bowed down with age, being full of the Holy Ghost, predicted whatsoever should befall his posterity unto the latest generation. These things were all written in the book of Enoch, and are to be testified of in due time.

"30. It is the duty of the twelve, also, to ordain and set in order all the other officers of the church, agreeably to the revelation which says,

"31. To the church of Christ in the land of Zion, in addition to the church laws respecting church business—Verily, I say unto you, says the Lord of hosts, there must needs be presiding elders to preside over those who are of the office of an elder; and also priests to preside over those who are of the office of a priest, and also teachers to preside over those who are of the office of a teacher in like manner, and also the deacons: wherefore, from deacon to teacher, and from teacher to priest, and from priest to elder, severally as they are appointed, according to the covenants and commandments of the church. Then comes the high priesthood, which is the greatest of all; wherefore it must needs be that one be appointed of the high priesthood to preside over the priesthood, and he shall be called president of the high priesthood of the church; or, in other words, the presiding high priest over the high priesthood of the church. From the same comes the administering of ordinances and blessings upon the church, by the laying on of the hands.

" 32. Wherefore the office of a bishop is not equal unto it; for the office of a bishop is in administering all temporal things; nevertheless a bishop must be chosen from the high priesthood, unless he is a literal descendant of Aaron; for unless he is a literal descendant of Aaron he cannot hold the keys of that priesthood. Nevertheless, a high priest that is after the order of Melchizidek, may be set apart unto the ministering of temporal things, having a knowledge of them by the spirit of truth, and also to be a judge in Israel, to do the business of the church, to sit in judgment upon transgressors, upon testimony as it shall be laid before him according to the laws, by the assistance of his counsellors whom he has chosen, or will choose among the elders of the church. This is the duty of a bishop who is not a literal descendant of Aaron, but has been ordained to the high priesthood after the order of Melchizidek.

" 33. Thus shall he be a judge, even a common judge among the inhabitants of Zion, or in a state of Zion, or in any branch of the church where he shall be set apart unto this ministry, until the borders of Zion are enlarged, and it becomes necessary to have other bishops or judges in Zion, or elsewhere; and inasmuch as there are other bishops appointed they shall act in the same office.

" 34. But a literal descendant of Aaron has a legal right to the presidency of this priesthood, to the keys of this ministry, to act in the office of bishop independently, without counsellors, except in a case where a president of the high priesthood, after the order of Melchizidek, is tried, to sit as a judge in Israel. And the decision of either of these councils, agreeably to the commandment which says,

" 35. Again, verily, I say unto you, the most important business of the church, and the most difficult cases of the church, inasmuch as there is not satisfaction upon the decision of the bishop or judges, it shall be handed over and carried up unto the council of the church, before the presidency of the high priesthood; and the presidency of the council of the high priesthood shall have power to call other high priests, even twelve, to assist as counsellors; and thus the presidency of the high priesthood and its counsellors shall have power to decide upon testimony according to the laws of the church. And after this decision it shall be had in remembrance no more before the Lord; for this is the highest council of the church of God, and a final decision upon controversies in spiritual matters.

" 36. There is not any person belonging to the church who is exempt from this council of the church.

" 37. And inasmuch as a president of the high priesthood shall transgress, he shall be had in remembrance before the common council of the church, who shall be assisted by twelve counsellors of the high priesthood; and their decision upon his head shall be an end of controversy concerning him. Thus, none shall be exempted from the justice and the laws of God, that all things may be done in order and in solemnity before him, according to truth and righteousness.

" 38. And again, verily I say unto you, the duty of a president over the office of a deacon is to preside over twelve deacons, to sit in council with them, and to teach them their duty—edifying one another, as it is given according to the covenants.

" 39. And also the duty of the president over the office of the teachers is to preside over twenty-four of the teachers, and to sit in council with them, teaching them the duties of their office, as given in the covenants.

' " 40. Also the duty of the president over the priesthood of Aaron is to preside over forty-eight priests, and sit in council with them, to teach them the duties of their office, as is given in the covenants. This president is to be a bishop; for this is one of the duties of this priesthood.

" 41. Again, the duty of the president over the office of elders is to preside over ninety-six elders, and to sit in council with them, and to teach them according to the covenants. This presidency is a distinct one from that of the seventy, and is designed for those who do not travel into all the world.

" 42. And again, the duty of the president of the office of the high priesthood is to preside over the whole church, and to be like unto Moses. Behold, here is wisdom; yea, to be a seer, a revelator, a translator, and a prophet, having all the gifts of God which he bestows upon the head of the church.

" 43. And it is according to the vision, showing the order of the seventy, that they should have seven presidents to preside over them, chosen out of the number of the seventy; and the seventh president of these presidents is to preside over the six; and these seven presidents are to choose other seventy besides the first seventy, to whom hey belong, and are to preside over them; and also other seventy until seven times seventy, if the labour in the vineyard of necessity requires it. And these seventy are to be travelling ministers unto the Gentiles first, and also unto the Jews; whereas other officers of the church, who belong not unto the twelve, neither to the seventy, are not under the responsibility to travel among all nations, but are to travel as their circumstances shall allow, notwithstanding they may hold as high and responsible offices in the church.

" 44. Wherefore now let every man learn his duty, and to act in the office in which he is appointed, in all diligence. He that is slothful shall not be counted worthy to stand, and he that learns not his duty and shows himself not approved, shall not be counted worthy to stand. Even so. Amen."

The importance of the above extract will atone for its length. It contains nearly the whole of the Mormon Ecclesiastical Polit y Subsequent sections make provision for the most minute particulars —relative not only to things sacred, but things secular—such as farm and store taking, printing and publishing of books, building and the raising of the requisite funds.

These, of course, have excited much ridicule. Certain technical religious doctrines have also met with little mercy from Mormon antagonists. It is sufficient here to allude to their distinctive tenets on prophecy, the religious and divine right of revenge, the baptism of the dead, and the revived Roman Catholic dogma of Baptismal Regeneration. It is possibly more important to consider at its due length the philosophical system promulgated by Mr. Orson Pratt, whose name we have already mentioned, as the learned apostle of the Mormon pretensions.

According to the " Lectures on Faith," and in accordance with the high tone assumed by the Mormons in their Materialism, they invariably give a literal interpretation to the Hebrew Scriptures. That is their cardinal point,—no mysticism ;—the plain meaning of plain words.

God, by the Mormons, is described through his personal attributes, and these, again, are resolved into corporeal characteristics. " The first thought that there ever existed in the mind of any individual that there was such a being as a God, who had created and did uphold all things," was owing to and " by reason of the manifestation which he first made to our father, Adam, when he stood in his presence, and conversed with him face to face, at the time of his creation."

This materialistic view makes the Mormon very angry with the Orthodox dogma, that commences the thirty-nine articles of the Church of England. The Mormon author of ",The Absurdities of Immaterialism"* expresses his contempt of the article in question, in these terms :—" The Immaterialist says, there is such a substance as God, but it is *without parts*—(first of the 39 Articles ; also, Art. Methodist Discipline ;)" and on all such Immaterialism the Mormons unscrupulously stamp the brand of Atheism. Of Atheists, they tell us, there are two classes in the world—one denying the existence of God in the most positive language ; the other denying his existence in duration or space. One says, " There is no God ;" the other says,

---

* *Absurdities of Immaterialism ;* or, A Reply to T. W. P. Taylder's Pamphlet, entitled, " The Materialism of the Mormons or Latter-day Saints, Examined and Exposed."

" God is not *here* or *there*, any more than he exists *now* and *then*."
The Infidel says, adds the writer, " God does not exist anywhere."
Tne Immaterialist says, " He exists *nowhere*." Upon the ingenuity or
absurdity of these statements it is needless to remark.

" The Immaterialist," says Mr. Orson Pratt, " only differs from the
other class of atheists, by clothing an indivisible unextended NOTHING
with the powers of a God. One class," continues Mr. Pratt, " believes
in no God; the other class believes that NOTHING is God, and wor-
ships it as such. There is no twisting away from this. The most
profound philosopher in all the ranks of modern Christianity, cannot
extricate the Immaterialist from atheism. He cannot show the least
difference between the idea represented by the word *Nothing*, and the
idea represented by that which is unextended, indivisible, and without
parts, having no relation to space or time. All the philosophers of
the universe could not give a better or more correct definition of
Nothing. And yet this is the God worshipped by the Church of England — the Methodists — and millions of other atheistical idolators,
according to their own definitions, as recorded in their respective
articles of faith. An open Atheist is not so dangerous as the Atheist
who couches his atheistical doctrines under the head of ' ARTICLES OF
RELIGION.' The first stands out with open colours, and boldly avows
his infidelity; the latter, under the sacred garb of religion, draws into
his yawning vortex, the unhappy millions who are persuaded to believe in, and worship an unextended indivisble *nothing* without parts,
deified into a god. A pious Atheist is much more serviceable in
building up the kingdom of darkness than one who openly, and without any deception, avows his infidelity.

" No wonder that this modern god has wrought no miracles and
given no revelations since his followers invented their ' Articles of
Religion.' A being without parts must be entirely powerless, and
can perform no miracles. Nothing can be communicated from such a
being; for, if nothing give nothing, nothing will be received. If, at
death, his followers are to be made like him, they will enjoy, with
some of the modern Pagans, all the beauties of annihilation. To be
made like him! Admirable thought! How transcendantly sublime to
behold an innumerable multitude of unextended nothings, casting their
crowns at the feet of the great, inextended, infinite Nothing, filling all
space, and yet ' without parts!' There will be no danger of quarrelling
for want of room : for the Rev. David James says, " Ten thousand
spirits might be brought together into the smallest compass imaginable,
and there exist without any inconvenience for want of room. As
materiality,' continues he, ' forms no property of a spirit, the space
which is sufficient for one, must be amply sufficient for myriads, yea,

for all that exist.'* According to this, all the spirits that exist, 'could be brought together into the smallest compass imaginable;' or, in other words, into no compass at all; for, he says, a spirit occupies 'no room, and fills no space.' What an admirable description of Nothing! *Nothing* occupies no room, and fills no space.' If myriads of Nothings were 'brought together into the smallest compass imaginable,' they could 'there exist without any inconvenience for want of room.' Everything which the Immaterialist says, of the existence of *spirit*, will apply, without any variation, to the existence of *Nothing*. If he says that his god cannot exist ' *Here* ' or ' *There*,' the same is true of *Nothing*. If he affirms that he cannot exist ' *Now* ' and ' *Then*,' the same can, in all truth, be affirmed of *Nothing*. If he declares that he is ' *unextended*,' so is *Nothing*. If he asserts that he is ' *indivisible*,' and ' *without parts*,' so is *Nothing*. If he declares that a spirit ' occupies no room and fills no space,' neither does *Nothing*. If he says a spirit is ' *Nowhere*,' so is *Nothing*. All that he affirms of the one, can, in like manner, and with equal truth, be affirmed of the other. Indeed, they are only two words, each of which express precisely the same idea. There is no more absurdity in calling *Nothing* a substance, and clothing it with Almighty powers, than there is in making a substance out of that which is precisely like nothing, and imagining it to have Almighty powers. Therefore, an immaterial God is a deified Nothiag, and all his worshippers are atheistical idolators."

Skilfully, however, as the Mormon writer puts his argument, it has no novelty. The celebrated Soame Jenyns, whose life was written by Dr. Johnson, has anticipated the whole of it. He (like the Mormon in regard to an Immaterial substance) supposed that he had disproved the existence of Eternity, by proving that its definition was identical with that of Nothing. It is true, that both the Mormon's "Immaterial Substance" and Jenyn's "Eternity" suffer under this apparent confutation. After all, the controversy only regards a matter of definition : What is nothing? Mr. Orson Pratt presents us with a series of " six definitions," as so many aids to the exposition of his own idea. Here they are :—

Definition 1.—Space is magnitude, susceptible of division.

Definition 2.—A Point is the negative of space, or the zero at which a magnitude begins or terminates; it is not susceptible of division.

Definition 3.—Duration is not magnitude, but time susceptible of division.

Definition 4.—An Instant is the negative of duration, or the zero of which duration begins or terminates ; it is not susceptible of division.

Definition 5.—Matter is something that occupies space between any two

---

* Rev. David James on the Trinity, in Unitarianism Confuted. Lect. VII., page 382.

instants, and is susceptible of division, and of being removed from one
portion of space to another.

Definition 6.—NOTHING is the negative of space, of duration, and of matter; it is the zero of all existence.

A Point, Instant, and Nothing, here enjoy an identity of definition. Neither of these are "susceptible of division." It is scarcely
conceivable how an elaborate thinker, such as Mr. Orson Pratt evidently is, could thus have committed himself, by actually recognising
the Idea, not of one Substance only, but of three Substances " without
Parts." A " Point," an " Instant," and a " Nothing,"—each insuscep-
tible of division ? He appears not to have been aware that he had
reached the conception of the most abstract Being, in thus identifying
it with Nothing, an Instant, and a Point, and had made an Affirma-
tion of which an Euclid or a Hegel might be proud; that, in fact, he
he had proved the very case that he sought to subvert, and demonstrated that he could not conduct his argument without inferring,
and indeed presuming, the existence of that " Substance without Parts,"
against which he was expressing such a holy horror, when proposed
to his belief in the language of a system different from his own.

Philosophers who have been led, in their investigation of truth,
not by a desire to establish the system of the Mormons, but to interpret the system of the universe by the light of a Divine intelligence,
have from Plato to Oken, recognised the difficulty which so puzzles
the Mormon materialist. But they have seen in it only a proof that
the Substances so identified with Nothing, are not such as can be
identified with any Thing—that is, with aught that occupies place or
time ; that therefore, they cannot be properly called Things at all ;
and that a higher term must be found to distinguish them from all
possible objects of sense, and to class them in a " cage of rushes", a
category of their own. In fact, the mind has been justly lead, by
contemplations, such as these, to the apprehension of the idea of Being
in itself, which, though in the carnal conception, identical with
nothing, is the basis, the boundary, the origin, and the terminus of
all ; at once the " Zero of all existence," and the plenum. It is in
this sense, that we may understand the leading postulate of Hegel,
that " Seyn und nicht ist dasselben." " *Being and Nothing is the
same.*"

The Mormons have shown themselves, in accordance with their
Materialism, to be practical political economists. The ordinary statesman is too apt, in the affairs of the world, to make little account of
men of their order of mind. Yet have they been, at all times, the
men of a crisis—the fomenters of revolutions—the authors of new
is_ isations. Pious frauds to such individuals are no more than

legal fictions to the lawyer. They serve them in the place of axioms and postulates; they are assumptions which enable them to take the first step in the practical argument which they mean to maintain against the world. To them they are unquestionable data, and the more supernatural their character the more unquestionable do they become. Frequently there is some shadow of a fact, which serves as the original basis; this soon, however, becomes modified into fiction; and ultimately completed in a well-rounded myth.

Whatever Joseph Smith may have been, the present race of Mormons are satisfied with him. They say—"There is our statement; there are the witnesses; there is the book." Armed with these credentials, the Apostles of the new belief have at last founded, not only a Church, but a State.

The longer the original imposture has remained before the world, the more difficult it has become to overthrow it. Joseph Smith was slain, and it acquired sanctity in the eyes of his followers. Other " witnesses drop off, and the myth becomes more and more mythological. Thus, we learn from an obituary in the *Millennial Star* (July 1st, 1850), that one of the " three witnesses" has lately died. " Elder Wallace informs us, that Oliver Cowdery died last February, of consumption. Brother Cowdery is one of the ' THREE WITNESSES' to the BOOK of MORMON. For rebellious conduct he was expelled from the Church some years since. Although he stood aloof from the Church for several years, he never, in a single instance, cast the least doubt on the truth of his former testimony. Sometime in 1847 or 1848, he sought to be re-admitted to the fellowship of the Saints. His return to the fold was hailed with great joy by the Saints, who sti l remembered him with a kindly recollection, as one who had suffered much in the first rise of the Church. He has now gone the way of all the earth. May he rest in peace, to come forth in the morning of the first resurrection unto eternal life, is the earnest desire of all Saints."

A similar record will shortly, in the natural course of things, be made of the other witnesses; the seal of the grave will be set upon their testimony; and thus Mormonism—even if Sidney Rigdon should divulge his secrets—will, to the hearts of thousands, who would believe it on far less evidence—stand as firm as Buddhism stands, or Mahomedanism, or any other false creed, which millions believe to be true.

The objections to Mormonism, however, are not of a purely doctrinal character, or dependent upon the truth or falsehood of the Book of Mormon. It is alleged that the Mormons both tolerate and practice polygamy and seduction. This charge has been made against them in many quarters.

According to Mr. Bowes, the author of the pamphlet from which we have already quoted, the social life of the Mormons is an extensive and well organised system of licentiousness. Joseph Smith, he tells us, taught a system of polygamy; that he sought to seduce Nancy Rigdon, Sarah M. Pratt, and others; that, in some instances, he was repulsed, in others, he succeeded. Joseph Smith is also accused of having endeavoured to secure Martha H. Brotherton, once of Manchester, for his friend Brigham Young; in both cases attempting to influence his victims by persuading them that he had received a revelation from God, justifying adultery, seduction, and other sins. A letter from Martha Brotherton sets forth the whole charge against Joseph Smith and Brigham Young, and if to be believed, proves it:—

" I had been at Nauvoo near three weeks, during which time my father's family received frequent visits from Elders Brigham Young and Heber C. Kimball, two of the Mormon Apostles; when, early one morning, they both came to my brother-in-law's (John M'Ilwrick's) house, at which place I then was on a visit, and particularly requested me to go and spend a few days with them. I told them I could not at that time, as my brother-in-law was not at home; however, they urged me to go the next day, and spend one day with them. The day being fine, I accordingly went. * * * * He led me up some stairs to a small room, the door of which was locked, and on it the following inscription: ' Positively no admittance.' He observed, ' Ah! brother Joseph must be sick, for, strange to say, he is not here. Come down into the tithing-office, Martha.' He then left me in the tithing-office, and went out, I know not where. In this office were two men writing, one of whom, William Clayton, I had seen in England; the other I did not know. Young came in, and seated himself before me, and asked where Kimball was. I said he had gone out. He said it was all right. Soon after, Joseph came in, and spoke to one of the clerks, and then went up stairs, followed by Young. Immediately after, Kimball came in. ' Now, Martha,' said he, ' the Prophet has come; come up stairs.' I went, and we found Young the Prophet alone. I was introduced to the Prophet by Young. Joseph offered me his seat; and, to my astonishment, the moment I was seated, Joseph and Kimball walked out of the room, and left me with Young, who arose, locked the door, closed the window, and drew the curtain. He then came and sat before me, and said, ' This is our private room, Martha.' ' Indeed, sir,' said I, ' I must be highly honoured to be permitted to enter it.' He smiled, and then proceeded—' Sister Martha, I want to ask you a few questions; will you answer them?' Yes, sir, said I.' * * * * * ' To come to the point more closely,' said he, ' have not you an affection for me, that, were it lawful and right, you could accept of me for your husband and companion?' * * * * * I therefore said, 'If it was lawful and right, perhaps I might; but you know, sir, it is not.' 'Well, but,' said he, 'brother Joseph has had a revelation from God that it is lawful and right for a man to have two wives; for, as it was in the days of Abraham, so it shall be in these last days, and whoever is the first that is willing to take up the cross will receive the greatest blessings; and if you will accept of me, I will take you straight to the celestial kingdom; and if you will have me in this world, I will have you in that which is to come, and brother Joseph will marry us here to-day, and you can go home this evening, and your parents will not know anything about it.' 'Sir,' said I, 'I should not like to do anything of the kind without the permission of my parents.' * * * * 'Well,' said he, 'I will have a kiss, any how,' and then rose, and said he would bring Joseph. He then unlocked the door, and took the key, and locked me up alone. He was absent about ten minutes, and then returned with Joseph. 'Well,' said Young, 'sister Martha would be willing if she knew it was lawful and right before God.' 'Well, Martha, said Joseph, 'it is lawful and right before God—I *know* it is. Look here, sis; don't you believe in me?' 'I did not answer. 'Well, Martha,' said Joseph, 'just go a-head, and do as Brigham wants you to—he is the best man in the world, except me.' 'O!' said Brigham, 'then you are as good.' 'Yes,' said Joseph. 'Well,' said Young, 'we believe Joseph to be a Prophet. I have known him near eight years, and always found him the same' 'Yes,' said Joseph, 'and I know that this is lawful and right before God, and if there is any sin in it, I will answer for it before God; and I have the keys of the kingdom, and whatever I bind on earth is bound in heaven, and whatever I loose on earth is loosed in heaven; and if you will accept of Brigham, you shall be blessed—God shall bless you, and my blessing shall rest upon you; and if you will be led by him you will do well; for I know Brigham will take care of you; and if he don't do his duty to you, come to me, and I will make him; and if you do not like it in a month or two, come to me, and I will make you free again; and if he turns you off, I will take you on.'"

Another deposition, sworn by Melissa Schindle, describes similar practices. Mr. Bowes also describes certain hidden orgies practised in the Nauvoo Temple, which are sufficiently suspicious. The statement is sworn to by J. M. Gee Van Dusen and Maria Van Dusen, who profess to have been initiated into the mysteries. The seventh degree in the temple relates to "the Spiritual Wife Doctrine."

"Those who have attained to this are taught," say these witnesses, "that they are no more under obligations to their husband, if they have one. and it is their privilege to leave their lawful husband, and take another;" and, "it is the privilege of some kings to have scores, yes, hundreds of queens, especially the King of kings, Brigham Young. the present Mormon god in California,—(or devil, I should say, for I have reason to believe he is the wickedest man now on the face of the earth;) and, further, as we are all made kings and queens by this secret farce the foundation for a kingdom is laid also. And here is the secret of the Spiritual Wife Doctrine:—Their kingdom is to consist in their own posterity, and the more wives the greater opportunity of getting a large kingdom, of course ; so it is an object to one who holds this doctrine sacred, as thousands do, to get all the women he can, consequently it subjects that portion of the female sex which he has influence over eventually to literal ruin."

This reason, which may hold good for polygamy, obviously does not for adultery or fornication, into one or both of which the Spiritual Wife practice resolves itself. There is. in such an erroneous argument, ground for suspicion of prejudice in relation to the statement adduced as its basis. And as the Mormon authorities positively deny that Joseph Smith was guilty of the charge often alleged in justificating his murder, it is a motive of caution in the receipt of evidence. We must remember. too, that Smith universally, in all his letters, revelations, and speeches, denounced adultery and fornication. Subject as all founders of religious systems are to calumny, we cannot resist the doubt that there may have been misrepresentation and exaggeration, both as to the character of Joseph Smith and the cause of his untimely end. At any rate. and under any circumstances. it is impossible to justify the acts of his enemies, either in the persecution of his followers, or in the circumstances of his death. The fanaticism that destroyed him is to be condemned quite as strongly as his own.

It is further stated, that the Mormon candidate for holy orders, among other promises, makes oath, that he " will never touch a daughter of Adam, unless she be given him of the Lord ." - thus consecrating licentiousness with the holiest sanctions. But it must be remarked that these charges are given under cover of " secret revelations of the church—none but the faithful being permited to have the privilege" of prostituting the daughters and wives of their friends and acquaintances. It is affirmed, on this covert evidence. that the Mormons "teach that this system is what we are to understand by the blessings of Abraham, Isaac, and Jacob" We are further told that there is an institution of " Cloistered Saints," which forms " the highest order of tl e Mormon harem, and is composed of women, whether married or unmarried, as *secret* spiritual wives." This is Mr Bowes's statement ; who likewise requires us to believe that " When an apostle, high priest, elder, or scribe, conceives an affection for a female, and has ascertained her views on the subject, he communicates confidentially to the prophet his love affair, and requests him to inquire of the Lord whether or not it would be right and proper for him to take unto himself this woman for his spiritual wife. It is no obstacle whatever to this spiritual marriage if one or both of the parties should happen to have a husband or wife already united to them according to the laws of the land."

" The prophet," continues Mr. Bowes, " puts this singular question to the Lord, and if he receives an answer in the affirmative, which is always the case where the parties are in favour with the president, the parties assemble in the lodge-room, accompanied by a duly authorized administrator, and place themselves, kneeling, before the altar, the administrator commences the ceremony by saying.—

" ' You, separately and jointly, in the name of Jesus Christ, the Son of God, do solemnly covenant and agree that you will not disclose any matter relating to the sacred act now in progress of consummation, whereby any Gentile shall come to a knowledge of the secret purposes of this order, or whereby the saints may suffer persecution, your lives being the forfeit."

After the vow of assent is given by each of the pair, the administrator proceeds to pronounce them " *one flesh*, in the name of the Father, and of the Son, and of the Holy Ghost."

" The parties," it is said, by the same authority, " leave the cloister with generally a firm belief, at least on the part of the female, in the sacredness and validity of the ceremonial, and consider themselves as united in spiritual marriage, the duties and privileges of which are in no particular different from those of any other marriage covenant."

Among the stray statements quoted on more or less evidence touching this subject, we find that William Arrowsmith, before mentioned, " talked to Joseph Smith about Martha Brotherton's case. Smith did not deny what Martha relates, but stated that Brigham Young and he did it to try her, as they had heard an evil report of her. We are told, also, upon the same sort of authority, that " Whelock," another Mormon leader, married three wives, the first Parish, the second Rose. Grand jury took him up for bigamy. He married a decent girl at Birmingham, and she would have to live with the American wives, educated in bad families "

Accusations like these naturally lead us to look into the recognised

documents of the Mormons themselves for corroboration and support. We turn, accordingly, to " The Book of Doctrines and Covenants," for such articles of law and regulation as may relate to these alleged practices. These revelations, it should be observed, notwithstanding the limitation in the title-page, are not all given to Joseph Smith, but are extended to divers of his apostles likewise. In one purporting to be received by Martin Harris, the opulent Mormon already spoken of as one of the witnesses, and who is warned in it " not to covet" his " own property, but impart it freely to the printing of the Book of Mormon," we find this admonition published :—
" And again I command thee, that thou shalt not covet thy neighbour's wife, nor seek thy neighbour's life." Not less explicit is the revelation vouchsafed to Joseph Smith himself.

" And again, I say, thou shalt not kill; but he that killeth shall die. Thou shalt not steal ; and he that stealeth and will not repent, shall be cast out. Thou shalt not lie; he that lieth and will not repent, shall be cast out. Thou shalt love thy wife with all thy heart, and shalt cleave unto her and none else ; and he that looketh upon a woman to lust after her, shall deny the faith, and shall not have the Spirit, and if he repents not, he shall be cast out. Thou shalt not commit adultery; and he that committeth adultery and repenteth not shall be cast out; but he that has committed adultery and repents with all his heart, and forsaketh it, and doeth it no more, thou shalt forgive; but if he doeth it again, he shall not be forgiven, but shall be cast out. Thou shalt not speak evil of thy neighbour, nor do him any harm. Thou knowest my laws concerning these things are given in my scriptures; he that sinneth and repenteth not, shall be cast out.

" And, verily, I say unto you, as I have said before, he that looketh on a woman to lust after her, or if any shall commit adultery, in their hearts, they shall not have the Spirit, but shall deny the faith and shall fear: wherefore I, the Lord, have said that the fearful, and the unbelieving, and all liars, and whosoever loveth and maketh a lie, and the whoremonger, and the sorcerer, shall have their part in that lake which burneth with fire and brimstone, which is the second death. Verily I say, that they shall not have part in the first resurrection."

Here, too, is an ordinance directing the manner of proceeding with adulterers.

" And if any man or woman shall commit adultery, he or she shall be tried before two elders of the church or more, and every word shall be established against him or her by two witnesses of the church, and not of the enemy ; but if there are more than two witnesses it is

better. But he or she shall be condemned by the mouth of two witnesses. and the elders shall lay the case before the church, and the
church shall lift up their hands against him or her. that they may be
dealt with according to the law of God. And if it can be, it is necessary that the bishop is present also. And thus ye shall do in all
cases which shall come before you."

Here is another with the same purport, but including the forni-
cator.

" Behold, verily I say unto you, that whatever persons among you,
having put away their companions for the cause of fornication, or in
other words. if they shall testify before you in all lowliness of heart
that this is the case, ye shall not cast them out from among you; but
if ye shall find that any persons have left their companions for the
sake of adultery, and they themselves are the offenders, and their
companions are living. they shall be cast out from among you. And
again, I say unto you. that ye shall be watchful and careful, with all
inquiry. that ye receive none such among you if they are married;
and if they are not married, they shall repent of all their sins. or ye
shall not receive them."

Here likewise is an ordinance relating to marriage.

" And again, I say unto you, that whoso forbiddeth to marry is not
ordained of God, for marriage is ordained of God unto man; wherefore
it is lawful that he should have one wife, and they twain shall be one
flesh, and all this that the earth might answer the end of its creation, and that it might be filled with the measure of man, according
to his creation before the world was made."

Finally, the charge with which we are dealing is met in a direct
and positive manner, as follows :—

" All legal contracts of marriage made before a person is baptized
into this church should be held sacred and fulfilled. Inasmuch as
this church of Christ has been reproached with the crime of fornication, and polygamy ; we declare that we believe that one man should
have one wife ; and one woman but one husband, except in case of
death, when either is at liberty to marry again. It is not right to
persuade a woman to be baptized contrary to the will of her husband ;
neither is it lawful to influence her to leave her husband. All children are bound by law to obey their parents ; and to influence them
to embrace any religious faith, or be baptized, or leave their parents
without their consent, is unlawful and unjust. We believe that hus
bands, parents. and masters, who exercise control over their wives,
children. and servants. and prevent them from embracing the truth
will have to answer for that sin."

Several of the Epistles which are to be found scattered through the publications of the sect, show that those in authority are actuated by an earnest desire to remove all cause for scandal in reference even to the most ordinary intercourse between the sexes, and if they are to be judged by their writings, we may assume that their efforts are continually directed towards the attainment of a higher system of morality than that commonly in vogue. For instance, in a letter to the Saints by Orson Pratt and Orson Spencer, we find the writers addressing those under their charge in the following terms:—

"The sharp edge of persecution is whetted to unwonted keenness by *lewd* men, who turn the grace of God into lasciviousness, and bring scandal and stigma upon that priesthood which is ordained to save the human family. When one member of the priesthood is polluted, however obscure, the whole body is sickened by the contagion. Speedy amputation often becomes painfully necessary. All heaven is pervaded with one common spirit of indignation. We feel as though something like fratricide, or slaying of our brethren had been attempted: the wound is in the house of our friends. But Zion will not always mourn. Judgment is now given into her hand, and the workers of iniquity shall be cut off, and the stench of their detestable deeds will follow them: and when the seducer's and adulterer's bones are mouldering in the dust, the scent of his abominable deeds will bring upon his memory the bitter imprecations of the righteous. While the law of God has been but imperfectly appreciated, even by many of the Church, these things may have been bearable through false tradition; yet, the time is now, when the cloak of charity cannot, and will not, screen such offenders. Two instances of gross lewdness have occurred among the elders of this land, and we have strictly enjoined the prohibition of their re-baptism or reunion with the Church, without a verbal application to the First Presidency, residing far distant in Zion. Although the spirit of seduction and lewdness has occasionally invaded the Church in its purest state, it has never obtained a particle of fellowship, neither will it do so in any future time, from any faithful servant of God. And we distinctly say to the Saints in Britain, let no artifice or cunningly devised tale ever be regarded as any apology for this gross immorality. No grade of office whatever will ever authorize any one to teach or practise this abomination. This Church is a purifier, and will refine its members as silver; and men must not think to bring into its sacred enclosure the abominations of the Gentiles, who are an adulterous and wicked generation—strange children—conceived in sin and shapen in iniquity.

"Not so with the Church of the living God. Their marriage vows are sacred, and cannot be violated with impunity: their offspring are legitimate, and not bastards conceived in sin, but holy unto the Lord; and the man or woman in this Church that contributes to illegitamacy, thereby entailing upon his or her offspring the curse of exclusion from the congregation of the Lord, to the third generation, he or she that does it becomes detestable in the eyes of the Lord and all good people, and their condemnation will not slumber. Let none be deceived in this matter for the eyes of the Lord will penetrate every work, and the spirit that is confirmed upon the Saints will bear witness against all such like abominations, and no work of iniquity will or can possibly escape detection in due time. The nations of the earth are corrupt and abominable in these things ; but they that bear the message of the Lord must be clean : they must keep themselves undefiled, or share in the plagues of Babylon. Pitiable is the condition of that man who has made commerce of the gifts of the priesthood, like Esau. His strength is gone, like unto Sampson's when shorn of his locks, and he becomes an easy prey to his enemies. Who then, among the sons and daughters of men, will lay hold upon the skirts of such fallen reprobates in order to obtain salvation? Let those who have already spotted their garments with these Gentile practices, prove a sufficient ensample to deter all others. Let the beacon-light of a few examples keep others from the rocks and quicksands where scattered wrecks fearfully remonstrate and warn !

"Dear brethren, no false delicacy shall forbid us from speaking plainly to you upon this subject. Lust, when it is conceived, bringeth forth sin. The pure in heart have no occasion to mistake this infallible precursor and antecedent to sin : it is easily discoverable. It is only when the invading foe is welcomed and cherished that sin can ever be the result. *Here* is opportunity afforded for to consider, reflect, and *beware !* Whatever of sexual manners, dress, or intimacy is known to cherish forbidden or ungovernable lusts, may be as surely known to produce sin. The familiar usages of one nation may not be equally compatible with the purity of another people, accustomed to other usages. We do not complain of the manners and dress of any nation, so long as they are compatible with purity and the law of God. The salutation by kissing was practised in the Jewish nation, and it was tolerated among the members of the primitive Church of Christ ; but it was by no means a law or necessary duty.

"The first transgression introduced the necessity of a covering, and urged the importance of fresh laws regulating acts of decency. Perfect purity would require no law to determine what is modest or what is perilous to virtue. The law is made for transgressors. When men can keep themselves pure in body, soul, and spirit, they then become as wise virgins, and emerge into the perfect law of boundless liberty. No person can be a successful candidate for the celestial prize that does not keep the law in all these respects. Men must learn to approximate to that state of perfect purity in which the law is written upon their hearts, so as to supersede the necessity of outward ordinances which will perish with the using.

"The pure in heart, who are fully established in the law of continency, might use the ancient salutation of a holy kiss, and other innocent familiarities of a kindred nature, with perfect impunity. But not so with all. We have need to write unto some, even as carnal and babes in Christ. Such have not already attained that steadfastness to which the Gospel calls them. What then ? Is it not better that the strong bear the infirmities of the weak, and forego any practise that may cause their brother to offend?

"We therefore think it wise and expedient, and give it as our counsel accordingly, to the English Saints, to abstain entirely from these unbecoming familiarities through which some have been already led into gross transgression.

" If the elders wish to save their congregations, and obtain a good degrees for themselves and others in the kingdom of God, let them abstain, rather, from all appearance of evil. Let those familiarities which are often the legitimate expression of innocence and the purest love, be avoided, because they may be spoken evil of by those that are without, and because the inexperienced confidence of young members is liable to be betrayed, and made a bait to folly and crime. We write unto presidents of conferences as unto wise men, to whom a hint will be sufficient, and who will readily understand what the will of the Lord is in such matters. We do not wish to multiply arbitrary laws among a people that are destined by the grace of God, and and their own trustworthiness, to rise above all law into the region of ineffable light, purity, and glory. But we do, nevertheless, intend to establish laws against the invasion of the unruly and transgressors. And we wish the elders and holy women who are mothers, to co-operate with us against the intrusion of Gentile abominations. And we do declare, with all sobriety in the fear of God, and by the authority we hold from God in the holy priesthood, that a curse shall rest upon transgressors, who, with knowing wickedness, shall hereafter violate the laws of virtue and chastity. This is the voice of the priesthood in Zion, and the voice of God, from the foundation of the world. Hear it, oh ye Saints throughout the British isles and adjacent countries ! While God is gathering, and will continue to gather his sons from afar, and his daughters from the ends of the earth, he will not tolerate the obstruction of the great and last gathering by the abominations of reprobates, that have been cast out as refuse silver, and by their slanderous tales of abomination, palmed upon his infant cause."

In the Third General Epistle of the Presidency we find some regulations which redound highly to the credit of the Mormon authorities. But leaving the question of the polygamy and seduction alleged to have been, or to be still practised by the Mormons, to be decided by the reader, upon the evidence on both sides which we have produced, we proceed to other points.

" Many brethren having gone to the Gold Mines, and many are about going. and all ' by counsel,' as they say, and, no doubt, truly. A few have gone according to the advice of those whose right it is to counsel the saints, and such are right, inasmuch as they do right : but much the greater portion have gone according to the counsel of their own wills and covetous feelings. Such might have done more good by staying in the Valley, and labouring to prepare the way for the reception of the brethren : but it is not too late for them to do good and be saved if they will do right in their present sphere of action, although they will not get so great a reward as they would have done had they performed the greater good.

" If, at the mines they will listen to the counsel of those men who have been appointed to counsel them, and they return work righteousness, and do as they

would be done unto, and acknowledge God in all their ways, they may yet attain
unto great glory ; but if they shall cease to hearken to counsel, and make gold
their god, and return among the Saints, filled with avarice, and refuse to lend, or
give, or suffer their money to be used unless they can make a great speculation
thereby, and will see their poor brethren, who have toiled all the day, in want
and in perplexity, and they will not relieve, but keep the dust corroding in their
purses, it had been better for them if a mill stone had been hanged about their
necks, and they had been drowned in the depths of the sea, before they had departed from the right ways of the Lord ; for if they sha'l continue thus to harden
their hearts ; and to shut up their bowels of compassion against the needy, they
will go down to the pit with all idolaters, in a moment they are not aware, with
as little pity as they have manifested to their poor brethren, who would have
borrowed of them but have been sent empty away.

Gold is good in its place —it is good in the hands of a good man to do good
with, but in the hands of a wicked man it often proves a curse instead of a blessing. Gold is a good servant, but a miserable, blind, and helpless god, and at last
will have to be purified by fire, with all its followers.

Now, it would be easy to charge the cupidity of the individuals
here reproved on the Mormon community, but it would be manifestly
unjust. We must recognise in such aberrations the inevitable
struggle between self-will and newly established law. Further provision is made against the evil complained of in the following express
rules and statement :- –

" Elders Amasa Lyman and Charles C. Rich will continue their operations at
Western California, according to previous instructions, and not only keep an accu-
rate account of all tithings and of the general proceedings of all faith'ul brethren,
that we may know of their good works, and hail them as brethren when we meet,
but keep a perfect history of all who profess to be Saints and do not follow their
counsel, pay tithing, and do their duty, and report the same to us every mail
that they and their works may be entered in a book of remembrance in Zion,
that they may be judged therefrom, and not impose upon the faithful ; for it is
not uncommon for men to say, " I can do more good if I go to the mines, than I
can to stay here," and we want to prove such, and know whether they are true
men or liars.

" When men, professing to be brethren, go to the mines according to their own
counsel, we want them to stay until they are satisfied—until they have obtained
enough to make them comfortable, and have some to do good with and a disposition to use it for that purpose, and not run back here in a few months, lock up
their gold, boast how much they have made, doing no good themselves, and hin-
dering every body else from doing good over whom they have an influence ; curse
God, deny the Holy Ghost, and when spring opens, run to the mines again, as
some have done. Let such men remember that they are not wanted in our midst ;
for unless they speedily repent, the wrath of an offended Creator will suddenly
overtake them, and no power can stay it. Let such leave their carcases where
they do their work; we want not our burial-grounds polluted with such hypocrites ;

but we have it in our hearts to bless all men who will do right, whatever their occupation, and our arms are ever open to embrace such, and we pray for all men who are ignorant, or out of the right way, that our Heavenly Father will give them his spirit, that they may learn and do right."

Some other points of social economy are touched on with like wisdom ; such as the emigration fund, and the establishment of the Deseret University.

" We would urge upon all Saints the importance of keeping in view the Perpetual Emigrating Fund, and of adding thereto, all in their power the present season ; for every succeeding year will be more and more eventful in the progress of the work of God, and more and more Saints will be ready, and want to gather to Zion. We warmly anticipate that such will be the interest felt, and the funds collected in the British Isles, that we can commence bringing forward the Saints, from that region, one year hence ; and the Presidency in England will take special care to be ready to act on future instructions on the subject.

" Elders of Israel be faithful in your calling, feed the sheep, feed the lambs of the flock, and proclaim the gospel in all simplicity, meekness, and love, whenever you have the opportunity as it shall be given you by the power of the Holy Ghost which you will always have for your counsellor if you are faithful ; and let all the Saints give diligent heed unto the counsel of those who are over them in the Lord, upholding them by the prayer of faith, keeping themselves pure and humble. and they will never lack wisdom from above, and by faith and works search out your way to Zion.

" Several elders have been appointed missions to England. Scotland, the Society Islands, the States, and Western California, as will be seen by the minutes of the General Conference, of the 6th of April, to which we refer for particulars concerning any business then transacted.

" We are happy in saying to all, that a brighter day is dawning on the intellectual prosperity of Zion ; that the University recently established by the State of Deseret, bids fair to accomplish the object for which it was instituted ; that it is under the supervision of faithful and intelligent men, who will consider no labour too great to carry out the wishes and greatest possible good of those for whose benefit the institution was founded : and we earnestly solicit the co-operation of all the Saints, and particularly the elders in all nations, to gather, as they may have the opportunity, books in all languages, and on every science, apparatus, and rare specimens of art and nature, and every thing that may tend to beautify and make useful; and forward or bring the same to the Regents of our University, for the benefit of all such as may hereafter seek intelligence at their hands. '

Mr. Orson Pratt, in an " Epistle to the Saints throughout Great Britain," is solicitous for the purification of both the state and church from unworthy members. The following are extracts :—

" About two years have elapsed since I was appointed to preside over the Saints in this land. I have endeavoured, during the time, to inform myself concerning your condition, and to offer such counsel as I thought best adapted to your circumstances. If, in the multiplicity of business which has pressed my mind, I have at any time erred, it has not been intentionally. It has been my constant prayer and study to know the will of God concerning you. It affords me great pleasure to know that the churches have greatly flourished since I have been in your midst, and that many thousands have been added to your numbers. Peace and union have also prevailed in almost every branch; while the Holy Spirit has been abundantly poured forth upon you, as is evident from the miraculous manifestation of the healing power, together with numerous other blessings enjoyed throughout the land. These tokens of the goodness of God towards his Saints are calculated to make the faithful servants of God rejoice.

" The wise and judicious management displayed by the presidents of conferences, and the travelling elders under them, has been the principal means in the hands of God in extending the cause of truth in the British Isles. The extensive circulation of the printed word has also given an impetus to the rolling of the great wheel of salvation. *Strictness of discipline in plucking off dead branches —in purifying the church of corrupt members —and in laying the axe at the very root of every species of wickedness, has also had a powerful tendency to strengthen and confirm the meek and humble, and to enlighten the eyes of the honest inquirer.*"

" Let the presiding elders of every conference endeavour to inform their minds relative to the condition of every branch under their respective jurisdictions. See whether your flocks are in a healthy condition or not. The Lord has made you the shepherds over his sheep: if you lose the sheep, or suffer them to perish through your neglect, they will be required at your hands. Teach the presidents of branches to look diligently after all the members. Counsel them to enforce strict discipline, and to root out all backbiting and evil-speaking one against another; for this is a great evil, and tends to quarrels, divisions, strifes, apostacy, and death. If the backbiter or evil-speaker will not, after proper admonitions, reform and cease his evil practices, let fellowship be withdrawn from him, and let all know that the church of God is not the place to injure and devour one another. If any officer or member under your charge be found teaching or practising unvirtuous doctrines, let him be dealt with strictly by the law of God; and if the president of a conference shall transgress, or teach or practice any iniquity, let the same be reported to us, accompanied with the proper evidences; and if one of the Twelve, or the president of the Saints in Great Britain, shall transgress the law of virtue, and teach or practise unrighteousness, let the presidents of conferences inquire into the same, and collect the testimonies thereof, and forthwith transmit the documents unto the First Presidency at head quarters, that all may be dealt with according to the law of heaven. The time is come when too much light and knowledge have been given to the Saints for them to suffer themselves to be imposed upon by men who are carried away with their lusts. And we say, in the name of the Lord, that the displeasure of heaven shall overtake the adulterer unless he speedily repent, and his name shall be blotted out from among the people of God. " Woe unto them that commit whoredoms, saith the Lord God Almighty, for they shall be thrust down to hell." Woe unto them who shall betray the confidence reposed in them, and shall make use of their authority to seduce and lead astray ignorant and silly women, for, except they repent, their authority shall perish quickly like the dry stubble before the devouring flame.

U

Woe unto them who lie and bear false witness against their brother or sister to their injury ; it were better for them that they were sunk in the depths of the mighty ocean than to offend the children of God. Woe unto them who steal, for their deeds shall be made manifest, and justice and judgment shall lay hold on them in an hour they think not. Woe unto them who love slander, and will not cease to speak evil of their brother and sister, for they shall be hated of God and man, and their hopes shall wither away and perish. Woe unto all those among the Saints who shall turn from their righteousness and do iniquity, for the great day of the Lord is at hand, and their portion shall be among hypocrites and un-believers.

Such language as this in their public documents, together with the recorded facts of the excision and excommunication of offending mem-bers, would seem to exonerate the Mormon system from the vices of Mormon members. They also prove, whatever may have been the moral state of Mormon society in time past, that it has al-ready greatly improved. And as to the accusations against their founders, even when made by undoubtedly pious men, the Mormons have an indisputably valid answer, which they have thus worded for themselves.

" Pious men, who prayed often and fasted frequently, affirmed that Jesus and His apostles were foul impostors, vile sabbath-breakers, gluttons, wine-bibbers, treasonable persons, not fit to live. Do you judge Jesus by the testimony of pious enemies? No, you judge his character, &c., by the testimony of friends. Pursue the same line of judgment toward Joseph Smith, and the issue is triumph : his bosom burned with a love to humanity, manly, frank, and Godlike. You believe in the testimony of Moses as to the won-ders recorded in the Pentateuch, yet Moses killed the Egyptian and hid his body in the sand ! Joseph Smith never did anything like that. You believe and receive the Psalms and Proverbs, yet David and Solomon sinned foully and fearfully. Let your reason and common sense speak and judge righteous judgment. A false prophet will ever teach something false : Joseph taught in perfect accordance with Scripture, just as a true prophet must do."

The enmity excited among the pious, too, had its natural ground in the peculiar doctrines taught by the new sect. These we will also take in their own words :—

" Some of the leading characteristics of the Latter-Day Gospel were as follows : It declared all the earth, Christian, Jew, Heathen, and Pagan, to be living in wickedness, unbelief, and without a knowledge of God. It declared that the religion of Jesus established upon the earth in the days of the primitive apostles, had been long perverted into human institutions, without either the form or power, and consequently were not acknowledged of God. It declared, that all those calling themselves Christians in the nineteenth century, were nothing less than idolators, and living under a broken covenant. It declared that God had now spoken from the heavens, and given a commission to man to go forth and usher in the dispensation of the fulness of times, by opening the kingdom of God to Gentile and Jew. It declared that all who would not humble themselves, and go forth and be baptized for a remission of their sins, and have the imposition of hands for the reception of the Holy Ghost, by those whom God had called, would never enter into the kingdom of God, or be saved with an everlasting salvation. It declared that all who were without prophets and apostles—the spirit of inspiration and immediate revelation from God, together with the Holy Ghost, which would enable men to dream dreams, see visions, and prophesy; speak in unknown tongues, and work miracles; were not yet fellow-citizens with the Saints, or of the household of God. It declared that this was the stone cut out of the mountain without hands, spoken of by Daniel and the prophets, and that it would roll on until every hostile power upon the earth had fallen before it, and it had become a great kingdom and filled the whole earth. Let us here pause, and inquire: Was there anything in all this, to pamper the prejudices of the public mind, and thereby gain the applause of the world? On the contrary; it is obvious, that had the inhabitants of some other world laid their heads together, to concoct such a story to palm upon this world, as would stir up the bitterest spirit of hatred and persecution, they could not have hit upon one more effectual than the principles embodied in the Latter-Day Gospel.

" We accordingly find that the gospel met the opposition and contempt naturally to be expected. No sooner was its first proclamation made, than both earth and hell were in a stew to find adequate means to put a stop to such a work; all manner of lies and slanderous reports were put in circulation to the prejudice of those who obeyed it, everywhere. The whole artillery of the learned world was put in requisition to bolster up such lies and slanders, and men were warned, both from pulpit and press, to beware of the impostors. The servants of the Lord knew and felt they were so treated; but still they preached and still they determined to know, and to glory in nothing else. Why this, if they were impostors, they must have yielded to the contempt it called forth. But no, they preached it, and succeeded. And yet Jew and Gentile hated it. What could carry it above that hatred but the power of God? For, as was to be expected from a religion of this description, making such pretensions, and with a world hostile and already entrenched in power, it met with most formidable opposition and violent persecution from all ranks, orders, classes, and individuals whose interests were endangered or craft disturbed. From governors, rulers, inferior magistrates; from priests and the whole train of idolatrous worshippers; from a lawless rabble multitude, the victim and sport of every passion and prejudice; the ready instruments of party violence; the easy dupes of designing men, and the tumultuous and eager executioners of wrath, against those who had become the object of their hatred. That the Latter-Day Saints have suffered horrible persecutions is a fact not to be denied, after all the publications upon the subject, and the thousands of living witnesses who at this moment attest its truth, and mourn over their martyred relatives.

" As an outline of what is contained in our records upon this subject, we may notice, that no sooner were a few thousands of the Saints settled on the western frontiers of Missouri, having provided themselves with comfortable, and many of them with large possessions, and having by industry greatly improved their estates, and were beginning to enjoy something like real comfort, than the storm that had been brewing against them in the hearts of their enemies broke out with uncontrollable force; and large bodies of Christians, armed with the powers of mobocracy, and headed by their ministers, with the Bible in one hand and the sword in the other, endeavoured to annihilate the poor, peaceful, unoffending Latter-Day Saints; and in the most savage, barbarous manner did they drive them from their lands and possessions in the midst of a severe North American winter, burning their dwelling-houses and other buildings, murdering them and their families, first ravishing and then murdering their wives and daughters. In one case nineteen of them had hid themselves in an old smithy, but their ruthless pursuers found them out and butchered them to a man; and just when about to leave, thinking that the work of slaughter was done in this place, one of them discovered a little boy hid behind the bellows; him they dragged forth, and while his little eyes and hands were raised to heaven in earnest entreaty that these christian savages might have mercy upon him, one of them, in whose heart the last spark of humanity was not wholly extinguished, ventured to plead for the life of the little boy; but the ready reply of one and all was, ' Away with him ; d—n him, if he lives he'll be a Mormon like his father,' and a ball from a gun quickly scattered his brains upon the floor.

" My heart sickens, and the blood freezes in my veins while I write, and while I contemplate the worse than savage atrocities inflicted upon the most law-abiding, peaceful, unoffending people that ever graced the footstool of God. Yes,—they drove them from their homes, their lands, and their possessions. Stript, wounded, and beaten, they were compelled to flee from all they had in or of the world, in the midst of a very rigorous winter. It would have sickened the heart of the wildest savage of the forest to see their young infants, their old men and women, their sick and infirm, with many of their women suffering from the pangs of child-birth, many of them too premature to look, or even hope for their recovery, lying scattered here and there across the bare prairies, without the slightest covering to shelter them from the pitiless pelting storm, or the bitter frost and snow; so that many more were they who fell martyrs to the inclemency of winter, than they who perished by the sword, and much more bitter and torturing to the feelings was their fate.

"It will not be expected that I could write one-thousandth part of the sufferings of the Saints at the period alluded to, neither is it my present intention so to do; suffice it to say, that the readiest pen, or the most eloquent tongue, would come far short of the reality. To know would be to have felt; and even then the knowledge would be all your own—you could not communicate it to another.

"But the question now is, did these cruelties destroy the work of God? No,—so far from destroying, it did not so much as retard it a single moment. Nay, it went on with accelerated speed; and at the very moment the Saints were being butchered for the testimony of Jesus and the word of God, that testimony was boldly and undauntedly borne throughout all parts of the land. Is it possible to look upon facts like these, and still hold the idea that these poor persecuted people were impostors, or under a delusion? Reasoning from such a state of things, and the results flowing from it, we cannot, as reasonable beings, hold the idea a single moment. They must either have obtained a knowledge of that God whom to know is life eternal, and which served to support their sinking spirits, and bear them up under all they were called upon to suffer, or they must have given way to the popular wrath, and thrown up their imposture as a thing altogether unfit to succeed in the world."

We have now brought to a close the few observations which we have thought it necessary to make upon the evidence by which the present believers in the mission of Joseph Smith support his claims; as well as upon the theology which has gradually grown out of the remarkable imposture, of which the *Book of Mormon* is the root. We have, at the same time, investigated the charges of vice and criminality brought against Smith and his disciples. We have also considered Mormonism as a social and secular institution, which already plays a very note-worthy part, both in this country and in America. The West has had its prophet as well as the East; and whatever may

have been the original character of the man, the sect which he founded
has arrived at such a growth, that no arguments founded upon the
fraud or absurdity of his pretensions will be of the slightest avail in
preventing the development of Mormonism. The sect—established
in its own home—treats all adverse criticism with the same indiffer-
ence as the Mahometans or Buddhists show to all who impugn the
truth of their religions. They pity the objectors—treat their arguments either as folly or blasphemy, and entrench themselves in the
impregnable fortress of their own faith. If this were not the natural
course of things, and strictly in accordance with all experience, there
would at this time be but one form of religion in the world. That
there are many forms of religion, each of which believes itself, and it
alone—to be the true one, may explain, though it will not justify, the
faith and position of the Latter-Day Saints. Whatever the world
may say of the Mormons, the Mormons may say of themselves, that
they have succeeded in establishing the third political system that
has grown out of Christianity. The Pope, the Queen of England,
and Brigham Young, are alike heads of States and of Churches: and,
what is perhaps as remarkable a fact, the only State Church in
America is that which has been founded by Joseph Smith.

The great impetus given to the trade and population of the Pacific,
by the discovery of the golden treasures of California,—a discovery
partly owing to the Mormons—will doubtless lead to a more rapid
development of the resources of the new and peculiar community of
Deseret or Utah, than might otherwise have been anticipated. Their
past history has been a singular one. Their future history promises
to be even more remarkable.